Glue & Go
Costumes for Kids

Glue & Go
Costumes for Kids

Super-Duper Designs with Everyday Materials

Holly Cleeland

photographs by Larry Lytle

Sterling Publishing Co., Inc.
New York

illustrations by Colin Hayes
edited by Isabel Stein
designed by Wanda Kossak

Library of Congress Cataloging-in-Publication Data

Cleeland, Holly.
    Glue & go costumes for kids : super-duper designs with everyday
materials / Holly Cleeland ; photographs by Larry Lytle.
        p. cm.
     Includes index.
     ISBN 0-8069-9283-2
     1. Children's costumes. I. Title: Glue and go costumes for kids. II.
Title.
    TT633 .C58 2004
    646.4'78–dc22

                                2003024266

10 9 8 7 6 5 4 3 2 1

Published in paperback in 2006 by Sterling Publishing Co., Inc.
387 Park Avenue South, New York, NY 10016
© 2004 by Holly Cleeland
Distributed in Canada by Sterling Publishing
c/o Canadian Manda Group, 165 Dufferin Street,
Toronto, Ontario, Canada M6K 3H6
Distributed in the United Kingdom by GMC Distribution Services,
Castle Place, 166 High Street, Lewes, East Sussex, England BN7 1XU
Distributed in Australia by Capricorn Link (Australia) Pty. Ltd.
P.O. Box 704, Windsor, NSW 2756, Australia

Sterling ISBN-13: 978-0-8069-9283-9 Hardcover
       ISBN-10: 0-8069-9283-2
       ISBN-13: 978-1-4027-4053-4 Paperback
       ISBN-10: 1-4027-4053-0

For information about custom editions, special sales, premium and
corporate purchases, please contact Sterling Special Sales
Department at 800-805-5489 or specialsales@sterlingpub.com.

Contents

Introduction

Ready for a creative adventure? Plug in the hot glue gun, grab the packing tape, clean out the plastic cups, and prepare to build fabulous memories with lots of laughs along the way.

Costume-making means a lot to me because I was the child who wanted to win the costume contest. I was tired of being the child that circled the costume parade as people scratched their heads every time I passed by, not knowing what I was.

As I grew older, I created costumes for kids in the neighborhood. During one contest, my neighborhood friend circled around in the costume parade as people pointed and stared at the costume I made. It was delightful to see my friend's face when he realized he stood out as the winner. The smile on his face grew bigger and brighter with each lap that he made. For that moment in time he was outstanding. A memory was created that would last a lifetime.

Several costume contests and lots of happy memories later, I bring the fun to you. I hope that you too will enjoy stimulating your creative imagination, broadening your reach as an artist, and developing memories with family and friends as you build prize-winning costumes together.

Before You Start

Building costumes can be a lot of fun. When there are young children around, there are a few do's and don'ts to keep in mind. Do keep all sharp tools, pins, hot glue guns, power tools, etc., out of the reach of very young children. For the parts of the projects that demand your focused attention, such as cutting foam core board, try to find a time when you aren't distracted by small persons asking for apple juice or jumping off chairs. Read through a project entirely before you get started and be sure you have all the tools and supplies that you need on hand. Protect your work surface with a few layers of scrap cardboard when you are cutting. Work in a place with good ventilation when you are using materials whose vapors or dust could be irritating.

To enlarge patterns, reproduce the grid given in the book with light pencil lines on the foam core or cardboard, making the boxes the size indicated on each grid. Then redraw the enlarged pattern on the cardboard or foam core board, using the small pattern as a guide, working box by box.

While you work on the costume, very young children can help by making collages of wrapping paper or crepe paper decorations for a party area. They can make drawings of costumes they'd like to see, cut out pictures of dressed-up people from an old magazine, or make an accompanying paper costume for a favorite doll or bear. Older children can help with measuring and enlarging patterns, painting costumes, taping and gluing, and cutting paper and other things, as long as they are closely supervised. You know best what your children can do. Don't expect perfection from yourself or from them, but share the fun of creating something together.

If children will be walking around in their costumes in the dark, add some reflective tape so they can be seen easily. If a child is wearing a costume that cuts off the child's vision, plan to accompany the child as he or she walks around. (You probably would want to do this anyway.) Be sure children won't be near open flames in flammable costumes. For a party, plan the clothes underneath the costume so the child will still look festive if he or she takes off the large parts of the costume.

Where to Find Materials

You'll probably find a wealth of materials you can use for costumes. Here are some places to look:

- acrylic paint: art supply store or craft store
- cardboard tubes: center core of wrapping paper or paper towels
- clear packing tape: office supply or shipping store
- colored tape: hardware store
- corrugated cardboard: art supply store; or use disassembled boxes (lay them flat and tape together in the shape that the costume requires)
- drywall screws: hardware store
- polyester batting: fabric store
- flexible polyurethane foam: craft store, upholstery store
- foam core board: art supply store
- polyurethane foam: foam store, mattress company
- Plastifoam™: craft supply store
- Plexiglas®: hardware store
- polyethylene tubing: hardware store, pet store
- PVC tubing and connectors: hardware store, craft store
- modeling clay: craft store
- ricrac: fabric store
- Mylar™ sheets: art supply store or sign shop
- star decorations, bows, bunting: party supply store
- Styrofoam® balls, eggs, cones: craft store

Artist's Palette

MATERIALS

- 33" × 48" (84 × 122 cm) white foam core board, ½" (1.5 cm) thick
- acrylic paint: red, orange, yellow, green, blue, purple, and hot pink
- seven 6" (15 cm) diameter balloons
- seven 12" × 12" (30.5 × 30.5 cm) pieces of white fabric
- 12 oz (360 mL) white glue
- 2 rolls of 1" (2.5 cm) wide white tape
- roll of 2" (5 cm) wide clear tape
- 3 black 12 oz (360 mL) plastic cups
- 36" (92 cm) strong white ribbon for strap, 1" (2.5 cm) wide
- 24" (61 cm) cardboard tube, 1½" (3.8 cm) wide
- 6" × 24" (15 × 61 cm) yellow wrapping paper
- Styrofoam coffee cup
- aluminum foil to wrap coffee cup
- newspaper

TOOLS: craft knife, paintbrush, scissors, large bowl, hot glue gun, pencil, ruler

CHILD WEARS: black clothes and red beret

DIRECTIONS

1 Draw the enlarged palette shape on foam core board and cut the palette shape out with a craft knife.

2 Tape over edges with 1" (2.5 cm) wide white tape for a clean line around palette and circle.

3 To make a strap for the costume, find the top center and poke two holes in the top edge of the palette, centered on the width, with a 12"

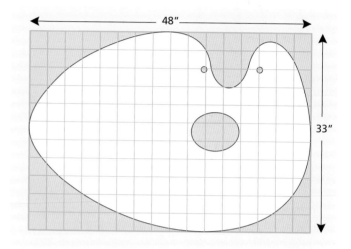

Step 1. Pattern for palette. 1 box = 3" (7.6 cm). Cut away blue parts. Dots indicate holes for straps.

(30.5 cm) gap between the holes (see pattern). Tie the white ribbon through the holes. Try it on the child and be sure it is the correct length. Tape down the ribbon ends with clear tape.

4 Protect work surface with newspaper or plastic. Take cap off of white glue and pour all of the glue into a large bowl. Fill the empty glue container with water (so you have an equal amount of water to glue), and stir all of the water into the glue until the glue is completely dissolved. Blow up balloons until they are 6" (15 cm) in diameter and tie off. Soak the white sheets of fabric in the glue mixture, one at a time, and wrap each balloon with one. Let dry overnight.

5 Once they are completely dry, use something sharp to pop the balloons, leaving the stiff outer shells of fabric. With your hands, scrunch and shape the shells so they look like paints on a palette. Paint these shells with the acrylic paints, a different color for each shell. When the paint is dry, hot-glue the shells to the palette.

6 Wrap the 24" (61 cm) cardboard tube with yellow wrapping paper.

7 Tape the Styrofoam coffee cup to one end of the cardboard tube, with the open end of the coffee cup facing out. Cover the cup all over outside and on its edge with aluminum foil. Together these will become the handle and ferrule for the paintbrush.

8 Take 3 black 12 oz (360 mL) plastic cups. Use scissors to make vertical cuts ½" (1.5 cm) apart from the rim of each cup to the base. These cups will be the bristles for the paintbrush.

9 Tape one black cup inside the cup covered in aluminum foil at the end of the paintbrush. Tape the second black cup inside the first black cup. Repeat with the last cup.

10 Tape the artist's brush to the palette so the brush extends about 12" (30.5 cm) above the top of the palette.

Paint me a rainbow.

Bacon and Eggs

MATERIALS

- 30" × 42" (76 × 107 cm) piece of foam core board, ½" (1.2 cm) thick
- two 2-quart (1.9 L) plastic bowls
- two 12" × 30" (30.5 × 76 cm) white sheets of polyurethane foam, 1" (2.5 cm) thick
- 6" × 30" (15 × 76 cm) strip of scrap cardboard
- 1" (2.5 cm) wide roll of white tape
- acrylic paint: yellow, red, tan, and white; 2.5 oz (75 mL) of each
- roll of 2" (5 cm) wide clear packing tape
- red baseball cap
- 5 yards (4.6 m) of thin (20 gauge) wire
- two 18" (45 cm) pieces of strong white ribbon for ties

TOOLS: craft knife, small cotton paint roller, scissors, paintbrush, pencil, marker

CHILD WEARS: white T-shirt, black pants, and black shoes

DIRECTIONS

1 Draw the shape of fried egg whites on the 30" × 42" (76 × 107 cm) foam core board and cut out the white shape (see pattern).

2 Place the 2 plastic bowls on the egg white shape (see photo). Trace around the bowls, and use a craft knife to cut out slightly smaller circles from the foam core board.

3 Tape around the outside edges of the foam core board with white tape.

4 Poke two small holes for straps in the top of the egg white (see pattern), with a 12" (30.5 cm)

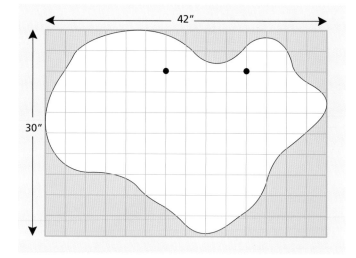

Step 1. Pattern for egg whites. 1 box = 3" (7.5 cm). Dots indicate holes for strap. Cut away blue parts.

gap between the holes. Tie an 18" (45 cm) piece of white ribbon through each of the holes and tape down the tied ends with clear tape. The ribbons are ties that will hold the costume on the child's neck.

5 Use the small cotton paint roller to cover the front of the foam core board with white acrylic paint. Let dry.

6 Mix a little red acrylic paint into your yellow paint to give it the orange tinge of an egg yolk and paint the undersides of the plastic bowls. Let dry.

7 Fit the bowls into the big holes in the egg white shape so that the rims are at the back and the rounded parts stick out the front, and tape to board from behind with the clear packing tape.

Start your morning off right!

8 Take the two sheets of polyurethane foam and use a marker to mark a wavy line on each long edge, like the edges of a strip of bacon (see photo for example). Cut on these lines with scissors.

9 To make a clean line while painting the foam strips to look like bacon, cut the 6" × 30" (15 × 76 cm) strip of cardboard so that it has a wavy line that roughly follows the edge of the foam. Then push the cardboard edge almost flush to the edge of the foam, leaving about 1" (2.5 cm) of the foam edge uncovered. Paint the uncovered foam edge with the red acrylic paint. Repeat this process on each side of each bacon strip. Paint a wavy red stripe down the middle of each piece to finish the bacon. Let dry.

10 Mix the tan paint with water. Make this very transparent. Lightly brush the foam bacon strips with this mixture to make the red paint and foam look tan. Let dry.

11 Run a piece of thin wire all around the edges of each foam bacon strip to help stiffen it, taking large running stitches with the wire along the edges as if it were thread. Twist wire ends together and cut off excess. Be sure to cover any wire ends with tape so they don't scratch anyone.

12 Poke two holes through the middle of each of the foam bacon strips with a short piece of wire. Take one of the bacon strips and wire it to the baseball cap in front (poke holes through the cap); it should balance well when the cap is on the child, and the child should be able to see easily when he is wearing the cap.

13 Wire one of the bacon strips to the bottom of the egg white shape by poking holes through the foam core and feeding the wire ends through to the back. Twist the wire's ends together to hold the bacon to the foam core, cutting off any excess. Tape down the wire ends so they won't stick the wearer.

Birdhouse

MATERIALS

- two 29" × 24" (73.5 × 61 cm) pieces of corrugated cardboard
- 24" × 40" (61 × 101.5 cm) piece of corrugated cardboard
- 24" × 24" (61 × 61 cm) piece of corrugated cardboard
- two 18" × 18" (45.5 × 45.5 cm) pieces of corrugated cardboard
- 28" × 36" (71 × 91.5 cm) yellow wrapping paper
- 28" × 72" (71 × 183 cm) green wrapping paper
- 24" × 72" (61 × 183 cm) white butcher paper
- 12" × 18" (30.5 × 45.5 cm) sheet of construction paper in each color: pink, purple, orange, yellow, red
- 12" × 12" (30.5 × 30.5 cm) sheet of blue construction paper (for bird in hair) or toy bird for hair ornament
- 12" (30.5 cm) cardboard tube, 1" (2.5 cm) wide
- lime green acrylic paint
- 2" (5 cm) wide roll clear packing tape
- white glue
- piece of newspaper
- bobby pin

TOOLS: scissors, craft knife, ¼" (5 mm) paintbrush, pencil, ruler, ruling compass

CHILD WEARS: black or white shirt, shoes in a neutral color

DIRECTIONS

1 Draw pattern and cut out the front and back of the birdhouse from the 29" × 24" (73.5 × 61 cm) cardboards.

2 Cut an 8" (20 cm) diameter circle out of the center of the front panel to create the door for the bird. Just below the door, cut out a 1" (2.5 cm) circle to hold the perch.

3 Tape an 18" × 18" (45.5 × 45.5 cm) side cardboard panel to the front panel, using clear tape, working from the bottom up; see diagram. Tape the back panel to the 18" × 18" side panel also. Tape the other 18" × 18" side panel to the other side of the front and back panels.

4 Once the cardboards are taped together, cover the front with yellow wrapping paper; tape the paper in place. Cover the sides with green wrapping paper; tape it in place.

5 Fold a 24" × 40" (61 × 101.5 cm) piece of cardboard in half so it is 24" × 20" (61 × 51 cm) to create the roof of the birdhouse. Flatten it out and wrap it with white butcher paper, taped in

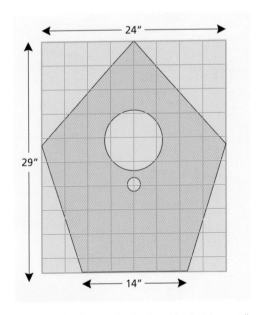

Steps 1 and 2. Pattern for front and back. 1 box = 3" (7.5 cm). Holes should be cut out only on front part. Cut away blue parts.

Make a birdhouse and see who shows up!

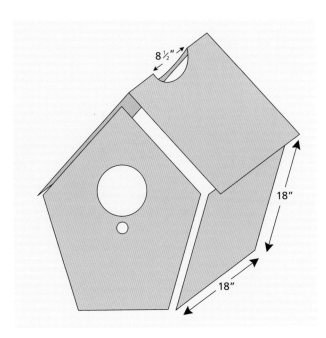

Step 3. Tape sides to front and back. Tape on roof in Step 5.

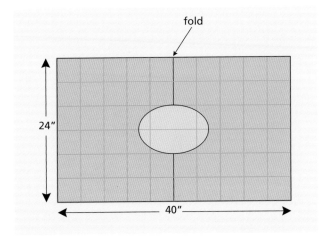

Step 5. Pattern for roof. 1 box = 4" (10 cm). Cut away oval.

place. Cut out an 8½" × 10" (21.5 × 25.5 cm) oval hole centered on the crease. The oval should extend about 5" (12.5 cm) on either side of the crease so that there will be room for the child's head once the roof has been folded and attached to the birdhouse. Try the roof on the child; enlarge oval if needed. Tape the roof to the top of the house, being sure the roof overlaps all around (see Step 3 diagram).

6 Stand the house on top of the 24" × 24" (61 × 61 cm) piece of cardboard (which will become the floor), leaving a 5" (12.5 cm) edge at the front. Trace a line around the base of the house onto the cardboard, and cut the house outline out of the cardboard floor with a craft knife to provide a space for the child to stand in inside the costume.

7 Cover the floor of the house with white paper, cutting away the paper over the inner space, and tape the floor with clear tape from inside the house to the sides of house. Glue a rolled-up newspaper to the front of the house (see photo).

8 Stack the 12" × 18" (30.5 × 45.5 cm) sheets of pink, purple, and red construction papers. On a separate piece of scratch paper or cardboard, draw a 3" (7.5 cm) flower shape and cut it out. Use that as a template to draw flower shapes with a pencil on the stacked construction paper. Cover the papers with as many flower shapes as can fit. Cut out the flowers, being careful to keep the stack of construction paper aligned, which keeps you from having to mark and cut each piece of construction paper separately.

9 Stack the 12" × 18" (30.5 × 45.5 cm) yellow and orange construction papers. Cover the top paper with 1" (2.5 cm) circles. Cut them out through all layers, being careful to keep the stack aligned.

10 Glue the pink, purple, and red flower shapes all over the roof and sides of birdhouse as seen in photo. Glue yellow and orange circles on top of flowers.

11 Insert and tape in the cardboard tube below the large hole to serve as bird perch.

12 Use the lime green paint and paintbrush to paint little stems and leaves around the flowers at the bottom of the birdhouse.

13 Fold a bird out of 12" × 12" (30.5 × 30.5 cm) blue construction paper, or use a toy bird for a hair decoration, bobby-pinning it in place.

Black Widow Spider

MATERIALS

- thirty-two 12 oz (360 mL) black plastic cups
- four 10" (25.5 cm) black plastic plates
- 10" (25.5 cm) red plastic plate
- four 1" (2.5 cm) wide × 24" (61 cm) black ribbons
- black baseball cap
- two black pipe cleaners
- ½" (1.2 cm) wide black tape
- 2" (5 cm) wide clear packing tape
- ¼" wide × 48" (0.5 × 122 cm) red ribbon for hair bows (optional)

TOOLS: scissors, ruler

CHILD WEARS: extra-large black sweatshirt, pillow, red tights, black shoes, red bows in hair

DIRECTIONS

1 With clear packing tape, tape together 4 black plastic plates into a diamond shape. On the upper black plate, cut 2 holes for straps, about 8" (20 cm) apart. Repeat this on the bottom of the diamond (the lower black plate). Tape the red plastic plate in the center of the diamond shape.

2 For a leg, tape 4 black plastic cups, one inside the next, in a stack, making a curved shape. Repeat this 7 times to make a total of 8 legs.

3 Tape 4 legs on the left side and 4 legs on the right side of the diamond shape with clear tape.

4 For straps, tie a black ribbon through each of the top holes in the plates and one through each of the bottom holes; they will hold the costume in place.

5 With black tape, make balls on the ends of the pipe cleaners and tape the pipe cleaners to the black baseball cap.

6 After the child has dressed in the oversized sweatshirt, put a pillow inside the sweatshirt on her back. Arrange the costume on the front of the child. Criss-cross the ribbon straps against her back to hold the pillow in place and to secure the costume on her shoulders and waist.

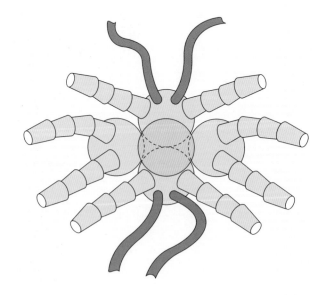

Steps 1 to 4. Make diamond of 4 black plates and a central red one. Attach legs as shown. Straps tie around child.

*Welcome to
my web.*

Cell
Phone

You rang?

MATERIALS

- twelve 12 oz (360 mL) white plastic cups
- two 6½" × 27" (16.5 × 68.5 cm) pieces of foam core board
- 6½" × 15" (16.5 × 38 cm) foam core board
- 15" × 27" (38 × 68.5 cm) foam core board
- 2" × 15" (5 × 38 cm) foam core board
- 12" × 15" (30.5 × 38 cm) foam core board
- 9" × 15" (23 × 38 cm) foam core board
- two 12½" × 7" (32 × 18 cm) pieces of foam core board
- 12½" × 15" (32 × 38 cm) foam core board
- 3" × 10" (7. 5 × 25.5 cm) cardboard tube
- 12" × 28" (30.5 × 71 cm) black wrapping paper
- three rolls of ½" (1.2 cm) wide black tape
- 8 oz (240 mL) bottle black acrylic paint
- 3 oz (90 mL) bottle white acrylic paint
- 4" × 4" (10 × 10 cm) disposable plastic container with lid
- white glue
- 2" (5 cm) wide clear packing tape
- computer printout or hand-lettered sign with the word "TALK" (letters about ¾" or 2 cm tall)
- computer printouts or hand-lettered keypad numbers and letters (numbers should be 1" or 2.5 cm tall and letters, ½" or 1 cm).

TOOLS: craft knife, medium-wide paintbrush or 3" (7.5 cm) cotton roller, ruler, pencil, scissors

CHILD WEARS: black shirt, red or contrasting color pants, black shoes

DIRECTIONS

1 Lay out the number pad with ruled pencil lines as shown in the diagram:

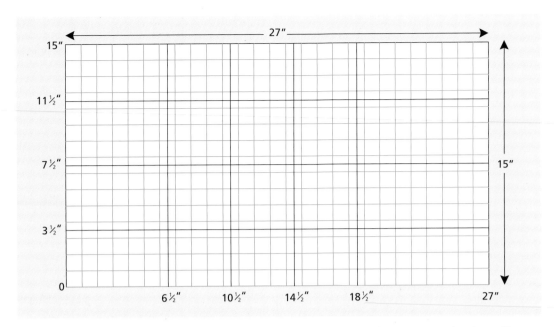

Step 1. Rule foam core board as shown. 1 box = 1" (2.5 cm). Places where black lines cross are locations of buttons.

1a Take the 15" × 27" (38 × 68.5 cm) foam core board and lay the board with the long edge facing you. Place marks on both the near and far long edges at 6½" (16.5 cm), 10½" (26.5 cm), 14½" (37 cm), and 18½" (47 cm) from the left edge.

1b Connect these marks by drawing lines from the 6½" (16.5 cm) near mark to the 6½" far mark. In the same way, connect the near and far marks at 10½", 14½", and 18½", leaving you with four 15" (38 cm) long parallel lines that are 4" (10 cm) apart from each other.

1c Next place marks at 3½" (9 cm), 7½" (19 cm), and 11½" (29 cm) on the left and right edges, measuring from the bottom edge up.

1d Connect the marks on the left edge to the marks on the right edge by ruled lines, leaving you with three 27" (68.5 cm) long parallel lines connecting the two sides, with 4" (10 cm) between them.

1e The left edge will be the top of the number pad and the right edge will be the bottom of the number pad.

2 You should have 7 lines that cross at 12 points. Use the bottom of one of your 12 oz (360 mL) cups to trace a circle that is centered over every crossing point. Cut out the circles with a craft knife. These circles will be where you will put your buttons for the number pad.

3 Clear-tape one long edge of each 6½" × 27" (16.5 × 68.5 cm) piece of foam core to each long edge of the 15" × 27" (38 × 68.5 cm) number pad.

4 Tape a long edge of the 6½" × 15" (16.5 × 38 cm) piece of foam core to the bottom edge of the number pad and to the bottom edges of the sides of the number pad to complete the main frame of the phone.

5 To create the earpiece (where the face hole is), refer to diagrams for Steps 5 and 6:

5a Make a 7½" × 8½" (19 × 21.5 cm) oval cutout in the center of the 12½" × 15" (32 × 38 cm) piece of foam core board (see diagram).

5b Tape the long edge of the 2" × 15" (5 × 38 cm) piece of foam core board to the lower 15" (38 cm) edge of the piece of foam core board with the oval cutout. (All taping joins boards at right angles.) The 2" wide piece will act as the bottom edge of the earpiece.

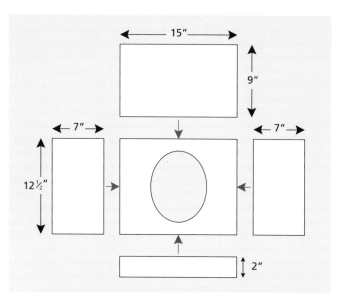

Step 5b, c, d. Assemble earpiece as shown, taping sides at right angles to central panel.

5c Tape one long edge of each 7" × 12½" (18 × 32 cm) piece to the 12½" sides of the piece with the cutout and to the 2" bottom (see diagram).

5d Then tape one 15" (38 cm) edge of the 9" × 15" (23 × 38 cm) piece of foam core to the top 15" edge of the piece with the oval cutout. Tape the 9" sides to the 7" sides of the 7" × 12½" pieces. See diagram.

6 Tape the earpiece to the number pad with the earpiece's 2" (5 cm) side towards the number pad (see diagram).

7 Paint the entire phone black. Let dry.

8 Use black tape on all of the corners and edges to make nice clean lines (don't forget to tape the edges of the oval).

9 From the back of the costume, push the plastic cups though the holes in the number pad to create the buttons for the phone and tape them in place on the back, using the 2" (5 cm) wide clear packing tape.

10 Paint the 4" × 4" (10 × 10 cm) lid and container with the white acrylic paint and let dry.

11 Glue the painted 4" (10 cm) container in the upper left portion of the number pad, above the #1 button. This container will be the "push to talk" button.

12 Glue the painted 4" lid to the bottom middle portion of the number pad (below the 0 button). This will be the mouthpiece of the phone.

13 Use the 3" × 10" (7.5 × 25.5 cm) tube to trace a circle on the top of the earpiece where an antenna would go. Cut out the circle.

14 Wrap the 3" × 10" tube with black wrapping paper. Push tube through the antenna hole and tape from the inside with the 2" (5 cm) wide clear packing tape.

15 Cut out and paste the word "TALK" on the "push to talk" button, and then cut out and paste the numbers and letters for the keypad on the appropriate buttons.

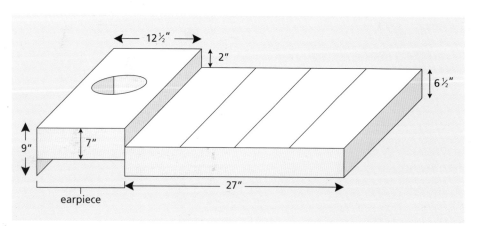

Step 6. Side view of cell phone, showing earpiece attached to body of phone.

Corn on the Cob

You could be accused of being corny.

MATERIALS

- 24" × 48" (61 × 122 cm) piece of corrugated cardboard
- 20" × 20" (51 × 51 cm) piece of corrugated cardboard
- four 2" × 30" (5 × 76 cm) strips of cardboard
- roll of clear packing tape
- two hundred ¾ oz (22 mL) plastic soufflé cups (the kind used for salad dressing)
- 8 oz (237 mL) yellow acrylic paint
- four packages (of at least 12 sheets each) green tissue paper 24" × 36" (61 × 91.5 cm)
- three packages (of at least 12 sheets each) yellow tissue paper 24" × 36" (61 × 91.5 cm)
- bottle of white glue

TOOLS: scissors, craft knife, paintbrush, ruler, pencil

CHILD WEARS: jeans, boots, white T-shirt

This is a great costume for your harvest parade. Dress the other kids as scarecrows and old black crows to make it fun for all members of the family.

DIRECTIONS

1 Create a cylinder with the 24" × 48" (61 × 122 cm) piece of cardboard and secure it by taping the 24" edges together from top to the bottom.

2 Place the cardboard cylinder on top of the 20" × 20" (51 × 51 cm) piece of cardboard. Trace around the cylinder and cut the circle out to make a lid. Tape the lid to the top of cylinder.

3 Attach the four 2" × 30" (5 × 76 cm) strips of cardboard around the lid, folding in the middle to make a point; this will make the top of the corn.

4 To fit the costume to the child, cut a 1" (2.5 cm) peephole where you think his face will be when he will wear the costume. Then place the cylinder over the child's head to figure out where to cut out the final holes for the face and arms. Look in the peephole that you cut in the costume and use a pencil to draw an oval on the outside of the cylinder that is approximately the size of your child's face. Also try to see where you want the armholes to be and trace the circles that you will cut out. Remove the costume and cut out the holes.

5 Make a center panel on the cylinder about 8" (20 cm) wide and 24" (61 cm) tall by taping down the yellow tissue paper. Tape yellow tissue paper to the top of the costume, covering the entire point.

6 Cover the rest of the costume with green tissue paper, taking care to keep it all flat and maintain clean lines. Tape using the 2" (5 cm) clear packing tape.

7 You will now need to glue the soufflè cups (representing corn kernels) to the yellow tissue. Lay the cylinder flat on your work area. Glue on the soufflé cups in rows. The soufflé cups will need to dry overnight. Prop your cylinder so it won't move.

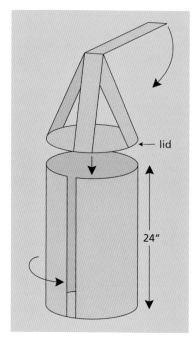

Steps 1 to 3. Making the cylinder. Fold strips in half and tape to the lid to make the point.

8 The next day, paint your soufflé cups with yellow acrylic paint. Cover all visible sides of the soufflé cups completely. Let this dry for an hour.

9 To make the corn silk, layer three sheets of yellow tissue paper and fold in half so that you have a folded stack that is 12" × 36" (30.5 × 91.5 cm). Cut these stacks into thirty-six 1" × 12" (2.5 × 30.5 cm) folded stacks of strips, being careful to keep the sheets together. Repeat the process until you've cut up four 3-sheet stacks of tissue paper. Tape the folded end of each bundle of strips to the point of the cylinder. Cover the whole top point of the costume with yellow strips, allowing the edges to fall outwards from the point. Use all of the bundles.

10 Using three sheets of tissue paper at a time, cut out thirty 6" × 18" (15 × 45.5 cm) strips of green tissue. Round one end on all of the green strips that have been cut out. This goes quicker if you keep the sheets stacked while cutting.

11 Start at the top of costume. Scrunch the green tissue in one hand to give it body and tape the 6" × 18" (15 × 45.5 cm) strips to cover the upper part of the ear of corn, with the rounded edges up and fluttering. Then, taping on row by row of green tissue paper, work down the costume, keeping ½" (1.2 cm) between rows, until you reach the bottom of the costume.

12 Tape any leftover green tissue strips to the costume near the bottom edge, allowing them to hang off the costume.

Cupcake

Just as cute as a cupcake!

MATERIALS

- circular plastic laundry basket, 24" (61 cm) in diameter*
- 18" (46 cm) white shoelace
- 5" × 24" (12.4 × 61 cm) piece of white cotton fabric
- 24" (61 cm) red ricrac
- 24" × 24" (61 × 61 cm) piece of corrugated cardboard
- 2" (5 cm) diameter cardboard tube, 24" (61 cm) long
- one sheet of 12" × 18" (30.5 × 45.5 cm) construction paper in: yellow, blue, and orange
- 7" × 28" (18 × 71 cm) yellow wrapping paper
- 2" (5 cm) wide clear packing tape
- roll of 18" (30.5 cm) wide aluminum foil, enough to surround basket twice
- 28" × 28" (71 × 71 cm) piece of polyurethane foam batting
- 28" × 28" (71 × 71 cm) pink T-shirt fabric
- plastic headband

*Laundry basket should be wide enough to fit around child's torso.

TOOLS: saw, scissors, marker, craft knife, pencil, hot glue gun, ruler, ruling compass

CHILD WEARS: white tights and shoes

DIRECTIONS

1 Cut out bottom of laundry basket with saw.

2 Turn basket upside down and lay the top edge of laundry basket flush on a 24" × 24" (61 × 61 cm) piece of cardboard, or whatever size will be larger than the top of the opening. Trace around the basket edge with pencil. Cut the traced circle out.

3 Cut out a 9" (23 cm) diameter circle right in the center of the circle you just cut from the piece of cardboard.

4 Using 2" (5 cm) wide clear packing tape, carefully tape the cardboard circle to the top of the laundry basket.

5 Lay foam batting on the work table. Turn the basket upside down on it. With a marker, trace around the cardboard circle onto the batting. Draw another circle 3" (7.5 cm) wider than the circle outline, and cut the wider circle out of the batting.

6 Use hot glue to attach the T-shirt material to the top of the foam batting, trimming the fabric's edges into the circle shape.

7 Turn the basket right-side up and hot-glue the foam batting to the top of the cardboard on the basket, turning the edges of the batting and fabric underneath while gluing to give a fluffy appearance. Cut out an 8" (20 cm) diameter hole in the center of the fluffy batting for the child's head. Turn any excess batting to the inside of the cardboard circle and hot-glue it to the cardboard circle so there are no loose edges.

8 Stack the 12" × 18" (30.5 × 45.5 cm) yellow, blue, and orange sheets of construction paper. Draw 1" (2.5 cm) diameter circles all over the top sheet. Keeping the sheets carefully stacked, cut out the 1" (2.5 cm) circles so that you have some colorful decorations to put on top of the cupcake.

9 Take the 18" (45.5 cm) wide aluminum foil and fold in each short side 1" (2.5 cm) to round off the edges. Then use the 2" (5 cm) packing tape to tape the aluminum foil to the sides of the laundry basket. To create a ridged look like a cupcake wrapper, as shown in the photo, tape every 3" (7.5 cm) and fold the aluminum foil like an accordion as you go around the cupcake (see photo).

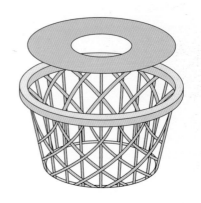

Steps 1 to 3. Basket has bottom carefully cut away. Circle for top has 9" (23 cm) diameter circle cut away in center.

10 Hot-glue the orange, yellow, and blue construction paper circles to look like confetti all over the top of the foam batting.

11 Take the 2" × 24" (5 × 30.5 cm) cardboard tube and wrap with yellow wrapping paper to make a candle for the cupcake.

12 Drip hot glue on the top and sides of the yellow candle to imitate melting wax. Let dry.

13 Tape the bottom of the candle to the headband with 2" (5 cm) wide clear packing tape.

14 To make the ruffled collar, take the 5" × 24" (12.5 × 61 cm) white cotton fabric and fold in 1" (2.5 cm) on the long side. Hot-glue the edge down along the 24" (61 cm) side to make a 1" wide casing for the shoelace. On the other long side of fabric, hot-glue the strip of ricrac. Let dry.

15 Slip the shoelace through the casing. Tie the collar around child's neck after she slips the cupcake costume on.

Cyclops

MATERIALS

- two sets of knit black gloves
- 12" (30.5 cm) diameter plastic trick-or-treat pumpkin
- two $3/8$" × 48" (1 × 122 cm) wooden dowels
- $1/2$" × 32" (1.2 × 81 cm) wooden dowel
- $1/2$" (1.2 cm) black tape
- 12 oz (360 mL) black plastic cup or black paper
- $1/2$" (1.2 cm) wide red tape
- letter-size piece of green paper
- acrylic paint: white, green, and black
- six 1 oz (30 mL) parfait cups
- 8 oz (237 mL) plastic bowl
- seven 18" (45.5 cm) black pipe cleaners
- 3 oz (90 mL) bag white marabou feathers
- 28" × 36" (71 × 91.5 cm) fuzzy orange fabric
- two 100" (254 cm) lengths of 18 gauge wire
- two 30" (76 cm) lengths of wire to attach head
- $3/4$" (2 cm) × 12" (30.5 cm) PVC pipe
- $3/4$" (2 cm) PVC T connector
- $3/4$" (2 cm) PVC 4-way connector
- two 2" × 56" (5 × 142 cm) black fabric strips
- two 8" × 36" (20 × 91.5 cm) pieces of black/white striped fabric (stripes go across 8" dimension) for sleeves
- black thread
- 24" × 36" (61 × 91.5 cm) piece of colorful striped fabric for body
- PVC pipe glue (optional)
- tacky glue
- three sheets of newspaper

TOOLS: wire cutters, drill with $1/8$" (3 mm) drill bit, needle, hot glue gun, paintbrush, ruler

CHILD WEARS: orange long-sleeved sweatshirt, black pants and shoes

DIRECTIONS

1 Drill six $1/8$" (3 mm) holes in the plastic pumpkin, just below the rim, spaced evenly around the opening, near the edge.

2 Drill four $1/8$" (3 mm) holes, $1/2$", $3/2$", 12", and $13/2$" (4 cm, 9 cm, 30 cm, and 34 cm) down from one end of the $1/2$" (1.2 cm) wide dowel. The dowel will be the body on which the head and arms are mounted.

3a To attach the head, take a 30" (76 cm) piece of wire and feed it halfway through the top hole in the dowel; then twist the wire parts together close to the dowel, leaving two equal lengths of wire facing out from the sides of the dowel. Feed one wire end through each of two holes on one side of the pumpkin (see diagram),

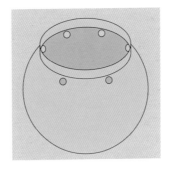

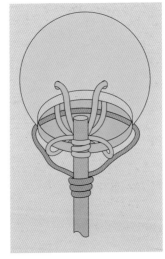

Step 1. Make 6 holes, evenly spaced, around the rim of the pumpkin.

Step 3a and b. Attach pumpkin to dowel with 2 pieces of wire.

Beware of one-eyed monsters!

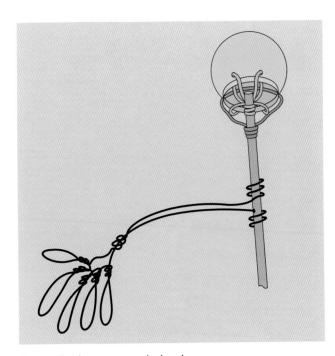

Step 4. Shaping an arm and a hand.

securing it around the dowel. Feed the other wire end through two holes on the other side of the pumpkin in the same way.

3b Take another 30" (76 cm) long wire and feed through the two remaining holes in the pumpkin. Feed one of the wire ends through the second hole in the dowel and twist the wire around dowel to secure. Bring the remaining wire end back to the dowel and twist around it for extra strength. Head should bobble.

4 Take a 100" (254 cm) piece of wire and thread one end a few inches (5 or 7 cm) through the third hole in the dowel. Twist the short end of the wire around the dowel to anchor it. This wire will become one arm and hand of the costume.

5 About 22" (56 cm) down the 100" (254 cm) wire, start to shape a hand. After shaping each finger, twist wire together at base of finger. When finished with hand, twist wire around where wrist would be. Bring excess wire back to

dowel. Twist remaining wire around dowel. Shape the second hand and arm using the second piece of 100" wire, the same way as the first one, but starting the wire in the fourth hole down on the dowel.

6 Hot-glue seven black pipe cleaners to the top of the orange head. Hot-glue white feathers to the ends of the black pipe cleaners.

7 Cover plastic pumpkin with hot glue. Drape the 28" × 36" (71 × 91.5 cm) fuzzy orange fabric over pumpkin so it covers the whole thing, and hot-glue in place, shaping the fabric around the pipe cleaners and letting some fabric hang down a few inches (5 or 7 cm) below the pumpkin edge to form a neck and cover the wires.

8 Paint the plastic bowl and six parfait cups white with acrylic paint on the undersides. Let dry.

9 From a black plastic cup or black paper, cut out six ¼" × 4" (0.5 × 10 cm) pointed shapes (see photo). Tape one sharp black point to the center of each white 1 oz (30 mL) parfait cup with red tape.

10 Tacky-glue parfait cups to the front of the orange fuzzy head in the shape of a smile.

11 To make the eye, on the bottom of the white plastic bowl, paint a green circle; then paint a black circle dead center of the green circle. Tacky-glue the bowl above the smile on the fuzzy orange head to create the Cyclops' eye.

12 Fold an 8" × 36" (20 × 91.5 cm) black-and-white striped piece of fabric in half so that it is 4" × 36" (10 × 91.5 cm). Sew the 36" (91.5 cm) edges closed to create a sleeve for one of the arms of the costume. Repeat on the other 8" × 36" (20 × 91.5 cm) piece of fabric.

13 Turn the black-and-white sleeves right-side out so that stitching is on the inside. Slip one over each wire arm. Sew one sleeve end to the base of the orange head on the orange fabric.

Does someone need his morning coffee?

5 Wrap the whole "V" frame with red wrapping paper. Cut away the paper covering the hole for child's head and tape down loose paper.

6 On the inside of the "V" frame, near the front, glue white cones for fangs, two on top in front, and two on bottom (see photo). Glue in Styrofoam cups to look like teeth also. Let dry.

7 Take a 2" × 10" (5 × 25.5 cm) piece of cardboard and stick a toothpick straight through the cardboard into a 6" (15 cm) Styrofoam ball to make an eye. Place the other 6" ball next to the first eye (leave a little room in between for a nose) and join it to the cardboard in the same way. Glue the toothpicks in place so they stay well.

8 Paint a Styrofoam egg orange and attach it with a toothpick and glue in between the 6" (15 cm) Styrofoam balls, for a nose.

9 Tape the 2" × 10" (5 × 25.5 cm) cardboard that has the eyes and nose to the top edge of the "V" frame, near the front, using red tape.

10 With hot glue, stick a blue Easter egg onto each 6" (15 cm) Styrofoam eyeball.

11 Cut out two 2" × 8" (5 × 20 cm) black strips from black plastic plates or cardboard. Hot-glue each to the top of a 6" (15 cm) Styrofoam eye ball to be an eyebrow.

12 For claws, mark out twelve 4¼" × 4¼" × 6" (10.8 × 10.8 × 15.2 cm) triangles on the 6" × 18" (15 × 45.5 cm) white construction paper and cut them out.

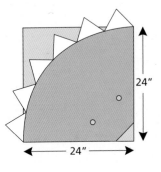

Step 13. Grid for drawing and cutting out paw boards. 1 box = 4" (10 cm). Black dot = hole for ribbon. Swing an arc from corner to corner that fits all the claws. Cut away gray parts.

13 For paws, lay 6 claw triangles on a 24" × 24" (61 × 61 cm) piece of cardboard (see diagram). Draw an arc from one corner of the cardboard to its diagonally opposite corner to make a quarter circle. This should make a large paw, large enough to fit all 6 claws, but don't attach them yet. Cut out the paw shape, trimming off the corner (see diagram). Make another paw on the other 24" × 24" (61 × 61 cm) cardboard.

14 Cover each paw board front and back with part of the orange tablecloth, gluing and taping it in place.

15 Glue and tape 6 white triangles as claws on each paw board.

16 Tape a 1" (2.5 cm) tall red tip around the point of each claw with red tape.

17 Poke 2 holes about 4" (10 cm) apart, about 8 inches (20 cm) in from the end of the paw (see diagram for Step 13). String a ribbon through the paw holes and tie each paw to the child's arm (see photo).

Fireworks

Start the celebration!

MATERIALS

- 17" × 17" (43 × 43 cm) piece of corrugated cardboard
- two 14" × 36" (35.5 × 91.5 cm) pieces of corrugated cardboard
- lightweight wire tomato tower (trellis), round or square
- seven rolls of decorative star wire garland
- four 20" (51 cm) shooting star cone decorations
- 28" × 6' (71 × 183 cm) aluminum foil
- four 1" × 2" × 16½" (2.5 × 5 × 42 cm) wooden stakes
- four 2" (5 cm) diameter × 6" (15 cm) wooden dowels
- four large screw eyes (trellis leg must fit through eye)
- 28" × 6' (71 × 183 cm) red wrapping paper
- eight 1" (2.5 cm) drywall screws
- four 2" (5 cm) drywall screws
- 12" × 18" (30.5 × 45.5 cm) sheets of construction paper: 1 of yellow, 1 of red; 1 of blue, 2 of gold, 2 of silver, 1 of white
- white glue
- Chinese style rice-farmer's straw hat, or paper hat
- 2" (5 cm) wide clear packing tape
- two 36" (91.5 cm) lengths of strong ribbon for shoulder straps; color to match shirt

TOOLS: pliers, diagonal-cutting pliers or wire cutters, staple gun, screwdriver, drill and drill bits, scissors

CHILD WEARS: a silver top or red shirt covered in silver stars, blue jeans, and white shoes

DIRECTIONS

1 Pinch off the lowest horizontal round or bar on the tomato trellis all around, leaving the top three so there is room for the child to stand.

2 Turn the tomato trellis upside down and trace the top of the trellis (may be a circle or another shape) onto a 17" × 17" (43 × 43 cm) piece of cardboard, or whatever size you need for the top. Cut out the traced shape and wrap with aluminum foil. This will be the top of the fireworks.

3 Poke 3 holes in the top of the fireworks. Insert the bottoms of the 20" (51 cm) shooting star decorations into the fireworks top so they hang upside down, and clear-tape them to the fireworks top. Set aside the top of the fireworks for now.

4 Wrap the entire tomato trellis with star garlands.

5 Stack the red, yellow, silver, gold, white, and blue construction paper. On the top sheet draw as many star shapes as will fit, and cut out the stars through all layers.

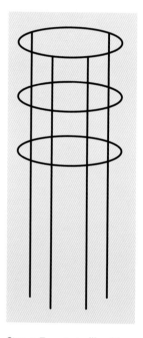

Step 1. Tomato trellis with one round cut away, or as many as are needed for child to have room to stand.

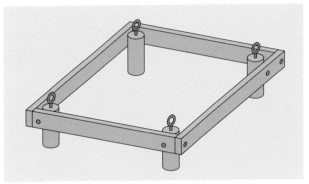

Step 9. Assembled frame has dowels with screw eyes in their tops.

6 Wrap the straw hat with aluminum foil and secure the foil with clear tape.

7 Wrap each of the 14" × 36" (35.5 × 91.5 cm) cardboard pieces with red wrapping paper and tape paper in place. Glue large white and blue paper stars in a row to the middle of the covered cardboard. These pieces of cardboard will be stapled to the wooden frame for sides to the box part of the costume.

8 Place silver stars and gold stars back to back and glue to wire garlands on the tomato trellis. The more stars glued, the merrier.

9 With the four wooden stakes, create a wooden frame on which to mount the tomato trellis, using two of the 1" (2.5 cm) drywall screws to join the stakes together at each corner. Glue a dowel section inside each corner, adding a 2" (5 cm) screw through the frame near each corner for added strength.

10 Drill a hole in the top of each dowel section and insert a screw eye in each. These screw eyes will be used to anchor the trellis in the wooden frame.

11 Flip the tomato trellis and wooden frame onto their sides. Using the pliers, wrap the wire end of each leg of the tomato trellis through one of the screw eyes on the dowels and around itself to secure it. Cover any sharp ends with tape. Be sure all the trellis legs end up being the same length.

12 For straps, tie two 36" (91.5 cm) lengths of strong ribbon to the front of the wooden frame, about 10" (25 cm) apart. Then cross them diagonally and tie them onto the back of the frame, adjusting them to your child's height so they hold the costume on the shoulders.

13 Using the staple gun, staple the 14" × 36" (35.5 × 91.5 cm) cardboard pieces you decorated in Step 7 to the wooden frame as box sides, bending them as necessary to go around corners. Cover all 4 sides of the frame. The cardboard should extend up a few inches (3 to 6 cm) above the frame, so the dowels and frame don't show.

14 With clear packing tape, attach the aluminum-foil-covered top of the trellis from Step 3.

15 Make the costume as festive as you want by scattering stars around the costume.

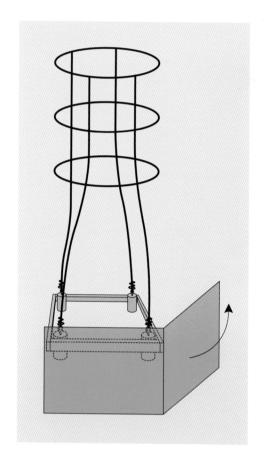

Step 13. Staple cardboard side to frame so it hides dowels; bend cardboard at corner.

Basket of Flowers

MATERIALS

- 24" (61 cm) wide wicker laundry basket*
- fifty-six 8 oz (240 mL) Styrofoam coffee cups
- five 1-gallon (3.8 L) plastic water jugs
- twenty-eight colored plastic Easter eggs
- acrylic paint, 2.5 oz (75 mL) size: yellow, orange, pink, and purple
- fifty-six green pipe cleaners
- twenty 12" × 18" (30.5 × 45.5 cm) sheets of green tissue paper
- 2" (5 cm) wide clear packing tape
- plastic headband
- two 2" × 24" (5 × 61 cm) strips of strong green cotton fabric or green ribbon
- tacky glue
- 1" (2.5 cm) wide green tape

*Laundry basket must be wide enough for child to wear around torso.

TOOLS: scissors, saw, ruler, paintbrush

CHILD WEARS: green or black sweatshirt, tan pants, and white shoes

DIRECTIONS

1 Cut away the bottom from a 24" (61 cm) laundry basket with a saw. Make sure to cut away only the inside of the bottom; cut as close to the edge binding as possible without cutting the binding.

2 To make small flowers, cut ½" (1.2 cm) wide strips into the Styrofoam cups, starting around the rim and stopping about ½" (1.2 cm) up from the bottom of cup. Do this to all 56 cups.

3 Paint the insides of the small flower cups with hot pink, purple, orange, and yellow acrylic paint. Use one color per cup. Do not paint the white edges of cup. Let dry.

4 Take one-half of a colored Easter egg and run tacky glue around the open edge of the egg. Glue each half in the center of a painted Styrofoam cup. Let dry. Repeat this for all 56 cups. Make sure that the color of the egg is not the same as the color of the inside of the cup. A good combination is a light color on top of a dark color or a dark color on top of a light one.

5 Cut the green tissue paper into fifty-six 4" × 12" (10 × 30.5 cm) strips for leaves. Fold each tissue paper strip in half and tape it with green tape along with a green pipe cleaner end to the back of a cup. The green pipe cleaners will be the flower stems. Do this to all 56 cups. Set aside.

6 Take all five 1-gallon (3.8 L) water jugs and cut the bottom off each. Shape the sides with scissors to look like tulip petals. Paint the

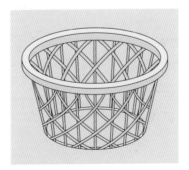 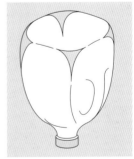

Step 1. Bottom of basket is cut away.

Step 6. Trim the sides of the water jug to make a tulip shape. Shaded parts and bottom are cut away.

Win someone's heart by bringing her flowers.

petals with color. Let dry. Tape the mouth of the water jug with green tape to look like the stem of a tulip. Tie pipe cleaners and green tissue paper around the mouth of each water-jug tulip.

7 Decide which side will be the front of costume. Insert the green pipe cleaner stem of each small flower in the basket rim and twist the pipe cleaner around itself to hold it in place. Attach your flowers side by side in the same way until they go completely around the front of basket.

8 Make another row of flowers above the first row. Lightly tape the rows together with clear packing tape to secure. Be sure to save some flowers for the headband.

9 For shoulder straps, take 2" × 24" (5 × 61 cm) strips of green fabric or ribbon and tie one end of each onto the front of the basket through the rim. They should be about 10" (25 cm) apart. Slip the loose end of one strip of the green fabric through the handles of half the water-jug tulips. Do the same thing for the second fabric strip with the rest of the water-jug tulips. Criss-cross the straps and tie the loose ends of the green fabric strips onto the rim at the back of the basket, about 10" apart from each other. Slip the basket over the child's head and adjust the strap length as needed.

10 Fold twelve 4" × 12" (10 × 30.5 cm) strips of green tissue paper in half. Wrap tissue paper around the straps; this is easiest to do when child is already in costume.

11 Wrap the headband with green tape. Twist the pipe cleaner stems of a few flowers made of Styrofoam cups around the headband, and tape flowers in place with clear packing tape (see photo).

Frankenstein's Monster

MATERIALS

- 8" × 14" × 16" (20 × 35.5 × 40.6 cm) cardboard box
- 12" × 12" × 30" (30.5 × 30.5 × 76 cm) cardboard box
- 6" × 10" × 32" (15 × 25.5 × 81 cm) cardboard box
- 18" × 24" (45.5 × 61 cm) piece of corrugated cardboard
- 54" × 108" (137 × 274 cm) green plastic tablecloth
- 54" × 108" (137 × 274 cm) purple plastic tablecloth
- two 8 oz (240 mL) purple plastic bowls
- eight 10" (25.5 cm) black plastic plates
- 10" (25.5 cm) yellow plastic plate
- 10" (25.5 cm) white plastic plate
- four 8" (20 cm) diameter orange plastic plates
- two 12 oz (360 mL) black plastic cups
- five 12 oz (360 mL) red plastic cups
- dome lid for 12 oz (360 mL) plastic cup
- two 3 oz (90 mL) plastic cups
- 24" × 24" (61 × 61 cm) piece of aluminum foil
- 2" (5 cm) wide clear packing tape
- ½" (1.2 cm) wide yellow tape
- tacky glue
- white glue
- red acrylic paint

TOOLS: scissors, pencil, ½" (1.2 cm) paint-brush, ruler, 3" (7.5 cm) paint roller, craft knife

CHILD WEARS: black pants, black shirt and shoes

DIRECTIONS

1 Tape all the boxes so that their flaps are closed. Lay the 12" × 12" × 30" (30.5 × 30.5 × 76 cm) box on the work surface on its largest side, so its length is vertical to you; it will become the face box. Place the 8" × 14" × 16" (20 × 35.5 × 40.6 cm) box horizontally on the work surface with one 16" (40.6 cm) side on the table, centered above the top end of the 12" × 12" × 30" box (see diagram). The smaller box will be the forehead of the costume. The forehead will stick out about 2" (5 cm) over the face and will extend beyond the sides of the face box. Tape the boxes together, using the 2" (5 cm) wide clear packing tape.

2 On the right side of the face box and 2" (5 cm) back from the front surface, mark a 6" deep and 10" wide (15 × 25.5 cm) rectangle, and cut it into the face box. Its lower edge should be flush with the bottom of the face box (see diagram). Its back edge should be flush with the back of the face box. Cut another rectangle the same way on the left side of the face box. The spaces you have cut will hold the shoulder box.

3 For the shoulders, push the 6" × 10" × 32" (15 × 25.5 × 81 cm) box into the spaces cut for the shoulders so that the long side of the box is running across

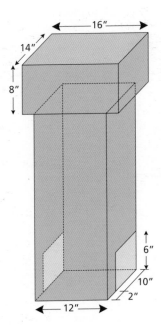

Step 2. Assembly of forehead box and face box. Gray part is cut away in face box to hold shoulder box.

inside and is centered in the face box. The 6"
(15 cm) side of the shoulder box should be
flush with the back of the face box. When
placed properly, the shoulder box should be
about 2" (5 cm) set back from the front of the
face box, and the shoulders should stick out 10"
(25.5 cm) to either side. Don't glue in place yet.

4 To lay out the 8" × 11" (20 × 27.5 cm) hole for
the mouth in the front of the face:

4a Make rules across the front of the face box,
7" (17.6 cm) and 18" (45.7 cm) up from the
bottom edge of the face box.

4b Measure in 2" (5 cm) from the edges of the
box on both lines and make marks for the
corners of the rectangle that you will cut out for
the mouth.

4c Rule vertical lines between the top (7") and
bottom (18") lines to finish the mouth
rectangle. Cut out the mouth from the cardboard.

4d Stand the costume upside down so its
lower end is up. In the bottom of the face box
and the shoulder box, cut a space that is large
enough for the child to fit in when he is wearing
the costume. Try the costume on the child;
be sure the child can see out and wear it
comfortably.

5 Remove the shoulder box from the costume.
Use the 3" (7.5 cm) paint roller to cover the
boxes for the face and forehead with white glue.
Then cover both boxes with large rectangles
cut from the green tablecloth. Tape the edges of
the tablecloth down with 2" (5 cm) wide clear
packing tape to create clean lines for the
costume. (Cover over the mouth hole when
wrapping.)

6 Clear the mouth hole by cutting through the
green tablecloth and trimming it to near the
edges of the hole. Then fold the excess tablecloth inside the box to create a clean edge, and
tape excess inside, using 2" (5 cm) wide clear
packing tape. Cut away the green tablecloth
that covers the side holes in the face box also.
Cover the shoulder box with part of the purple

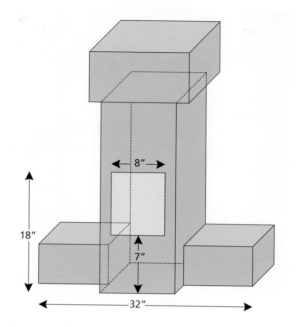

Steps 4 and 5. Shoulder box is inserted in face box. Window
for face is cut out (gray area).

tablecloth in the same way as for the other
boxes, and reinsert the shoulder box in position. Reserve enough purple plastic for the
chestplate.

7 Cut a 10" (25.5 cm) yellow plastic plate in
half. Then cut deep zigzags in each half to
create the monster's teeth.

8 Tape the half-plates with teeth inside the
mouth, using the yellow tape. Be careful to
make the teeth look menacing from the outside.

9 Paint the dome lid for the 12 oz (35.5 mL)
plastic cup using the red acrylic paint. Let it dry.

10 To create the nose, tape together three
12 oz (360 mL) red cups, stacking and taping
one inside of the other. Snap the dome lid on
the last cup to finish the nose.

11 Glue the nose to the center of the face
above the mouth with tacky glue (see photo).

12 Tacky-glue the purple bowls to each side of
the nose for eyes.

13 Cut out circles from white plastic plates to
make the whites of the monster's eyes. Tacky-
glue these to the eyes (purple bowls).

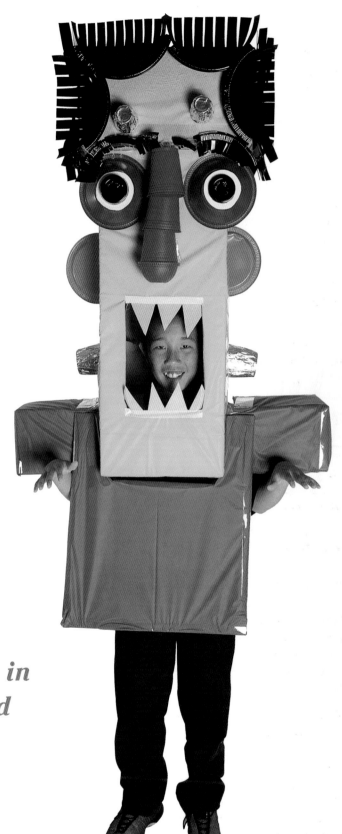

You are really in over your head this time!

14 Cut off bottoms of two 12 oz (360 mL) black plastic cups to make ½" (1.2 cm) tall black plastic disks for the centers of the eyes. Tacky-glue these to the white circles on the eyes.

15 Cover two 3 oz (90 mL) plastic cups and two 12 oz (360 mL) plastic cups with aluminum foil.

16 Tacky-glue the two 3 oz (90 mL) foil-covered cups to the forehead to look like bolts.

17 Use the bottoms of the 12 oz (360 mL) aluminum-foil-covered cups to trace circles 3" (7.5 cm) above the shoulders on the sides of the face box. Use scissors to cut out the circles. Then push the 12 oz (360 mL) foil-covered cups through the holes to make bolts for the sides of the face. Use 2" (5 cm) wide clear packing tape on the inside of the costume to secure the cups.

18 Cut a ¾" × 8" (2 × 20 cm) slit on each side of the head that is parallel to the face, starting 5" (12.5 cm) above the neck bolts. These slits will be used to hold the monster's ears.

19 Hold two 8" (20 cm) orange plastic plates face to face; then push these partway into one of the ear slits until the plates are properly seated. Tape them on the inside using 2" (5 cm) wide clear packing tape. Repeat the process for the second ear.

20 For the hair, cut six 10" (25 cm) black plastic plates in half. Cut ¾" (2 cm) wide strips down each half, starting from the straight edge, about 2½" (6.4 cm) deep. Don't cut the plate rims. Repeat this for all 12 halves.

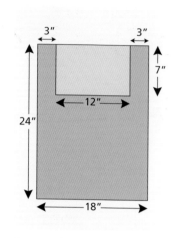

Step 23. Chestplate of costume. Gray area is cut away.

21 Tacky-glue the hair circle halves around the top of the forehead as shown in photo, being sure they adhere well to the box.

22 Cut the other two black plastic plates in half and cut out the half-circle bottoms; reserve the rims for eyebrows. Use the four half-circles to fill in extra spaces between the cut black plates, as needed. This should leave you with four half-rims from the plate edges. Without cutting all the way through to the outer edges, cut narrow strips into the ring, ¼" or ⅛" (5 mm or 3 mm) wide. Use for eyebrows. Trim to the right size and tacky-glue above the eyes.

23 Cut a rectangle 12" (30.5 cm) wide and 7" (18 cm) deep from one 18" side of the 18" × 24" (45.4 × 61 cm) cardboard, centering the rectangle on the width (it is 3" or 7.5 cm in from each edge). Cover the piece of cardboard with the remaining purple tablecloth. Trim and tape the edges of the tablecloth in place, using 2" (5 cm) wide clear packing tape. Try to keep clean lines on the edges. This will be the monster's chestplate.

24 You can tacky-glue the chestplate to the shoulders of the costume under the chin, to help stabilize the costume when it is worn. You can also attach a strap to the chestplate to go around the child's shoulders if you find that you need it.

Heart Box of Candy

MATERIALS

- two 36" × 36" (91.5 × 91.5 cm) pieces of corrugated cardboard
- 36" × 36" (91.5 × 91.5 cm) white paper
- two 12" × 48" (30.5 × 122 cm) pieces of corrugated cardboard
- 7' × 36" (213 × 91.5 cm) red wrapping paper
- three 24" × 24" (61 × 61 cm) sheets of black paper
- acrylic paint: 2.5 oz (75 mL) each of brown, hot pink, red, orange, and green
- 3 oz (85 g) acrylic gel medium
- 2" (5 cm) wide roll clear packing tape
- seven blocks of polyurethane foam, 2" × 5" × 8" (5 × 12.5 × 20.3 cm)
- four circles of polyurethane foam, 7" (18 cm) diameter × 2" (5 cm) thick
- glue

TOOLS: craft knife, scissors, small paintbrush, pencil, ruler

CHILD WEARS: white pants or tights, black shoes

DIRECTIONS

Making the Heart Box

1 On a 36" × 36" (91.5 × 91.5 cm) piece of cardboard, draw a large heart shape that uses as much of the area as possible, all the way out to the edges.

2 Cut out the heart shape to be the front panel of the heart and lay it on the second 36" × 36" (91.5 × 91.5 cm) piece of cardboard. Trace around the heart shape and cut out the heart to be the back of the box. On the 36" × 36" (91.5 × 91.5) white paper, trace and cut out a third heart. Set the paper heart aside.

3 On the front panel cardboard only, cut an 8" × 8" (20 × 20 cm) square out of the upper left area (see pattern). This will be where the child's face looks out of the costume.

4 Take a 12" × 48" (30.5 × 122 cm) piece of cardboard and start taping one long edge to the edge of the rear heart panel; continue taping it around the right half of the rear panel to make the side of the box. Tape it on the inside and

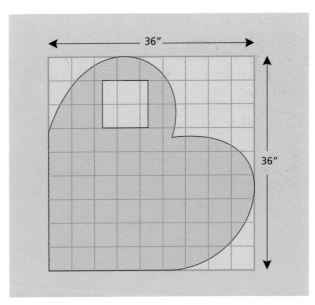

Step 1. Pattern for heart box front and back. 1 box = 4" (10 cm). Cut window in front only. Gray parts are cut away.

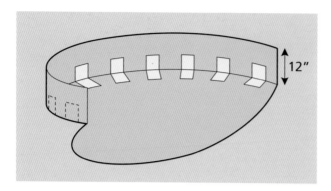

Step 4. Taping the edge to the back of heart.

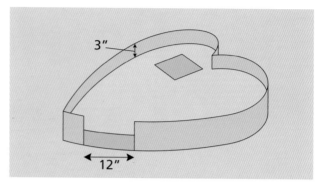

Steps 5 and 6. Front of heart box is recessed 3" (7.5 cm). Opening in side for child to stand is 12" (30.5 cm).

outside of the heart. Tape the other 12" × 48" (30.5 × 122 cm) piece of cardboard to the left half of the rear panel. Trim excess of 12" × 48" cardboard, if any.

5 Tape the front heart panel to the sides of the box, but be sure the front heart panel is recessed 3" (7.5 cm) from the side edges. The distance between the front and back will be 9" (23 cm).

6 On the bottom right of the heart, cut a 12" × 12" (30.5 × 30.5 cm) hole in the side wall of the box for the child's legs. This hole should be directly below the face hole in the top left corner. Try costume on child to see if she can fit into it, and check that the face can look out of the hole. Make any adjustments necessary.

7 After you are happy with the fit and have the costume taped solidly together, tape the white paper heart you made in Step 2 over the front panel of the heart and cut out the 12" × 12" (30.5 × 30.5 cm) window for the face hole.

Decorating and Finishing

8 Wrap the sides and back of the heart with red wrapping paper. When wrapping the heart around the sides, make sure you have enough width; allow an extra 4" (10 cm) of paper to wrap around the front edges of the heart box, all the way down to the white paper heart.

9 From the three sheets of black paper, cut the following: seven 6" × 9" (15 × 23 cm) rectangles; four 8" (20.3 cm) diameter circles; and twelve 2" × 24" (5 × 61 cm) strips of black paper.

10 Fan-fold a 2" × 24" (5 × 61 cm) strip of black paper by folding it back and forth in 2" (5 cm) wide folds. Do this for all 12 strips. They will be the papers around the candies.

11 Tape fan-folded black paper strips around the outside of each 6" × 9" (15 × 23 cm) black paper square and 8" (20.3 cm) diameter circle. These circles and squares will be the candy wrappers. Tape one fan-folded paper around the face window opening also.

12 Glue each candy wrapper onto the front of the heart box.

13 Paint all 5" × 8" (12.5 × 20.3 cm) blocks of foam with brown acrylic paint. Let dry. Glue the blocks into their wrappers.

14 Paint the 8" (20.3 cm) circles of foam with acrylic paint; make 2 red and 2 orange. Let dry. Glue the foam circles into the round candy wrappers.

15 Using hot pink, red, and green acrylic paint mixed with gel medium to add thickness, decorate the "candies" with heart shapes, curlicues, zigzags, and roses with stems (see photo). Let dry.

Who wouldn't want to be a big sweetheart?

Hot Air Balloon

MATERIALS

- round wire tomato tower (trellis)
- 20" (51 cm) diameter inflatable beach ball
- round wicker or plastic basket 12" to 15" (30.5 to 38 cm) tall × 20" (51 cm) diameter*
- duct tape
- clear tape
- roll of twine
- four pink preassembled ribbon bows
- four yellow preassembled ribbon bows
- spool of curly orange ribbon
- spool of curly pink ribbon
- four small brown paper bags
- two 36" × 1" (91 × 2.5 cm) lengths of strong ribbon for straps of costume
- 6' (about 2 m) of nylon fishing line
- a few pieces of paper

*Basket should be large enough to fit around child, and basket edges should line up with trellis legs.

TOOLS: diagonal-cutting pliers, saw, pliers, scissors, ruler

CHILD WEARS: white or black pants and shoes. This will keep the color focus on the costume. Cute long-sleeved striped shirt on top. A boy might wear a beanie and a painted-on French mustache. Girl could wear hair pulled back with festive ribbons.

DIRECTIONS

1 Take the tomato trellis and cut the last 2 circles off the frame with diagonal-cutting pliers to assure enough room for the child to stand and move comfortably, but leave the uprights.

2 Cut out the bottom of the basket with the saw. Cut just inside of the frame; don't cut the frame or the basket will fall apart.

3 Tape any rough edges on the tomato trellis with duct tape to make all edges smooth.

4 To attach the tomato trellis to the basket, start by slipping all four upright wire legs from the tomato trellis into the top of the basket. Keep the wires aligned and about a foot (30 cm) apart from each other. Measure down from the second circle on the tomato frame to the top of

Steps 4 and 5. Trellis leg is slipped through basket, bent up, and twisted around itself.

Up, up, and away!

the basket. This distance should be the same on all 4 legs of the trellis to keep the tomato trellis circles parallel to the top of the basket. Put the beach ball in the upper circle of trellis. Adjust the height of the costume so the child can stand in it without the ball hitting her head. Make sure the costume is not top-heavy.

5 Once the height is determined, bend each wire leg through the basket and twist each leg back up and around the wire frame.

6 Duct-tape these four attachments. Make sure all wire ends are covered by tape.

7 Measure out five 36" (91 cm) strands of twine at a time. Tie them in groups of 5 in a knot at the top of the tomato trellis. Wrap the tomato trellis with the twine. Make sure the tomato trellis does not show through. Measure out additional 36" lengths of twine as needed.

8 Open up the pink ribbon bows and tape on the top circle of the tomato trellis, evenly spaced around the top, about 10" (25 cm) apart.

9 Cut about five 18" (45.5 cm) strands of curly orange ribbon and hang these like bunting between the pink bows (see photo).

10 Use yellow ribbon bows and pink curly ribbon for bunting to decorate the lower circle of the tomato trellis, the same way you did in Step 9.

11 Fill the small brown bags with paper. Tie off the top of the bags with twine. These will be the sandbags. Then use twine to tie each bag to one of the four uprights of the trellis.

12 Tie the strong ribbons through the top edge of the basket in front and in back, about 10" (25 cm) apart, to make two shoulder straps that will fit over your child's clothes. Criss-cross straps in back before tying. Have child stand in the basket and adjust the straps to the child's height. Distribute the weight evenly.

13 Place the beach ball in the frame and secure it with a few pieces of nylon fishing line attached to the frame and over the ball.

Lemonade Stand

MATERIALS

- 24" × 36" (61 × 91.5 cm) white foam core board, ¼" (0.6 cm) wide
- 27" × 48" (68.5 × 122 cm) piece of corrugated cardboard
- two 14" × 14" (35.5 × 35.5 cm) pieces of corrugated cardboard (sides)
- 48" (122 cm) strong curly white ribbon for straps, ½" (1.2 cm) wide
- five red paper cups
- two ⅜" (1 cm) diameter 48" (122 cm) wooden dowels
- 4 yards (3.7 m) thin red ribbon
- 28" × 7' (71 × 213 cm) yellow wrapping paper
- roll of 1" (2.5 cm) wide yellow tape
- roll of 2" (5 cm) wide clear packing tape
- tacky glue
- red, light yellow, dark yellow, white, and black acrylic paints
- 20" × 30" (51 × 76 cm) white butcher paper

TOOLS: ¼" (0.5 cm) paintbrush, craft knife, scissors, ruler

CHILD WEARS: blue shirt, pants, and sandals, or goes barefoot

DIRECTIONS

1 Cut a 13" × 27" (33 × 68.4 cm) rectangle of cardboard and cover with white butcher paper for a sign.

2 Paint "Lemonade" across the sign in red paint. Let dry.

3 Cut a 4" × 27" (10 × 68.5 cm) rectangle of cardboard and cover with white butcher paper. It will be the shelf.

4 Cut a 10" × 27" (25.5 × 68.5 cm) rectangle of cardboard and cover with yellow wrapping paper to be the front of the stand.

5 Cut a 14" × 27" (35.5 × 68.5 cm) rectangle of cardboard and wrap one side with yellow wrapping paper. This will be the back wall.

Lemonade

1⁰⁰

When life brings you lemons, make lemonade.

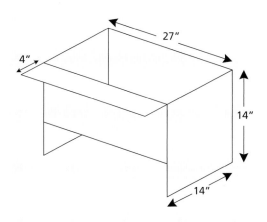

Steps 9 to 11. The stand with its shelf.

6 Take the two 14" × 14" (35.5 × 35.5 cm) squares of cardboard and cover each with yellow wrapping paper.

7 Cover the 2 dowels with white butcher paper by twisting and taping a thin strip of paper around each dowel.

8 Tape the red ribbon at top of dowel and twist it around dowel. Tape at bottom also. Repeat this on the other dowel.

9 Tape the white 4" × 27" (10 × 68.5 cm) shelf panel on its long side to the yellow 10" × 27" (25.5 × 68.5 cm) front panel on its long side, using 2" (5 cm) wide clear tape. The 4" × 27" shelf panel extends out from the front panel.

10 Tape a yellow 14" × 14" (35.5 × 35.5 cm) side panel to each side of the yellow front panel, using 2" (5 cm) clear packing tape.

11 Tape the 14" × 27" (35.5 × 68.5 cm) back wall from Step 5, with its yellow side facing front (inward), to each of the 14" × 14" (35.5 × 35.5 cm) side panels. This should leave you with a rectangular box shape that is open at the bottom and top.

12 Tape a dowel inside each front corner of the box. As much as possible of the dowel should be taped inside the box, so the structure will be strong.

13 Tape the "Lemonade" sign near the top of the dowels.

14 Glue red paper cups to white ledge of the stand.

15 Cut out two 8" (20 cm) diameter circles of foam core board for lemon slices. Cut three whole lemon shapes out of foam core board. Cut out one glass with a lemon slice shape (see photo) out of foam core board.

16 Paint the whole lemon shapes dark yellow. Let dry and tape edges with yellow tape.

17 Paint the lemon slice circles with light yellow. Let dry. Then paint their outer edges with dark yellow paint. Paint 1" (2.5 cm) white lines around the insides (see photo) of the slices for highlights. Let dry. Tape outer edges with yellow tape. Paint the glass of lemonade, straw, and ice cubes as shown in photo. Outline with black paint.

18 Cut one lemon slice circle in half. Tape its cut edges with yellow tape.

19 On one circle, paint "$1.00" or another price.

20 Tape three lemons and two slices with clear tape to the stand (see photo).

21 Paint and tape the lemonade glass shape and the circle with the price to the top of the sign.

22 Poke a hole on the front of the stand about 9" (23 cm) in from the right corner of the stand and an inch (2.5 cm) down from the counter. Poke another hole about 9" in from the left corner. Do the same on the back of the stand. Take a 48" (122 cm) length of white ribbon and knot it on the outside of the stand. Thread the ribbon through a hole in the front. Do the same with the second length of ribbon. These ribbons will be the straps that rest on the child's shoulders. Criss-cross the ribbons. Tie off the ribbons on the back of the stand, after adjusting the straps to your child's height.

Lobster

MATERIALS

- 2" (5 cm) wide clear packing tape
- fifteen red plastic plates, dinner size
- twenty-four 12 oz (360 mL) red plastic disposable cups*
- four to six pieces of 12" × 12" (30.5 × 30.5 cm) red felt for claws
- 16" × 16" (40.5 × 40.5) red felt for hat
- red tape
- clear packing tape
- 24" × 24" (61 × 61 cm) piece of corrugated cardboard
- 8 oz (240 mL) bottle of white glue
- red thread
- 6 yards (5.5 m) thin wire
- red ribbon, ½" (1.2 cm) wide: 96" (243 cm) to tie on claws, for hat ties, and for straps

*Science buffs may notice that our lobster is missing two legs. Actually, lobsters have 8 legs plus two claws. If you wish, add another two legs, in which case you need 8 more cups and more wire.

TOOLS: scissors, craft knife, ruling compass, wire cutter, hole punch, ruler, sewing needle, straight pins

CHILD WEARS: red sweatshirt, red sweatpants, red tennis shoes

DIRECTIONS

1 For the breastplate, arrange 4 or 5 plates on a table by partially overlapping one on the next in a row, with the backs of the plates up. Use red tape to attach the bottom of the first plate to the top back of the next plate. Repeat this with the rest of the plates. You might need 4 or 5 plates, depending on the child's height. The breastplate should cover the child from the collar to the thighs. Make a second row of plates for the backplate in the same way.

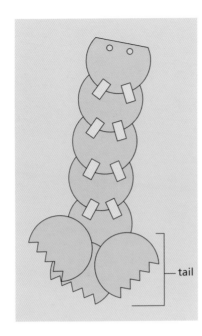

Steps 1 to 3. Assembly of plates to make the breastplate and backplate. Dots at top are holes where ribbons will go. Extra 3 plates for tail are added to the back only.

tail

2 Cut across the first (top) plate of the breastplate about 3" (7.5 cm) down to make a flat top. Tape the cut edge with clear tape to keep it smooth. With a hole punch, punch two holes on the taped edge, about 1" (2.5 cm) in from the edge and 3" (7.5 cm) apart. These holes are for the straps that will go over the child's shoulders. Cut and tape the first (top) plate of the backplate in the same way, and punch 2 holes in the top of the first plate of the backplate also.

3 For the tail, cut a jagged, sawtooth edge across each of 3 plates, about ⅓ of the way up. Tape the 3 sawtooth plates to the lowest plate in the backplate stack you made.

4 There will be 6 legs, 3 on each side (or, if you prefer, make 4 on each side). To make a leg, poke 2 holes about an inch (2.5 cm) apart through the bottom of each of 4 red cups. Cut a 36" (91.5 cm) piece of wire. Fold wire in half. Then slip the ends of the wire in the holes on the bottom of the cup, starting from outside the cup. Twist the wires together in the inside of the cup. Then slip the wires into the holes of the next cup. Make a circle with the tape, leaving the sticky side out, and stick the tape on the inside bottom of the first cup. Press the

next cup to the sticky tape. This will help your lobster legs to have shape. Attach 4 cups in total for each leg. Make a total of 6 legs (or 8, if you prefer). Don't trim off the excess wire; you'll need it to attach the legs to the rest of the costume.

5a To attach the legs to the front of the costume, poke 2 holes on the left and 2 on the right side of each of the first 3 plates. Take a leg you made earlier. Thread the loose wire ends through a set of 2 holes, working from the front of the breastplate, and twist the wires together on the back of the breastplate. Cut off the excess wire and tape the wire ends safely in place.

5b To join the front and the back, cut a 24" (61 cm) piece of red ribbon. Tie one end through the left hole in the top plate of the breastplate. Try the costume on the child and tie through the left hole in the top backplate, adjusting length to fit child. Repeat for the right side of the breastplate and backplate.

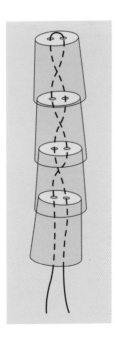

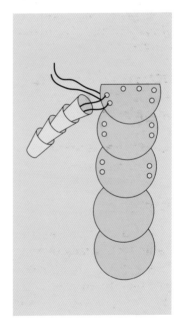

Step 4. Assembling a leg. Twist wires around each other inside each cup before adding the next one.

Step 5a. Leg being attached to side of breastplate by wires.

6 For each lobster claw, cut two 10" (25.5 cm) diameter circles from cardboard. Cut away one-fourth of each circle. Use the remaining three-fourths circle as a pattern to cut four claw shapes of red felt. Fold the remaining three-fourths cardboard circle in half, and glue the felt claw shapes on its front and back. Punch holes about 3" (7.5 cm) apart on each, near the fold (see diagram). Cut two 12" (30.5 cm) long red ribbons. Pull a red ribbon through the holes on one claw. Tie it around the child's wrists. Repeat for second claw.

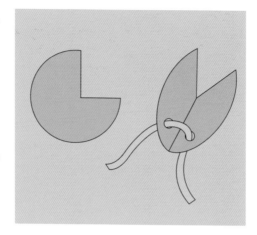

Step 6. A three-quarters circle becomes a claw when it is bent.

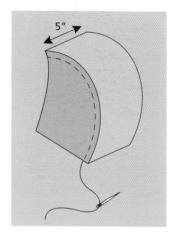

Step 7. For the hat, stitch the straight 5" x 14" (12.7 x 35.5 cm) strip of felt to each side piece.

Hat

7 To make the hat, cut the following from the 16" x 16" (40.5 x 40.5 cm) piece of red felt: 5" x 14" (12.7 x 35.5 cm) strip, two 7" x 8" (17.8 x 20.3 cm) pieces, and two 1" x 12" (2.5 x 30.5 cm) strips. To make the hat sides, round one corner of each of the 7" x 8" hat side pieces by trimming away a corner. With needle and thread, sew the long edge of the 5" x 14" strip around the edge of each 7" x 8" hat side piece of felt on the two rounded sides, with about ¼" (6 mm) seam allowance. Turn right-side out so seams are inside.

8 Fold the 1" x 12" (2.5 x 30.5 cm) strips in half so the width is ½" x 12" (1.2 x 30.5 cm), pin, and sew up the short edge and the long edge. Turn right-side out. This will make one antenna. Repeat to make a second antenna. Stitch antennae to top of hat.

9 Cut two 12" (30.5 cm) pieces of red ribbon for ties, and sew a ribbon tie to each of the corners of the hat that will be near the child's chin, if desired.

Octopus

MATERIALS

- 16" (40 cm) string
- two 23" × 25" (58.5 × 63.5 cm) pieces of corrugated cardboard
- 24" × 24" (61 × 61 cm) piece of corrugated cardboard
- plastic purple tablecloth
- two hundred ¾ oz (22 mL) plastic soufflé cups (used in take-out restaurants for salad dressing)
- sixty-four 8 oz (240 mL) plastic purple drinking cups
- 5 oz (148 mL) tacky glue
- roll of 2" (5 cm) wide clear packing tape
- two white 8" (20 cm) plastic plates
- two 16 oz (480 mL) black plastic cups
- eight 48" (122 cm) long wires

TOOLS: pushpin, craft knife, scissors, wire cutters, pencil, ruler

CHILD WEARS: purple or black long-sleeved shirt, black pants, and black shoes, or all white

DIRECTIONS

Making the Shoulder Circle

1 To make the shoulder circle, draw a circle of radius 12" (30.5 cm) on the 24" × 24" (61 × 61 cm) cardboard (diameter of circle will be 24"). To do this, draw diagonal lines on the cardboard, connecting both corners to make an "X" in order to find the center. To draw the circle,

get a piece of string and stick the pushpin into one end of the string and then into the center point of the cardboard. Tie the other end of the string to a pencil, making sure the string length is exactly 12" (30.5 cm) from the pin. Hold the pin down with one hand. With other hand, bring pencil right to the edge (string should be taut) and swing an arc around the cardboard so the pencil marks a circle. Adjust the string to 4" (10 cm) long and mark another circle of 4" radius, keeping the pin in the center. Diameter will be 8" (20 cm). You will have drawn a doughnut shape on your cardboard.

2 With a craft knife, cut the 24" (61 cm) diameter shoulder circle out of the cardboard. Cut out the center 8" (20 cm) diameter circle also.

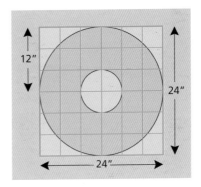

Steps 1 and 2. Pattern for shoulder circle. 1 box = 4" (10 cm). Gray parts are cut away.

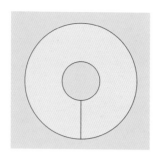

Step 3. Cut a slit in shoulder circle so wearer can get into and out of costume.

3 Make a straight slit through the cardboard from the inner circle to the outer circle. Cover one side of the shoulder circle with a piece of purple plastic tablecloth, using the tape to secure it. Slit open the plastic over the cardboard slit, so the child can get in and out easily. Cut away the plastic over the inner circle and tape any ends in place.

Making and Attaching Legs

4 Fold each of the eight 48" (122 cm) wires in half.

5 Take the sixty-four 8" (20 cm) purple plastic cups and poke two holes at the bottom of each cup, about 1" (2.5 cm) apart. Put the ends of one wire into each of the holes at the bottom of a cup, starting from the outside. Inside the cup, twist the two wire ends together twice. Slip another cup onto the wire so it looks as though you are stacking the cups. Keep adding cups until you have a strand of 8 cups. That will be one leg. Don't cut off the extra wire. Make the other 7 legs the same way.

6 You can use packing tape inside of the cups that make up the legs to hold the legs in whatever position you want.

7 To attach the suckers, lay all legs on the table. Place 200 soufflé cups upside down and tacky-glue the bottoms. Let the tacky glue set for a few minutes. Then take some soufflé cups and place 20 to 25 on one of the 8 arms, bottoms down. Attach the cups side by side in rows to look like the suction cups of an octopus. Do this to all 8 legs. Let the legs dry overnight.

8 To attach the legs to the shoulder circle, poke two holes that are 2" (5 cm) apart near the outer edge of the shoulder circle that you cut out earlier. Turn the shoulder circle purple-side down. Put the wires from one leg up through the holes, twisting them together tightly and taping the wire down on the upper (uncovered) side of the circle. Make sure the last cup that makes up the leg is flush against the covered underside of the shoulder circle. Spacing the remaining 7 legs evenly around the shoulder circle, attach them in the same way. Cut off any excess wire.

9 Once all the legs are attached to the shoulder circle, cover the top side of the circle with part of the purple plastic tablecloth. Cut a slit in the plastic over the slit in the cardboard. Trim off the unused plastic that extends beyond the edges and cut away the excess tablecloth in the center, close to the inside edge of the inner circle. Tape down any loose edges.

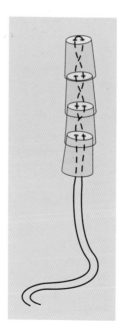

Step 5. Assembling a leg. Twist wires around each other inside each cup before adding the next one.

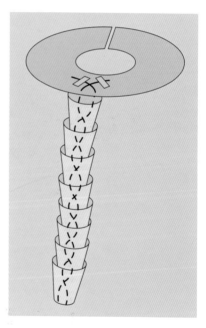

Step 8. Leg attached to underside of shoulder circle; wire ends twisted together and taped in place on top.

Always ready to lend a hand.

Making the Head

10 On a 23" × 25" (58.5 × 63.5 cm) piece of cardboard, draw a petal shape that tapers to be 12" (30 cm) across at the face end (see diagram). Cut the shape out and trace and cut out the same shape on another 23" × 25" piece of cardboard.

11 Tape these two petal shapes together, one on top of the other, to create the octopus's head. At the narrow end of the shape, we need to cut out an upside-down "U" that is about 9" wide × 5" tall (23 × 12.5 cm) for the face opening. Measure your child's head before cutting to be sure this octopus head will fit well, and adjust the opening size to your child's face.

12 Cover the whole cardboard head with purple plastic tablecloth, trimming the plastic to shape and taping and gluing edges down.

13 For the eyes, glue two white plates side by side above the face opening. Cut down two black cups to be 2" (5 cm) tall and glue them, with the bottoms facing up, on top of the white plates to finish the eyes. Try the hat on the child; add strings to hold it on if necessary.

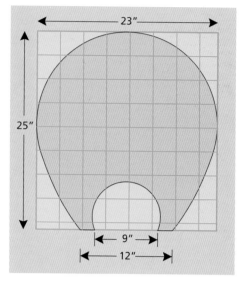

Step 10. Pattern for head. 1 box = 3" (7.5 cm). Gray parts are cut away.

Paper Airplane

MATERIALS

- eight 15" × 96" (38 × 244 cm) pieces of white butcher paper
- four 34" × 50" (86 × 127 cm) pieces of corrugated cardboard or two 64" × 50" (163 × 127 cm) pieces
- roll of 2" (5 cm) wide clear packing tape
- 2 oz (56 g) white glue
- two 72" (182 cm) lengths of strong white 1" (2.5 cm) wide ribbon for straps
- 8½" × 11" (21.5 × 28 cm) white paper for hat
- two 18" (46 cm) pieces of thin cord to tie on paper hat

TOOLS: scissors, craft knife, pencil, yardstick

CHILD WEARS: clothes that contrast with paper

DIRECTIONS

1 Lay the four 15" × 96" (38 × 244 cm) pieces of butcher paper side by side on their long sides and tape together, using 2" (5 cm) wide clear packing tape. This gives you a large piece of paper, 60" × 96" (152.4 × 244 cm).

2 Fold this sheet in half so that you have a folded piece of paper that is 60" × 48" (152.4 × 122 cm). This first fold line is the spine of the airplane.

3a Open up fold and align paper so the first fold runs from left to right on the table. Then take the lower left corner and fold up so what was the paper's left edge aligns with the spine.

3b Repeat with the upper left corner, folding it in and aligning its former left edge with the spine. This leaves a point at the end of a triangular shape on the left side of the paper. This point will be the front of the airplane.

4 Now re-crease the spine so its fold is sharp.

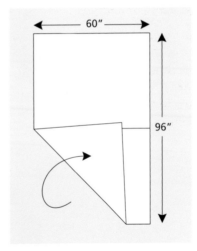

Step 3a. Fold corner up to align with spine fold.

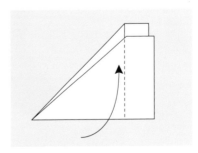

Step 4. Re-crease spine.

Check out this flight suit!

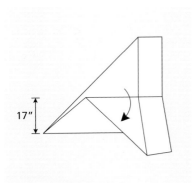

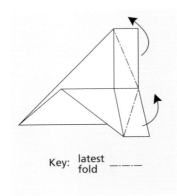

Key: latest fold ─·─·─

Step 5a. Measure up 17" (43 cm) from spine, and fold wing down.

Step 5b. Fold up back corners of wings.

5a Measure up 17" (43 cm), about one-third the way up from the spine, and fold the wing nearest you down towards the spine, making sure the crease of the wing fold is parallel to the spine. Fold the wing on the other side of the plane down in the same way.

5b Fold the back corners up from the end of the overlapped paper to the 17" (43 cm) line (see diagram).

6 Spread out the spine and wing folds so you see a flattened, almost triangular plane shape. Set aside.

7 Arrange the 34" × 50" (86 × 127 cm) cardboards together to be larger in area than the spread-out plane. Overlap the cardboard sections 2" (5 cm) on each other and tape them together, using 2" (5 cm) wide clear packing tape. Don't overlap the cardboards at the spine, however; just tape the upper and lower boards right next to each other there. Using the spread-out airplane as your template, cut two joined wing shapes from cardboard, tracing the shape of the wings from the plane (see diagram), but not including the folded-up back corners from Step 5b. The spine is the dividing line between the two wing shapes.

8 Piece together four 15" × 96" (38 × 244 cm) pieces of white butcher paper on their long sides and wrap the cardboard shape you just cut in the butcher paper, cutting off excess and taping paper in place. Insert the wrapped cardboard plane shape in the paper plane, using glue to attach it to the paper airplane. Refold plane.

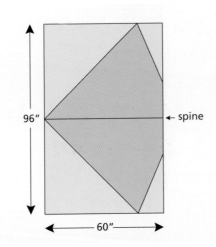

Step 7. Cut cardboard shape same size as flattened plane. 1 box = 12" (30.5 cm). Gray areas are cut away.

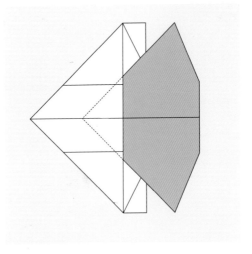

Step 8. Insert wrapped cardboard into the paper plane made in Step 5.

9 Draw a 12" (30.5 cm) diameter circle, centered on the airplane's spine, about 32" (81 cm) back from the nose point of the airplane. Extend this into an oval shape 12" × 48" (30.5 × 122 cm). This oval will be the place in which the child will stand. Cut away the oval from the paper and cardboard. Try the costume on the child to be sure he has room to stand; widen oval if needed. Use 2" wide (5 cm) clear packing tape to tape down the paper around the hole to get clean lines. While the child is still in the costume, mark the position of two holes in front of the oval and two in back of the oval on the wings, to position the straps.

10 Have the child take off the airplane. Poke the strap holes through the paper and cardboard. Feed the ribbons through the holes and tie them on. Adjust their length to child.

11 When the costume is refolded into the airplane shape and the child is wearing costume, you can tape the two halves together above the spine in the rear and middle of the plane, so that the costume will hold its shape.

12 Cutting the oval through the spine weakens the airplane, making it tend to droop in the back. You can fix this by taping a small card-

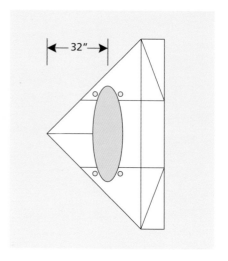

Steps 9 and 10. Make oval cutout so child can wear costume. Small dots indicate holes for ribbons.

board box to the spine of the airplane for support against the back of the child. Do this while fitting the costume to be certain of the best effect. Turn the wing tips up as in photo.

13 Make a little paper airplane in the same way from an 8½" × 11" (21.5 × 28 cm) piece of paper. Punch two holes in it for strings and tie it on for a hat.

A group of friends in their costumes.

Pencil

MATERIALS

- 24" × 48" (61 × 122 cm) piece of corrugated cardboard
- 20" × 54" (51 × 137 cm) piece of corrugated cardboard
- 14" × 14" (35.5 × 35.5 cm) piece of corrugated cardboard
- 12" × 30" (30.5 × 76 cm) piece of corrugated cardboard
- 11" × 54" (28 × 137 cm) polyurethane foam, ½" (1.2 cm) thick
- 2" (5 cm) wide clear packing tape
- ½" (1.2 cm) wide black tape
- 13" × 56" (33 × 142 cm) piece of pink cotton knit (T-shirt material)
- 48" × 24" (122 × 61 cm) yellow wrapping paper
- 10" × 54" (25.5 × 137 cm) silver Mylar sheet or duct tape
- two large brown paper bags

TOOLS: craft knife, scissors, yardstick or long ruler, pencil, hot glue gun

CHILD WEARS: neutral or dark-colored pants, shirt, shoes

DIRECTIONS

1 Take the 24" × 48" (61 × 122 cm) corrugated cardboard and mark and crease every 8" (20 cm) on the 48" (122 cm) side. Tape the 24" sides together to make a six-sided tube.

2 Lay down a piece of 14" × 14" (35.5 × 35.5 cm) cardboard. Stand your six-sided tube on top of the cardboard and trace around the bottom hexagon shape.

3 Cut out the traced hexagon and tape it on the top of the cardboard tube.

4 Cut six 2" × 30" (5 × 76 cm) strips of corrugated cardboard from the 12" × 30" (30.5 × 76 cm) piece. Fold the strips in half and tape these in a teepee shape around the top of the tube to form a point (see diagram). The strips will overlap each other.

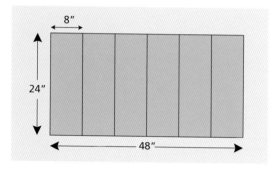

Step 1. Rule and crease lines as shown.

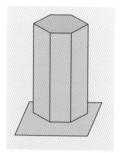

Step 2. Trace around hexagonal tube to make the top for the pencil.

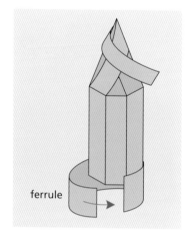

Steps 4 to 6. Folded strips of cardboard form the point. A rounded strip of cardboard, partly overlapping the hexagonal tube, forms the ferrule.

5 Fill in open spots in between the cardboard strips with more cardboard. Tape and fit the pieces together smoothly.

6 To make the ferrule (the "metal" part), cut an 8" × 52" (20 × 132 cm) rectangle of corrugated cardboard from the 20" × 54" (51 × 137 cm) piece. Bend and tape it securely to the open end of the tube with clear tape, overlapping the cardboard at least 1" (2.5 cm) over the end of the tube.

*Pencil
me in.*

7 For an eraser, cut an 11" × 54" (28 × 137 cm) rectangle of cardboard. Bend and tape it below the ferrule you just attached. Let the new cardboard overlap the end of the ferrule at least 1" (2.5 cm).

8 Take an 11" × 54" (28 × 137 cm) piece of polyurethane foam. Using hot glue, cover the foam with pink T-shirt material, folding the excess material around to cover the edges of the foam. Then hot-glue the pink-covered foam all the way around the part of the cardboard you are using as an eraser, tucking in and gluing under any loose edges.

9 To fit the costume to the child, have the child hold the costume; mark a small hole where you think the child's face will be when he is wearing the costume. Remove the costume and cut the hole for the child's face. Then place the cylinder over the child's head to figure out where to cut out the final holes for the face and arms. Look in the peephole you cut in the costume, and use a pencil to draw a circle on the outside of the tube that is about the size of the child's face. Also try to find out where you want the armholes to be, and trace the circles that you will cut out for them. Remove the costume and cut out the circles.

10 Cut open the two brown paper bags and make 3" (7.5 cm) wide strips from it. Wrap the point of the cylinder with the strips, taping and gluing them on. This will be the tip of pencil.

11 Now cover the main 24" × 48" (61 × 122 cm) barrel of the pencil with yellow wrapping paper, up to the ferrule, overlapping the brown paper point with yellow paper by 5" (12.5 cm). Tape and secure the yellow paper to the cylinder on the sides, and scallop (cut curved edges, as seen in photo) the overlapping yellow paper on the top, taping the yellow paper to the brown paper to make the pencil look as though it has been sharpened.

12 Take the 10" × 54" (25.5 × 137 cm) silver Mylar sheet and adhere it to the costume on the ferrule, overlapping the pink eraser on one side and the yellow wrapping paper on the other. Circle the entire cylinder with Mylar. If you don't have Mylar, you can use duct tape.

13 Cover each edge of the Mylar with thin black tape.

14 Wrap the point of the pencil with 6" (15 cm) of black tape to make a "lead" for the pencil.

Piggy Bank

MATERIALS

- pushpin
- string 30" (76 cm) long
- five 24" × 48" (61 × 122 cm) pieces of corrugated cardboard
- 15' × 28" (4.6 m × 71 cm) pink wrapping paper
- 2" (5 cm) wide roll clear packing tape
- three 8" × 12" (20 × 30.5 cm) pieces of pink felt
- black acrylic paint
- gold-colored cardboard cake plate
- plastic headband
- glue

TOOLS: paintbrush, craft knife, scissors, ruler, pencil

CHILD WEARS: pink top under costume and cute shoes, dark pants

DIRECTIONS

1 On the first 24" × 48" (61 × 122 cm) cardboard, draw and cut out two 24" (61 cm) diameter circles (radius 12" or 30.5 cm). See page 53 for general instructions on drawing circles.

2 Bend the spine of a second 24" × 48" (61 × 122 cm) piece of cardboard to shape it into a cylinder, and tape one 48" edge to a 24" circle, using 2" (5 cm) wide clear tape. Tape the other 24" circle to the other cylinder end. This makes the body of the piggy bank. On what will become the top center of this cylinder, cut a round hole big enough for the child's head. About 6" (15 cm) to one side of the hole, make a 2" × 10" (5 × 25 cm) coin slot. Below it, on the opposite side of the cylinder, cut a space big

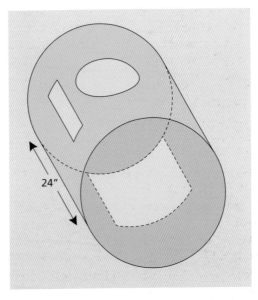

Step 2. Body cylinder has cutouts for child's head, legs, and a coin slot (gray areas).

enough for the child to stand. Try the costume on the child to be sure it fits well.

3 From the third 24" × 48" (61 × 122 cm) cardboard, cut two 7" × 48" (18 × 122 cm) strips (one for the head and one for the snout), a 10" (25 cm) diameter circle for the head, and four 8" (20.3 cm) diameter circles for feet.

4 From the fourth 24" × 48" cardboard, cut four 5" × 48" (12.7 × 122 cm) strips for feet.

5 From the fifth 24" × 48" cardboard, cut an 18" (45.5 cm) diameter circle to create the head of the pig. Save the rest for later.

6 For each of the 7" × 48" (18 × 122 cm) strips of cardboard, bend and break down the spine of the cardboard. Tape one 7" × 48" strip on its

See what saving money can do?

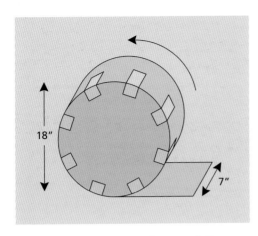

Step 6. Tape a strip on the 18" (45.5 cm) diameter circle as shown.

long side to the 18" (45.5 cm) circle to create the head of the pig. Use part of the next 7" (18 cm) wide strip to complete the head.

7 For the snout, in the same way, tape the rest of the 7" × 48" (18 × 122 cm) cardboard strip to the 10" (25.5 cm) diameter circle until the ends meet; cut off any excess from the strip.

8 For the feet, take the four 5" × 48" (12.5 × 122 cm) cardboard strips. In the same way as for the head of the pig, break the spine of the cardboard and tape one long side around each 8" (20 cm) diameter circle until the ends meet; cut off the excess strip.

9 Wrap each pig piece with pink wrapping paper. The easiest way is to measure, wrap, and tape the paper around the cylinders and cut out the circles separately. Tape the circles on the fronts of the cylinders.

10 Once everything is wrapped with pink paper, tape the head (18" or 45.5 cm diameter), centered on the body cylinder's front, as shown in the photo.

11 Tape on the snout (10" or 25.5 cm cylinder), centered on the front of the head, as shown in the photo.

12 Tape the feet on the underside of the pig (see photo).

13 For ears, cut two 8" (20 cm) triangles from cardboard. Cover with pink wrapping paper on outside and pink felt on the inside. Tape ears to top of the head.

14 Cut four 2" × 8" (5 × 20 cm) strips of pink felt, and cut a "V" in the center of each strip on one long side. Glue one strip on the front of each of the pig's feet for a hoof.

15 With black paint, paint on eyes and nostrils as shown in the photo.

16 Paint the number "25" on the gold cake plate. Let dry. Tape the cake plate to the head-band with clear tape.

Popcorn

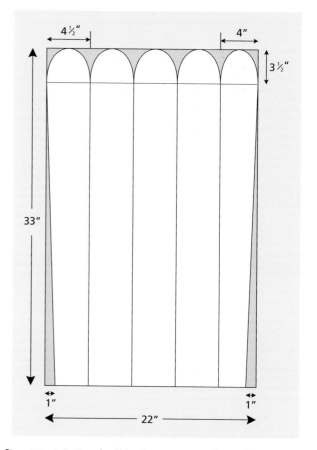

Steps 2 to 4. Pattern for side of popcorn container. 1 box = 3" (7.5 cm). Cut away excess above scallops and taper sides as shown (gray areas).

MATERIALS

- 48" × 96" (122 × 244 cm) white foam core board, ¼" (0.5 cm) thick
- 22" × 22" (56 × 56 cm) square of foam core board for top
- pencil
- 6 oz (180 mL) red acrylic paint
- black marker
- roll of 1" (2.5 cm) wide white tape
- roll of 1" (2.5 cm) wide red tape
- roll of 2" (5 cm) wide clear packing tape
- roll of masking tape
- 24" × 36" (61 × 91.5 cm) yellow construction paper
- 24" × 36" (61 × 91.5 cm) black construction paper
- 24 oz (720 mL) bag of Styrofoam packing popcorn
- yellow baseball cap
- glue

TOOLS: ruling compass, craft knife, yardstick or long ruler, narrow (¼" or 6 mm) paintbrush, hot glue gun, and narrow cotton paint roller for the stripes

CHILD WEARS: whatever she prefers under costume, since most of her clothes will not show, but cute shoes and bright-colored socks

DIRECTIONS

1 Cut foam core board down to 33" × 88" (84 × 223.5 cm). Divide board into four pieces that are 22" × 33" (56 × 84 cm) each. These will be the sides of the container.

2 On one short end of each 22" × 33" board, mark down 3½" (9 cm). Draw a line across the 22" width at 3½". Repeat on all four pieces.

3 Divide the line you just drew into four 4½" (11.4 cm) wide segments and one segment that is 4" (10 cm) wide. With a compass, mark scallops above the line. You should have five scallops. Cut away the board above the scallops with a craft knife. Repeat this on the tops of the other three 22" × 33" (56 × 84 cm) pieces of foam core board.

4 With a pencil, mark a short line 1" (2.5 cm) in from each side at the bottom of each 22" × 33" (56 × 84 cm) board. Then align the yardstick from the top corner on the right side to the 1" (2.5 cm) mark on the bottom right and draw the line between to taper the side. Cut off the excess with the craft knife. Repeat on the left side. Taper each of the three remaining 22" ×

Step 5. Angle the paint lines of side sections as shown (red lines).

Got butter?

33" sides the same way. Each side section should now be 20" (51 cm) at the bottom; the top should have 5 scallops.

5 On the 20" (50.8 cm) edge of each container side, measure in 4" (10 cm) from each of the two outer edges and make a small mark. With a yardstick, draw a line from each mark you just made to the corresponding mark at the lowest point between the first and second and fourth and fifth scallops on the top edge (see diagram). Repeat this on each board. These new lines are the paint lines for the outer sections.

6 Lay one of the 20" × 33" (50.8 × 84 cm) sides of the box on a work table. Run a strip of masking tape on the sides of each area where a red stripe will go. This will keep any excess paint from getting on the sections that are supposed to be white. Use the narrow cotton roller to paint the red sections. See photo; colors alternate. Two box sections start and end with red, and two start and end with white. Prepare and paint all three remaining 20" × 33" panels. Let paint dry. Then gently remove the masking tape.

7 Place all four side sections on the floor, face down. Join the sides together with tape on the long sides, making a box shape, taping on the unpainted side of the boards so the container ends up straight when standing upright.

8 Take the 22" × 22" (56 × 56 cm) square of foam core board, and cut a circle out of the center big enough for your child's head to go through. Tape this square inside the assembled popcorn box, just below the scallops.

9 With your red tape, cover the top edges of all the red scallops. With your white tape, cover the top edges of all the white scallops. Cover the seams where the sides meet on the outside with either red or white tape, whichever matches best.

10 On a piece of yellow paper, draw letters saying POPCORN. Cut out the letters and trace around them on the black paper. Cut out the letters from the black paper. Glue the letters to the popcorn box with the yellow letters partly overlapping the black ones (see photo).

11 Hot-glue little Styrofoam popcorn pieces all over the baseball cap.

12 Have the child stand in the costume and fill the top with Styrofoam packing popcorn.

Race Car

MATERIALS

- 14" × 3" (35.5 × 7.5 cm) piece of corrugated cardboard (front, headlights)
- two 36.5" × 9" (93 × 23 cm) pieces of corrugated cardboard (for sides)
- 9" × 20" (23 × 51 cm) piece of corrugated cardboard (rear panel)
- 36" × 20" (91.5 × 51 cm) piece of corrugated cardboard (top panel)
- 8" × 20" (20.3 × 51 cm) piece of corrugated cardboard (spoiler)
- two 8" × 8" (20.3 × 20.3 cm) pieces of corrugated cardboard (pylons for spoiler)
- two 6" × 8" (15.2 × 20.3 cm) pieces of cardboard (fins for spoiler)
- 28" × 2' (71 × 61 cm) black wrapping paper
- 28" × 5' (71 × 153 cm) red wrapping paper
- four disposable round covered Styrofoam containers, about 8" (20 cm) across (for wheels)
- eight 12 oz (360 mL) black plastic cups
- ½" (1.2 cm) wide roll of black tape
- black acrylic paint
- white acrylic paint
- ½" (1.2 cm) diameter × 28" (71 cm) wooden dowel
- ½" (1.2 cm) diameter × 33" (84 cm) wooden dowel
- 24" × 24" (61 × 61 cm) sheet of silver stick-on Mylar
- 2" (5 cm) wide roll clear packing tape
- tacky glue
- 1" × 48" (2.5 × 122 cm) piece of black ribbon
- 12" × 18" (30.5 × 46 cm) black construction paper
- 12" × 18" (30.5 × 46 cm) white construction paper

TOOLS: black marker, pencil, long ruler, craft knife, scissors, paintbrush, ruling compass

CHILD WEARS: white shirt, black pants, and black shoes

DIRECTIONS

For layout of all lines, use a long ruler and a pencil. Refer to the diagrams as you rule and cut the pieces to shape with a craft knife.

Top of Car

1 To lay out the top panel of the car, take the 36" × 20" (91.5 × 51 cm) cardboard and lay it on the work surface so that one longer edge is closest to you. Then:

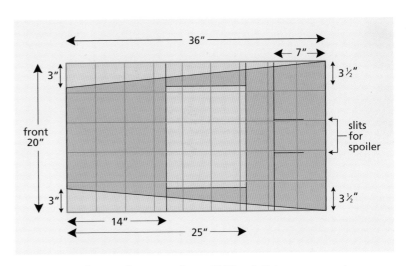

Step 1. Pattern for top of race car. 1 box = 4" (10 cm). Cut away gray parts.

Gentlemen, start your engines!

1a Lay out the points and lines indicated in the Step 1 diagram. The front of the car is at the left in this diagram.

1b Cut along the angled lines to cut away the excess from the cardboard, and cut away the 11" × 13" (28 × 33 cm) rectangle that is in the center of the panel, where the child will stand.

1c Use the craft knife to cut 4" (10 cm) long slits, which later will hold the pylons for the spoiler near the back. The slits start 7" (18 cm) in from the back edge (see diagram). Make sure not to cut all the way out to the edge. You should leave 3" (7.5 cm) uncut at the edge of the panel. Set the top aside for now.

Side Panel

2 To shape the side panel, lay a 36½" × 9" (93 × 23 cm) cardboard on your work surface with a long side closest to you. Rule the side panel as shown in the diagram for Step 2. Repeat this procedure for the second side panel. Cut away the excess part of the side panels as shown.

3 With clear tape, attach the front (14" × 3" or 35.5 × 7.5 cm) and rear panels (9" × 20" or 23 × 51 cm) to the side panels. Then tape on the top panel with 2" (5 cm) wide clear packing tape to complete assembly of the frame for the car (see diagram).

4 Wrap the frame of the car with red wrapping paper, using the 2" (5 cm) clear packing tape to tape inside the frame, taking care to keep clean lines on the car.

5 Mark and cut out holes for the ribbon straps near the corners of the center cutout. Cut the ribbon into two pieces, tie each in front, criss-cross them, and tie each in place at the back of the cutout.

6 Cut all eight 12 oz (360 mL) black plastic cups down to 2" (5 cm) height. These will be used as the headlights on the front panel and as hubcap centers.

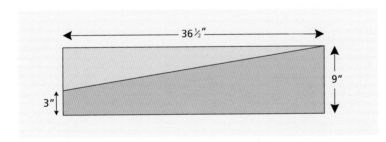

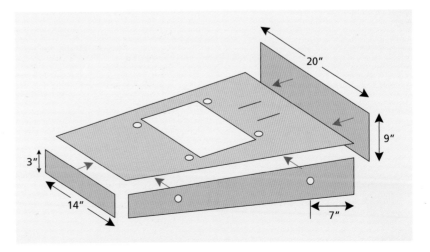

Step 2. Pattern for side panel of car. 1 box = 4" (10 cm). Cut away gray parts.

Step 3. Assembling the parts of the car body. Small dots indicate holes for axles and straps.

7 Cut eight 1½" (4 cm) diameter circles out of the sheet of Mylar. Pull off the paper protecting the sticky surface of the Mylar circles and stick them to the headlights and hubcap centers (the bottoms of the black plastic cups).

8 Draw and cut out four 7" (18 cm) diameter circles from the Mylar. Inside each 7" Mylar circle, draw another circle that is 4" (10 cm) in diameter and cut it out, leaving a Mylar donut that is 1½" thick (4 cm). This donut will be used as a decoration on the tires.

9 Paint all of the round disposable containers (which will be wheels) with the black acrylic paint. Let dry.

10 Mix black and white and paint a gray 6" (15 cm) diameter circle in the center of one side of a disposable container (choose either the top or the bottom of the container). Let dry. These will represent the hubcaps of the wheels.

11 Tape black tape around the edges of the round 8" (20 cm) Styrofoam containers where the lid and base meet.

12 Lay the 7" Mylar donuts cut in Step 8 on the wheels over the place where the gray and black paint meet.

13 Tacky-glue four 2" (5 cm) black cups (from Step 6) to the front panel of the car to act as headlights. Use black tape on the headlights where they meet the front panel to create clean lines.

14 For the rear axle, cut ½" (1.2 cm) diameter holes that are 7" (18 cm) in from the rear edge and 2½" (6.3 cm) up from the bottom on both sides of the car (see diagram with Step 3). Feed the longer (33") dowel through both rear holes until the dowel is centered in the car. Repeat this for the front axle, using the 28" (71 cm) dowel and measuring back 7" (18 cm) from the front of the car and up 2½" (6.3 cm).

15 Cut a ½" (1.2 cm) hole in the center of each of the Styrofoam container wheels, cutting the container and lid. Slip each wheel onto one of

the dowels, having some of the dowel protrude. Tacky-glue a 2" (5 cm) black cup onto the center of each wheel, over the dowel.

Decorations

16 Cut the decorative ovals used for the race car from the construction paper, as follows:

For Small Ovals:
- two 5½" × 6" (14 × 15 cm) black ovals
- two 4½" × 5½" (11.4 × 14 cm) white ovals
- two 3¼" × 3½" (8.25 × 9 cm) black #3's

For Large Oval:
- 10" × 12½" (25.5 × 32 cm) black oval
- 8½" × 10" (21.5 × 25.5 cm) white oval
- 6" × 6" (15 × 15 cm) black #3

To assemble the number ovals, glue the small white ovals on the small black ovals. Then glue the small numbers on the white ovals. Do the same for the large oval. Glue the small ovals to each side of the car, and glue the large oval to the hood.

17 To mount the spoiler, you will need to make two pylons. To make each pylon:

17a Measure and rule up the 8" × 8" (20.3 × 20.3 cm) cardboard as shown in the diagram. Cut out the pylon.

17b On the left edge of the pylon, mark a point that is about ¾" (2 cm) up from the bottom. Use the scissors to cut a slit 2" (5 cm) across, parallel to the bottom edge, starting from this mark on the pylon.

17c Wrap the pylon in black wrapping paper, using black tape to create clean lines.

18 Make two triangular fins for the spoiler from 6" × 8" (15.2 × 20.3 cm) cardboard pieces (see diagram). Wrap both fins in black wrapping paper and use black tape to secure it with clean lines.

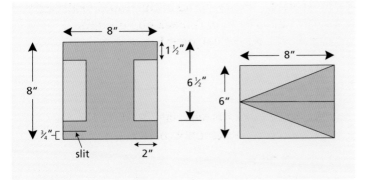

Steps 17 and 18. Left, pattern for pylon. Right, pattern for fin.
1 box = 2" (5 cm). Cut away gray parts.

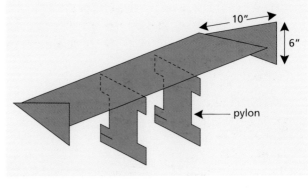

Step 21. Pylons with spoiler and fins attached.

19 Wrap the 8" × 20" (20 × 51 cm) cardboard panel for the spoiler with black wrapping paper, using black tape to hold it with clean lines. Tape the spoiler to the pylons and tape the fins to the spoiler with black tape.

20 Use the craft knife to feel for 4" (10 cm) pylon slits at the back of the car top, and cut the wrapping paper

there. Do the same to find and cut a slit in the paper over the slit at the bottom of each pylon.

21 Slip each pylon into its slit on the car top and slide it forward until the slit on the bottom of the pylon overlaps the frame of the car and the pylon is seated properly.

Reduced pattern for ovals.

Snowflake

MATERIALS

- 48" × 48" (122 × 122 cm) foam core board, ¼" (0.6 cm) thick
- four rolls of ½" (1.2 cm) wide white tape
- 3 oz (90 mL) white acrylic paint
- 12 oz (360 mL) crystal clear glitter
- 4½ oz (135 mL) silver glitter
- 3 oz (90 mL) blue glitter
- white glue
- two 36" (91.5 cm) pieces of strong white ribbon for straps

TOOLS: craft knife, scissors, ruler, pen, pencil, 3" (7.5 cm) wide cotton roller

CHILD WEARS: all white, or light blue or gray sweatshirt and pants

DIRECTIONS

1 Copy the snowflake pattern on the foam core board. Make sure the pattern touches each edge of the board at its widest point.

2 Trace around the edges of the snowflake with pen.

3 Draw the inside designs (where the glitter will be) with pencil (see photo).

4 Cut the snowflake out of the foam core board with a craft knife. Cut out a 9" wide × 12" long (23 × 30.5 cm) oval right in the center of the snowflake. The oval will be a space for the child's face.

5 Tape with white ½" (1.2 cm) wide tape all the way around the outside edge of snowflake. Tape around the oval's edge also.

6 Place the snowflake flat on your work table where it will dry. With the 3" (7.5 cm) roller, roll white acrylic paint across the face (front) of the

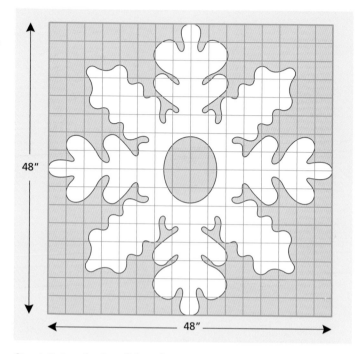

Step 1. Pattern for Snowflake. 1 box = 3" (7.5 cm). Cut away gray parts.

entire snowflake. Let dry. Then roll glue across the face of the snowflake and completely the cover face of the snowflake with crystal clear glitter. Let dry (takes about 2 hours).

7 Dump off the glitter that doesn't stick. With the bottle of white glue, trace around the inside designs, applying glue heavily. Sprinkle silver glitter on the areas you just glued.

8 Take the bottle of glue and highlight the edges of glitter designs you drew (see photo). Sprinkle blue glitter on those areas. Let dry.

9 Have the child hold the snowflake up to her face. Mark a spot near each of her shoulders where a strap can be attached. Poke a hole in the snowflake, and push one ribbon end through to the front and tie there. Tie the long ribbon ends in the back over the child's back, to help support the costume.

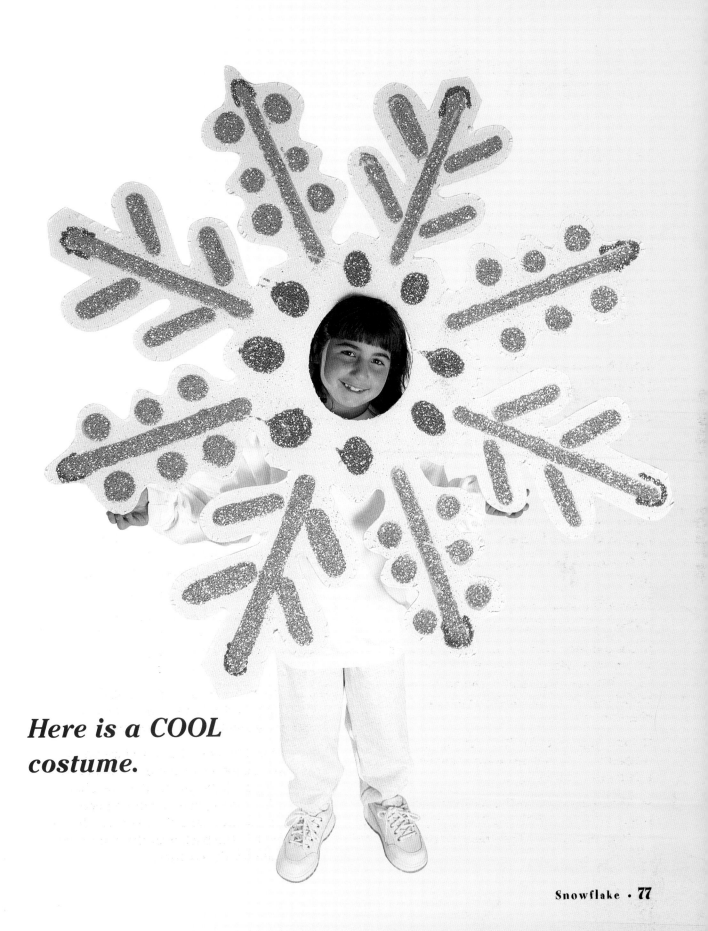

Here is a COOL costume.

Plate of Spaghetti

MATERIALS

- 28" (71 cm) piece of string
- 40" × 40" (101.5 × 101.5 cm) foam core board, ¼" (0.5 cm) thick
- 40" × 10" (101.5 × 25.5 cm) piece of foam core board, ¼" (0.5 cm) thick
- 6 oz (177 mL) red acrylic paint
- 3 oz (90 mL) brown acrylic paint
- 2" (5 cm) wide roll of clear packing tape
- ½" (1.2 cm) wide roll of red tape
- two ½" (1.2 cm) wide rolls of white tape
- two 36" (91.5 cm) pieces of strong red ribbon for straps, 1" (2.5 cm) wide
- red baseball hat
- two 6" (15 cm) diameter Styrofoam balls
- 40' (12 m) polyethylene tubing, ⅜" (1 cm) wide*
- red modeling clay, about a half-pound (224 g)
- four 2" (5 cm) paper clips

*The kind used for fish tank filters

TOOLS: long ruler, pushpin, pencil, pen, craft knife, plastic or rubber glove, sponge (to spread paint), scissors

CHILD WEARS: red sweatshirt, black pants, and black shoes

DIRECTIONS

We will cut two rings out of foam core board. The largest ring will become the outer rim of the plate and the smaller one will become the center of the plate. There will be a space in the center of the plate for the child to stand.

1 Find the center of the 40" × 40" (101.5 × 101.5 cm) foam core board by measuring in 20" (51 cm) on each side. Draw 3 circles—radius 20" (51 cm), radius 13½" (34.3 cm), and radius 7" (18 cm), all with their centers in the center of the foam core board. Use the string, pencil, and pushpin method described on page 53.

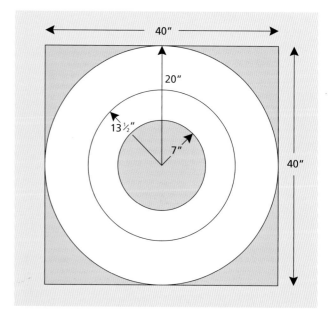

Step 1. Pattern for spaghetti plate. Cut on circles; discard gray parts.

Here's one time your child won't want a second helping.

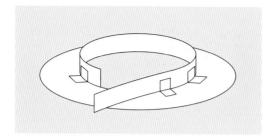

Step 3. Tape the 2" (5 cm) strip of foam core around the inside of the large ring.

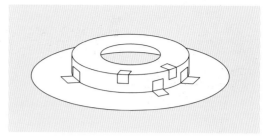

Step 4. Tape the 13½" (34.3 cm) ring onto the strip already in place.

2 Cut along all the circular lines using a craft knife to make rings. Be careful to keep the rings intact as you cut. Discard the 7" (18 cm) radius circle.

3 Cut three 2" × 38" (5 × 96.5 cm) strips of foam core from the 40" × 10" (101.5 × 25.5 cm) foam core board. Tape the ends of the strips together to make one long continuous strip. Break the spine of the foam core by bending the strips into a circle. Tape the strip to the inner circle of the 20" radius (51 cm) ring (see diagram). Cut off any excess strip.

4 Tape the outside of the 13½" (34.3 cm) radius ring to the unattached long edge of the 2" (5 cm) wide foam core strip you just added (see diagram), reinforcing it with 2" (5 cm) wide clear tape. The 13½" ring will become the center of the plate.

5a Turn the assembly you have made upside down, so the lower part is in the center. Tape around the outer edge of the 13½" (34.3 cm) ring with red tape. Tape around the inside circle of the 13½" diameter ring with red tape. Tape around the outer edge of the plate with white tape.

5b To make holes for shoulder straps, poke two holes about 8" (20 cm) apart, about 1" (2.5 cm) out from the inner edge of the red ring, in what will be the front of the costume. Poke two more in what will become the back. Thread a red ribbon through each set of holes in front,

criss-crossing straps, and tie them through the holes in back. Adjust length to your child's height. Pull straps out of the way for Step 6.

6 Wearing a plastic glove, use a sponge to rub red acrylic paint all over the central ring to look like spaghetti sauce. Let dry.

7 Cover both 6" (15 cm) foam balls with red clay to make "meatballs" for your plate. Paint the clay meatballs with brown acrylic paint, letting some of the red show through. Let dry.

8 Partially unbend 2" (5 cm) paper clips, and poke one end up through the bottom of the red foam core ring into each meatball, to secure it.

9 With the child in the red sweatshirt, slip the costume over his head and rest the straps on the shoulders. Cut strips of tubing about 3' (91 cm) long. Twist around the child's body and arms like spaghetti. Don't twist anything around the child's neck.

10 Twist a piece of tubing around the baseball cap and tape in place.

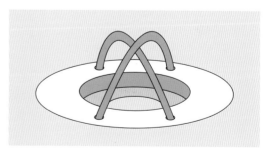

Step 5a and b. The spaghetti plate, turned right-side up, with straps attached.

Speedboat

MATERIALS

- 24" × 48" (61 × 122 cm) piece of corrugated cardboard
- two 7½" × 51" (19 × 129.5 cm) pieces of corrugated cardboard
- 15½" × 18" (39.5 × 46 cm) piece of corrugated cardboard
- 4" × 15" (10 × 38 cm) piece of corrugated cardboard
- 18" × 18" (46 × 46 cm) sheet of red tissue paper
- 28" × 5' (71 × 153 cm) blue wrapping paper
- roll of aluminum foil
- 2" (5 cm) wide clear packing tape
- tacky glue
- ½" (1.2 cm) wide roll of black tape
- acrylic paint: red, white, yellow, and orange
- 3½" × 17" (9 × 43 cm) piece of clear Plexiglas
- twenty-four 3 oz (90 mL) plastic cups
- two pieces of ½" × 24" (1.2 cm × 61 cm) strong black ribbon for straps

TOOLS: ruler, pencil, craft knife, ¼" (0.5 cm) wide paintbrush

CHILD WEARS: orange T-shirt, beach clothes, sandals (or is barefoot)

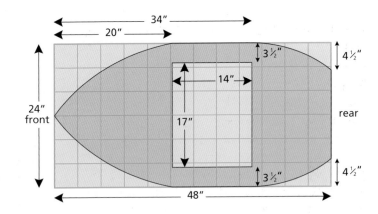

Step 1. Pattern for top of boat. 1 box = 4" (10 cm). Cut away gray parts.

DIRECTIONS

Top of Boat

1 On the 24" × 48" (61 × 122 cm) piece of cardboard, use a pencil to lay out the boat top as shown in the diagram for Step 1, using a ruler for straight lines and drawing the curves freehand.

2 The midpoint on the short side at the left is the front of the boat. The 14" × 17" (35.5 × 43 cm) rectangle in the center of the boat top is the place for the child to stand in while wearing the costume. Cut this rectangle away.

3 Then cut along the sweeping curves to remove the excess cardboard and you will have a piece of cardboard with the general outline of the top of a boat. Set it aside.

Sides and Rear of Boat

4 Lay out the side of the boat as follows:

4a Take one of the 7½" × 51" (19 × 129.5 cm) pieces of cardboard and set it so that one of the long edges is nearest you. Using pencil and a ruler, lay out the side of the boat as shown in the diagram for Step 4. Cut along the curved lines to shape the boat's side.

4b Repeat Step 4a to make the second side in the same way.

Make a splash without leaving dry land.

Assembly and Finishing

5 Starting from the front point of the boat top, tape each side to the boat top with packing tape. Remember that the long straight edge (51" or 129.5 cm) of the side is the one that should be taped to the boat top. The narrowest (3½" or 9 cm) portion of the boat side should connect to the front of the boat, and the 4½" (11.4 cm) deep portion of the boat side should end up at the rear. Take care to break the spine of the cardboard sides as you go to make it easier to match the curve in the top. Trim any excess off the side at the rear, as needed.

6 The 4" × 15" (10 × 38 cm) piece of cardboard completes the rear portion of the frame. Tape it to both sides in the rear and to the boat top with 2" (5 cm) wide clear packing tape.

7 Cover the entire boat frame with blue wrapping paper, taping it on the inside.

8 Using the 2" (5 cm) wide clear packing tape, attach the piece of Plexiglas to the front of the 14" × 17" (35.5 × 43 cm) opening in which the child will stand. The Plexiglas serves as a windshield. Use black tape around edges of the Plexiglas and in the places that it connects to the blue wrapping paper, to create the appearance of a window frame. You may need to build up the tape on the sides to get the windshield to the desired angle.

9 Mark out the outlines of flames along the boat sides with a pencil; then fill in with the colors of acrylic paint as shown, using one at a time and letting each dry before proceeding (see photo). Let dry.

10 Cut twenty-four 9" × 9" (23 × 23 cm) squares of aluminum foil.

11 Individually wrap each 3 oz (90 mL) plastic cup with an aluminum square.

12 Tacky-glue four cups together, angling each cup up a bit so that you get the appearance of a bent engine pipe (see photo). Repeat this process to make the five other engine pipes. Let dry.

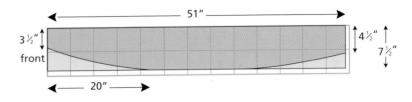

Step 4. Pattern for side of boat. 1 box = 4" (10 cm). Cut away gray parts.

13 Use the 15½" × 18" (39.5 × 46 cm) rectangle of cardboard to cut out an open box that measures 4" × 7½" × 10" (10 × 19 × 25.5 cm) for the engine. Lightly score along the ruling lines and cut away the corners as shown in diagram, but don't fold the box shape yet.

14 Outline and cut out three circular holes on each of the 4" × 10" (10 × 25.5 cm) sides of the engine box, using the bottom of a 3 oz (90 mL) plastic cup as a template; these holes will hold the engine pipes. After cutting the holes, fold the box sides down and tape them together to keep their shape.

15 Cover the engine box in aluminum foil. Tacky-glue a pipe (see Step 12) into each hole. Tear red tissue paper and glue it in the end of each pipe to create the effect of fire coming from the engine pipes.

16 Tape the finished engine box to the top back of the boat with 2" (5 cm) wide clear packing tape.

17 To support the costume, poke one hole into each front and rear corner of the 14" × 17" opening in the top of the boat, a few inches in (5 or 7 cm). Tie the black ribbons through the front holes to create straps to hold the costume on the child. Criss-cross them and tie each off in one of the back corner holes.

Step 13. Pattern for engine box of boat. 1 box = 4" (10 cm). Cut away gray parts; lightly score lines for folding.

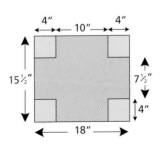

Tic Tac Toe

MATERIALS

- 33" × 34" (84 × 86.4 cm) white foam core board, ½" (1.2 cm) thick
- 11" × 11" (28 × 28 cm) piece of white foam core board, ½" (1.2 cm) thick
- two 1" (2.5 cm) wide rolls of white tape
- four 1" (2.5 cm) wide rolls of red tape
- four 1" (2.5 cm) wide rolls of blue tape
- clear packing tape
- acrylic paints, 3 oz (84 g) of each: white, red, blue, and black
- plastic headband
- 24" (61 cm) curly white ribbon, strong enough for a strap

TOOLS: pencil, long ruler, craft knife, ¼" (0.5 cm) wide paintbrush, scissors, pencil, compass

CHILD WEARS: white shirt, red sweatpants, black shoes

DIRECTIONS

See the diagram to clarify all the measurements discussed below.

1 Orient the foam core board so the 33" (84 cm) side is nearest to you. Rule your 33" × 34" (84 × 86.4 cm) piece of foam core into thirds on its 33" side by marking a line 11" (28 cm) in from the left 34" side and another line 22" (56 cm) in from the same side.

2 By marking an inch (2.5 cm) on either side of the 11" (28 cm) and 22" (56 cm) lines, you will create 2" (5 cm) wide lattice bars for the tic tac toe.

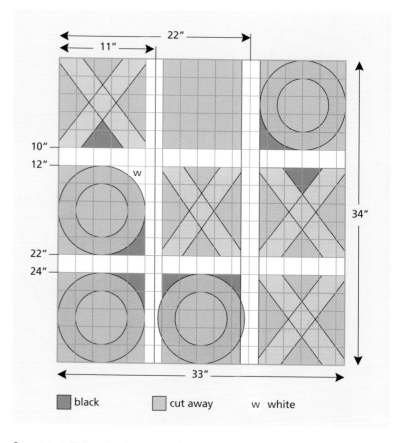

Steps 1 to 7. Pattern for tic tac toe. 1 box = 2" (5 cm). Rule board as shown and follow key that indicates where to paint and where to cut away.

3 From the top, measure down 10" (25.5 cm) on both 34" (86.4 cm) sides and draw a line across the width of the board. Draw another line 2" (5 cm) below it at 12" (30.5 cm) down. Draw another line at 22" (56 cm) down and one at 24" (61 cm) down. These lines mark the horizontal parts of the lattice between the squares.

*What's your
winning strategy?*

4 In four boxes of the lattice (see diagram), draw circles of diameter 10" (25.5 cm). Draw 8½" (21.5 cm) diameter circles inside the 10" ones. Circles must touch or overlap the lattice on 2 or 3 sides so they stay attached. Mark the areas around the "O"s that are to be cut away and the ones to paint black (see diagram). The top central box will be cut away so the child can look out there.

5 On the same cardboard, draw a large "X" in each of 4 remaining boxes (see photo). Each "X" should have sides that are 2½" (6.3 cm) thick and should be the full size of its box.

6 To paint, let each color dry before applying the next. Paint the tic tac toe lattice white. Paint the "O"s red. Paint the "X"s blue. Paint the corners marked black on the diagram black.

7 With a craft knife, carefully cut away the cardboard around the "X"s and "O"s where it is indicated on the diagram to cut, but never cut the letter attachments away from the white lattice.

8 Tape all the cut edges, using tape that matches the color of the letter. Use white tape on the lattice edges.

9 For the headband, draw a 10" (25.5 cm) circle on the 11" × 11" (28 × 28 cm) foam core board. Draw an 8½" (21.5 cm) circle inside it. Cut out the center circle. Paint the "O" red. Let dry. Tape the edges with red tape. Tape the red "O" to the headband with clear tape.

10 Tie white ribbon for a strap around the top bar of the lattice in the center in two places. Hang the tic tac toe sign around the child's neck.

Witch on Broom

MATERIALS

- four 1" × 1" × 16½" (2.5 × 2.5 × 42 cm) pieces of wood
- ten 1" (2.5 cm) drywall screws
- two 2" (5 cm) drywall screws
- 40" long (101.5 cm) small broom
- 5 oz (140 g) bag of purple feathers
- two 8" × 38" (20 × 96.5 cm) strips of striped fabric for legs
- small size 6 children's tennis shoes (thrift store)
- 10 oz (280 g) bag polyester batting
- 20" × 72" (51 × 183 cm) black fabric
- 17" × 40" (43 × 101.5 cm) black fabric
- 40" (101.5 cm) black ribbon, ½" (1.2 cm) wide
- 50" (127 cm) black ribbon, ½" (1.2 cm) wide
- witch's hat

TOOLS: screwdriver, drill, hot glue gun, scissors, needle and thread, saw, staple gun

CHILD WEARS: purple long-sleeved top, black shorts or skirt, white tights, and black shoes

DIRECTIONS

1 Use the four pieces of wood to create a rectangular frame by joining the pieces of wood together at their ends with 1" (2.5 cm) drywall screws. Use two drywall screws at each corner.

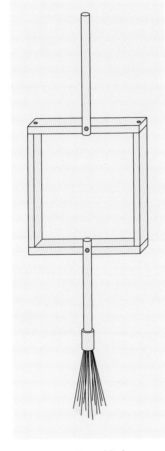

Steps 1 to 3. Assemble frame as shown and attach 2 pieces of broomstick.

2 Cut off the top 16" (41 cm) of the broomstick with a saw.

3 Mark the midpoint of one side of the frame. Drill a hole through the frame at the midpoint for a 2" (5 cm) drywall screw. Place one end of the 16" length of broomstick flush behind the wood frame, centering it on the tip of the drill, and drill through the broomstick also. Attach the 16" broomstick piece to the frame with a 2" (5 cm) drywall screw. On the opposite side of the frame, attach the remaining, lower portion of the broomstick in the same way. There is no broomstick inside the frame, leaving room for the child to stand.

4 To make the witch's legs, fold each of the 8" × 38" (20 × 96.5 cm) pieces of striped fabric in half to 4" × 38" (10 × 96.5 cm), with right sides of fabric facing in. Sew the long sides closed with needle and thread. Stitch one short end closed also. Repeat for the second piece of striped fabric.

5 Turn the leg right-side out and fill solidly with batting.

6 On the sides of the wooden frame that don't have any broomstick attached, attach a small tennis shoe on the outside of frame, close to the bristly end of the broom (see photo), by screwing it into the frame with a 1" (2.5 cm) screw.

*Better lie low . . .
the witch flies
tonight!*

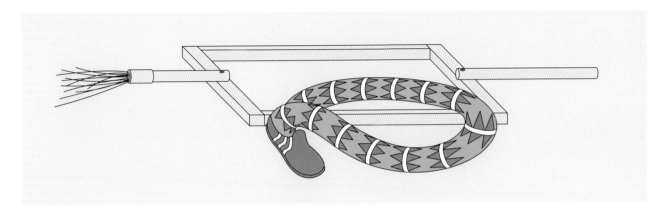

Steps 6 and 7. After sneaker is nailed to frame, stuffed leg is bent, part is inserted in sneaker, and the leg is stapled onto the frame in 2 places.

7 Stick the closed end of the batting-filled leg into the hole in the shoe to act as a foot. Align the leg on the side of the frame and staple it to the side of the frame near the front. Bend the rest of the leg back over the shoe and staple the leg to the top of the wooden frame. Repeat this on the opposite side of the frame with the second leg.

8 To make the skirt, fold the 20" × 72" (51 × 183 cm) black fabric in 1" (2.5 cm) on one side to make a 19" × 72" (48 × 183 cm) piece with a 1" hem. Sew down the hem near its edge to make a 1" tube for the ribbon.

9 Slip the 50" × ½" (127 × 1.2 cm) ribbon through the tube, gathering the fabric of the skirt as you go, until the ribbon has been fed all the way through. Leave excess ribbon to tie the skirt onto the child, around the waist.

10 Wrap the black skirt around the outside of frame, folding it back to leave the legs and

shoes exposed. Bring a little of the fabric under and inside the frame and staple it on the inside of the frame. The skirt should hang approximately 14" (35 cm) from waist to bottom of frame.

11 Take the witch's hat and hot-glue purple feathers around the top brim of the hat.

12 To make the cape, fold the 17" × 40" (43 × 101.5 cm) piece of black fabric to make a 14" × 40" (35.5 × 101.5 cm) shape with a 3" (7.5 cm) hem. Then fold over another 3½" (9 cm) to make an 11½" × 40" (20 × 101.5 cm) shape.

13 Sew across the cape fabric ½" (1.2 cm) in from the last fold, all the way across the 40" (101.5 cm) width to make a ½" (1.2 cm) wide tube to thread the ½" × 40" ribbon through, leaving you with a cape with a collar.

14 After the child is dressed, tie the costume on around her waist and tie the cape around her neck.

Lollipops and Sugar Sticks

MATERIALS

- three pieces of ¾" × 12" (1.9 × 30.5 cm) PVC pipe (for uprights)
- two pieces of ¾" × 18" (1.9 × 45.5 cm) PVC pipe (sides)
- two pieces of ¾" × 36" (1.9 × 91.5 cm) PVC pipe (for lollipop sticks)
- ¾" × 22" (1.9 × 56 cm) PVC pipe (for lollipop stick)
- ¾" × 9" (1.9 × 23 cm) PVC pipe
- seven pieces of ¾" × 2½" (1.9 × 6.4 cm) PVC pipe
- four ¾" (1.9 cm) PVC elbows: 3 regular elbows and 1 side outlet elbow*
- six ¾" (1.9 cm) PVC straight-through T connectors
- PVC pipe glue
- 2" (5 cm) wide red tape
- 2" (5 cm) wide clear packing tape
- four 15" (38 cm) diameter disposable see-through dish covers, the kind used for catering (for large lollipops)
- two 12" (30.5 cm) diameter disposable see-through dish covers (for small lollipop)
- five round 5" (12.5 cm) diameter see-through disposable containers (for round candies)
- acrylic paint, 6 oz (177 mL): white, hot pink, orange, yellow, and red
- plastic headband
- two pieces of 40" (102 cm) white ribbon for straps, 1" (2.5 cm) wide
- two 12" × 18" (30.5 × 45.5 cm) sheets of shiny hot pink wrapping paper
- three 12" × 18" (30.5 × 45.5) sheets of shiny deep purple wrapping paper
- 10' (300 cm) purple ribbon, ½" (1.2 cm) wide
- 10' (300 cm) hot pink ribbon, ½" (1.2 cm) wide
- 10' (300 cm) ribbon, ¼" (6 mm) wide, in each of the following: green, red, pink, blue, light green, yellow
- one each of 2" (5 cm) wide cardboard tubes, wrapped in white butcher paper, in the following lengths: 18" (45.5 cm), 12½" (32 cm), 17" (43 cm), 23" (58.4 cm)**
- two 2" wide × 17½" (5 × 44.5 cm) cardboard tubes wrapped in green wrapping paper**
- one each of 1½" (3.8 cm) wide cardboard tubes wrapped in green paper, in the following lengths: 11" (28 cm), 12" (30.5 cm)**
- one each of 1½" (3.8 cm) wide cardboard tubes, wrapped in yellow wrapping paper, in the following lengths: 14" (35.5 cm), 22" (56 cm), 23" (58.4 cm), 13" (33 cm)**
- ½" (1.2 cm) wide × 8" (20 cm) cardboard tube (e.g., fax paper roll) covered in white butcher paper (for hairband)**
- tacky glue

*The side outlet elbow has an extra hole at the top for a pipe.
**Before starting the steps below, wrap each cardboard tube neatly in paper and tape the paper ends inside the tube.

TOOLS: scissors, paintbrushes, ruler, craft knife

CHILD WEARS: solid bright colors and white shoes, or just socks

DIRECTIONS

Basically, you will assemble a frame from PVC components that is about 20" (51 cm) deep and 21" (53.3 cm) wide. The lollipops (suckers), round candies, and candy sticks all will be

*Life is sweeter
with a little
extra sugar.*

attached to this frame. The child will stand inside the frame. There are some extra decorations on the headband. We give you the basic instructions, but improvise as you see fit. Unless otherwise noted, all taping is done with clear tape. Gluing of PVC parts to each other should be done with PVC pipe glue.

Candies

1 Take all wrapped cardboard tubes and wind them with ribbons of different colors and thicknesses: Tape one end of each ribbon using 2" (5 cm) clear packing tape and twist ribbon around the tube to create a spiral pattern, cutting and taping the ribbon's end at the other end of the tube. Use any ribbons or combination of ribbons that look good to you.

2 To make the round wrapped candies, wrap each of three plastic 5" (12.5) circular containers in a 12" × 18" (20.5 × 45.5 cm) sheet of shiny deep purple wrapping paper. Twist ends of wrapping paper so the containers look like wrapped candies (see photo); tie each end closed with ribbon.

3 Repeat Step 2 for two more containers, but use shiny hot pink wrapping paper instead. Set them aside.

4 Lollipops: Paint a spiral onto the inside of both halves of each of the large (15" or 38 cm diameter) plastic dish covers, using a bright color of acrylic paint. After the spirals you have painted have dried, coat the entire inside of the container with either a darker or lighter color of acrylic paint. You could use a red spiral with a solid white background or an orange spiral with a yellow background, for example. Do the same for the 12" (30.5 cm) diameter see-through dish covers, which will become the smaller lollipop. Use your imagination and have fun. There are two sides to every lollipop, so

paint these in pairs, using the same color scheme. Let the covers dry. From the outside, you will see the original spiral; the rest of the cover will appear to be filled with the second color. Glue the two matching lollipop sides together. For each lollipop, cut a small hole in the seam to hold a ¾" (1.9 cm) PVC pipe section (the lollipop stick). Set these parts aside.

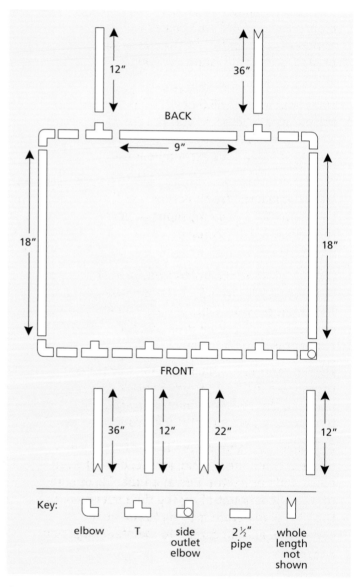

Step 5. Assembly diagram for PVC frame. Turn T connectors and side outlet elbow so openings are facing up.

Frame for Costume

5 Follow the Step 5 diagram to lay out the frame for the costume, but don't glue the pieces together yet:

5a On a flat work surface, connect a PVC elbow to each end of an 18" (45.5 cm) pipe; this will become the side of the frame on your left.

5b To make the back of the frame, working from your left to right, attach a 2½" (6.4 cm) piece of pipe, a T connector, a 9" (23 cm) piece of pipe, another T connector, another 2½" piece of pipe, and finally another elbow.

5c For the side of the frame on your right, add an 18" (45.5 cm) PVC pipe to the elbow at the back, and then add a side outlet elbow at the front. (The side outlet elbow has an extra hole for an upright.)

5d To make the front, connect all 5 remaining 2½" (6.4 cm) pipes between the remaining 4 T connectors (see diagram).

5e Attach the assembled front piece to the sides of the frame, at the elbows. With the frame flat on your work surface, rotate your T connectors so that all the open holes on the connectors are facing straight up.

5f Slide the 17½" (44.5 cm) green cardboard tubes over the two 18" (45.5 cm) pipes that make up the sides of the frame; you must temporarily disconnect the pipes to do this.

5g Once you have gotten the frame pieces well aligned, disconnect, glue, and reconnect each piece and connector, one at a time. Make sure to wait the amount of drying time specified on the PVC glue before moving to the next connector, and be careful to maintain alignment as you go.

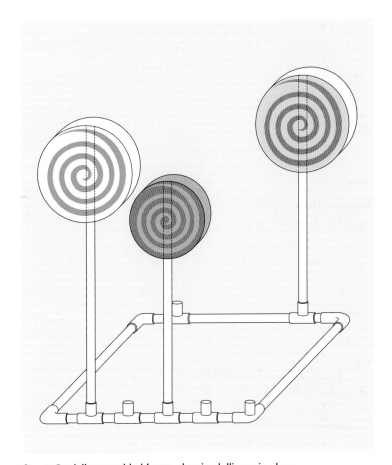

Step 7. Partially assembled frame, showing lollipops in place.

6 While you are facing the front of the frame, insert two 12" (30.5 cm) PVC pipes in the T connector and the side outlet elbow on the front of the frame (see diagram for Step 5) and one 12" pipe in the T connector on the left rear of the frame. All inserted pipes should be upright (vertical). Once you have them in position, disconnect, glue, and reconnect.

7 Twist ribbon around the two 36" (91.5 cm) PVC pipes and insert one pipe into a T connector in the back to your right and one in the front at your left. Disconnect, glue, and reconnect. These are the sticks for the large lollipops.

8 On the front of the frame, starting from the 12" pipe at your right front:

8a Slip the 2" diameter × 18" (5 × 45.5 cm) white cardboard tube over the 12" (30.5 cm) upright pipe (in the elbow).

8b On the first T connector from the right, tape the 2" × 12½" white cardboard tube with clear tape, holding it at an angle (see photo). This cardboard tube is taped directly onto the T connector.

8c Slip the 1½" diameter × 22" (3.8 × 56 cm) yellow cardboard tube over the upright pipe in the second T connector from the right.

8d The 1½" diameter × 12" (3.8 × 30.5 cm) green cardboard tube goes over the upright PVC pipe in the third T connector from the right.

8e The large lollipop top (15" or 38 cm diameter) gets attached to the 36" (91.5 cm) PVC pipe in the fourth T connector from the right. Insert the unattached 36" pipe end through the hole in the center seam of the lollipop top and push the top down as far as it will go. Then tape the top in place with clear tape.

8f Glue and tape the 12" (30.5 cm) diameter lollipop top to the 22" (56 cm) piece of PVC pipe in the second T connector from the right.

9 Facing the front of the costume and starting on your right in the front, tape the 1½" × 11" (3.8 × 28 cm) green cardboard tube, the 1½" × 14" (3.8 × 35.5 cm) yellow cardboard tube, and the 2" × 23" (5 × 58.4 cm) white cardboard tube in a bunch to the 2" × 18" white cardboard tube

in the right front elbow. Tape a hot pink round candy (see Step 3) to the frame in front of those tubes you just attached.

10 Tape the 2" × 17" (5 × 43 cm) white tube horizontally along the front left part of the frame (as you face it), below the upright pipes (see photo).

11 Tape a round purple candy (from Step 2) above the white tube you just attached to the frame, and tape one in front of the smaller lollipop.

12 Tape a hot pink candy to the front of the green post between the two purple candies you just attached.

13 Cover the 12" (30.5 cm) upright pipe at your left at the back of the costume with the 1½" diameter × 23" (3.8 × 58.4 cm) yellow cardboard tube.

14 Tape and glue a 15" (38 cm) diameter lollipop to the top of the 36" (91 cm) tall PVC pipe at the back on your right. Set the costume aside.

15 Cover the headband in red tape. With clear packing tape, tape the 1½" × 13" (2.5 × 33 cm) yellow cardboard tube to the headband. On top of the yellow tube, tape the ½" (1.2 cm) × 8" (20 cm) white cardboard tube. Tape a round purple candy on top of the tubes on the headband.

16 Have the child stand in the costume, holding it at about hip height. Tie the white ribbons on the front frame corners, criss-cross them behind her shoulders, and tie the other ends on the frame corners at the rear to support the costume.

About the Author

Growing up in Burbank, California, Holly Cleeland was exposed to the art of costume at an early age. The youngest of five children, she frequently accompanied her mother, Arden Cleeland, a costumer for many famous movie and television stars, to the stars' homes and movie sets. In this way, she met famous actresses including Elsa Lanchester, Susan St. James, Nancy Walker, and Stella Stevens. As a child of 4, Holly got to see a dragon for Disneyland being built in her own front room.

Being around creative activities and creative people inspired her in all areas. With such role models, it wasn't long before Holly started making costumes for family members and neighborhood friends, sharing in their delight when her creations won prizes.

During her high school years, Holly made money by painting T-shirts, designing store windows at holiday time, and drawing portraits, among other things. After attending Los Angeles Trade Tech and the Pasadena Art Center, in 1988 Holly started creating and selling Lawn Cheers, outdoor lawn displays for the holidays, an activity that takes her to many large art shows up and down the California coast. She also markets Lawn Cheers through many mail order catalogs. Her unique and easy-to-make costumes and lawn decorations have been featured on "The Rosie O'Donnell Show" and on HGTV's "The Carol Duvall Show." Holly lives in North Hollywood with her cat, Pumpkin.

Index

IN APPRECIATION

Our sincere thanks are extended to the over-200 individuals who have contributed to this cook book...California winemakers, their wives and families, their colleagues and companions, who have shared with us their love of cooking. They are the authors of this book, which is dedicated to a simple truth known for thousands of years in countless countries: that good food is even better with wine.

As the book's title implies, the recipes are not necessarily original. Some are, of course; and many of the dishes have been developed through generations within a family, made without written aid and perfected only by loving practice over the years.

Where recipe wording has been changed in this book, therefore, it has been to insure clarity of meaning and present-day cooking convenience. We have also tried to avoid duplication of recipes as far as possible, although the large number of our contributors will make a few savory similarities inevitable.

The assistance of Home Advisory Service of Wine Institute is gratefully acknowledged. We are particularly pleased by receipt of favorite recipes and wine choices from staff members of the Department of Viticulture and Enology and the Department of Food Science and Technology of University of California where research and teaching of viticulture (grape growing) and enology (science of wine making) were established by the State legislature in 1880. The work of the University has contributed greatly to the high quality of California wines. We express thanks for participation by staff members of the Department of Viticulture and Enology of Fresno State College, which started viticulture classes in 1929 and added enology courses in 1949.

WINE ADVISORY BOARD

D. C. Turrentine

WINE APPRECIATION GUILD

K. R. Hoop

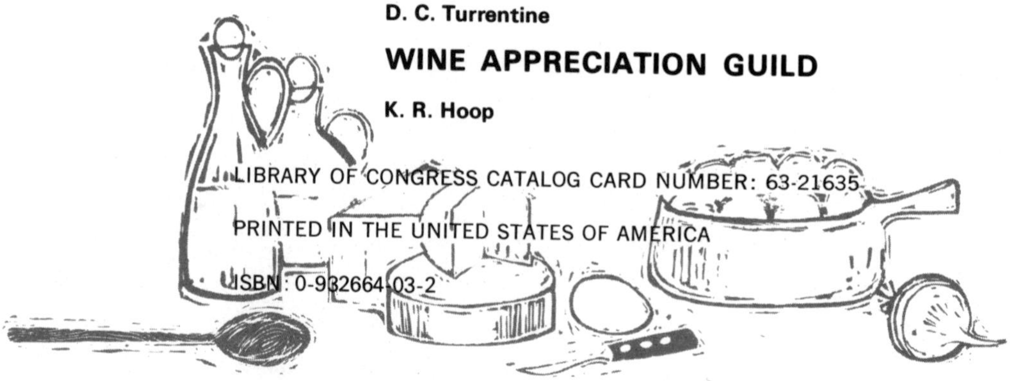

LIBRARY OF CONGRESS CATALOG CARD NUMBER: 63-21635

PRINTED IN THE UNITED STATES OF AMERICA

ISBN: 0-932664-03-2

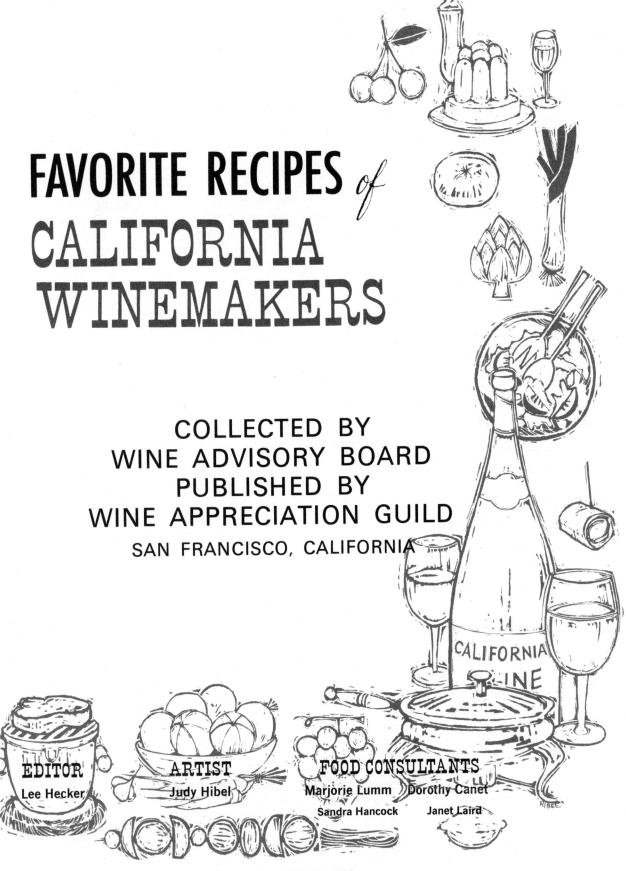

FAVORITE RECIPES *of* CALIFORNIA WINEMAKERS

COLLECTED BY
WINE ADVISORY BOARD
PUBLISHED BY
WINE APPRECIATION GUILD

SAN FRANCISCO, CALIFORNIA

EDITOR
Lee Hecker

ARTIST
Judy Hibel

FOOD CONSULTANTS
Marjorie Lumm Dorothy Canet

Sandra Hancock Janet Laird

THE LORE AND LURE OF WINE COOKERY

The use of wine in cooking is surely the happiest—and probably one of the oldest—of mankind's culinary discoveries: almost as old as wine itself, or its use in medicine. Whoever first discovered the sudden flowering of flavor from pouring a little wine into the pot remains unknown, an unsung genius in gastronomical history. But legions of chefs and good home cooks would salute and bless his name if we knew it. It is a name lost in the fragrant vinous mists from millions of kitchens ever since, throughout the ages.

Homer tells us the earliest civilized Greeks used wine for cooking as well as for quaffing. Later, under the Romans, wine was ever more at home on the range, improving pot roasts, stews, vegetables, sauces. As the basic drink throughout this ancient world, wine was even supplied regularly to slaves, to keep them in good health.

So entwined is the vine in western cultures, spreading northward from the Mediterranean, that by the 18th century we read quite naturally in the early English cook books of lamb marinated in white wine, pears done in Port, wine soup, Sherry-flavored puddings, Isaac Walton's own fish poached in wine, relishes and sauces containing wine and wine vinegar, swan or beef or hare with Claret, and such goodies. Wine flowed freely into the cooking pots of Europe, and its use was important also to many of our own nation's great. George and Martha Washington took pride in the wine cookery and wine service of their household. Thomas Jefferson selected carefully the wine-cooked dishes (as well as wines) for state dinners at the White House. So universal a custom must be soundly based on a more enjoyable cuisine.

Thus cooking with wine cannot be set off as a specialized field of cookery. It is too old a practice, too international, too intrinsic; it is merely the **best** way to cook. And no collection of wine cookery recipes could ever begin to cover all the marvels of taste created every day from simple dishes when the cook experiments. One of the beauties of wine cookery is that adding wine can only improve a dish. Itself a food, wine inevitably blends with the flavors of other foods. So use whatever wine you have on hand; and try wine in more kinds of dishes. This book shows some of the wide variety possible.

Another fact is revealed in the wine types recommended to accompany most of these foods, as beverage: the fact that there is no rule on choice but that of personal preference. If your wine is from California, whatever its type you can enjoy it with confidence. For California provides wines made 100% from the juice of true **vinifera** grapes, used for great wines for centuries in famous wine-growing regions of the world. And the strictest of all quality regulations are those imposed by the State of California for California wines.

Serve them with pride and cook with them, too—and you'll explore more fully the fine old-time pleasures of the table.

LEE HECKER

CONTENTS

Five Wine Classes	Best-Known Types

APPETIZER WINES

To enjoy before dinner or as a refreshment anytime

SHERRY	
VERMOUTH	*(vur-mooth)*
FLAVORED WINES	

RED DINNER WINES

BURGUNDY	
Similar Types:	
Pinot Noir	*(pea-no no-ahŕ)*
Gamay	*(ga-maý)*
Red Pinot	*(red pea-no)*
CLARET	
Similar Types:	
Cabernet	*(kab-er-naý)*
Zinfandel	*(ziń-fan-dell)*
Grignolino	*(green-yo-leeń-oh)*
ROSÉ	*(roh-zaý)*
"VINO" TYPES	*(vee-no)*
CHIANTI (Red)	*(kee-ahń-tee)*

WHITE DINNER WINES

SAUTERNE	*(so-tairń)*
Similar Types:	
Semillon	*(saý-mee-yonh)*
Sauvignon Blanc	*(so-vee-nyonh blanh)*
RHINE WINE	
Similar Types:	
Riesling	*(reeź-ling)*
Traminer	*(trah-meeń-er)*
Sylvaner	*(sil-vah́-ner)*
CHABLIS	*(shah-bleé)*
Similar Types:	
Pinot Blanc	*(pea-no blanh)*
Pinot Chardonnay	*(pea-no shar-doh-naý)*
White Pinot	*(white pea-no)*

DESSERT WINES

To enjoy after dinner or as a refreshment anytime

PORT	
TOKAY	*(toh-kaý)*
MUSCATEL	*(muss-kah-telĺ)*
ANGELICA	*(an-jelĺ-ee-cah)*
CREAM (SWEET) SHERRY	

SPARKLING WINES

CHAMPAGNE	*(sham-paiń)*
(White or Pink)	
Brut (very dry)	*(brewt)*
Sec (semi-dry)	*(sehk)*
Doux (sweet)	*(doo)*
SPARKLING BURGUNDY	

The more popular distinct types are shown above in ALL CAPITAL LETTERS.

WINE TYPES AND WINE USES

Type Characteristics			Favorite Uses *
SHERRY: Rich, nutlike flavor; from dry to sweet, pale to dark amber. Sweet or Cream Sherry is more dessert or refreshment wine.	**VERMOUTH:** Spicy, aromatic, herbal flavor. Dry is pale amber or almost colorless, light-bodied. Sweet is darker, medium-bodied.	**FLAVORED WINES:** Smooth, clear, with natural pure flavors added.	*Serve chilled, without food or with* **HORS d'OEUVRE OR SNACKS** Popular in 2½ to 4-ounce servings either straight or "on-the-rocks." Flavored wines are also served as tall mixed drinks.
BURGUNDY: Dry, robust; traditionally fuller-bodied and deeper in color than Claret. Pinot Noir, Red Pinot and Gamay are "varietal" Burgundies, named for their grape varieties. Pinot Noir is especially soft and velvety, with superb bouquet. Gamay is often a little lighter in body and color.	**CLARET:** Dry, tart, zestful; usually light or medium-bodied, ruby red. Cabernet, Zinfandel and Grignolino are varietals, named for their grapes. Zinfandel is fresh and fruity; Grignolino often more like a Rosé. Cabernet differs from most Clarets in its fuller body, deeper, more sumptuous color and bouquet.	**ROSÉ:** Gay pink, fruity, light-bodied, dry or slightly sweet. **"VINO" TYPES** often have Italian names, are mellow, soft in flavor, slightly sweet, quite full. **CHIANTI:** Dry, slightly tart, full-bodied, "Italian" in flavor.	*Serve at cool room temperature, in 6 to 9-ounce glasses, with* **STEAKS, ROASTS, CHOPS, CHEESES OR SPAGHETTI** Also good as part of the liquid in stews, pot roasts; in marinating economy meats; and in making delicious wine jellies and punches. *(Exception is Rosé or pink: serve chilled, with all foods.)*
SAUTERNE: Golden-hued, full-bodied, fragrant, ranging from dry to sweet. Semillon (dry or sweet) and Sauvignon Blanc (usually dry) are varietal Sauternes, named for their grapes. Haut Sauterne is sweet, with delightfully rich aroma. This type is also popular as a dessert wine.	**RHINE WINE:** Thoroughly dry, tart, with flowery bouquet, light body; pale or green-gold in color. Rieslings are Rhine-type varietals, delicate in flavor, usually named for their grapes, such as Johannisberg (White) Riesling or Grey Riesling. (Sylvaner is a Franken Riesling.) Traminer is another varietal, spicy, fresh.	**CHABLIS:** Soft, dry, less tart and fuller-bodied than Rhine Wines. The delicately flavored and smoothly aristocratic Pinots are the best-known varietals, named for the grape varieties from which they are made.	*Serve well chilled, in 6 to 9-ounce glasses, with* **SEAFOODS, CHICKEN, OMELETS OR OTHER LIGHT DISHES** Also used in cooking fish, white meats; and in making punches.
PORT: All Ports are rich, sweet, fruity, fairly full-bodied. They may be deep red, white (pale gold) or tawny (autumn-leaf color). The red is usually heavier-bodied.	**MUSCATEL:** Sweet, fruity, full-bodied, with the pronounced flavor and aroma of Muscat grapes. Color may range from golden and dark amber to red.	**TOKAY:** Pinkish amber, with slightly "nutty" or Sherry-like flavor. Less sweet than Port. **ANGELICA:** Straw or amber-colored. Very sweet, resembling White Port.	*Serve chilled or at cool room temperature, in 2½ to 4-ounce servings, with* **FRUITS, COOKIES, NUTS OR CHEESES** Also used in cooking, like basting ham or making wine jellies; or poured over fruit desserts.
CHAMPAGNE: Gay, festive, naturally effervescent. Ranges from very dry ("brut") to semi-dry ("sec") to sweet ("doux"). The pink is sometimes called Sparkling Rosé.	**SPARKLING BURGUNDY:** Ruby-red, sweet or semi-sweet, fruity, gay and bubbling, from the same type of natural secondary fermentation that produces Champagne.		*Serve well chilled, in 5 to 9-ounce glasses. Good with all foods:* **APPETIZERS, MAIN COURSE OR DESSERTS** And especially fine for festive "special occasion" punches.

Most people prefer the combinations shown in the right-hand column. But the "correct" wine is the one YOU like best.

A Note to the Reader

- Wine "bottle" when mentioned in this book means 25.6 fluid ounces. This size is also referred to as a "fifth," meaning 1/5 gallon, or 4/5 quart, or simply "large bottle."

- Where the word "NOTE" appears **under** recipes, the comment that follows is the editor's. Other comments are by recipe donors.

- Towns mentioned in most cases indicate location of winery referred to.

- For quick cooking tips and general hints for beginner cooks, see Page 120. A chart is also given on Page 121 which shows the amount and type of wine to add to your **own** recipes, to make them even more flavorful.

- This book is designed to **let you look while you cook.** Keep it in your kitchen where you'll see and use it often; it's made for everyday cooking convenience. You can fold it back and lay it flat. Or, you can fold it back and stand it up. (Slip a rubber band around each side to keep pages upright when book is standing.) Whichever way you prefer, you'll find it easy to use where you need it most — in your kitchen.

PUNCHES

Also Cocktails, Coolers and Hot Drinks with Wine

Entertaining with wine has become a widespread custom in this country in recent years. The wonderful flavor-variety and reasonable cost of good California wines have made them favorites everywhere with knowing hosts and hostesses. For the door to the wine cupboard is the gateway to delightful entertaining in every conceivable situation. With wine on hand, you can whip up a colorful, crowd-pleasing punch (hot or cold), that makes partying easier every way. Or you can greet guests with lively wine cocktails, that spark the conversation but protect the palate, insuring full appreciation of your delicious wine-cooked dinner. These recipes are only a sampling of the many delights of mixed wine drinks. Try them as an introduction to wine's great versatility.

FOR "LARGE BOTTLE" SIZE, SEE NOTE TO READER ON PAGE 8, OPPOSITE.

5-STAR FINAL PUNCH

(About 60 servings, 3-oz. size)

C. E. Gibson, Weibel Champagne Vineyards, Mission San Jose

> 2 (6-oz.) cans frozen orange
> juice concentrate, or 6 cups
> freshly squeezed orange juice
> 2 large bottles California Sauterne
> or other white dinner wine
> 1 large bottle California brandy
> 1 cup orgeat syrup
> 2 large bottles California Champagne

Reconstitute thoroughly the frozen orange juice, according to directions on can. In punch bowl, mix orange juice, white wine, brandy and orgeat syrup. Add cracked ice; let stand an hour or two. Just before serving, add more ice and pour in Champagne. Serve in punch cups.

NOTE: *If orgeat syrup is not available, substitute equal amount of simple syrup (2 parts sugar and 1 part water, boiled together 5 minutes), or light corn syrup, plus drop or two of almond extract. A small amount of this punch can be pre-tested before your party by combining 1 cup each orange juice and white wine, ½ cup brandy and 2 tablespoons orgeat. Add 1 cup Champagne just before testing.*

PUNCH IN THE PINK

(About 35 servings, 3-oz. size)

Brother Timothy, Mont La Salle Vineyards, Napa

This is delightful for afternoon parties or receptions where a light beverage is desired. It's also wonderful summer-evening-in-the-garden refreshment, with cookies, wafers, cake or canapés. It has been a great success wherever served.

> 1 small pkg. (about 3 tablespoons)
> "red-hot" cinnamon candies
> ¼ cup sugar
> ½ cup warm water
> 1 (46-oz.) can pineapple-grapefruit drink,
> chilled
> 1 qt. bottle ginger ale, chilled
> 1 large bottle California Light Muscat,
> chilled

Cook candies, sugar and water together over low heat, stirring constantly until candies are dissolved. Cool; combine with chilled ingredients.

PERFECTION PUNCH

(About 45 servings, 3-oz. size)

Hanns Kornell, Hanns Kornell Cellars, St. Helena

1 (6-oz.) can frozen lemonade concentrate
6 cups (1 large can) pineapple juice,
   well chilled
2 large bottles California Riesling
   or other white dinner wine, well chilled
1 large bottle California Champagne,
   well chilled
   Orange slices, maraschino cherries or
   strawberries for garnish

Mix frozen lemonade concentrate and pineapple juice in punch bowl. Add Riesling; blend well. Add 1 tray of ice cubes. Just before serving, pour in Champagne. Garnish as desired.

NOTE: *This is one of the simplest and most satisfying of all Champagne punches. It may be made entirely from California Champagne, of course—3 bottles total—added to fruit juice mixture just before serving.*

CHAMPAGNE RANGES from very dry (usually labeled "brut" or extra dry) to semi-dry (usually labeled "sec" or dry) to sweet ("doux"). Sparkling Burgundy is generally sweet or semi-sweet.

MAY WINE (MAI BOWLE)

(About 25 servings, 3-oz. size)

Dino Barengo, Dudenhoefer Co., Inc., Acampo

This is a very old, traditional punch for spring or summer. Place 1 small bunch of woodruff (OR 1 small bunch of mint and 6 crushed whole cloves) in punch bowl. Add 1 large bottle California Rhine or other white dinner wine. Steep 1 hour, then remove flavorings and pour in 2 more bottles of the same wine, chilled. Add 2 tablespoons simple syrup or sugar to taste. Stir well. If desired, add 2 cups halved sugared strawberries. Just before serving, add block of ice or several trays of ice cubes. Float some flowers, whole strawberries and mint sprigs on top.

NOTE: *You can get dried woodruff from some herb dealers or pharmacies, if fresh woodruff is not available. Another delightful way to serve this drink is to surround the punch bowl with an assortment of sliced or cubed sugared fruits and whole sugared berries, on the punch bowl tray. (In this case you would not add berries to the punch itself.) Guests then select and add their own fruit garnish to the punch cups, as desired.*

PRE-BREAKFAST PUNCH

(4 servings)

Mrs. Albert Cribari, Evergreen Vineyards, San Jose

In each of 4 large glasses, place 1½ to 2 jiggers (3 or 4 tablespoons) California brandy. OR, use 1 jigger (2 tablespoons) **each**: California Sherry and brandy. Set aside. Combine 1 pt. vanilla ice cream and 1 cup milk, using rotary beater or electric blender. Blend to consistency of a thick milk shake. Pour over brandy in glasses; stir. Top with nutmeg. (Pitchers of this milk shake can be made ahead of time and stored in refrigerator, if desired.)

NOTE: *This is wonderful before a late, festive breakfast or brunch. The punch can be thinned as desired, using more milk and less ice cream.*

SANGRIA

(About 10 servings, 3-oz. size)

Doris Paulsen, Wine Institute, San Francisco

This is the famous Spanish pitcher drink—really delicious and refreshing, and quite easy to mix.

1 large bottle California Burgundy
   or other red dinner wine
1 orange
1 lemon or 2 limes, sliced
   Variety of fresh fruit (such as 1 or 2
   sliced fresh peaches, 1 or 2 sliced
   plums and ½ cup fresh berries
1 jigger (3 tablespoons) California brandy
   Sugar (optional)
1 (7-oz.) bottle sparkling water

Pour wine into glass pitcher. Peel orange in one long spiral strip. Put peel in wine, with one end of spiral curled over spout of pitcher. Squeeze orange; add juice to wine along with lemon and lime slices and brandy. For best flavor, allow to stand several hours. About 1 hour before serving, add remaining fresh fruit. Taste; add sugar, if desired. (The traditional Spanish Sangria is refreshingly fruity but not too sweet.) Just before serving, add sparkling water. Pour Sangria into tall glasses or large wine glasses, half-filled with ice cubes. Pieces of fruit may be added to each glass.

NOTE: *When no suitable fresh fruit is in season, frozen fruit may be substituted, with lemon juice added to balance the frozen fruit sugar. Serve as soon as defrosted. Still another version of Sangria, without fruit, is made using juice of 4 lemons for fruitiness and ½ cup sugar.*

DON'T BE AFRAID to experiment with punch recipes. If you like the flavor of a particular recipe that calls for white dinner wine, such as Sauterne, substitute California Rosé if you would prefer a gay pink color. Pink Champagne or Sparkling Rosé may also be used in place of regular Champagne. Or, introduce extra color by means of fruit or berry garnishes, or ice cubes made of frozen fruit juice.

BLOSSOM HILL CHAMPAGNE PUNCH

(25 servings, 3-oz. size)

Mrs. E. Jeff Barnette, Martini & Prati Wines, Inc., Santa Rosa

This idea came from South America, where I lived for eight years. It has been worked out and perfected here at Blossom Hill Ranch, and is delicious for any occasion, especially for holidays and receptions. The basic ingredients may be combined and refrigerated for days ahead, with the Champagne added just prior to serving.

      2 cups frozen pineapple juice
      1 cup sugar
    1½ cups California brandy
    1½ cups California Sauterne, Chablis
        or other white dinner wine
      ½ cup lime or lemon juice
    2¼ teaspoons Angostura bitters
      1 large bottle California Champagne,
        chilled

Combine all ingredients except Champagne in a half-gallon jar or large mixing bowl. Cover; refrigerate overnight or at least 8 hours. Just before serving, pour mixture over block of ice in punch bowl; add Champagne.

SUMMER HOUSE TEA makes unforgettable cool refreshment for about 6 wilted friends. To 1 pint strong hot tea, add 1 cup California Claret (or other red dinner wine), 1 cup orange juice, ¼ cup lemon juice and sugar to taste. Chill well. Pour over ice cubes in tall glasses. Garnish with orange slices or mint for color and a flavor fillip.

SOUTHLAND CHAMPAGNE PUNCH

(27 servings, 3-oz. size)

Mrs. Cesare Vai, Cucamonga Vineyard Co., Cucamonga

    2 large bottles California Champagne,
      chilled
    1 large bottle California Sauterne
      or other white dinner wine, chilled
    1 cup California brandy, chilled
    ½ (1-qt.) bottle sparkling water,
      chilled
    1 cup simple syrup (see below)
    1 qt. lightly sugared strawberries
      with stems

Combine chilled ingredients with simple syrup in punch bowl. Add a small block of ice; garnish with strawberries.

SIMPLE SYRUP: Combine 6 cups sugar with 2⅔ cups water. Let stand at room temperature, stirring occasionally, until dissolved. Use at room temperature. See also Note, Page 9.

BOWLE

(About 20 servings, 3-oz. size)

The Marquise de Pins, Beaulieu Vineyard, Rutherford

This "bowle" is delicious and refreshing before lunch or dinner.

    4 or 5 medium-size peaches
      5 apricots (if available)
      1 large banana
    1½ cups strawberries
      2 rounded tablespoons sugar
      ¼ cup California brandy
      2 large bottles California
        Brut Champagne, chilled

Slice fruit into large bowl. Add sugar, brandy and 1½ cups Champagne, or just enough to not-quite-cover the fruit. Stir; marinate in refrigerator about 2 hours, stirring several times. Just before serving, add rest of chilled Champagne; mix well. Strain; pour into well-chilled glasses. Serve immediately.

NOTE: *A really excellent combination.*

SPARKLING BURGUNDY CUP

(About 8 servings, 3-oz. size)

Dino Barengo, Barengo Cellars, Acampo

    1½ cups water
      3 whole sticks cinnamon
      6 whole cloves
      ½ teaspoon ground nutmeg
      4 thin lemon slices
      3 tablespoons sugar
      1 large bottle California
        Sparkling Burgundy, well chilled

First make spice syrup as follows: Boil water, spices, lemon slices and sugar together in covered saucepan about 10 minutes. Strain through very fine strainer; discard spices and lemon; chill liquid thoroughly. When ready to serve, pour about 1 tablespoon (or more, to taste) of spice syrup into each cup. Fill with Sparkling Burgundy. (Leftover syrup can be stored in refrigerator.)

ORANGE-FROSTED CHAMPAGNE PUNCH is cooling and colorful for a small group of card-players. To make 16 servings, 3-oz. size: Dilute 1 (6-oz.) can frozen orange juice concentrate with ice water, as directed on label. Add ½ pint orange sherbet and stir until melted. Add 1 pint California Champagne and mix gently. Add ½ pint more sherbet by spoonfuls, to float in punch bowl. Serve at once. An economical way to be lavish.

INSTANT SPARKLER

(Any amount)

Dr. W. V. Cruess, U.C. Dept. of Food Science & Technology

This recipe is excellent between meals as a thirst-quencher or pickup; and **with** meals, as a starter, or in place of dinner wine in warm weather. Simply pour dry red or white dinner wine (such as Burgundy or Sauterne) into tall glasses, about half-full. Fill with chilled, plain carbonated water. For persons who prefer a little sweetness, add a small amount of sugar; or use a carbonated drink containing some sugar, such as ginger ale or one of the lemon-flavored carbonated drinks.

NOTE: *Always dependably refreshing, yet moderate. For those with a sweet tooth, dessert wines such as Port or Muscatel are also good mixed with the sparkling water. It pays to experiment to find the type of Wine Cooler you prefer.*

THE SPRITZER goes on generation after generation as a favorite summer beverage. It's for people who prefer their drinks very dry. Simply mix a California Rhine wine type with unsweetened sparkling water, half-and-half, over ice cubes in a tall glass.

THE BASIL BOWLER is a really fresh, different drink, to surprise and delight your guests. Mr. and Mrs. W. W. Owen, of California Grape Products Corporation, Delano, enjoyed it in a French vineyard region. Here's an adaptation of the recipe, to make about 6 generous servings: Pick fresh basil leaves from stems; wash and crush leaves lightly. Use about 1 cup of leaves, loosely measured, to 1 large bottle California Muscatel. Steep leaves in wine 1 or 2 hours. Strain; pour wine over ice in tall glasses. Add squeeze of fresh lemon juice to each glass, stir to blend, and garnish with additional basil leaf, if desired.

SUMMER COOLER

(4 servings)

Mrs. Guy Baldwin, Jr., Mont La Salle Vineyards, Napa

    2 cups California
       Light Muscat wine, chilled
    2 cups lemon-flavored
       sparkling water, chilled

Combine wine and lemon beverage. Pour over cracked ice in tall glasses.

NOTE: *A pleasant variation on the standard Wine Cooler or Wine-and-Soda combination — and nothing could be easier.*

ROSÉ CREAM is lovely to look at, and sip, on a warm afternoon. To make about 8 tall servings: Blend 2 cups chilled California Rosé with 1 pint strawberry ice cream, in blender or bowl with rotary beater. Put about ½ cup of mixture in each tall glass. Pour in chilled sparkling water or ginger ale to fill glass. Stir gently, admire and enjoy.

FRENCH 75 PITCHER

(About 10 servings, 3-oz. size)

Albert B. Cribari, Evergreen Vineyards, San Jose

This is a fine, well-tested drink for serving to rather large parties. It's best with a stiff, formal or unhappy crowd!

  ½ cup California brandy
  3 dashes Angostura bitters
  3 twists lemon peel
  1 large bottle California Demi-sec
     Champagne, chilled

Fill a large pitcher with ice cubes. Add brandy, bitters and lemon peel (that has first been twisted over ice cubes). Stir; set aside. Just before serving, pour Champagne rapidly over ice cubes. (DO NOT STIR.) Pour into Champagne or cocktail glasses; garnish with orange slices or maraschino cherries. (If a drier Champagne is used, you may want to add about ½ teaspoon sugar.)

SPARKLING QUININE water makes a good Wine-and-Tonic drink for warm afternoons or evenings. Use any favorite California wine (try Sherry or a flavored wine), half-and-half with quinine water, over ice. Squeeze of lemon or lime is optional.

SHERRY SOUR

(9 to 10 servings, 3-oz. size)

Mrs. Albert Cribari, Evergreen Vineyards, San Jose

> 1 large bottle California Dry Sherry
> ½ to 1 (6-oz.) can frozen lemonade concentrate

Combine ingredients in pitcher and mix well. Amount of lemonade concentrate depends on lemon flavor desired. Store in refrigerator overnight or longer. When ready to serve, add a few ice cubes and serve in cocktail glasses.

NOTE: *This is a version of the famous SHERRY SHRUB, a favorite wine cocktail—a superb refresher, and one that improves with age. The longer you store it in the refrigerator (up to a month or more), the better it gets. Variations on this recipe are numerous. Some like to add juice of 2 lemons to the full 6-oz. can of lemonade concentrate. Others vary the recipe as follows:*

SHERRY FRAPPÉ. Joseph Aime of Assumption Abbey Winery, Guasti, adds plenty of crushed ice to the basic mixture above just before serving, then blends in electric blender until drink is "soupy thick." He serves it in a daiquiri-type glass and garnishes edge of glasses with bar sugar, also adding sprig of mint, cherry or orange slice.

ANOTHER FRAPPÉ EFFECT is made by Mrs. Kenneth O. Dills of Charles Krug Winery, St. Helena, by freezing the Sherry-lemonade for about 24 hours, until mushy. She also adds a bottle of lemon-flavored carbonated soft drink to her mixture. The drink is served in a Champagne glass with a short straw. (Mrs. Dills also likes the unfrozen but long-mellowed Sherry Sour version. When making this she uses 1 cup fresh lemon juice and ½ cup sugar to 1 large bottle Dry Sherry—no lemonade concentrate.)

BLOSSOM HILL SHERRY SOUR, made by Mrs. E. Jeff Barnette of Martini & Prati Wines, Inc., Santa Rosa, combines 1 cup California Cream Sherry (instead of Dry Sherry) with juice of 1 lemon or lime, 1 tablespoon sugar, and crushed ice. Shake well; add cherry or mint sprig if desired. This makes 4 small Sherry Sours.

LADIES' DELIGHT. Mrs. E. A. Mirassou of Mirassou Vineyards, San Jose, uses pink lemonade concentrate (1 6-oz. can to 1 large bottle Dry Sherry) in her version of the Sherry Sour. She freezes the drink, as does Mrs. Dills, then defrosts to sherbet consistency and serves with straws in Champagne glasses. Another who likes pink lemonade in the mixture is Mrs. Sydney Whiteside of Del Rio Winery, Lodi, who says, "A real good drink for the girls!"

SHERRY DAIQUIRI. Mrs. Joseph S. Concannon, Jr., of Concannon Vineyard, Livermore, follows the blender procedure given above for Sherry Frappé. She prefers to use a 6-oz. can of frozen daiquiri mix or frozen limeade (in place of regular lemonade concentrate) with 1 large bottle of Dry Sherry. All of which shows that some delightful and varied cocktails are possible, with even one single type of California wine! Think what you could do with a full assortment in your kitchen wine cupboard.

CLASSIC CHAMPAGNE COCKTAIL

(1 serving)

Hanns Kornell, Hanns Kornell Cellars, St. Helena

First put ½ teaspoon sugar in a traditional Champagne glass. Add dash of bitters, and twist of lemon or orange peel if you like. Fill with icy-cold California Champagne and stir very lightly; serve. (If you want special elegance, frost the glasses first, by cooling them in refrigerator, rubbing rim with lemon slice, then dipping rim in powdered sugar for a minute or two. Shake off excess sugar, then make cocktail.)

NOTE: *Variations on the traditional Champagne cocktail are many, and fun to try. One, the CHAMPAGNE JULEP, adds fresh mint sprigs, an ice cube and 2 oz. California brandy (optional) to the sugar in the glass, without bitters, before filling with Champagne. Top is garnished with fresh fruit. The MAHARAJAH'S BURRA PEG follows the regular Champagne cocktail procedure, with sugar–soaked bitters, then adds 1 part brandy and 4 or 5 parts Champagne. This one is served in a tall glass, decorated with spiral of lime or lemon peel.*

SHERRY MANHATTAN

(10 servings, 3-oz. size)

Sandra Hancock, Wine Institute, San Francisco

This is not only a very good drink, but an extremely easy recipe to enlarge and make ahead of time for a party.

> 1 large bottle California Dry Sherry
> 1 cup California Sweet Vermouth
> ½ teaspoon grenadine syrup
> 1 small orange, sliced

Combine all ingredients 3 or 4 days before serving. Store in glass, ceramic or plastic container in refrigerator until ready to serve.

THE ASH BLONDE COCKTAIL is a growing favorite. As originally devised by Mr. and Mrs. Jack F. M. Taylor of Mayacamas Vineyards, Napa, this sprightly pre-dinner drink combined 5 parts of chilled California Dry Vermouth to 1 part Sweet Vermouth, with a twist of lemon peel, in a chilled glass (or over ice). Over the years the Taylors have been making the cocktail drier and drier— until now they estimate they use 20 parts Dry Vermouth to 1 part Sweet. The important fact is that Vermouth tastes so good by itself, whatever the proportions. In Europe, of course, it has long been a popular aperitif.

A TRADITIONAL VERMOUTH COCKTAIL mixes 1 or 2 dashes bitters and twist of lemon peel with California Sweet Vermouth, well-chilled. And Sherry-and-Bitters combines 2 or 3 dashes bitters with each jigger of California Dry Sherry. Quick and good before dinner.

WINE COLLINS

(1 serving)

Paul Kershaw, Jr., Mills Winery, Sacramento

Fill tall glass with ice. Squeeze ½ lime into glass, also adding rind. Add 3 oz. (6 tablespoons) California flavored specialty wine. Fill remaining half of glass with lemon-flavored soda. Garnish with a cherry.

BAMBOO COCKTAIL

(1 serving)

Joseph Aime, Assumption Abbey Winery, Guasti

Mix 1½ ounces California Sherry with same amount of Vermouth. Add 1 dash of bitters and several dashes of grenadine and/or maraschino syrup, to taste. Add cracked ice, and stir with vigor. Strain into cocktail glass and garnish with green olive. This is a well-known old cocktail, with several variations. You can use Dry or Cream Sherry, and Dry or Sweet Vermouth, whatever type you prefer.

THE OLD MONTANA COCKTAIL combines 1 part California Dry Vermouth, 1 part California Port and 4 parts California brandy. Stir with ice cubes.

VERMOUTH OLD-FASHIONED is a welcome change. For 1 serving, dissolve ¼ teaspoon sugar in 1 tablespoon water with dash of bitters in old-fashioned glass. Add ice cubes and ¼ cup **each** California Dry Vermouth and sparkling water. Stir to blend; garnish with cherry and orange slice.

EASY WINE LEMONADE

(1 serving)

Don Gregg, Mendocino Grape Growers, Inc., Ukiah

Dissolve 1 tablespoon sugar in juice of ½ lemon (or about 1½ tablespoons juice), in bottom of tall glass or large wine glass. Add ice cubes and ½ cup of any type of dinner wine (Burgundy, Sauterne, Rosé, etc.). Add plain ice water or chilled sparkling water to fill; stir and serve. (If an appetizer or dessert wine is used, such as Sherry, Port or Muscatel, decrease sugar.)

WINE SNOW CONES

(Any amount)

Mrs. Larry Cahn, Wine Institute, San Francisco

Bowl of shaved or crushed ice
Assortment of full-bodied
  California wines
Straws

Inspired by children's snow cones, these are for adults. Fill each guest's glass nearly to the brim with ice. Let each guest pour the wine of his choice over the ice (about 3 oz.). Insert straw and sip, or serve with a spoon and nibble, for a wine-flavored ice cooler. Easy and refreshing.

NOTE: *Offering a choice of several California wine types adds special interest for guests, and extra color.*

HOT CLAM-TOMATO COCKTAIL is a perfect appetizer before a big dinner. To make about 6 servings, 3-oz. size, combine the following: 1 cup tomato juice, 1 (9-oz.) can clam juice, ¼ cup California Dry Vermouth, few drops Tabasco sauce and 2 tablespoons fresh lemon juice. Add salt and pepper to taste. Heat just to boiling and serve in small heat-proof or preheated glasses.

TROCADERO COCKTAIL is ½ jigger **each** of California Dry and Sweet Vermouth, with a dash **each** of grenadine and orange bitters. Stir well with ice; strain and add twist of lemon peel.

CALIFORNIA CAFÉ BRULOT

(About 8 demi-tasse cups)

Albert E. Moulin, Jr., Wine Advisory Board, New Orleans

This flaming coffee is a version of a very old New Orleans drink. It serves as both dessert and coffee.

- 15 whole cloves
- 3 sticks cinnamon, broken in pieces
  Peel of ½ orange and ½ lemon, cut in nickel-size pieces
- ½ cup California brandy
- 1 tablespoon California Sherry
- ⅔ cup sugar (or at least 20 cubes)
- 4 cups hot strong black coffee

Combine spices, peel, brandy, Sherry and sugar; let stand about 4 hours before using. Place in a Brulot bowl, a large Pyrex bowl or a copper-base silver bowl. (Do not use a sterling silver bowl.) Ignite the mixture (during cold weather this works best if mixture is pre-warmed before igniting). Stir the flaming liquid with a long-handled spoon or ladle. When flames begin to die down, add piping hot coffee and serve immediately. (To preserve the brandy taste, do not burn too long. Plenty of sugar is required for the rich flavor.)

NOTE: *Some versions of this classic add pieces of vanilla bean. There are also many variations in serving. A favorite one is to light a candle and douse the lights. Heat the spoon or ladle over the candle flame, and with it dip up some of the brandy mixture (not yet flaming) with one or two brandy-soaked lumps of sugar. Touch these off with the candle, then lower the flaming ladle into the bowl to set off the remaining brandy mixture. Add coffee, as above. Great showmanship to climax a special dinner!*

AFTER-DINNER PEACHIE

(4 generous servings)

Paul R. Heck, Korbel Champagne Vineyards, Guerneville

- 4 small (half-dollar size) ripe peaches, peeled
- ¾ cup California brandy
- 1 tablespoon powdered sugar
- 1 large bottle California Sec or Brut Champagne, chilled

Pierce peeled peaches thoroughly with a fork. Place in small glass bowl. Pour over brandy; sprinkle with powdered sugar. Refrigerate overnight. When ready to serve, place each peach in a tall, clear, zombie-type glass. Gently pour Champagne over peach, filling glass ⅔ full. If peach is small enough to move in glass, the effervescence of the Champagne will cause the peach to swirl.

NOTE: *This is a traditional combination serving as both dessert and after-dinner drink. It is also attractive served in a regular wine glass or a Champagne glass. Guests eat the peach with a spoon, then drink the Champagne.*

SHERRIED COFFEE DESSERT

(1 serving)

Elie Skofis, Roma Wine Company, Fresno

In a coffee cup put 1 tablespoon California Sherry, 1 tablespoon California brandy and 3 to 4 tablespoons chocolate ice cream. Fill cup with strong hot coffee and serve at once.

NOTE: *A luscious idea that would fill two purposes very well indeed — dessert and coffee, all in one. For an even simpler after-dinner drink, J. B. Cella, II, of Cella Wineries, Fresno, suggests adding California brandy to coffee — a famed combination that always pleases guests.*

SHERRY BANANA SHAKE

(2 to 4 servings)

Dino Barengo, Barengo Cellars, Acampo

- 2 large bananas
- 1 cup milk
- 1 pint vanilla ice cream
- ⅛ teaspoon salt
- ⅓ to ½ cup California Sherry
- ¼ teaspoon nutmeg

Peel bananas. Combine with all remaining ingredients in electric blender. Blend until smooth and foamy. (If blender is not available, mash banana and beat all ingredients together with a rotary beater until smooth; **or,** shake vigorously in a covered container.)

SHERRY FLIP

(1 serving)

Gertrude Harrah, Wine Institute, San Francisco

- 1 egg
- 1 teaspoon fine granulated sugar
- 2 jiggers (3 oz. total) California Dry Sherry
  Ice, cracked or crushed

Shake all together, then strain into glass and top with dash of nutmeg. A famous traditional drink, and delicious as a brunch feature or night-cap — or anytime. Make the popular Port Flip the same way, but without the sugar.

HOT MULLED WINE

(12 servings, 3-oz. size)

Mrs. Joseph S. Concannon, Jr., Concannon Vineyard, Livermore

This can be made well in advance and reheated when ready to serve. We serve it at Christmas when friends drop in. We always have plenty of Christmas cookies, sugared nuts and Grandmother's fruit cake to offer with the mulled wine.

1½ cups boiling water
½ cup granulated sugar
½ lemon, sliced
3 sticks cinnamon
3 whole cloves
1 large bottle California Burgundy, Claret or other red dinner wine
Nutmeg

Combine boiling water, sugar, lemon, cinnamon and cloves; stir until sugar dissolves. Add wine; simmer 20 minutes. (DO NOT BOIL!) Strain. Serve hot with a sprinkling of nutmeg.

HOT LEMON SWIZZLE EGGNOG

(About 16 servings, 3-oz. size)

Dino Barengo, Barengo Cellars, Acampo

1 quart commercial eggnog
1 cup milk
1 cup California Muscatel
¼ teaspoon salt
2 teaspoons grated lemon rind
Nutmeg
Curls of lemon peel

Combine eggnog and milk. Slowly beat in Muscatel. Stir in salt and lemon rind. Heat gently to just below boiling. Top each serving with a dash of nutmeg and a lemon peel curl.

HOT CRANBERRY-WINE CUP

(About 28 servings, 3-oz. size)

Elie Skofis, Roma Wine Company, Fresno

2 (1-pt.) bottles cranberry juice cocktail
2 cups water
1½ cups sugar
4" stick cinnamon
12 whole cloves
Peel of ½ lemon
2 large bottles California Burgundy or other red dinner wine
¼ cup lemon juice
Nutmeg

Combine cranberry juice cocktail, water, sugar, cinnamon, cloves and lemon peel in saucepan. Bring to boil, stirring until sugar is dissolved; simmer 15 minutes and strain. Add wine and lemon juice; heat gently. (Do not boil.) Serve in preheated mugs or cups, with a little nutmeg sprinkled over top of each serving. Very flavorful in cold weather.

HOT SPICED (or mulled) wine drinks were quaffed even in Charlemagne's day, as an apéritif. They're one of the oldest of mixed wine drinks known to Northern Europe. And with good reason, you'll know—if you've ever enjoyed a steaming wine bowl on a cold, rainy or snowy night.

HORS D'OEUVRE

And "Anytime" Refreshments with Wine

At cocktail time, wine itself, alone, can serve as appetizer. The nutlike tang of a chilled California Sherry, or the piquancy of a Vermouth or flavored wine on-the-rocks, can make the dinner to follow even more enjoyable. But a few nibbles or snacks are also often desirable. These appetizers can be the simplest. Even cheese spread out of a jar has a festive flavor when it has been mixed with wine in the kitchen — and served with wine in the living room. Wine-flavored cheese spreads are also delightful as a dessert or any-hour refreshment, served with fruit and California Port (or with other dessert wines).

WINEMAKER COCKTAIL 'BURGERS

(About 4½ dozen)

Richard Norton, Fresno State College Dept. Vitic. & Enology

    1   lb. ground beef chuck or round steak
    ½   cup fine dry bread crumbs
    ¼   cup California Sherry
    ¼   cup milk
    1   tablespoon instant minced onion
        or 3 tablespoons finely chopped
        green or mild onion
    1   teaspoon seasoned salt
    1   teaspoon seasoned pepper
        Heated shortening or oil
    4½ dozen tiny biscuits (see below)
        Dipping Sauce (see below)

Combine meat with bread crumbs, Sherry, milk, onion, salt and pepper. Mix until well blended. Shape into bite-size meat balls. Cover and refrigerate until ready to use. Sauté meat balls in a little heated shortening or oil, until cooked and nicely browned. Drain on paper towels and keep hot until ready to serve. Serve each meat ball on a tiny biscuit, secured by a toothpick, with Dipping Sauce on the side.

COCKTAIL BISCUITS: Separate biscuits from 8-oz. pkg. refrigerated biscuits. Flatten to about ¼" and cut into tiny biscuits with 1" cutter (or, divide each biscuit into quarters and round up into small balls). Bake in a hot oven (450°) until crisp and nicely browned, about 5 minutes. Makes about 4½ dozen.

DIPPING SAUCE: Blend 1 cup chili sauce or catsup with 2 tablespoons prepared mustard. If thinner sauce is desired, add a little California Sherry. Makes about 1¼ cups sauce.

My choice of wine to accompany this dish:
CALIFORNIA SHERRY OR VERMOUTH

EASY LOBSTER CANAPÉS

(About 1½ cups of spread)

Robert S. McKnight, Di Giorgio Wine Company, Di Giorgio

This recipe is a bachelor's delight. You can make it in five minutes and it's wonderful!

    ⅓   cup mayonnaise
    3 or 4 tablespoons California Dry Sherry
        Salt and paprika
    1   cup canned or fresh cooked lobster meat

Combine all ingredients in mixer or blender; mix well. Chill; serve as a spread, on crackers or toast rounds.

My choice of wine to accompany this dish:
CALIFORNIA CHAMPAGNE COCKTAIL, DRY SHERRY OR VERMOUTH COCKTAIL (DRY OR MIXED WITH SWEET)

HOT SHERRIED CHICKEN LIVERS

(About 16 livers, for 4 to 8 persons)

J. B. Cella, II, Cella Wineries, Fresno

We enjoy these as hors d'oeuvre at our home during "Champagne Hour" before dinner.

    1   pound chicken livers
    4   tablespoons butter
    ½   cup California Dry Sherry or brandy
    2   teaspoons chopped parsley
    ½   teaspoon salt
        Few grains pepper

Sauté livers in butter over low heat until brown. Add other ingredients; simmer for 10 minutes. Serve hot with cocktail pick in each piece.

MUSHROOMS MAGNIFIQUE

(About 30 mushrooms)

Marvin B. Jones, Gibson Wine Company, Elk Grove

These are especially nice served in a chafing dish, and the recipe is easy to enlarge in any amount.

    1   (4-oz.) can button mushrooms, or
        30 fresh cooked button mushrooms
    ¼   cup butter or margarine
    ⅓   cup California Sherry
        Finely chopped fresh parsley or chives

Drain mushrooms; heat in butter in shallow pan. Add Sherry; simmer gently until liquid is almost completely evaporated. Sprinkle with chopped parsley or chives. Serve hot with cocktail picks.

NOTE: Always a winner at any cocktail-hour gathering. Serve with Vermouth or Sherry on-the-rocks, or California Champagne.

TOASTED MUSHROOM ROLLS are different and delicious. (Make in advance and toast just before serving.) To make filling: Sauté sliced fresh mushrooms in butter, with chopped shallots or finely minced green onion. Add flour to thicken, then equal parts of chicken broth and cream. Cook, stirring constantly, until reduced and thickened, and finally add a few tablespoons California Marsala or Sherry. Mixture should be like a thin paste in consistency. Spread on thin slices of white bread with crusts removed. Roll up, fasten with cocktail picks, and place on buttered cookie sheet. Bake in moderately hot oven (375°) until bread is toasted. Serve hot with glasses of chilled Sherry.

ANCHOVY WINE CHEESE SPREAD

(About 1½ cups)

Peter Scagliotti, Live Oaks Winery, Gilroy

    1   (2-oz.) can anchovies, drained
    2   (8-oz.) pkgs. cream cheese
    ¼   cup California Sherry
    2   tablespoons finely chopped
        stuffed green olives

Mash drained anchovies. Soften cheese and blend into fish. Beat in Sherry until mixture is smooth. Add olives. Cover and chill several hours to blend flavors. When ready to serve, pile into bowl and place bowl in cracked ice, if desired. Garnish spread with strips of anchovy and pimiento and top with a stuffed green olive. (Or, sprinkle with finely chopped green onion or chopped hard-cooked egg.) Serve as an appetizer with buffet rye bread or crackers.

My choice of wine to accompany this dish:
CHILLED CALIFORNIA SHERRY OR DRY VERMOUTH
ON-THE-ROCKS, OR CHAMPAGNE

GOLD COAST NUGGETS

(About 36 cubes)

Mrs. Stanley Strud, California Wine Association, Lodi

    2   (5-oz.) jars Cheddar cheese spread
    ¼   cup California Sherry
    2   tablespoons mayonnaise
    ½   teaspoon Worcestershire sauce
        Salt
        Dash of cayenne pepper
   36   (1-inch) bread cubes (approximately)
        (see below)
        Paprika

Place cheese spread in mixing bowl; gradually blend in Sherry. Add mayonnaise, Worcestershire sauce, salt and cayenne; mix well. With a fork, dip each cube into cheese mixture, coating all but one side. Place cubes, uncoated side down, on greased baking sheet. Sprinkle with paprika. Broil until delicately browned. Serve hot.

TO MAKE BREAD CUBES: remove crusts from unsliced loaf of sandwich bread. Cut bread in 1-inch slices; cut each slice into 1-inch squares.

NOTE: A refreshing change at hors d'oeuvre time, and ideally teamed with chilled California Sherry.

PICKLED FISH MADERA

Mrs. David Ficklin, Ficklin Vineyards, Madera

This was originally a Minnesota recipe, that has been adapted to use wine. It's superb when made with pike, but excellent also with sole. The dish can be served as an appetizer, or as a cold fish dish for a buffet dinner or smorgasbord.

        Sole, pike or other firm-fleshed fish,
        cut in 1" strips
    1   onion, sliced
        Several bay leaves
    ½   pkg. pickling spices
        (with hot peppers removed)
        California white wine vinegar
        California Sauterne or other
        white dinner wine

Weave 1" strips of fish onto wooden cocktail picks. Place onion slices, bay leaves, pickling spices and equal amounts of wine vinegar and wine in an open kettle. Simmer slowly until onion is clear. Add fish; simmer until barely tender. Cool; chill in refrigerator until time to serve.

My choice of wine to accompany this dish:
CALIFORNIA SEMILLON OR SAUTERNE

HOT SHRIMP APPETIZER

(6 to 8 servings)

Esther Gowans, Glen Ellen Winery & Distillery, Glen Ellen

1½ lbs. raw shrimp or prawns
¼ cup California Dry Sherry
¼ cup butter or margarine
½ teaspoon garlic salt
¼ cup grated Parmesan cheese

Peel and devein shrimp; place in bowl. Pour over Sherry; marinate several hours. Melt butter in heavy skillet over low heat; add shrimp and Sherry. Sprinkle with garlic salt; simmer 10 to 15 minutes. Just before serving, sprinkle cheese over shrimp; place under broiler for 2 or 3 minutes or until cheese is lightly browned. Serve hot, with cocktail pick in each, and cold Shrimp Sauce on side.

SHRIMP SAUCE: Combine ½ cup mayonnaise, 1 tablespoon tomato paste, 1 teaspoon Worcestershire sauce and 1 teaspoon prepared mustard. Refrigerate until ready to serve.

NOTE: Different and good. Delectable with any favorite California appetizer wine or Champagne.

SHRIMP COCKTAIL SAUCE or dip (great also for crabmeat or lobster) blends 1 cup bottled cocktail sauce with ⅓ cup California Claret or other red dinner wine, ¼ cup cream, 1 teaspoon lemon juice and salt to taste. This makes about 1⅔ cups for zestful dipping.

STUFFED CELERY is better than ever when the cheese stuffing is blended from a jar cheese spread and California wine. Try White Port, Port or Sherry with Cheddar or American; Claret or Burgundy with blue cheese; and Chablis or Sauterne with pimiento. Usual proportion: 2 tablespoons wine to each 5-oz. jar. Thinned down still more with wine, these cheeses also provide enjoyable dips for potato chips or crackers. It's fun to provide an assortment of several flavors.

CARAWAY CHEESE LOG

(1-lb. log; about 20 servings)

C. E. Gibson, Weibel Champagne Vineyards, Mission San Jose

1 (8-oz.) pkg. cream cheese
⅓ cup California Sauterne, Rhine or other white dinner wine
½ lb. Jack or Swiss cheese, grated
1 tablespoon caraway seed
1 (2½-oz.) jar shredded Parmesan cheese

Beat cream cheese until soft; blend in wine. Add Jack cheese and caraway seed. Sprinkle layer of Parmesan cheese in an unfolded 1-lb. butter carton; spoon the caraway-cheese mixture over Parmesan cheese to form brick. Pat top and sides of brick with remaining Parmesan cheese. Close butter carton; chill until firm enough to slice (about 1 hour). Garnish with chopped parsley, if desired. Serve with crackers.

NOTE: This is a soft, creamy cheese mixture, and may be packed into any suitable container, or rolled up in foil, to chill. Served with California Champagne, it would be a delightful hors d'oeuvre for a festive dinner.

3-CHEESE RING WITH FRUIT

(1 quart mold)

Philo P. Biane, Assumption Abbey Winery, Guasti

1 lb. Cheddar cheese, grated
½ lb. Jack cheese, grated
4 oz. blue cheese
½ cup mayonnaise
¼ cup California Sherry
¼ teaspoon curry powder
½ teaspoon grated lemon rind
Melon balls (cantaloupe, Persian, honeydew) or other bite-size pieces of fruit

Combine grated Cheddar and Jack cheeses with crumbled blue cheese and mayonnaise; beat until blended thoroughly. Beat in Sherry, curry and lemon rind. Pack into buttered 1-quart tube mold. Chill, covered, in refrigerator several hours or overnight, so that mold becomes firm and flavors blended. Turn out onto serving dish. Fill center of mold with melon balls or other fruit. Serve with crackers, for a dessert or evening refreshment.

My choice of wine to accompany this dish:
CALIFORNIA PORT OR OTHER DESSERT WINE

MODESTO CHEESE MASTERPIECE

(About 2 cups)

Mrs. Charles M. Crawford, E. & J. Gallo Winery, Modesto

This makes a good cheese spread for a snack anytime, or before dinner.

    1 lb. ripe Camembert cheese
    ½ cup California Dry Sherry
    1 lb. unsalted butter
    3 tablespoons dry bread crumbs

Remove rind from cheese, press into bowl and cover with Sherry; let stand in cool place overnight. Cream unsalted butter in a warm bowl. Drain Sherry from cheese and reserve. Mash the cheese with fork, add butter and blend thoroughly. Blend in Sherry; place bowl in refrigerator about an hour, or until cheese sets. Immerse bowl to rim in warm water to unmold neatly onto serving plate. Garnish with dry bread crumbs, and serve with melba toast or crackers.

My choice of wine to accompany this dish:
CALIFORNIA PALE DRY COCKTAIL SHERRY

NOTE: Chopped toasted almonds would also be an interesting garnish for this sophisticated mixture.

MINIATURE TURKEY TURNOVERS

(48 turnovers)

W. E. Kite, Alta Vineyards Company, Fresno

Prepare pastry crust, using 2 (9-oz.) pkgs. pie crust mix; follow directions on carton. Roll out thin and cut in 3" rounds. Place some Turkey Filling (see below) in center of each round. Moisten edges with water; fold pastry over to form a semi-circle; press edges together and prick tops with fork. Brush tops with milk, for glaze. Bake in hot oven (450°) 15 to 20 minutes. Serve hot.

TURKEY FILLING: Melt 3 tablespoons butter, stir in same amount flour. Add ⅓ cup **each** chicken stock and California Sauterne, or other white dinner wine. Cook, stirring constantly, until mixture boils and thickens. Stir in 1 cup finely chopped cooked or canned turkey (or chicken); ½ cup finely chopped canned or sautéed fresh mushrooms; ¼ cup grated Parmesan cheese; 2 tablespoons chopped parsley; ½ teaspoon **each** lemon juice and Worcestershire sauce; dash of mace; and salt and pepper to taste. Refrigerate until ready to make turnovers.

NOTE: Hot hors d'oeuvre such as these are always favorites. Keep them hot, or bake only half a batch at the start of your party, and the other half later on for a second serving. Wonderful with chilled California Sherry or other appetizer wine.

HOT MINIATURE TURNOVERS such as the above are an international favorite for the Sherry hour. Other fillings, popular in the Latin American version (empanadas), include ground beef moistened with Burgundy; or grated Cheddar cheese moistened with Sherry or Sauterne. Follow same procedure above, and serve very hot, with any chilled California appetizer wine or Champagne.

HERBED CHEESE SPREAD CHABLIS

(3 cups)

Keith V. Nylander, Di Giorgio Wine Company, Di Giorgio

    ½ lb. Port d' Salut or Jack cheese
    2 (8-oz.) pkgs. cream cheese
    1 (2½-oz.) jar shredded Parmesan cheese
    ½ teaspoon crumbled dry marjoram
    ½ teaspoon dried dill
    ½ teaspoon hickory smoke salt or
        seasoned salt
    3 tablespoons soft butter
    ½ cup California Chablis or other
        white dinner wine
        Crisp crackers and fresh grapes

Grate very finely the Port d' Salut or Jack cheese; soften cream cheese. Combine all cheese with herbs, salt and soft butter. Beat until well blended. Beat in wine until mixture is quite smooth. Pack into lightly oiled 3-cup mold. Cover and chill in refrigerator several hours or overnight, until mold firms and flavors mellow. Turn out on serving platter; surround with crisp crackers and tiny bunches of fresh grapes. Serve as a refreshment anytime or dessert.

My choice of wine to accompany this dish:
A MELLOW CALIFORNIA PORT

HOT SEAFOOD TARTLETS (36 total) are also made from a 9-oz. pkg. pie crust mix. Cut unbaked crust in 2½" rounds; fit over **backs** of tins for tiny 2" muffins. Prick pastry and bake in hot oven (450°) 10 to 12 minutes or until lightly brown. Cool and fill with seafood filling, made as follows: Melt 4 tablespoons butter, stir in same amount flour, add ½ cup **each** cream and chicken stock. Stir constantly until mixture boils and thickens, then stir in ½ cup California Sauterne or other white dinner wine. Add ½ cup finely diced celery, 2 tablespoons chopped parsley, ¼ teaspoon grated lemon rind, salt, pepper and paprika to taste. Add 1 cup flaked crabmeat (6½-oz. can) and 1 cup shrimp (5-oz. can). (Cut up shrimp if large.) Fill tartlet shells; bake 10 to 15 minutes at 350° or until hot.

SHRIMP MOUSSE

(6 servings)

Mrs. August Sebastiani, Samuele Sebastiani, Sonoma

This is an excellent hors d'oeuvre to serve before any type of meal, as a cracker spread. It may also be used as a salad.

   1½ teaspoons plain gelatin
   ½ cup cold water
   ¾ cup California Chablis or
        other white dinner wine
   1 (7-oz.) can shrimp
   1 tablespoon chopped onion
   1 teaspoon lemon juice
   ½ teaspoon dry mustard
   1 cup mayonnaise
        Salt and pepper
        Dash cayenne pepper

Soften gelatin in water. Heat wine; stir in gelatin until dissolved. Put remaining ingredients in blender; mix until smooth. Stir in wine mixture; pour into mold. Chill until firm. Unmold on cold platter garnished with lettuce. Decorate with capers and lemon peel, if desired.

NOTE: A very pleasing flavor. Would be enjoyable with Sherry, Vermouth-on-the-rocks or Champagne.

CHRISTMAS CHEESE BALL

(1 ball, about 3" diameter)

Mrs. Pete Peters, Fresno

This may be made up several days ahead and refrigerated, with the rolling in chipped beef (if desired) done just before serving. It's good anytime guests serve themselves: as a prelude to dinner, or on a buffet. I usually double the recipe, for a larger-size cheese ball.

   ½ lb. Cheddar cheese, grated
   1 (3-oz.) package cream cheese
   ¼ cup California Sherry
   ¼ cup coarsely chopped pitted black olives
   ½ teaspoon Worcestershire sauce
        Dash each: Onion, garlic and celery salts
   ½ cup coarsely snipped dried beef (optional)

Have cheeses at room temperature. In large bowl, combine cheeses, Sherry, olives, Worcestershire sauce and salts; mix with electric beater at medium speed. Shape mixture into a ball; wrap in foil; refrigerate until needed. Before serving, remove foil and roll ball in dried beef.

NOTE: The dried beef would be an attractive finishing touch for a Christmas cocktail party. The recipe would be perfect any time of year, however; the cheese ball could also be rolled in finely chopped parsley, sesame seeds or caraway seeds. Chilled California Sherry would be an appetizing accompaniment.

PARTY PATÉ

(1 large loaf pan)

Mrs. Jack F. M. Taylor, Mayacamas Vineyards, Napa

   1½ lbs. liver (see Note below)
   ½ cup California Sweet Vermouth
   ½ cup water
   1 (5-oz.) jar sweet pickled onions
   ¼ lb. boiled ham
   1½ cups bacon fat or margarine
   2 tablespoons mixed herbs, such as
        rosemary, marjoram and basil
   4 teaspoons savory salt
   ¼ cup California brandy
   1 small can chopped ripe olives

Slice liver; simmer very gently 15 minutes in Vermouth and water. Meanwhile chop onions and ham very fine. When liver is done, place in blender, adding a little of the cooking liquid as needed for easy blending. (If any liquid is left, save for soup.) Melt fat; combine with liver and all other ingredients; mix well. Press firmly into a large loaf pan lined with waxed paper or saran. Chill until firm. Remove from pan; cut into 4 or 5 small cakes. Wrap each cake and freeze, to be used as needed as a very special hors d'oeuvre. To serve, slice very thin and serve on melba toast or crackers.

NOTE: Or let guests spread their own; it spreads easily. Wonderful with a dry California Sherry, Vermouth-on-the-rocks or, of course, Champagne. (Mrs. Taylor says that she has made this recipe with many kinds of liver. She prefers venison liver, if available; or, next best, chicken livers. Baby beef, calves or pork liver may also be used.)

NIPPY WINE-CHEESE SAUCE also provides a good dip for little hot cocktail sausages, or chunks of hot frankfurters. Start with your favorite "store-bought" cheese sauce, and blend in California Sherry to taste, or Claret or Burgundy. Keep sauce hot over a candle-warmer or in chafing dish.

HOT CRAB HORS D'OEUVRE

(16 servings)

Tony Kahmann, Wine Public Relations Consultant

½ cup butter
4 small onions, minced
1 lb. sharp Cheddar processed
  cheese, cubed
¾ cup catsup
¼ cup Worcestershire sauce
  Cayenne pepper
4 (7-oz.) cans crabmeat, drained
¼ cup California Sherry
  Crackers or melba toast

In blazer or top pan of chafing dish, over direct heat, melt butter and sauté onions slightly. Add cheese; stir until melted. Blend in catsup, Worcestershire sauce, cayenne and drained crabmeat. When hot, add Sherry. Set blazer over hot water to keep warm. On individual serving plates, put crackers or melba toast. Spoon hot crab mixture over and serve with a fork. Thin mixture with additional Sherry if it becomes too thick. Makes about 5 cups.

NOTE: Your favorite California appetizer wine could be served with this. A Dry Vermouth on-the-rocks would be particularly good with it. Tony says the recipe is extremely simple to make and serve; guests always enjoy it.

MOLDED CRAB CANAPÉS are an easy do-ahead party pleaser. To make 36 to 40: Soften 2 envelopes unflavored gelatin in ⅓ cup California Sherry 5 minutes; then dissolve in top of double boiler, over hot water. Cool. Blend 1 cup mayonnaise, 2 tablespoons chili sauce, 1 tablespoon lemon juice and 2 tablespoons chopped parsley. Stir in cooled gelatin mixture. Fold in ½ cup heavy cream, whipped; add salt and pepper to taste. Chill until mixture begins to thicken, then fold in 1 (6½-oz.) can crabmeat, flaked, **or** 1 cup fresh crabmeat. Spoon mixture into 4 (5-oz.) cheese glasses, lightly oiled. Chill several hours or overnight. Just before serving, unmold and slice in thin slices, to top toast rounds or crackers.

SONOMA STEAK POT

(8 to 10 servings)

John Pedroncelli, John Pedroncelli Winery, Geyserville

2 lbs. tender beef steak
  (cut about 1" thick)
¼ cup butter
1½ teaspoons plain or seasoned salt
⅔ cup California Sauterne or other
  white dinner wine, or Rosé
¼ cup catsup
2 teaspoons cornstarch
¼ teaspoon dried dill
  Freshly ground black pepper
  Assorted Go-Alongs (see below)

Trim all excess fat from meat. Cut steak into bite-size cubes, about ½" thick (should be about 48 cubes). Brown steak quickly in heated butter, turning and sprinkling meat with salt during browning. Do not crowd skillet; meat should brown nicely, just to rare or medium-rare stage. Remove steak cubes to heated chafing dish or other serving dish over a candle-warmer. Blend wine, catsup, cornstarch, dill and pepper to taste; stir into rich pan drippings. Cook and stir until mixture boils and thickens. Pour over steak cubes, stirring to combine meat and sauce. Serve with fondue forks or bamboo picks or other cocktail picks for spearing meat. Each guest spears a piece of meat and dips it into desired Go-Along.

GO-ALONGS: Finely chopped green onion or parsley; toasted sesame seeds; half-and-half mixture of prepared mustard and catsup or chili sauce; sour cream mixed with chopped chutney or canned green chile.

NOTE: This is a great conversation dish, and one that men particularly like. Good with any appetizer wine: California Sherry, Vermouth or flavored wine over ice.

NO-FUSS COCKTAIL SPREAD combines deviled ham with California Sherry, blended in seconds. Or, mix deviled ham with cream cheese and moisten with Sauterne.

RIPE OLIVES, drained and marinated in California Sherry mixed with a little salad oil, are extra good for before-dinner nibbling. Add a clove of garlic to the marinade, and marinate overnight in the refrigerator. Discard garlic just before serving, and drain off marinade.

THE TUNA-SHERRY CAPER

(About 3 cups)

Jessica McLachlin Greengard, Public Relations, Wines & Food

Serve this as a dip with chips, melba toast, crisp crackers or raw vegetables.

        1 (8-oz.) package cream cheese
        3 tablespoons mayonnaise
        5 tablespoons California Sherry
        2 (6 or 7-oz.) cans chunk-style tuna
        3 tablespoons capers
        3 tablespoons chopped parsley
        1 teaspoon Worcestershire sauce
        ½ teaspoon *each*: garlic salt
            and onion salt
            Dash Tabasco sauce
            Paprika

Mash cheese with fork; blend in mayonnaise. Gradually blend in Sherry, beating until smooth. Add the remaining ingredients; mix well. Heap in bowl; chill several hours. Dust with paprika.

My choice of wine to accompany this dish:
CALIFORNIA SHERRY

TUNA RAREBIT DIP

(About 3½ cups)

Mrs. Peter Mirassou, Mirassou Vineyards, San Jose

        1 (8-oz.) package process Cheddar cheese
        ⅓ cup California Sherry
        ⅓ cup evaporated milk
        1 (10½-oz.) can condensed tomato soup
        3 strips bacon, crisp cooked
        2 (7-oz.) cans tuna, drained and flaked

Slice cheese into top of double boiler; melt cheese over boiling water. Blend in Sherry, milk and soup. Crumble crisp bacon; add with tuna to cheese mixture. Serve hot in chafing or warming dish with cubes of French bread for dipping. Or, fill bite-size cream puffs or pastry shells with the mixture; heat through in moderate oven (350°).

NOTE: *Would be appetizing with a chilled California Sherry or Vermouth on-the-rocks.*

SONOMA SHRIMP-CRAB DIP

(About 2½ cups)

Rod Strong, Windsor Winery, Windsor

        1 cup mayonnaise
        1 teaspoon instant minced onion
        ¼ teaspoon Worcestershire sauce
        2 tablespoons finely chopped green pepper
        ¼ cup California Sherry
        1 (6½-oz.) can crabmeat
        1 (4½-oz.) can shrimp

Combine all ingredients, stirring lightly. Serve chilled with crisp crackers.

My choice of wine to accompany this dish:
CALIFORNIA JOHANNISBERG RIESLING

LODI BLUE CHEESE DIP

(About 1 cup)

Mrs. Alvin Ehrhardt, United Vintners, Inc., Lodi

        2 oz. blue cheese
        2 (3-oz.) pkgs. cream cheese
        California Dry Sherry

Combine cheeses in bowl; soften with Sherry; mix thoroughly. Let stand several hours before serving.

NOTE: *A perfect example of the great ease of blending cheeses with wine for a more tantalizing flavor. Another good blend is used by Mrs. Reginald Gianelli of East-Side Winery, Lodi, who mixes Sherry with a sharp Cheddar cheese spread (from a jar) until dipping consistency is reached, for either crackers or potato chips. Any appetizer wine would be good with these dips—chilled California Sherry or Vermouth, or a flavored wine on-the-rocks.*

CALIFORNIA BOUNTY BOWL combines chilled crab legs, lobster cubes, cooked prawns or shrimp, avocado balls, raw cauliflowerets, green and red pepper strips, and / or tiny red or yellow tomatoes, arranged on serving platter. (Insert wooden cocktail picks as needed.) In center of platter, place bowl of dipping mixture, made as follows: Mix 1 cup mayonnaise wtih ⅓ cup chili sauce and ¼ cup California Sherry. Add 2 tablespoons chopped parsley, 1 teaspoon grated onion, ½ teaspoon Worcestershire sauce and salt to taste. Blend mixture well and chill until serving time.

BLUE-CHEDDAR PARTY ROLLS

(2 or 3 rolls, about 1¼" diameter)

Mrs. Harold von der Lieth, Lodi

½ pound Cheddar cheese, grated
½ pound blue cheese, crumbled
2 (3-oz.) packages cream cheese
¼ cup California Port
1 cup finely chopped walnuts
½ cup chopped parsley
1 teaspoon grated onion
Dash cayenne pepper

Blend cheeses well; add Port, ½ cup of the walnuts, ¼ cup of the parsley, onion and cayenne. Chill until firm enough to shape into 2 or 3 rolls about 1¼" in diameter. Wrap in waxed paper and chill overnight. Unwrap; roll in mixture of remaining nuts and parsley. Slice thin and serve with crisp crackers.

NOTE: With glasses of California Port, this could be served anytime, as an afternoon snack or evening refreshment.

SHERRIED CLAM-CHEESE DIP

(About 2 cups)

Mrs. Julius Jacobs, Wine Institute, San Francisco

1 (8-oz.) can minced clams, undrained
1 (8-oz.) pkg. cream cheese
¼ cup California Dry Sherry
Worcestershire sauce
Paprika

Drain clams, reserving liquid; chop clams very fine. Soften cheese; thin with clam juice and Sherry. Add clams, Worcestershire sauce and paprika. Mix well; chill.

My choice of wine to accompany this dish:
CHILLED CALIFORNIA CHABLIS, ROSÉ OR SHERRY

SOUPS

Simplest Way to Explore Good Cooking with Wine

Few if any dishes ever set on a table provide more bountiful goodness, more warmth for both body and soul than a hearty soup. Whether served steaming hot in winter or refreshingly chilled on a warm day, a good soup relaxes the weary and revives the palate. An old and valued secret of soup cookery is to number wine among the most basic ingredients. Wine smooths out and "marries" the many competing flavors; wine adds a mellow aroma. Its alcohol vanishes quickly when the soup first simmers, well below the boiling point. Only the richness remains, and the satisfaction that *here* is a soup. If you've never cooked at all before with wine, soup provides the easiest test. Open a can for lunch and lace the soup with a California wine. (See chart on Page 121.) You'll make a simple but significant discovery.

CREAM OF FRESH MUSHROOM SOUP

(1¾ qts.)

Mrs. Lewis A. Stern, E. & J. Gallo Winery, Modesto

    1 lb. fresh mushrooms
    ¼ cup butter or margarine
    ¼ cup sifted flour
    6 cups scalded milk
    1 egg yolk, lightly beaten
    ½ cup California Dry Sherry
      Salt and pepper
      Croutons

Slice caps of mushrooms; chop stems. Sauté in melted butter, in a saucepan, until lightly browned. Stir in flour; cook 4 or 5 minutes over low heat. Add scalded milk; simmer about 10 minutes, stirring frequently. Combine lightly beaten egg yolk with Sherry; add to soup. Add salt and pepper; simmer 2 or 3 minutes longer. Top each serving with 4 to 6 croutons.

NOTE: A lusciously rich blend. Could serve as first course for a festive dinner, or as the main dish itself for a light supper — with a white dinner wine (such as California Chablis) accompanying.

NAPA OYSTER BISQUE

(5 or 6 servings)

Mrs. Robert Mondavi, Charles Krug Winery, St. Helena

    1 cup oysters
    ¼ cup cooked spinach
    2 cups milk
    1 cup heavy cream
    ½ teaspoon monosodium glutamate
    1 teaspoon meat sauce
      Dash garlic salt or tiny piece of
      pressed garlic
    2 tablespoons California Rhine
      or other white dinner wine
    2 tablespoons butter or margarine
      Whipped cream or sour cream

Puree oysters and spinach in blender. Heat milk and cream to simmering; blend in oyster puree, monosodium glutamate, meat sauce and garlic. Very slowly add wine, stirring constantly. When ready to serve, add butter; simmer a few minutes. Place in ovenproof serving dish; top with whipped or sour cream. Brown lightly under broiler and serve.

NOTE: An abundance of fine flavor, for a very special dinner. For complete dining pleasure, serve a chilled California Rhine or Chablis with the soup.

SHERRIED CRAB SOUP

(4 or 5 servings)

C. E. Gibson, Weibel Champagne Vineyards, Mission San Jose

> 1 (10½-oz.) can condensed tomato soup
> 1 (10½-oz.) can condensed pea soup
> 1½ cups light cream
> 1 cup cooked fresh or canned crabmeat
> ½ cup California Sherry
> 2 tablespoons chopped parsley
> ⅛ teaspoon curry powder
> Salt and pepper

Combine soups and cream in chafing dish or top of double boiler; heat just to simmering, stirring occasionally. Add crab, Sherry, parsley and seasonings; heat piping hot. Serve at once in heated soup bowls.

NOTE: *This would be a quick gourmet soup for unexpected guests or for Sunday suppers. To make it even more enjoyable, serve a glass of chilled California Sherry on the side—or a white dinner wine, such as Sauterne or Chablis, or a Champagne.*

EASY LOBSTER BISQUE

(About 2½ qts.)

Mr. & Mrs. Paul L. Halpern, Mission Bell Wineries, Madera

This can be a real "quickie" using prepared soups. It makes a hearty supper meal on a cool winter evening, and goes especially well with Champagne and candlelight. The recipe was given to us by a friend, Jack Alex, now retired from the wine business, who concocts some very tasty dishes.

> 1 (9-oz.) pkg. frozen lobster tails
> 1 (10½-oz.) can beef broth
> 1 (10½-oz.) can tomato soup
> 1 (17-oz.) can green split pea soup
> ½ cup California Dry Sherry
> 1 (17-oz.) can clam chowder, or
> 1 or 2 (8-oz.) cans minced clams
> 3½ cups light cream, or 1 (13-oz.) can
> evaporated milk and 2 cups whole milk
> Salt and pepper

Remove lobster meat from shells; cut into 1" chunks. Heat beef broth, tomato and split pea soups together. Add lobster and Sherry; simmer gently about 5 minutes. Add clam chowder; continue heating. Just before serving add milk; heat through. Season with salt and pepper. If desired, add ¼ cup more Sherry just before serving. Serve in chafing dish. (If minced clams are used, first sauté 1 finely chopped onion and 1 cubed medium-size potato in butter in soup kettle or large saucepan. Add ingredients in order given above.) Good with hot garlic French bread, and for dessert a huge bowl of fresh fruits in season.

Our choice of wine to accompany this dish:
CALIFORNIA CHAMPAGNE, RIESLING, CHABLIS, SAUTERNE OR ZINFANDEL

WEST COAST BOUILLABAISSE

(20 to 24 servings)

Mrs. Albert J. Puccinelli, Puccinelli Vineyards, San Mateo

> ½ cup sliced carrots
> ¾ cup chopped onion
> ½ cup olive oil
> 1 (No. 2½) can tomato puree
> 3 cloves garlic, diced
> 2 tablespoons parsley
> ¼ teaspoon oregano
> ¼ teaspoon thyme
> ¼ teaspoon marjoram
> ¼ teaspoon fennel (optional)
> 1 tablespoon salt
> Freshly ground pepper
> 8 lobster tails
> 7 cups water
> 1 cup California Sherry
> 8 slices sea bass, cut in 1" cubes
> 8 slices red snapper
> 1 lb. shelled deveined shrimp
> 1 (8-oz.) can whole clams

Sauté carrots and onions in oil about 10 minutes. Add tomato puree, garlic and other seasonings. Add lobster, water and Sherry; bring to boiling. Reduce heat; simmer 15 minutes. Add bass and snapper; cook 10 minutes. Add shrimp and clams; heat thoroughly. A green salad is optional with this, but make it plain. Serve with hot garlic bread. A whipped gelatin zabaglione would be a good dessert.

NOTE: *California red dinner wine, such as Burgundy, Claret or Zinfandel, would be a most agreeable accompaniment for this hearty traditional soup.*

GOLDEN GATE SHRIMP SOUP

(4 to 6 servings)

Tony Kahmann, Wine Public Relations Consultant

> 2 cans frozen cream of shrimp soup
> 1 soup-can milk
> 1 soup-can light cream
> 1 cup crabmeat
> Salt and pepper
> Dash nutmeg
> 2 teaspoons lemon juice
> 2 tablespoons California Sherry
> 1 ripe avocado, cubed

Place frozen soup in top of double boiler; blend in milk and cream, stirring until smooth and hot. Add crabmeat, seasonings and lemon juice. Just before serving, stir in Sherry and avocado.

NOTE: *A glass of chilled Sherry on the side would be the ultimate in enjoyment.*

CORN-CLAM CHOWDER CHABLIS

(4 or 5 servings)

John Pedroncelli, John Pedroncelli Winery, Geyserville

     3 slices bacon
     2 green onions
     1 (7-oz.) can minced clams
        and juice
     1 (No. 2) can yellow
        cream-style corn
    1½ cups rich milk
     ¼ cup California Chablis or
        other white dinner wine
     1 teaspoon salt
        Crackers

Fry bacon until crisp; drain and crumble. Chop onions very fine and cook in 1 tablespoon bacon drippings until soft but not browned. Add all other ingredients, except crackers, and bring just to boil. Simmer about 5 minutes. Crumble crackers in bottom of soup bowls. Pour in hot soup and serve immediately.

NOTE: An easy and savory home-made soup, that would go perfectly with any white dinner wine, such as the Chablis used in cooking.

VINTAGE-OF-THE-SEA CHOWDER

(4 to 6 servings)

Lee Hecker, Wine Advisory Board, San Francisco

This quick meal-in-itself chowder has a rich bouquet and flavor. It's an easy way to cook a mixed-up catch, when the fish are too small for baking.

     1 medium-size onion, finely chopped
     2 stalks celery, thinly sliced
     ½ green pepper, finely chopped
     3 tablespoons butter or margarine
     1 clove garlic, pressed (optional)
     2 (10¼-oz.) cans frozen potato soup, thawed
     2 cups rich milk
     2 cups California Rhine, Chablis or
        other white dinner wine
     1 (10-oz.) pkg. frozen mixed vegetables
     1 to 1½ lbs. fillets of fresh white-meat fish
        (bass, rockfish, eel, capezone, etc.,
        or a combination)
        Salt and pepper
     ¼ cup finely chopped parsley

In a large saucepan, sauté onion, celery and green pepper in melted butter, until barely tender. Add garlic, if desired. Remove from heat; stir in thawed potato soup and milk; blend until smooth. Add wine and frozen vegetables. Cut fish into small pieces; add to soup. Simmer over low heat 8 to 10 minutes, or until fish and vegetables are just tender. (Do not overcook!) Season with salt and pepper. Just before serving, add ½ to 1 cup more wine, depending on thickness of chowder. (It should not be too thin.) Serve very hot in large heated bowls, garnished with chopped parsley. No main course needed; simply add a salad of chilled tomato slices, marinated in oil and wine vinegar; and breadsticks or garlic bread.

My choice of wine to accompany this dish:
A CHILLED CALIFORNIA RHINE

BOOMBA POLIVKA SPANIELSKA

(4 servings)

Walter J. F. Weselsky, Jr., Mont La Salle Vineyards, Napa

This is an old Ruthenian peasant dish, very popular in the Carpathian Alps. The shepherds there like a hearty, tasty dish after a hard day, often in inclement weather. The Ruthenians use shiflicki, a very fine egg noodle cut diamond-shaped, instead of the substitute seashell macaroni in this modern adaptation. This is easy to prepare, and is good as a luncheon dish served with salad, or as a first-course soup served prior to a lighter entree.

     1 (1-lb.) can chili con carne with beans
     1 (10½-oz.) can tomato soup plus
        equal amount of water
     2 tablespoons Parmesan cheese
     ½ cup California Pinot Noir, Claret
        or other red dinner wine
     ⅛ teaspoon *each*: basil, oregano
        and rosemary
     ½ teaspoon parsley
     ½ teaspoon monosodium glutamate
     ¼ teaspoon garlic salt
     ¼ lb. seashell macaroni, cooked
        according to pkg. directions

Combine all ingredients except macaroni in a saucepan; bring to boiling. Reduce heat; simmer 15 minutes. Add cooked seashell macaroni to soup; heat a few minutes longer. Top each serving generously with Parmesan cheese. Very effective when served piping hot in earthenware bowls, and delicious with rye bread toast spread with melted garlic butter.

My choice of wine to accompany this dish:
CALIFORNIA CABERNET, PINOT NOIR OR CHIANTI

AN OLD COLONIAL RECIPE for fresh Maryland Turtle Soup calls for thickening the soup with mixed flour and butter about a half-hour before dinner. Just before serving, "add a glass of red wine."

CLASSIC FRENCH ONION SOUP

(6 servings)

Otto Gramlow, Beaulieu Vineyard, Rutherford

      ¼ cup butter or margarine
      6 medium-size onions, thinly sliced
      4 cups bouillon (canned or
         bouillon-cube broth may be used)
      1 cup California Sauterne or other
         white dinner wine
         Salt and pepper
      6 slices French bread, toasted
         and buttered
      ½ cup grated Parmesan cheese

Melt butter in large saucepan; saute onions until clear. Add bouillon; cover and cook slowly until onions are very tender. Add wine, salt and pepper; bring to boiling. Pour into 6 individual casseroles or 1 large one. Float pieces of buttered French bread toast on top; sprinkle with grated Parmesan cheese. Bake on upper rack of hot oven (450°) until cheese browns lightly (about 10 minutes).

NOTE: *A little Sauterne or Sherry may be added to each dish just before serving, if desired. This brings out a luxurious flavor and bouquet.*

GOLDEN CHEESE SOUP is a quick, creamy blend with a tantalizing flavor. To 1 (11-oz.) can Cheddar cheese soup, add ¼ cup California Dry Sherry, in saucepan. Stir in 1 cup thin cream or rich milk and heat slowly, stirring now and then. Meanwhile, blend ½ cup sour cream with ⅛ teaspoon celery seed and 1 tablespoon finely chopped parsley. Drop a spoonful of this mixture on top of each serving of the hot soup. Recipe will make 4 or 5 servings.

CREAMY CORN CHOWDER takes only a few minutes, yet tastes of old-time soup magic. To make about 1 quart: Blend in saucepan a 15-oz. can cream style corn, a 10½-oz. can cream of mushroom soup, 1½ teaspoons instant minced onion (or, 2 tablespoons minced green onion), ⅛ teaspoon nutmeg, salt and pepper to taste, 1½ cups rich milk and ½ cup California Sauterne or other white dinner wine. Heat slowly until very hot, stirring now and then. Especially good on a cold evening, with a glass of the same wine accompanying.

CURRIED CHICKEN SOUP

(2 quarts)

Mrs. Robert Weaver, U. of Calif. Dept. Viticulture & Enology

      4 (10½-oz.) cans cream of
         chicken soup or chicken broth
      1 (10½-oz.) can consommé
      ¼ cup California Sherry
      1 pint light cream
      1 to 3 teaspoons curry powder
         Diced raw red apple, unpeeled

Heat soups in top of double boiler. Add Sherry and cream, slowly, stirring constantly. Add curry powder; stir well. Serve in bowls, sprinkling each serving with diced apple. (Red apple peeling, left on, will add color.) Serve with anything but a chicken entrée.

My choice of wine to accompany this dish:
CALIFORNIA GREY RIESLING OR CHENIN BLANC

BACCHANALE CHICKEN SOUP

(8 generous servings)

Judy Hibel, Wine Advisory Board, San Francisco

This is an original recipe, improvised and revised over a period of time.

         Giblets, neck, back and wing tips
         from a 2½-lb. fryer
      3 qts. water
      2 fresh tomatoes, quartered, or
      1 (1-lb.) can whole tomatoes
      ½ teaspoon thyme
      ½ teaspoon dried parsley flakes
      1½ teaspoons salt
      ⅛ teaspoon pepper
      1 small onion, thinly sliced
      1 carrot, sliced
      ¼ cup mushrooms (optional)
      1 cup uncooked pasta (egg noodles,
         small macaroni, etc.)
      ½ cup California Chablis or other
         white dinner wine

Clean chicken parts; place in water along with all remaining ingredients except pasta and wine. Bring to boiling; reduce heat; simmer very gently, partly covered, about 2 hours. Remove chicken parts; cut into bite-size pieces, removing bones. Return to soup; simmer, partly covered, 1 hour longer. About 20 minutes before serving, add uncooked pasta and wine. Taste; correct seasoning.

My choice of wine to accompany this dish:
ANY CALIFORNIA WHITE DINNER WINE

FRESNO BORSCH

(6 servings)

Elie Skofis, Roma Wine Company, Fresno

1 soup bone or 1 lb. short ribs
½ lb. stewing beef
3 quarts water
3 medium onions, sliced
3 stalks celery, chopped
1 green pepper, chopped
2 cups cabbage, shredded
3 tomatoes, cut in pieces
3 cups cooked beets, grated
1 cup California Sauterne or other
    white dinner wine
    Salt and pepper
½ pint whipping cream or sour cream

Cook soup bone or short ribs, beef and onions in 3 quarts boiling water for 2 hours. Add celery, pepper, cabbage and tomatoes; cook 10 minutes. Add beets and wine and cook 5 minutes more. Serve hot, topping each serving with a generous spoonful of whipped or sour cream.

NOTE: *This may also be served cold, if desired. Especially good for a one-dish meal, with hot bread on the side and chilled California Rosé, Burgundy or Sauterne.*

INTERNATIONAL MINESTRONE

(8 servings)

Mrs. E. A. Mirassou, Mirassou Vineyards, San Jose

I would call this an international soup—of Italian origin, served to a Frenchman and concocted by an Irishman. It's a meal in itself, served with tossed green salad and crisp sour-dough French bread.

2 to 3 lbs. soup meat
6 carrots, diced
½ head cabbage, chopped
1 (1-lb.) can peeled whole tomatoes
1 (1-lb.) can new potatoes, halved
2 onions, chopped
2 cloves garlic, minced
3 slices bacon, chopped
½ teaspoon rosemary
½ teaspoon basil
½ cup chopped parsley
2 beef bouillon cubes
½ lb. uncooked macaroni
1 (1-lb.) can red kidney beans
1 cup California Burgundy or other
    red dinner wine
    Salt and pepper

Simmer soup meat in 2 gallons water for 1½ hours. Add carrots and cabbage; when carrots are almost tender add tomatoes and potatoes. Sauté onion and garlic with bacon; add to soup along with remaining ingredients. Simmer 25 to 30 minutes longer to blend flavors.

My choice of wine to accompany this dish:
A ROBUST RED WINE, SUCH AS CALIFORNIA
BURGUNDY OR CABERNET SAUVIGNON

QUICK FRIDAY MINESTRONE

(6 servings)

Mrs. August Sebastiani, Samuele Sebastiani, Sonoma

Minestrone is an old recipe that used to take about a half-day to prepare, starting with dry red beans. This is a modern version using canned kidney beans, and it is equally as good as the old. It's a terrific Friday dish; I usually serve it with garlic bread and a salad, and this makes a very nourishing meal.

1 (1-lb. 11-oz.) can red kidney beans
1 teaspoon salt
½ teaspoon garlic salt, or
    1 clove garlic (pressed)
¼ teaspoon pepper
1 small zucchini, cut in small cubes
2 stalks celery, chopped
2 green onions, chopped
1 small carrot, diced
2 tablespoons butter or margarine
1 (8-oz.) can tomato sauce
2½ cups water
½ cup California Dry Sherry
¼ cup cooked elbow macaroni (optional)

Place undrained beans in a large saucepan or kettle; mash about ⅔ and leave the rest whole. Add seasonings, vegetables, butter, tomato sauce and water. Simmer 1 hour; add Sherry and (if desired) cooked macaroni. Simmer 10 to 15 minutes longer.

My choice of wine to accompany this dish:
A DRY CALIFORNIA RED, WHITE OR ROSÉ

NOTE: *Mrs. Sebastiani says that any vegetable you have on hand may be used in this savory soup. Even a cut lettuce leaf or two will add to it.*

FOR A SPEEDY, fresh-tasting vegetable soup that serves 2 or 3: Heat a can of beef bouillon with ¼ cup California Sauterne or other white dinner wine. Add 1 cup of cooked mixed vegetables. Heat well and serve with sprinkling of grated Parmesan cheese.

CHICKEN IN THE POT (see Page 56) is also enjoyable as a soup. Remove the whole chicken from the pot when tender. Bone out the chicken meat and cut it into thin strips, which you return to the rich broth. You may wish to add more liquid—both Sauterne and water.

CHILLED CABERNET-CHERRY SOUP

(6 to 8 servings)

Brother Timothy, Mont La Salle Vineyards, Napa

This is an original recipe.

2 lbs. ripe red cherries, pitted
2 cups water
1 (3-inch) stick cinnamon
2 whole cloves
2 drops almond extract
¼ teaspoon salt
2 cups California Cabernet Sauvignon,
   Claret or other red dinner wine
1 tablespoon California brandy
   Sugar
2 egg yolks

Simmer cherries in water with cinnamon, cloves, almond extract and salt. When cherries are soft, rub through a sieve. Combine with wine, brandy and a little sugar to taste. Return to heat; blend in egg yolks; cook until slightly thickened. Serve well chilled.

NOTE: Reminiscent of Danish soups, and delicious on a warm day. A sour cream topping would be good, and a glass of chilled California Rosé on the side.

GAZPACHO

(About 1 qt.)

Elie Skofis, Roma Wine Company, Fresno

This is one of the many versions of the famous Spanish soup. Since it is served cold, it's ideal on a hot summer day.

1 cup California Sauterne or other
   white dinner wine
1 (No. 2) can tomato juice
1 cup fresh tomatoes, peeled and
   diced
⅓ cup fresh cucumber, peeled and
   diced
⅓ cup chopped green pepper
2 tablespoons finely chopped
   fresh parsley
2 tablespoons fresh lemon juice
1 teaspoon instant minced onion
   Salt to taste (about ¾ teaspoon)
   Ice

Chill wine and tomato juice; combine with all other ingredients except ice. Serve in large soup bowls with a chunk of ice in each bowl.

NOTE: Would be delicious and refreshing for lunch, with a chilled Sauterne or Rosé accompanying. Some other Gazpacho versions add such ingredients as chopped ripe olives, chopped hard-cooked eggs, chopped pimientos, basil and garlic. And some variations use Burgundy or other red dinner wine instead of the white. Use whatever you have on hand. The Spaniards do!

CUKE SOUP

(3 servings)

Robert S. McKnight, Di Giorgio Wine Company, Di Giorgio

2 cups chicken broth (canned or
   bouillon-cube broth may be used)
2 tablespoons butter, melted
2 cups coarsely chopped,
   unpeeled cucumbers
½ teaspoon salt
2 to 4 tablespoons California
   Cream Sherry
   Whipping cream or sour cream

Combine broth, butter, cucumbers and salt in mixer or blender. Mix until well blended. Pour into saucepan; bring to boiling. Stir in Sherry. Serve hot or well chilled, topped with cream or sour cream, if desired. Serve with small glasses of California Cocktail Sherry. Some add this to soup; others drink it on the side.

HOT-DAY COLD SOUP

(4 servings)

Mrs. Jack F. M. Taylor, Mayacamas Vineyards, Napa

2 (10½-oz.) cans chicken, turkey
   or beef consommé
¼ cup California Sherry
   Juice of 2 large lemons
2 (4-oz.) cans mushroom stems and pieces
1 teaspoon savory salt
8 small green onions
6 to 8 sprigs parsley
   Sour cream

Combine consommé, Sherry, lemon juice, juice from mushrooms and savory salt. Chop onions, parsley and mushrooms very fine; add to liquid. Cover; chill several hours. Stir before each serving. Top each bowl, cup or mug with a spoonful of sour cream.

NOTE: This soup would lend itself delightfully to the pleasant custom of adding additional Sherry at the table. Simply pass a small bottle or carafe of the wine and let guests pour their own final flavoring into the soup.

HERE'S ANOTHER easy cold soup for summer. Stir a bit of California Dry Sherry into chilled tomato juice. Top with some sour cream, flecked with dried dill or seasoned salt.

BEAN SOUP BURGUNDY

(4 or 5 servings)

Pat Gibbs, Wine Institute, San Francisco

This is an easy way to dress up a canned soup, with no trouble.

    1 large onion, minced
    2 tablespoons bacon drippings,
       butter or margarine
    2 (11½-oz.) cans condensed
       bean with bacon soup
    2 cups water
    ½ cup California Burgundy, Claret
       or other red dinner wine
    1 beef bouillon cube
    1 teaspoon Worcestershire
       Salt and pepper

Sauté onion gently in bacon drippings 5 minutes. Add soup, water, wine, bouillon cube and Worcestershire sauce. Bring to boil, then cover and simmer gently 15 minutes, stirring now and then. Season to taste with salt and pepper. Serve very hot in heated bowls or cups.

My choice of wine to accompany this dish:
CALIFORNIA BURGUNDY OR ROSÉ

OXTAIL SOUP ST. HELENA

(About 2 quarts)

Louis P. Martini, Louis M. Martini Winery, St. Helena

A pot of this thick soup makes excellent winter eating.

    1 oxtail
    1 tablespoon shortening
    1 quart hot water
 2½ teaspoons salt
    1 tablespoon instant minced onion
       or ¼ cup chopped raw onion
    ⅓ cup pearl barley
    ½ lb. peas, or ½ (9-oz.) pkg.
       frozen peas
    3 medium-sized carrots
    3 large stalks celery
    ½ cup California Chablis, Sauterne
       or other white dinner wine
    1 (10½-oz.) can bouillon or
       broth (optional)

Have oxtail cut in short lengths. Brown slowly in heated shortening. Add hot water, salt, onion and barley. Cover; simmer 1½ to 2 hours, until meat and barley are tender. Meanwhile, shell peas, pare and slice carrots, and slice celery. Add vegetables and wine to soup and simmer about 20 minutes longer. For thinner soup, add can of broth or bouillon, diluted, to the soup. Serve with crusty hot bread.

NOTE: *Robust enough for a California Burgundy or Zinfandel accompanying; or Rosé or white dinner wine, if preferred.*

QUICK GOURMET SOUP

(6 to 8 servings)

Mrs. Frank G. Cadenasso, Cadenasso Winery, Fairfield

This soup was purely an invention (for unexpected company) one noontime. Everyone enjoyed it, and we have used it many times since. It's especially good with cheese or fish entrees.

    1 (4-oz.) pkg. smoky green pea
       dry soup mix
    1 (1⅜-oz.) pkg. onion
       dry soup mix
 6½ cups water
    ⅓ cup California Sherry

Combine soup mixes with water; bring to boiling. Simmer 10 minutes. Add Sherry; simmer over very low heat 5 to 10 minutes longer.

My choice of wine to accompany this dish:
A CHILLED CALIFORNIA DRY WHITE DINNER WINE

MID-AFTERNOON REFRESHER: A glass of bouillon or consommé over ice cubes, with a squeeze of lemon and dash of California Sherry. This also makes a good pre-dinner drink.

WINE'S DELICATE FLAVOR and bouquet may be appreciated in soups even more if wine is added just before removing the soup from heat.

ANOTHER DELICIOUS RECIPE blends California Chablis (or other white dinner wine) with canned kidney beans and sliced frankfurters to make a hearty, filling soup. To make about 1 quart: Cook 2 thinly sliced green onions slowly in 1 tablespoon butter. Meanwhile empty a 15-oz. can kidney beans into blender jar, and blend until smooth (or puree). Combine bean puree, 2 cups tomato juice, ½ cup Chablis, salt to taste, and ⅛ teaspoon **each** of pepper and powdered thyme with onion. Heat slowly. Add 2 sliced frankfurters and heat a minute more.

VALLEY VEGETABLE CREAM SOUP

(4 or 5 servings)

W. E. Kite, Alta Vineyards Company, Fresno

1 (10-oz.) pkg. frozen
    peas and carrots
1 small onion, chopped
1 cup chicken stock (canned or
    bouillon-cube broth may be used)
1 cup light cream
¼ cup California Sherry
    Salt and pepper to taste
    Croutons and paprika for garnish

Cook peas and carrots with onion, covered, in 1 cup salted boiling water about 15 minutes, or until very tender. Force vegetables and liquid through sieve or food mill. Add stock, cream and wine. Heat gently to simmering; add seasoning. (Electric blender may also be used to blend cooked vegetables and liquids until smooth, before heating.) Pour into heated bowls or soup mugs; top each with croutons and dusting of paprika. Serve at once.

NOTE: *Preferably with a glass of chilled California Sherry, as a combination of appetizer and first course.*

YOUR OWN IMAGINATION can be especially rewarding, in experimenting with soups and wine. Sherry, of course, is the most versatile wine for cooking, and can be used in almost any type of soup. But don't overlook Dry Vermouth also, for its piquant herbal flavor. Even a few drops of California Port can do great things for a bean soup or cream soup. And red dinner wine, such as Burgundy, transforms a plain canned consommé into something very special, garnished with raw sliced mushrooms, chopped ham or grated carrot.

DON'T FORGET an interesting garnish for soups, if you're a perfectionist. Avocado balls, thinly sliced cucumber (with skin left on), very small sprigs of watercress (or slightly chopped cress), thin strips of cooked carrots, chopped chives or green onion tops, chopped hard-cooked egg yolks, very thin tomato slices topped with sour cream or chopped chives, whipped cream (slightly salted), roughly chopped walnuts—the list is endless. The garnish can also become an important flavor-accent.

MEATS

Beef, Veal, Pork, Lamb, Variety Meats with Wine

Here is probably the most important of wine's many functions in the kitchen: to enrich the flavor of meats, adding subtle new aromas and a succulent tenderness. There's no meat known that cannot easily be improved in some way by a little wine, whether directly applied during cooking, or stirred into the pan drippings to make a wonderful sauce or gravy. And, of course, served *with* a wonderful California wine at the table. (For favored sauce recipes, see section starting Page 79. Wild game meats start Page 65. Helpful marinating tips are on Page 120, and a quick-reference cooking chart on Page 121.)

BEEF WITH HORSERADISH SAUCE

(8 to 10 servings)

Dr. Emil M. Mrak, University of California, Davis

- 4 lbs. top round steak, cut in 1½" cubes
- 6 tablespoons butter or margarine
- 2 large onions, thinly sliced
- 2 teaspoons curry powder
  1-inch square fresh ginger root, pressed, or 1 teaspoon ground ginger
- 2 tablespoons Worcestershire sauce
- 1 teaspoon salt
- ½ teaspoon freshly-ground pepper
- ½ to 1 cup California Sauterne or other white dinner wine
- 1 cup sour cream
- 2 tablespoons prepared horseradish
- 2 tablespoons freshly-chopped parsley

Brown meat in 4 tablespoons butter; remove to casserole. Brown onions in remaining 2 tablespoons butter. Add to casserole along with curry powder, ginger, Worcestershire sauce, salt, pepper and wine. Bake, covered, in slow oven (300°) about 3 hours, or until meat is tender. Just before serving, combine sour cream and horseradish; stir into meat along with parsley. Serve on rice.

NOTE: *Mrs. Mrak says her husband always uses fresh ginger, put through a garlic press, for this dish. (Fresh ginger root can be sliced and frozen for use later, a slice at a time.) For an accompanying wine, California Burgundy would be perfect.*

A PRESSURE COOKER works quick magic on stews, for those who are short on cooking time. Cuts out hours. Even faster: canned or frozen stew, heated in oven, and sparked with California red dinner wine for flavor and that personal touch.

BEEF STEW BURGUNDY

(6 servings)

Mrs. Ronald G. Hanson, Di Giorgio Wine Co., Di Giorgio

- 5 medium-size onions, peeled and sliced
- 2 tablespoons bacon drippings
- 3 lbs. lean beef stew meat, cut in 1" cubes
- 1½ tablespoons flour
  Salt and pepper
  Pinch each of marjoram and thyme
- ½ cup beef bouillon (canned or bouillon-cube broth may be used)
- 1 cup California Burgundy, Claret or other red dinner wine
- ½ lb. fresh mushrooms, sliced

In a large heavy skillet, sauté onions in bacon drippings until brown. Remove onions. Brown meat on all sides in same drippings, adding a little more fat if necessary. When browned, sprinkle with flour and seasonings. Add bouillon and wine; mix well. Simmer very slowly 3¼ hours. (Add more bouillon or wine as necessary to keep meat barely covered.) Return onions to skillet along with mushrooms; stir well. Simmer 1 hour longer, or just until meat is tender.

NOTE: *Robust rich flavor. To bring out more wine taste, about ¼ cup of wine may be saved out and stirred in just before serving, if desired. Would be marvelous with rice or noodles and any of California's many good red dinner wines accompanying. Beef stew is one of the most popular dishes cooked with red wine. It's a favorite also with Mrs. E. F. Handel of East-Side Winery, Lodi; Mrs. Joseph Roullard of Petri Wineries, Escalon; and W. W. Owen of California Grape Products Corp., Delano.*

BOEUF MIRONTON

(8 servings)

Mrs. Walter H. Sullivan, Jr., Beaulieu Vineyard, Rutherford

This casserole of beef a la Mironton is an old Gascon recipe.

        1 (4-lb.) piece rump or cross rib of beef
        3 or 4 carrots
        7 to 9 medium-size onions
        1 bay leaf
        8 to 10 peppercorns
          Butter or margarine
          Salt and pepper
          California Chablis, Sauterne or other
          white dinner wine
          Bread crumbs

Place meat in large container; add carrots, 2 onions, bay leaf and peppercorns. Cover with water; simmer 3 to 4 hours. Skim off foam from time to time. Cool meat in cooking liquid. Remove meat, reserving broth; pick meat to pieces with two forks. (DO NOT CUT!) Thinly slice remaining onions; sauté in butter until golden brown. Mix well with shredded beef; season with salt and pepper. Place in 2 to 3-inch deep baking dish. Measure cooking broth; add an equal amount of wine. Pour into pan in which onions were sautéed. Bring to boiling twice; cook until liquid will cover ¾ of meat and onion mixture (about 5 minutes). Pour liquid over meat; sprinkle generously with bread crumbs; dot with butter. Bake in moderate oven (350°) about 45 minutes. Serve piping hot. Menu might include a jellied consommé with sour cream and caviar; mashed potatoes with the beef casserole; mixed green salad; sliced strawberries and toasted pound cake.

My choice of wine to accompany this dish:
CALIFORNIA BURGUNDY OR ROSÉ

VINTNER'S STEW

(6 servings)

Paul Huber, E. & J. Gallo Winery, Fresno

This is one of the easiest of all beef stews. The meat needs no browning before it is baked.

        2 lbs. stewing beef, cut in 1½" chunks
        1¼ cups California Burgundy, Claret
            or other red dinner wine
        2 (10½-oz.) cans condensed consommé,
            undiluted
        1 teaspoon salt
        ½ teaspoon garlic salt
        ¼ teaspoon pepper
        1 large onion, sliced
        ½ cup fine dry bread crumbs
        ½ cup sifted all-purpose flour

Combine beef, 1 cup of wine, consomme, salts, pepper and onion in a heavy casserole. Mix flour with crumbs; stir into casserole mixture. Cover; bake in slow oven (300°) for 3 hours, or until meat is tender. Just before serving, stir in remaining ¼ cup wine for additional wine flavor.

My choice of wine to accompany this dish:
CALIFORNIA BURGUNDY OR VIN ROSÉ

ANOTHER TRICK that adds subtle flavor to beef stew is to flame the meat with a little California brandy, just after browning it, before long cooking. Barely warm brandy first, carefully, in double boiler. Ignite and pour over meat. Spoon flaming brandy over meat until flames die out, then proceed with cooking. Two Wine Land cooks favoring this method are Mrs. Harold Berg, U. C. Dept. of Viticulture & Enology, Davis, and Mrs. Joseph Heitz, Heitz Wine Cellar, St. Helena.

EASY BAKED STEW

(6 to 8 servings)

Diana Herrin, California Growers Wineries, Cutler

        2 lbs. lean beef stew meat
          Salt, pepper and paprika
        2 tablespoons dry onion soup mix
        6 medium-size potatoes
        8 white boiling onions
        3 carrots, quartered
        1 (10½-oz.) can cream of celery soup
        ½ cup water
        ½ cup California Sherry

Season meat with salt, pepper, paprika and onion soup mix. Place meat in Dutch oven; add whole potatoes and onions and quartered carrots. Blend celery soup with water and wine; pour over meat. Cover; bake in slow oven (250 to 300°) for 5 hours.

NOTE: *This is an exceptionally easy recipe, with no browning of meat or watching necessary. For those who like increased wine flavor, a little extra wine could be poured over at the last minute. Would be tops with a hearty California red dinner wine such as Zinfandel, Claret, Burgundy, or a "vino" type, served with the meal.*

STEW WITH POLENTA

(7 servings)

Peter Scagliotti, Live Oaks Winery, Gilroy

For a cold-weather menu, Northern Italy style, this combination is wonderful. First make your favorite wild game stew, or one made of beef or veal. Use at least ¼ cup of California red dinner wine for each pound of meat, and not too many vegetables. Serve stew on top of thick slices of polenta, which is easy to make, as follows:

        3 quarts cold water
        4 cups yellow corn meal
        ½ cup butter or margarine
          Olive oil

Bring water to rolling boil in heavy kettle. (Copper kettle is traditional.) Stir corn meal in gradually. Cook over medium heat 1 hour, stirring often to prevent burning. Slice in butter, stirring until absorbed. Reduce heat; cook until very thick. Remove from heat and brush edges of polenta with a little olive oil, by pushing a spatula against side of pot and following with oil. Polenta will then drop out of pan in nice round firm mold. Slice at least 1" thick in 3" squares, to serve under stew. A romaine or endive salad made with good wine vinegar and a half-clove of garlic adds to the delicacy of this meal.

My choice of wine to accompany this dish:
CHILLED CALIFORNIA ROSÉ OR BURGUNDY

BEEF POT PIE

(6 servings)

Mrs. Robert Weaver, U. of Calif. Dept. Viticulture & Enology

    2 lbs. round steak, cut in 1-inch cubes
    1 teaspoon salt
    ¼ teaspoon pepper
    3 level tablespoons flour
    ¼ cup olive oil
    2 tablespoons butter or margarine
    4 cloves unpeeled garlic
    1 lb. fresh mushrooms, cut in halves
    1 (4-oz.) can green chiles, minced
    ¼ teaspoon marjoram
    ½ teaspoon dried dill weed
    1 cup California Burgundy or other
      red dinner wine
    1 (10½-oz.) can consommé
    1 tablespoon California wine vinegar
    2 (10-oz.) pkgs. frozen artichoke bottoms or
      hearts, cooked as directed on pkg.
      Parmesan Biscuit Crust (see below)

Sprinkle meat with salt and pepper; roll in flour. In large heavy skillet, heat oil and butter with garlic; brown meat. Remove meat to warm platter; discard garlic. In same skillet, add mushrooms; cover and simmer 7 minutes. Add chiles; return meat to pan. Add marjoram, dill weed, wine, consommé and vinegar; simmer, covered, very slowly for 1½ hours, stirring occasionally. Add cooked artichokes. Pour mixture into a 2 to 2½-qt. baking dish. Top with Parmesan biscuits around outer edge of casserole. Bake in moderately hot oven (400°) 10 to 15 minutes, or until biscuits are well browned. As the vegetables, meat and starch are already in the Pot Pie, I make a tangy tomato aspic with chopped celery, green pepper and chopped hard-cooked eggs in it, to add color served alongside; and plenty of Parmesan biscuits for the gravy.

PARMESAN BISCUIT CRUST: Separate 1 (8-oz.) pkg. refrigerator biscuits. Dip each biscuit in melted butter; roll in shredded Parmesan cheese; sprinkle lightly with dill weed. I make extra biscuits for bread and bake them on a cookie sheet, along with those on top of the Pot Pie.

My choice of wine to accompany this dish:
CALIFORNIA CABERNET SAUVIGNON OR BURGUNDY

MANY LIKE a pronounced wine flavor which can be added without fuss, at the very last minute, to any stew or meat dish where liquid or gravy is a basic element. Simply pour a little EXTRA wine into the dish, and serve promptly. Since this final wine is not cooked, the alcohol does not volatilize, hence flavor remains more intense. (Usually in cooking, the wine flavor does not dominate, but "marries" or blends with the other food flavors, bringing out their natural best, delicately enriched.)

BEEF MAGNIFIQUE

(8 servings)

Mrs. Frank H. Bartholomew, Buena Vista Vineyards, Sonoma

This Burgundian dish was served to us in the heart of the Cote d'Or vineyard district, when we were guests at Chateau Grivelet in Chambolle-Musigny.

    ½ lb. salt pork, thinly sliced
      and cut in 1" squares
    2 dozen small white onions
    4 lbs. lean beef, cut in 2" cubes
    1 teaspoon flour
    ½ teaspoon salt
    ¼ teaspoon freshly-ground pepper
    1 clove garlic, pressed
    1 slice orange peel
    1 bouquet garni (see below)
    2 cups California Pinot Noir,
      Burgundy or other red dinner wine
    1 cup fresh small button mushrooms, or
      1 (4-oz.) can button mushrooms, drained
      Fresh parsley, finely chopped

Brown salt pork in Dutch oven until crisp. Remove pork; brown onions in remaining fat. Remove onions. Brown meat on all sides in same fat. Sprinkle salt pork with flour; return to Dutch oven. Season with salt and pepper. Add garlic, orange peel and bouquet garni. Heat wine; pour over meat. Cover and place in slow oven (250 to 300°) about 3 hours. Add more wine as necessary. Meanwhile, sauté fresh mushrooms in a little butter, until soft. Add mushrooms and onions 15 minutes before beef is done. Before serving, remove herb bouquet and orange peel; sprinkle lavishly with parsley. Serve with hot, buttered, crusty, sour dough French bread.

TO MAKE BOUQUET GARNI, tie 2 small bay leaves, 1 sprig thyme, ½ teapoon freshly-ground nutmeg, ½ teaspoon marjoram and small bunch parsley in piece of cheesecloth.

My choice of wine to accompany this dish:
CALIFORNIA PINOT NOIR

EASY OVEN POT ROAST

(4 servings)

Mrs. Vincent Indelicato, Sam-Jasper Winery, Manteca

    3 lbs. chuck or pot roast
    1 (10½-oz.) can cream of mushroom soup
    1 cup California Burgundy or
      other red dinner wine
    1 large onion, finely chopped
    1 small clove garlic, crushed
    2 tablespoons finely-chopped parsley
      Salt and pepper
    4 medium-size potatoes
    4 medium-size carrots

Place meat in Dutch oven or small roaster. Blend soup and wine; pour over meat. Add onion, garlic, parsley, salt and pepper. Cover and bake in moderately slow oven (325°) 5 hours. During last hour, add potatoes and carrots. Serve with garlic bread, tossed green salad and gelatin dessert with fruit.

My choice of wine to accompany this dish:
CALIFORNIA BURGUNDY OR VIN ROSÉ

SWISS STEAK SUPREME

(6 servings)

Mrs. Allen Pool, Bear Creek Vineyard Association, Lodi

This is not an original recipe, but I have made it for years. When I became interested in wine cookery, I simply added wine to the recipe, and found that I liked it much better.

- ¼ cup flour
- 1 teaspoon salt
- ¼ teaspoon pepper
- 2 lbs. round steak, ¾ to 1" thick, cut in 6 serving-size pieces
- ¼ cup oil
- 1 onion, sliced
- 1 tomato, sliced (or 1 tablespoon tomato paste)
- 1 cup California Burgundy, Claret or other red dinner wine
  Pinch *each*: powdered bay leaf, oregano, rosemary
- 6 small potatoes, peeled
- 12 small carrots, peeled
- 12 small white onions, peeled
- 1 (10½-oz.) can cream of mushroom soup, or 1 (6-oz.) can whole mushrooms

Mix flour, salt and pepper; coat meat well, pounding in as much flour as possible. In a large heavy skillet, brown meat well in oil over high heat. Reduce heat. Top each piece of meat with a slice of onion and tomato; add wine and enough water to almost cover meat (or, if desired, use all wine). Add herbs. Simmer, covered, 2 hours. Place vegetables around meat; add mushroom soup or mushrooms. Simmer again until vegetables are tender (about 45 minutes). Since this is a whole meal in a skillet, menu might simply include a tossed green salad with wine vinegar and oil dressing and apple pie.

My choice of wine to accompany this dish:
CALIFORNIA BURGUNDY OR
ONE OF THE RED "VINO" TYPES

SWISS STEAK SAUTERNE

(6 servings)

Mrs. Louis W. Pellegrini, Sr., Italian Swiss Colony, Asti

- 2 lbs. round steak, cut ½" thick
- 1 teaspoon salt
- ⅛ teaspoon pepper
  Flour
  Oil
- ½ medium-size onion, chopped
- 1 cup California Sauterne or other white dinner wine
- 1 (6-oz.) can sliced mushrooms, undrained

Pound steak; cut in 6 serving-size pieces. Sprinkle with salt and pepper; dip in flour. In heavy skillet, brown meat in heated oil along with onions. When well browned, add wine and mushrooms. Cover; cook over low heat 1 to 1½ hours or until meat is tender.

My choice of wine to accompany this dish:
CALIFORNIA ROSÉ, BURGUNDY OR
SPARKLING BURGUNDY

BAKED SHORT RIBS

(4 servings)

Mrs. Joseph Stillman, Paul Masson Vineyards, Saratoga

This was my own experiment, and proved to be a favorite dish with my family.

- 2 pounds English-cut short ribs
- 2 tablespoons flour
- ½ teaspoon paprika
- 1 teaspoon salt
- ¼ teaspoon pepper
- 2 cups California Burgundy or other red dinner wine
- 1 clove garlic, diced

Roll ribs in flour seasoned with paprika, salt and pepper. Brown in hot fat. Place ribs in casserole; add wine and garlic. Cover and bake in slow oven (300°) 2½ hours, or until tender. Serve with baked potatoes, green beans, tossed green salad, French rolls, dessert.

My choice of wine to accompany this dish:
ANY CALIFORNIA RED DINNER WINE

ROUND OF BEEF WITH SHERRY

(6 servings)

Mrs. Alvin Ehrhardt, United Vintners, Inc., Lodi

- 4 lbs. bottom round steak
- 2 medium-size onions, sliced
- 1 clove garlic, chopped
- 1 bay leaf
- ¼ teaspoon thyme
- 1 teaspoon salt
  Dash Tabasco sauce
- ¾ cup California wine vinegar
- ¾ cup water
- 3 tablespoons fat from meat or shortening
- 8 small white onions
- 2 tablespoons flour
- ½ cup meat stock (may be made with 1 teaspoon meat-extract paste and ½ cup water)
- ¼ cup California Sherry

Trim fat from meat; wipe meat with damp cloth; place in small crock or covered dish. Combine onions, garlic, bay leaf, thyme, salt, Tabasco sauce, vinegar and water; pour over meat. Cover; refrigerate 2 days, turning several times each day. Remove meat, reserving marinade; drain. Brown well in heated fat in a heavy soup pot or Dutch oven. Add small onions; cover and cook over very low heat for 30 minutes, turning once. Remove meat. Add flour to fat in pan; cook, stirring constantly, 3 minutes. Strain marinade; stir into flour mixture along with stock. Simmer meat in thickened gravy, covered, 1½ hours. Add Sherry; simmer 1 hour more, or until meat is tender.

My choice of wine to accompany this dish:
CALIFORNIA BURGUNDY

SAUERBRATEN

(6 to 8 servings)

Mrs. Lewis A. Stern, E. & J. Gallo Winery, Modesto

Our friends usually look forward to some good old German cookery when they come to our house. This is Lew's favorite meal—the way "mother used to make it."

>   4 to 6 lbs. top round steak
>   4 slices bacon
> 1½ cups California wine vinegar
>   2 teaspoons salt
>   10 whole peppercorns
>   3 cloves
>   2 bay leaves
>   2 onions, chopped
>   2 carrots, sliced
>   3 tablespoons butter or margarine
>   ½ cup boiling water
>   1 cup California Burgundy or
>   other red dinner wine
>   1 cup sour cream

Lard meat by cutting a gash through the meat in about 6 places; insert a piece of bacon in each gash. In a saucepan, combine vinegar, salt, peppercorns, bay leaves, onions and carrots; bring to boiling. Remove from heat; cool about ½ hour. Place meat in glass or porcelain bowl; pour over vinegar mixture. Marinate 3 to 5 days in refrigerator, turning meat several times. Baste occasionally. Drain meat, saving marinade; blot dry with paper towels. Melt butter in Dutch oven. Brown meat all over. Add marinade and boiling water; simmer 2½ hours. Add wine; simmer 30 minutes longer, or until meat is tender. Add sour cream, stirring constantly; simmer 15 minutes longer. Slice and serve with the gravy and Potato Pancakes (Kartoffelpuffer—see below); also sweet-and-sour red cabbage, tossed green salad, French bread and apple pie with cheese.

POTATO PANCAKES (KARTOFFELPUFFER): Peel and grate 6 medium-size potatoes and ½ onion. Drain off liquid; combine potato-onion mixture with 2 tablespoons flour, 2 beaten eggs, 1½ teaspoons salt, ¼ teaspoon white pepper, ¼ teaspoon nutmeg and 2 tablespoons minced parsley. Beat well. Drop mixture by spoonfuls on hot, lightly buttered griddle; fry until brown and crisp on both sides, turning only once. Serve hot.

Our choice of wine to accompany this meal:
CALIFORNIA BURGUNDY OR CLARET

LOW BUDGET T-BONE STEAK

(2 or 3 servings)

Walter S. Richert, Richert & Sons, Morgan Hill

Buy tough chuck roast and serve meat as tender as T-bone. This method also works beautifully with any wild game: deer, rabbit, squirrel, duck, etc.

>   Chuck or pot roast, cut ¾" thick
> 1¾ cups California Burgundy, Claret
>   or other red dinner wine
>   ½ teaspoon salt
>   ½ teaspoon seasoned salt
>   ¼ teaspoon freshly-ground pepper

Cover meat with wine in glass or porcelain dish; marinate from 12 hours to 3 days, turning occasionally. (Marinate at room temperature for short period of time, or in refrigerator for longer period.) Remove meat from marinade, season and broil. Serve with tomato and onion salad marinated in wine vinegar: mayonnaise optional.

My choice of wine to accompany this dish:
ANY FULL-BODIED CALIFORNIA RED DINNER WINE

WINEBRATEN

(4 servings)

Mrs. Don Bonhaus, Wine Advisory Board, Detroit

This started in my mother's kitchen, as a substitute for Hasenpfeffer. By mixing recipes for Sauerbraten and Hasenpfeffer, and adding the most necessary "secret touch" of California Port, we have what I now call Winebraten.

>   2 cups "carelessly cut cubes" of
>   leftover pork or beef roast
>   ¼ cup California wine vinegar
>   2 tablespoons mixed pickling spices,
>   tied in small piece cheesecloth
>   ¼ teaspoon meat sauce
>   ½ teaspoon salt
>   ⅛ teaspoon pepper
>   ¼ teaspoon monosodium glutamate
>   1 cup leftover roast gravy or canned gravy
>   1 medium onion, chopped
>   ½ cup California Port
>   1 tablespoon cornstarch

Combine all in a saucepan. Simmer, covered, 1 hour or longer, stirring occasionally. If more thickening is desired, add a little more cornstarch blended with water; cook, stirring, until thickened. Serve over boiled noodles, with potato pancakes, small peas, lots of crisp celery, and fruit for dessert. Although this complete menu is not a balanced meal, it is a family tradition, and when it is served everyone forgets "the rules" and just enjoys it.

My choice of wine to accompany this dish:
CALIFORNIA CLARET, ZINFANDEL OR BURGUNDY

EASY CABERNET POT ROAST

(4 to 6 servings)

Mrs. Guy Baldwin, Jr., Mont La Salle Vineyards, Napa

4-lb. chuck or pot roast
2 tablespoons flour
2 teaspoons salt
3 tablespoons oil
1 (8-oz.) can tomato sauce
1½ cups water
1 cup California Cabernet Sauvignon,
  Claret or other red dinner wine
½ teaspoon dried oregano
½ teaspoon dried rosemary

Dredge meat with flour and salt. Brown on all sides in heated oil. Pour in tomato sauce, water and wine; add herbs. Cover and simmer gently 3 hours, or until meat is tender. Thicken gravy, if desired; add salt to taste; serve with meat. Menu could include noodles or rice; parsley-sprinkled carrots; tossed green salad; radishes, celery sticks and olives; buttered biscuits and strawberry preserves; and angel food cake.

My choice of wine to accompany this dish:
CALIFORNIA PINOT NOIR OR CABERNET SAUVIGNON

ROAST BEEF MAÑANA

(4 servings)

Mrs. Dale R. Anderson, Di Giorgio Wine Co., Di Giorgio

Mrs. Chet Steinhauer gave us this recipe several years ago when we lived in Delano, and it is our favorite way of using leftover roast beef—juicy and flavorful.

1 tablespoon butter or margarine
1 medium-size onion, chopped
1 level tablespoon flour
1 cup bouillon (canned or
  bouillon-cube broth may be used)
  Salt and pepper
  Worcestershire sauce
½ cup California Claret, Burgundy
  or other red dinner wine
  Thick slices cold cooked roast beef

Melt butter in saucepan; sauté onion until golden brown. Blend in flour. Slowly stir in bouillon; cook, stirring constantly, until well blended. Season with salt, pepper and Worcestershire sauce. Stir in wine. Add slices of cooked beef; heat thoroughly over low heat. Good with mashed potatoes, vegetable, tossed green salad and fruit for dessert.

My choice of wine to accompany this dish:
ANY CALIFORNIA DRY RED DINNER WINE

SAVORY ROAST OF BEEF

(16 servings)

Richard O'Hagan, Charles Krug Winery, St. Helena

9-lb. standing 3-rib roast of beef,
  with bones in
¼ teaspoon dried marjoram
¼ teaspoon dried thyme leaves
¼ teaspoon rubbed savory
¼ teaspoon dried basil leaves
½ teaspoon salt
⅛ teaspoon pepper
1 teaspoon meat extract paste dissolved
  in ½ cup hot water
1½ cups California Burgundy or other
  red dinner wine
6 tablespoons all-purpose flour
1¼ cups water

Preheat oven to 325°. Place beef, fat side up, in shallow roasting pan. Do not use rack; let beef rest on bones. Combine herbs, salt and pepper; mix well. Rub into surface of beef on all sides. Insert meat thermometer through outside fat into thickest part of muscle; point should not rest on fat or bone. Combine meat broth with ½ cup of wine; use a little to baste beef. Roast meat, uncovered, basting several times with remaining wine mixture. Roast until thermometer reads 140° for rare, 3¼ to 3¾ hours; 160° for medium, 3¾ to 4¼ hours; 170° for well done, 4½ to 4¾ hours. Remove meat to heated platter; let stand 20 minutes before carving. Meanwhile, make gravy. Pour off drippings from roasting pan into measuring cup. Return 6 tablespoons to pan; stir in flour until smooth. Gradually add water and remaining 1 cup wine, stirring until smooth and scraping up browned bits. Bring to boiling, stirring constantly, for 5 minutes. Taste; add more salt and pepper, if needed. Serve gravy along with beef. Preferred menu with this would include oven-browned potatoes, fresh steamed buttered carrots, combination vegetable salad, soft French rolls, and raspberry Bavarian cream for dessert.

My choice of wine to accompany this dish:
CALIFORNIA ROSÉ OR CABERNET SAUVIGNON

POT ROAST PIEMONTESE

(6 to 8 servings)

Ferrer and Mildred Filipello, Calif. Wine Association, Lodi

> **4 to 5-lb. beef rump roast**
> ¼ **lb. precooked ham, sliced
> into thin strips**
> 4 **strips bacon**
> 2 **cloves garlic, minced**
> 2 **medium onions, minced**
> 2 **stalks celery, minced**
> 2 **medium carrots, thinly sliced**
> 1 **cup California Chablis, Rhine
> or other white dinner wine**
> 1 **cup California Burgundy, Claret
> or other red dinner wine**
> 1 **teaspoon salt**
> ¼ **teaspoon pepper**
> 1 **sprig fresh rosemary**

Lard roast with ham strips. Line casserole or Dutch oven with bacon strips. Add meat; brown on all sides over high heat (about 10 minutes). Add remaining ingredients. Cover and simmer, turning meat occasionally, about 3 hours or until tender. This is best served with gnocchi on the side, covered with the meat sauce, or buttered tagliarini. A tossed green salad is always appropriate.

Our choice of wine to accompany this dish:
CALIFORNIA CLARET OR ZINFANDEL

LAZY SUNDAY OVEN DINNER

(4 to 6 servings)

Mrs. Richard Dettman, Mont La Salle Vineyards, Napa

This is a dinner which almost prepares itself—once it's in the oven, you can almost forget it.

> **4-lb. chuck roast**
> 4 **stalks celery, finely chopped**
> 6 **carrots, finely chopped**
> 2 **cloves garlic, finely chopped**
> **Salt and pepper**
> 1½ **cups California Burgundy or other
> red dinner wine**

Place roast on large piece foil in shallow baking pan. Brown meat well on both sides under broiler. Remove from oven; top meat with chopped vegetables and season with salt and pepper. Add 1 cup wine; fold foil tightly around meat. Bake in moderately slow oven (325°) for 2 hours. Half an hour before done, partially unwrap foil and add remaining ½ cup wine; rewrap. This is not absolutely necessary, but a certain amount of evaporation sometimes occurs and this eliminates any chance of dryness. Also, the added wine provides an excellent gravy when slightly thickened with flour. Good with corn soufflé, green salad, and ice cream or sherbet for dessert.

My choice of wine to accompany this dish:
CALIFORNIA BURGUNDY, PINOT NOIR OR
CABERNET SAUVIGNON

BARBECUED POT ROAST

(4 to 6 servings)

Phil Hiaring, Wine Institute, San Francisco

> 1 **(4 to 5-lb.) chuck or pot roast
> California Burgundy or other red
> dinner wine**
> 5 **cloves garlic, chopped
> Juice of 3 large lemons**
> 4 **tablespoons oregano**
> ¾ **cup olive oil**
> ¼ **cup chopped parsley
> Pinch of rosemary
> Salt and pepper**

Cover meat with wine; marinate several hours or overnight, turning occasionally. Combine remaining ingredients; use to baste meat while barbecuing over hot coals. (Or, combine wine with other ingredients and use as both marinade and baste.)

My choice of wine to accompany this dish:
THE SAME CALIFORNIA RED DINNER WINE

NOTE: *This is a man's dish, robust and aromatic from the garlic and oregano. Those who prefer milder seasoning might want to cut down a little on these two ingredients in the initial marinating. More can be added later to the baste, if you're brave.*

SPICY POT ROAST OF VEAL

(4 servings)

Mrs. Sydney Whiteside, Del Rio Winery, Lodi

> **5-lb. veal rump roast with bone**
> 1 **tablespoon dry mustard**
> 1 **teaspoon poultry seasoning**
> 2 **tablespoons flour**
> 1 **tablespoon brown sugar**
> 1 **tablespoon salt
> Pepper**
> 3 **tablespoons shortening or other fat**
> ½ **cup California Burgundy or other
> red dinner wine**
> 1 **onion, sliced
> Garlic (optional)**

Dredge meat with mixture of mustard, poultry seasoning, flour, brown sugar, salt and pepper. Brown well on all sides in heated shortening. Add wine, onion and garlic, if desired. Cover tightly; simmer about 2½ hours, or until meat is tender. Good with a corn casserole, any vegetable in season, green salad with your favorite dressing, hot biscuits and relishes, and warm apple pie.

My choice of wine to accompany this dish:
CALIFORNIA CLARET OR A ROSÉ

GROUND BEEF WITH GLAMOUR

(4 to 6 servings)

Mrs. Wm. V. Cruess, U. of Calif. Dept. of Food Technology

Lean ground beef or hamburger is not very glamorous or attractive in flavor. Wine adds "the touch," and greatly improves it.

        1 lb. ground lean beef
        1 egg, beaten
        1 cup cooked rice
        ½ onion, chopped
        1 small clove garlic, chopped
        ½ teaspoon salt
        ⅛ teaspoon pepper
        1 tablespoon oil
        ½ cup California Burgundy, Claret
            or other red dinner wine
        1 (10¾-oz.) can prepared gravy

Combine beef, beaten egg, rice, onion, garlic, salt and pepper; mix just enough to blend. Shape into thick patties and brown lightly in heated oil. Pour off excess fat; add wine and gravy. Simmer about ½ hour, basting often. Thicken gravy with a little cornstarch mixed with cold water before serving, if desired.

My choice of wine to accompany this dish:
ANY DRY CALIFORNIA RED OR WHITE, OR DRY SHERRY

WINEDERFUL MEAT LOAF

(6 to 8 servings)

Larry Cahn, Wine Institute, San Francisco

Our meat loaves had lacked a distinctive flavor, so one night I suggested we use wine rather than water in them. My wife hinted that as long as I didn't like the way she did it, why didn't I try it myself. No sooner said than done. The wine made all the difference, and if a testimonial is needed, my wife will happily supply same.

        2 lbs. ground beef
        1 (1⅜-oz.) pkg. onion soup mix
        1 cup California Burgundy, Claret
            or other red dinner wine
        1 cup tomato juice
            Bacon slices

Mix meat, soup mix, ½ cup wine and ½ cup tomato juice. Shape into loaf. Place in baking pan; top with bacon slices. Bake in moderate oven (350°) for 45 minutes. Drain off fat; add remaining wine and tomato juice. Bake and baste 15 minutes longer. If desired, thicken pan juices slightly with a little cornstarch mixed with cold water or additional wine. Serve with baked potatoes, buttered fresh peas, and hearts of lettuce with blue cheese dressing.

My choice of wine to accompany this dish:
THE SAME CALIFORNIA BURGUNDY

NOTE: *This easy-to-make meat loaf has unusual flavor, and is very moist, with lots of pan juices to make a luscious wine gravy. Another good red wine-flavored meat loaf is made by Mrs. Pete Peters, Fresno, who uses horseradish and chopped green pepper in hers.*

BEEF STROGANOFF

(6 to 8 servings)

Richard O'Hagan, Charles Krug Winery, St. Helena

        2 lbs. fillet of beef
        4 tablespoons butter or margarine
        1 cup chopped onion
        1 clove garlic, finely chopped
        ½ lb. fresh mushrooms, sliced ¼" thick
        3 tablespoons flour
        2 teaspoons meat-extract paste
        1 tablespoon catsup
        ½ teaspoon salt
        ⅛ teaspoon pepper
        1 (10½-oz.) can beef bouillon, undiluted
        ½ cup California Sauterne, Chablis
            or other white dinner wine
        1 tablespoon snipped fresh dill, or
        ¼ teaspoon dried dill
        1½ cups sour cream
            Wild & White Herb Rice (see below)

Trim fat from beef; cut fillet crosswise into ½" thick slices. Cut each slice, across grain, into ½" wide strips. Heat a large, heavy skillet; melt 1 tablespoon of the butter. Add beef strips a few at a time; brown quickly on all sides over high heat. Remove beef as it browns—should be browned outside and rare inside. Brown rest of meat; set aside. In same skillet, melt remaining 3 tablespoons butter; sauté onion, garlic and mushrooms until onion is clear—3 to 5 minutes. Remove from heat and add flour, meat-extract paste, catsup, salt and pepper. Stir until smooth. Gradually add bouillon; bring to boiling point, stirring constantly. Reduce heat; simmer 5 minutes. Stir in wine, dill and sour cream. Add beef strips; heat thoroughly. Serve with Wild & White Herb Rice (or fresh tagliarini, for a change). Menu might also include beef consommé with croutons, avocado and grapefruit wedges with French dressing, green beans with little white onions, hard French rolls and Grecian pears.

WILD & WHITE HERB RICE: Lightly toss 1½ cups cooked wild rice and 4 cups cooked white rice. Surround Beef Stroganoff with rice. Snip 2 tablespoons fresh dill or 3 tablespoons parsley over the top for garnish.

My choice of wine to accompany this dish:
CALIFORNIA JOHANNISBERG RIESLING,
ROSÉ OR CABERNET SAUVIGNON

NOTE: *This is an outstanding dish, well worth the price of the beef fillet indicated. However, for a lower cost Stroganoff, top sirloin may be used instead. Sherry may also be substituted for the white wine in the recipe, for a pleasant flavor variation. And an interesting Stroganoff is made with Burgundy by Mrs. L. J. Berg of Mont La Salle Vineyards, Napa.*

PAPER-THIN STEAKS POIVRADE

(4 servings)

Louis A. Benoist, Almaden Vineyards, Los Gatos

    2 lbs. boneless beef steak, cut ¼" thick
    1 teaspoon cracked black pepper
    ½ teaspoon soft butter or margarine
       for each side of each steak
    ⅛ teaspoon salt for each side
    ⅛ teaspoon ground pepper for each side
       Butter and oil (half and half)
    3 tablespoons butter or margarine
    1 teaspoon chopped green onions
    ½ cup California Burgundy, Claret
       or other red dinner wine
       Finely-chopped parsley

Sprinkle both sides of steaks with cracked pepper; press into meat. Cover each side of steaks with ½ teaspoon butter; sprinkle each side with salt and ground pepper. Heat butter and oil in large heavy skillet; brown steaks quickly over high heat. Place steaks on a hot platter. Discard cooking oil. In same skillet, blend 2 tablespoons butter with green onions, salt to taste and wine. Bring to boiling. Dip each steak into liquid for ½ minute. Boil liquid until almost all evaporated. Remove pan from heat; stir in remaining tablespoon butter a little at a time. Taste; correct seasoning. Pour sauce over steaks; sprinkle with parsley.

My choice of wine to accompany this dish:
CALIFORNIA CABERNET SAUVIGNON

NOTE: *These thin, well-seasoned steaks are really delicious. The sauce is a simplified version of the famous Marchand de Vin or Wine Merchant Sauce, traditional for many dishes.*

BOEUF SALMI

(4 to 6 servings)

Mrs. William Bonetti, Charles Krug Winery, St. Helena

This is an original recipe, and a very easy meat treatment.

    3-lb. chuck roast
       Salt
    1 carrot, diced
    1 small onion, chopped
    2 stalks celery, diced
       Sprig parsley
    ¼ teaspoon coarse black pepper
    3 cloves
       Pinch each: sage, rosemary, marjoram,
       sweet basil and bay leaf
    3 cups California Burgundy or other
       red dinner wine
    3 tablespoons butter or margarine

Season roast on both sides with salt. Place meat in a glass or porcelain dish. Add all other ingredients except butter (meat should be covered by wine). Cover dish; refrigerate 2 days, turning once a day. Drain meat, reserving marinade. Brown meat on both sides in melted butter; add wine marinade; simmer 2 to 2½ hours or until meat is tender. Serve with spaghetti, rice, mashed potatoes or polenta.

My choice of wine to accompany this dish:
CALIFORNIA CABERNET SAUVIGNON OR PINOT NOIR

NOTE: *For a good polenta recipe to go with the beef, see Page 34.*

PEPPER STEAK BARBECUED

(6 servings)

Mrs. John Paul, California Products Co., Fresno

    3 lbs. chuck or pot roast, 2" thick
    2 teaspoons unseasoned meat tenderizer
    2 tablespoons instant minced onion
       (or ½ cup finely-chopped onion)
    2 teaspoons thyme
    1 teaspoon marjoram
    1 bay leaf, crushed
    ½ cup California wine vinegar
    ½ cup California Burgundy or
       other red dinner wine
    ½ cup oil
    3 tablespoons lemon juice
    2 tablespoons coarse ground pepper

Sprinkle tenderizer on both sides of meat; pierce deeply with fork. Combine remaining ingredients; pour over meat in a glass or porcelain dish. Marinate the meat 1 to 2 hours, turning occasionally. Grill on rack about 6 inches above coals, 15 to 20 minutes per side. Baste with remaining marinade while cooking. Slice diagonally ½ inch thick to serve. Serve with rice baked in consommé, creamed spinach, tossed salad with tomatoes and apple pie.

My choice of wine to accompany this dish:
CALIFORNIA CABERNET SAUVIGNON

BEEF-RICE CASSEROLE

(6 to 8 servings)

Mrs. J. W. Fleming, Lockeford Winery, Lodi

    2 large onions, sliced
    1 green pepper, finely chopped
    3 tablespoons shortening
    ¾ pound ground beef
    1 cup raw rice
    ½ teaspoon chili powder
    2 teaspoons salt
    1½ cups tomato juice
    ¾ cup California Sauterne, Chablis
       or other white dinner wine

Sauté onions and green pepper in shortening until onions are clear. Add meat; cook until brown and crumbly. Add rice, chili powder, salt, tomato juice and ½ cup of wine. Turn into casserole, cover and bake in a moderate oven (350°) for 45 minutes. Remove cover, stir in remaining ¼ cup wine; cook, uncovered, 15 minutes more to brown.

NOTE: *A sprightly California Claret or Rosé served alongside would be the ultimate in appetite-appeal.*

BEEF ROLL-UPS, MILANESE

(6 to 8 servings)

Ferrer and Mildred Filipello, Calif. Wine Association, Lodi

- 3 lbs. round steak, cut in ¼-inch slices
- 2 tablespoons soy sauce
- 1 clove garlic, peeled
- 2 (12-oz.) pkgs. frozen chopped spinach, thawed
- 2 cups bread crumbs
- ½ cup chopped Italian salami
- 1 cup grated Parmesan or other dry cheese
- 1 teaspoon salt
- 1 teaspoon thyme
- ½ teaspoon pepper
- 1 teaspoon paprika
- 1 teaspoon monosodium glutamate
- 2 tablespoons oil
- 1 cup California Sherry
- 1 to 4 large sprigs fresh rosemary, or ½ to 1 teaspoon dried rosemary

Pound meat until quite thin; cut in 3-inch squares. Moisten each piece with a little soy sauce; rub with garlic. Set aside. Press out and discard excess liquid from thawed spinach. In a mixing bowl, combine bread crumbs, salami, cheese, salt, thyme, pepper, paprika and monosodium glutamate. Mix thoroughly with hands. Mix in spinach. Add a little Sherry while mixing to hold dressing together. Spread thin layer of dressing on each piece of meat. Roll up meat; tie both ends with string. Heat oil in large heavy skillet; add roll-ups; salt lightly. Brown meat on all sides over medium heat. Reduce heat to very low; add Sherry and rosemary. Cover; cook over low heat 30 minutes or until tender, turning occasionally. Add a little more Sherry if necessary. Remove strings, if desired, before serving. Serve with cauliflower, mixed tossed green salad and garlic bread.

Our choice of wine to accompany this dish:
CALIFORNIA CABERNET, CLARET OR ZINFANDEL

BAKED CORNED BEEF

(10 to 12 servings)

Mrs. Hans Hyba, Paul Masson Vineyards, Saratoga

- 6 lbs. corned beef
- 10 whole cloves
- ½ cup brown sugar (packed)
- 1 cup California Cream Sherry

Wash corned beef under running water to remove brine. In large kettle, cover with cold water; bring to boiling. Drain; cover with fresh water. Bring to boiling; simmer slowly until tender (about 6 hours). Remove from kettle; place in baking dish. Insert cloves in meat; sprinkle with brown sugar; slowly pour Sherry over meat. Bake in moderate oven (350°) until brown. Baste occasionally with Sherry syrup in bottom of pan until thickly glazed. Serve hot or cold.

NOTE: *This is a simple yet flavorful glaze. Would be a luscious main course dish served with chilled California Rosé.*

BEEF ROULADES IN RED WINE

(6 servings)

Mrs. Joseph S. Vercelli, Italian Swiss Colony, Asti

- 1½ lbs. round steak, very thinly sliced and cut in 6 pieces
- 1 clove garlic, cut in half
- 1 teaspoon salt
- ⅛ teaspoon pepper
- ¾ lb. ground sausage
- 2 tablespoons finely-chopped parsley
- 2 tablespoons finely-chopped onion
  Flour
- 1½ cups California Burgundy, Claret or other red dinner wine
- 1½ tablespoons tomato paste
- ½ cup pitted olives

Rub each piece of meat with cut clove of garlic. Season with salt and pepper. Spread a thin layer of sausage over each piece of meat. Sprinkle with parsley and onion. Roll up each piece; tie securely at both ends. Dredge the rolls in flour; brown well in heavy skillet. Discard any fat left in pan. Add wine. Mix tomato paste with a little of the wine; stir into wine in pan. Cover; cook slowly for 1 hour, or until meat is tender. About 15 minutes before meat is done, add olives. Good with steamed rice, green beans sautéed with almonds and mixed tossed green salad.

My choice of wine to accompany this dish:
CALIFORNIA CHIANTI

NOTE: *Still another good rolled beef dish is made by Mrs. Dan C. Turrentine, Wine Advisory Board, San Francisco. She uses a packaged bread stuffing and canned gravy with Burgundy and sour cream added — an "easy do-ahead recipe that seems company-prone."*

BURGUNDY MEATBALLS

(6 servings)

Mrs. John Parducci, Parducci Wine Cellars, Inc., Ukiah

- 1 lb. ground beef
- ½ cup fine dry bread crumbs
- 1 small onion, minced
- ¾ teaspoon cornstarch
  Dash allspice
- 1 egg, beaten
- ¾ cup light cream
- ¾ teaspoon salt
- ¼ cup oil
- 3 tablespoons flour
- 2 cups water
- 1 cup California Burgundy or other red dinner wine
- 2 beef bouillon cubes
- ½ teaspoon salt (additional)
- ⅛ teaspoon pepper

Combine beef, crumbs, onion, cornstarch, allspice, beaten egg, cream and ¾ teaspoon salt. Shape into small balls about the size of a walnut. Brown well on all sides in heated oil; remove from pan. Blend remaining ingredients into oil remaining in pan. Cook, stirring constantly, until smooth. Add meatballs to sauce. Cover and simmer 30 minutes. Serve with mashed potatoes, rice or noodles.

NOTE: *Would be perfect with the same good red wine on the table.*

RULADINI

(4 servings)

Mrs. Frank J. Pilone, Cucamonga Vineyard Co., Cucamonga

          2 to 2½ lbs. top sirloin, round or cube steak,
              cut in 12 pieces about 4" square and ¼" thick
          1 teaspoon butter or margarine
          ¼ cup chopped parsley
          1 clove garlic, minced
         12 thin slices onion
         12 thin slices carrot
         12 thin slices celery
         12 thin slices prosciutto or boiled ham
            Salt and pepper
            Flour
            Oil and butter
          ½ onion, chopped
          2 tablespoons chopped parsley
          1 (4-oz.) can sliced mushrooms, undrained
          ¼ cup California Sherry

Spread each piece of beef with butter, parsley and garlic, divided evenly. On each, place a slice of onion, carrot, celery and ham. Roll each slice; secure with a wooden pick or string. Roll in flour; brown in oil and butter. Remove rolls to baking dish. In same skillet, brown onion and parsley; sprinkle over meat. Add mushrooms and Sherry. Bake, covered, in moderate oven (350°) 1 hour, or until tender. Baste occasionally with Sherry. Preferred menu would include gnocchi, zucchini and green salad.

My choice of wine to accompany this dish:
CALIFORNIA BURGUNDY

VEAL SCALLOPINI MARSALA

(4 to 6 servings)

Mrs. Dorothy Winneberger, U. C. Dept. Viticulture & Enology

This Italian recipe is very simple to make, yet an exquisite main dish. Do actually squeeze the lemon wedges onto the meat; it adds a delightful touch of flavor.

          2 lbs. veal top round steak, thinly sliced
             and cut in 2" strips
            Flour
          ½ cup butter or margarine (or half oil)
          1 (4-oz.) can sliced mushrooms, drained
            California Marsala or Sherry
            Salt and pepper
            Lemon wedges

Pound veal strips with flour; brown meat quickly in heated butter. Cover with mushrooms; add wine to cover. Simmer, covered, 5 to 10 minutes or until tender. Season with salt and pepper; serve with lemon wedges. I usually also serve rice pilaf with it; very small frozen peas, buttered; a green salad; hot rolls; and an extravagant dessert, possibly angel food cake with chocolate whipped cream and slivered almonds.

My choice of wine to accompany this dish:
CALIFORNIA CABERNET SAUVIGNON OR PINOT NOIR

VEAL WITH ARTICHOKES

(6 servings)

Mrs. A. Jensen, Gemello Winery, Mountain View

This is a Gemello family recipe, which is a favorite of ours.

          2 cloves garlic
            Oil (half olive oil, if preferred)
          2 lbs. veal round (have butcher flatten to ¼")
            Flour seasoned with salt and pepper
          1 (1-lb.) can solid-pack tomatoes
          ½ cup California Sherry or Sauterne
          ¼ teaspoon oregano
          2 (10-oz.) pkgs. frozen artichoke hearts

In a heavy skillet, sauté garlic in oil. Dust veal with seasoned flour; brown in oil. Add tomatoes, wine and oregano; mix well. Add frozen artichoke hearts. Cover; simmer 45 minutes to 1 hour, or until meat is tender. Serve with steamed rice, tossed green salad, French bread and fresh fruit dessert.

My choice of wine to accompany this dish:
CHILLED CALIFORNIA VIN ROSÉ

***NOTE:** Lots of eye-appeal as well as taste in this one.*

BAKED VEAL SCALLOPINI

(6 servings)

Mrs. Allen Pool, Bear Creek Vineyard Association, Lodi

I acquired this recipe at a wine tasting luncheon, and have used it often during the last few years.

          ¼ cup chopped onions
          ¼ cup oil
          1½ lbs. boned veal steak,
             cut in serving-size pieces
          ¼ cup sifted flour
          ½ teaspoon salt
          ⅛ teaspoon pepper
          1 (4-oz.) can button mushrooms, drained
          1 cup tomato juice
          ½ teaspoon sugar
          1 cup California Sauterne, Chablis
             or other white dinner wine

Sauté onions in heated oil; remove to casserole. Roll veal in flour seasoned with salt and pepper; brown in oil. Add mushrooms and brown slightly. Arrange veal and mushrooms over onions. Combine other ingredients; pour over meat. Cover; bake in moderate oven (350°) for 1¼ hours or until veal is tender. Remove cover last ½ hour. Serve with baked potatoes, green peas, Perfection Salad and spumoni.

My choice of wine to accompany this dish:
CALIFORNIA BURGUNDY OR SAUTERNE

JOE'S VEAL CROQUETTES AU VIN

(6 to 8 servings)

Mrs. Cesare Vai, Cucamonga Vineyard Co., Cucamonga

- ¼ cup butter or margarine
- 2 tablespoons flour
- 1 lb. lean ground pork
- 1 lb. lean ground veal
- 4 eggs
- 1 cup grated Parmesan cheese
- ½ cup finely-chopped parsley
- ¼ teaspoon nutmeg
- 3 tablespoons California brandy
- 12 slices Provolone cheese, cut 2 x 1 x ¼"
- 6 slices prosciutto, cut in half
- ½ cup flour
- ½ cup bread crumbs
- ½ cup California Sauterne or other
  white dinner wine
  Sautéed sliced fresh mushrooms

Melt butter and stir in 2 tablespoons flour; cool. Combine butter-flour mixture with pork, veal, 2 eggs (beaten), ½ cup grated Parmesan cheese, parsley, nutmeg and brandy. Form meat mixture into thin patties. Top a patty with a slice of Provolone cheese, a piece of prosciutto and a second patty; pinch edges of patties together to hold filling. Repeat with remaining patties. In 3 separate bowls, place ½ cup flour, 2 beaten eggs and a mixture of bread crumbs and remaining grated Parmesan cheese. Dip each patty in flour, then egg, then crumb-cheese mixture. Fry patties in butter or margarine. Remove patties to shallow baking dish; add wine. Bake in slow oven (300°) for 30 to 40 minutes. Garnish with sautéed mushrooms. Menu might include linguini with tomato sauce, buttered green vegetable, tossed green salad with Italian dressing, fresh strawberries or sherbet and cookies.

My choice of wine to accompany this dish:
CALIFORNIA BARBERA

VEAL CHOPS TARRAGON

(2 servings)

Mrs. Joseph J. Franzia, Franzia Brothers Winery, Ripon

- 2 veal chops
- ¼ cup bread crumbs
- 3 tablespoons butter or margarine
- 2 shallots or green onions, chopped
- 1 tablespoon chopped parsley
- 3 or 4 leaves fresh tarragon, chopped,
  or 1 teaspoon dried tarragon
- ¼ teaspoon salt
  Few grains freshly-ground pepper
- ½ cup California Sauterne, Chablis
  or other white dinner wine

Roll chops in bread crumbs; press in as many as will stick to the surface of chops. (Do not use egg or milk.) Brown chops in butter. Add shallots or green onions, parsley, tarragon, salt and pepper. Cook 5 minutes. Reduce heat; add ¼ cup of the wine. Cover; simmer 15 to 20 minutes. Add remaining ¼ cup wine; continue simmering 10 to 15 minutes longer.

My choice of wine to accompany this dish:
CHILLED CALIFORNIA CHABLIS OR SAUTERNE

GOURMET VEAL BIRDS

(3 to 4 servings)

Mrs. William Bonetti, Charles Krug Winery, St. Helena

This is an original recipe, also entitled UCCELLI SCAPPATI.

- 8 very, very thin slices veal, cut 2 x 4"
- 8 very thin slices prosciutto
- 8 (½") cubes veal or chicken liver
- 8 wooden toothpicks
- 8 (¼") cubes salt pork
- 8 fresh sage leaves
- 2 tablespoons butter
- ¼ cup California Dry Semillon,
  Sauterne or other white dinner wine

Top each slice of veal with slice of prosciutto and cube of liver; roll up and secure with toothpick. Place cube of salt pork on one end of pick, and sage leaf on other. Melt butter in heavy skillet. Add veal rolls; brown slowly. Add wine. Cook 5 minutes, then cover; simmer slowly for 20 minutes more, or until fork-tender. Serve with whipped mashed potatoes or small buttered lima beans.

My choice of wine to accompany this dish:
CALIFORNIA JOHANNISBERG RIESLING

SALTIMBOCCA

(1 serving)

Mrs. Frank H. Bartholomew, Buena Vista Vineyards, Sonoma

This is a favorite dish at world-famous Giannino's in Milano. The chef there would tell you "the better the wine, the better the dish." This can, of course, be multiplied to serve any number of persons.

- 2 thin veal cutlets
  Salt and pepper
  Powdered sage
- 1 thin slice cooked ham or prosciutto
- 1 thin slice Jack, Provolone or other
  mild cheese
  Oil (half butter, if desired)
- 2 or 3 fresh mushrooms, chopped
- 2 teaspoons finely-chopped parsley
  Dash garlic
- 1 cup California Green Hungarian,
  Rhine or other white dinner wine
- 1 tablespoon butter

Season 1 cutlet with salt, pepper and sage. On top of cutlet, layer ham, cheese and other cutlet. Press edges of veal together firmly to hold filling; secure with wooden picks. Brown both sides well in heated oil. Remove to warmed shallow pan, or chafing dish, if preferred. In small pan, sauté mushrooms and parsley in butter with slight squeezing from garlic press. To pan in which meat was browned, add wine; heat, scraping up remaining browned bits into wine. Add mushrooms and parsley. Pour wine sauce over meat. Add 1 tablespoon butter; cook slowly over low heat until tender. Decorate with truffles, if desired.

My choice of wine to accompany this dish:
CHILLED CALIFORNIA GREEN HUNGARIAN

VEAL PAPRIKA

(6 servings)

W. W. Owen, California Grape Products Corp., Delano

        3 tablespoons oil
        2 pounds cubed veal
        ¼ cup flour
        1 cup hot water
        1 cup California Sauterne or
          other white dinner wine
        1 (4-oz.) can mushrooms, undrained
        2 tablespoons chopped parsley
        1 onion, thinly sliced
        1 teaspoon paprika
          Salt and pepper
        1 cup sour cream

Heat oil in heavy skillet. Add veal; brown slowly on all sides. Stir in flour, hot water and wine. Cook, stirring constantly, until mixture is thickened and smooth. Add mushrooms and liquid, parsley, sliced onion, paprika, salt and pepper. Simmer 1 hour, covered. Just before serving, pour in sour cream. Heat through.

NOTE: A chilled California Sauterne or Chablis would be an ideal wine-companion for this savory dish.

LUNCHEON CASSEROLE

(10 to 12 servings)

Mrs. Ernest A. Wente, Wente Bros., Livermore

        3 lbs. boneless veal, or 2 (2-lb.) pheasants,
          or 1 (4 to 5-lb.) stewing hen
        2 large onions
        6 stalks celery
        2 sprigs each: fresh rosemary
          and oregano, or 1 teaspoon
          dried rosemary and oregano
        1 teaspoon salt
        ⅛ teaspoon pepper
        2 cups California Sauterne or other
          white dinner wine
        ¼ cup oil
        ½ lb. fresh mushrooms, sliced
        2 (10½-oz.) cans cream of mushroom soup
        4 eggs, beaten
        4 cups (½ lb.) soda crackers,
          coarsely crushed

Place veal or poultry in large kettle with 1 onion (sliced), 2 stalks celery with leaves, herbs, salt, pepper and 1 cup wine. Add enough hot water to barely cover. Simmer 1 to 1½ hours, or until meat is tender. Cool; cut meat in bite-size pieces. Strain broth; set aside. Mince remaining onion; sauté in 2 tablespoons oil until soft. Mince remaining celery; add to onion along with 1 cup of reserved broth; simmer until celery is tender. Sauté mushrooms in 2 remaining tablespoons oil. Combine meat, onion and celery broth, mushrooms, soup, remaining 1 cup wine, 1 additional cup broth, eggs, crackers, salt and pepper. Place in large casserole. Put casserole in a pan of hot water (or place pan of hot water on lower rack of oven); bake in moderate oven (350°) for 1 hour.

NOTE: Would be marvelous with any chilled California white dinner wine, such as Sauterne, Chablis or Rhine Wine.

VEAL SUPREME

(8 servings)

Mrs. John G. Laucci, Franzia Brothers Winery, Ripon

        4 thin slices veal steak, cut in half
        ⅔ cup olive oil
        1½ tablespoons wine vinegar
        ¼ teaspoon oregano
        ¼ teaspoon sweet basil
        1 large onion
        1 large carrot
        1 small celery heart (or 3 stalks)
        2 sprigs parsley
        ½ cup dry mushrooms
        1 cup water
        2 eggs, beaten
          Fine, dry bread crumbs
          Salt and pepper
        ½ cup California Dry Sherry
        1 cup tomato juice
        8 to 10 potatoes, quartered

One hour before cooking, marinate veal in 3 tablespoons olive oil, wine vinegar, oregano and sweet basil. Meanwhile, finely chop onion, carrot, celery and parsley. Soak mushrooms in water 15 to 20 minutes; drain. Dip veal in beaten eggs, then coat both sides with bread crumbs. Heat remaining oil in large heavy skillet; brown veal over medium heat until golden. Remove veal to warm platter. Add to skillet the onions, celery, carrots, parsley, drained mushrooms, salt and pepper. Sauté over low heat, stirring often. Add Sherry and tomato juice; cook about 5 minutes. Return veal to skillet; simmer about ½ hour or until tender. Meanwhile, deep-fat fry quartered potatoes; add to veal; cook 5 to 10 minutes longer. Place veal on large platter, arrange potatoes around it and pour sauce over all. Garnish platter with large black olives and sprigs of parsley if desired.

NOTE: Wine accompaniment might be a hearty red, such as California Burgundy, or a mellow red "vino" type; or a chilled Rosé or white.

BAKED HAM SLICE SAUTERNE

(4 servings)

Mrs. E. F. Handel, East-Side Winery, Lodi

        1 (2-lb.) ham slice, cut 1½" thick
        ½ cup brown sugar, firmly packed
        3 tablespoons cornstarch
        1½ cups water
        1 tablespoon butter or margarine
        ½ cup raisins
        ½ cup California Sauterne or
          other white dinner wine

Cover ham with cold water; bring to boiling. Remove ham to oiled baking dish. Mix sugar and cornstarch in saucepan. Mix in water and butter; cook, stirring constantly, 5 minutes. Remove from heat; stir in raisins and wine. Pour over ham; bake, uncovered, in moderate oven (350°) for 45 minutes or until tender.

NOTE: Different and delightful, especially with the same good wine accompanying — or perhaps a chilled pink California Rosé. A very similar treatment is recommended by Mrs. James Concannon, Concannon Vineyard, Livermore.

HAM WITH ORANGES

(3 to 5 servings)

Brother Gregory, Mont La Salle Vineyards, Napa

    1 center slice of ham, ¾" thick
    2 tablespoons butter
    1 medium-size orange, peeled and sliced
    ½ cup California Light Muscat wine
      Salt, if desired

Trim any excess fat from ham. Brown ham in butter over moderately high heat. Add orange slices and cook about one minute (pushing ham to one side of pan). Add wine, lower heat and simmer 10 minutes. If wine cooks away, add just a little water, enough to capture essence in the pan. Remove ham; arrange on platter with orange slices. Scrape up gelatinous bits in pan; simmer until sauce is well blended (about 30 seconds). Ordinarily no salt is needed in sauce, but taste to make sure. Pour unthickened sauce over ham.

NOTE: A California white dinner wine, served well chilled alongside, would be the final touch of perfection.

BAKED HAM CHERRY-SHERRY

(8 to 10 servings)

Mrs. Otto E. Meyer, Paul Masson Vineyards, Saratoga

This recipe came from Finland. It is wonderful in cold weather.

    1 (1-lb.) can pitted black cherries
    2 oranges
    1 lemon
    1 teaspoon ginger
    1 cup dark brown sugar (packed)
    1 cup California Dry Sherry
    1 canned ham (about 6-lb. size)
    ¼ cup California brandy

Drain juice from cherries into saucepan. Blend with pulp and juice of oranges and lemon, ginger, brown sugar and Sherry. Simmer until sugar dissolves. Place ham in baking pan; pour on warm sauce. Bake, uncovered, in slow oven (300°) 25 minutes per lb. Baste with sauce every 15 to 20 minutes. About 15 minutes before done, pour brandy over ham. At end of cooking period, pour pan juices into saucepan and bring to boiling. Add cherries; simmer 5 minutes. Slice ham and serve with sauce. For first course with this menu I prefer broiled grapefruit, dotted with butter and brown sugar; then the Ham with Cherry-Sherry Sauce, with shredded carrots baked in a ring with petite green peas in center, and popovers. For dessert, perhaps a fresh fruit cup.

My choice of wine to accompany this dish:
CHILLED CALIFORNIA RIESLING

NOTE: An exceptionally fine ham treatment. If desired, sauce may be thickened slightly with a little cornstarch mixed with cold water. For Mrs. Meyer's fruit cup, see Dessert section.

BRAISED HAM FINANCIERE

(6 to 8 servings)

Rene Baillif, Buena Vista Vineyards, Sonoma

    4 or 5 lbs. uncooked smoked boneless ham
    1 medium-size onion
   12 whole cloves
    2 or 3 leeks
    1 bouquet garni (tie together few sprigs
        parsley, bay leaf and sprig of thyme
        or little powdered thyme)
    1 bottle California Sauterne, Chablis
        or other white dinner wine
   10 to 12 whole peppercorns
    2 cups California Sherry

Soak ham at least 24 hours, changing water several times. Place ham in large cooking utensil; cover with cold water; bring to boiling. Discard water; recover with fresh boiling water to which the onion (spiked with whole cloves), leeks and bouquet garni are added. Add white dinner wine; bring to boiling. Reduce heat; simmer 45 minutes to 1 hour. Add peppercorns last half hour of simmering. Remove ham to oven-proof dish or casserole; pour over Sherry. Bake covered in very slow oven (250°) 45 minutes to 1 hour longer, basting occasionally. Before serving, use remaining wine in pan as part of liquid to make a nice accompanying mushroom sauce, if desired. Should be served at a festive family dinner, with mashed potatoes, green beans and spinach.

My choice of wine to accompany this dish:
CALIFORNIA GREEN HUNGARIAN OR CABERNET ROSÉ

SHERRY-GLAZED HAM

(6 to 8 servings)

Mrs. Sydney Whiteside, Del Rio Winery, Lodi

    1 (3 or 4-lb.) canned ham
   1½ cups California Cream Sherry
    ½ cup apricot or peach jam
    ½ cup honey
      Dash nutmeg or cinnamon
    1 tablespoon cornstarch

Place ham in shallow baking pan and pour over ½ cup of the Sherry. Bake 1 hour in moderately slow oven (325°). Meanwhile, combine jam with honey and generous dash of nutmeg or cinnamon, in saucepan. Stir in cornstarch and remaining cup of Sherry. Cook, stirring constantly, until thick. Spoon sauce over ham and bake about 20 minutes more or until ham is glazed, basting occasionally. Good with candied sweet potatoes; hot fresh asparagus (if in season) or any other green vegetable; cinnamon apple salad, or fruit salad; relishes; rolls and pineapple sherbet.

My choice of wine to accompany this dish:
CHILLED CALIFORNIA ROSÉ

NOTE: Mrs. J. W. Fleming of Lockeford Winery, Lodi, recommends a very similar version of this taste-tempting sweet glaze. For a good sweet potato recipe for the menu, see Vegetable section.

HAM PORTUGUESE STYLE

(4 servings)

J. H. "Mike" Elwood, Llords & Elwood Wine Cellars, Fremont

½ cup dark brown sugar (packed)
1 lb. thick ham slice
4 tablespoons prepared mustard
2 tablespoons butter or margarine
¼ cup California Port

Rub sugar into both sides of ham; coat both sides with mustard. Melt butter in a heavy skillet; fry quickly, turning several times. Reduce heat; cover; cook slowly until tender, turning once. Remove to hot platter. Skim off fat from pan juices; stir in Port; heat to boiling. Pour over ham.

NOTE: A cool California Rosé would be fine with this unusually good ham.

FRUIT-SHERRY PORK CHOPS

(6 servings)

Mrs. Richard D. Dettman, Mont La Salle Vineyards, Napa

6 loin or rib pork chops, cut ¾" thick
¼ cup sifted flour
1½ teaspoons salt
½ teaspoon pepper
1 large orange
¼ cup brown sugar (packed)
2 tablespoons concentrated orange juice, undiluted
2 teaspoons concentrated lemon juice, undiluted
¾ cup California Dry Sherry
6 rings canned pineapple
½ cup juice from canned pineapple

Trim all but thin layer of fat from chops. In large heavy skillet, render some of the trimmed fat to coat pan lightly; discard excess fat. Rub flour seasoned with salt and pepper into both sides of meat; brown on both sides over medium heat. Cut 3 (¼") slices from center of orange; cut each slice in half; top each chop with piece of orange. Sprinkle with brown sugar. Combine concentrated orange and lemon juice with Sherry; pour over and around chops. Cover pan tightly; bake in moderately slow oven (325°) for 1 to 1½ hours, or until meat is fork-tender. Add pineapple rings and juice last half hour of cooking. Remove chops and fruit; thicken pan juices slightly with a little cornstarch mixed with cold water, if desired. With this I like to serve baked potatoes and fresh or frozen French-cut green beans, with a salad of cottage cheese, lime gelatin and crushed pineapple. Salad can be made a day ahead.

NOTE: A chilled California Sauterne or Vin Rosé would make beautiful sipping with this.

ROAST PORK ROSEMARY

(6 to 8 servings)

Mrs. Domenic E. Viotti, Jr., Viotti Winery, San Gabriel

This is a family recipe, taught to me by my mother-in-law, Mrs. Virginia Viotti.

2 tablespoons oil
1 (5 or 6-lb.) pork shoulder or pork loin roast
2 cups California Sherry
2 cups water
2 to 4 tablespoons fresh rosemary, or 4 to 6 tablespoons dried rosemary
1 tablespoon garlic powder, or 3 or 4 cloves garlic, minced
1 teaspoon monosodium glutamate
1 teaspoon salt
¼ teaspoon black pepper
½ cup flour
¼ cup butter or margarine

Heat oil in roasting pan or large Dutch oven. Brown roast slightly on all sides. Add Sherry, water and seasonings. Cook, covered, in slow oven (300°) for 4 to 5 hours (until very tender and meat pulls away from bone). Remove roast to platter. Skim off fat from pan juices; strain juices; set aside. Melt butter in saucepan. Blend in flour; mix well. Add juices slowly, stirring constantly. Cook over low heat until thickened. Thin to desired consistency with hot water or additional Sherry. Taste and correct seasoning, as desired. Slice onto serving platter, garnished with hot crab apples and parsley. Good with mashed potatoes, buttered green peas, mixed green salad and biscuits.

My choice of wine to accompany this dish:
CALIFORNIA CHAMPAGNE, SAUTERNE OR RHINE

EASY WINE PORK CHOPS

(6 to 8 servings)

Mrs. H. Peter Jurgens, Almaden Vineyards, Los Gatos

Trim excess fat from 6 to 8 thick loin pork chops; brown chops in heavy skillet. Season with salt and pepper. Add California Sauterne, Chablis or other white dinner wine to half-cover meat. Arrange quartered onions around chops. Bake in a moderate oven (350°) about 1 hour or until meat is fork-tender. Add more wine as needed.

NOTE: Sauterne is also used in PORK CHOPS ITALIANO, a recipe originated by Mrs. Domenic E. Viotti, Jr., of Viotti Winery, San Gabriel. Mrs. Viotti browns chops well, then transfers them to a casserole with a wine-tomato-garlic flavored sauce. She prefers either Rosé wine or Sauterne served alongside.

PORK TENDERLOIN IN WINE

(6 servings)

Mrs. Ronald G. Hanson, Di Giorgio Wine Co., Di Giorgio

> 6 serving-size pieces of
> pork tenderloin
> ½ teaspoon salt
> ⅛ teaspoon pepper
> 2 cups California Sauterne or
> other white dinner wine
> ½ bay leaf
> 1 onion with 2 cloves inserted
> 6 whole peppercorns
> 2 tablespoons butter or margarine

Lard pork; season with salt and pepper. Place in glass bowl; add wine, bay leaf, cloved onion, and peppercorns. Cover; marinate several hours. An hour before serving, remove meat, reserving marinade; drain and wipe dry. Heat butter in roasting pan; add meat. Roast in moderately hot oven (375°) until meat begins to brown, basting with pan drippings. Add 1 cup wine marinade, including spiced onion. Continue cooking until meat is tender and well done, basting frequently. Add more wine if necessary. Arrange on heated platter, garnished with border of cooked sauerkraut, plain boiled potatoes, and small glazed white onions.

NOTE: *And with a chilled bottle of California Sauterne or Rosé on the table, for maximum enjoyment. Pork chops may also be cooked this way.*

LODI JAMBALAYA

(4 to 6 servings)

Ferrer and Mildred Filipello, Calif. Wine Association, Lodi

This is a one-course meal.

> 1 lb. lean pork, cut in ¾" cubes
> 1 tablespoon olive oil
> 1 tablespoon butter or margarine
> 1 large onion, chopped
> 1 lb. ham, cut in ¾" cubes
> 4 cups water
> ½ cup California Sherry
> 1 teaspoon dry mustard
> 1 teaspoon celery salt
> ½ teaspoon savory
> ½ teaspoon thyme
> ¼ teaspoon black pepper
> 1½ cups long grain rice

In heavy skillet, brown pork in oil and butter; add onion and ham. Cook, stirring, until onion is soft (about 2 minutes). Remove meat and onion to large casserole. Combine water, Sherry and seasonings in saucepan; bring to boiling. Add rice to liquid, stir and remove from heat. Pour mixture over meat. Cover casserole; bake in moderate oven (350°) for 40 minutes. Stir once after 20 minutes.

Our choice of wine to accompany this dish:
CALIFORNIA CHABLIS OR ROSÉ

PEAS AND PORK ORIENTAL

(6 to 8 servings)

Mrs. William Perelli-Minetti, A. Perelli-Minetti & Sons, Delano

> 2 lbs. lean pork, cut in thin strips,
> about 2 x ¼ x ¼"
> 1 or 2 tablespoons oil
> 2 teaspoons salt
> ⅛ teaspoon pepper
> 3 tablespoons soy sauce
> ½ cup California Sherry
> 3 cups cold water
> 1 cup sliced onion
> 1 cup sliced celery
> 4 tablespoons cornstarch
> 2 vegetable bouillon cubes (optional)
> 2 (10-oz.) packages frozen peas,
> partially defrosted
> 1 (6-oz.) can sliced broiled-in-butter
> mushrooms, drained

Brown pork in oil. Add 1 teaspoon salt, pepper, 2 tablespoons soy sauce, ¼ cup Sherry and ½ cup water. Cover tightly; simmer 45 minutes to 1 hour, or until meat is tender. If needed, add more water, a tablespoon at a time. When tender, remove from pan. Blend remaining water with cornstarch, stirring until free of lumps. Stir into meat drippings. Add bouillon cubes, peas, and remaining teaspoon salt, ¼ cup Sherry and tablespoon soy sauce. Cook, stirring constantly, until sauce is thickened and peas are barely tender. Meanwhile, in second skillet, sauté onion and celery in a little hot oil until clear. Then add onions and celery to thickened sauce along with meat and mushrooms. Heat thoroughly. Good with rice or mashed potatoes, fruit salad or a rather bland molded salad, **or** fresh sliced tomatoes (no dressing) and cold, sliced marinated cucumbers.

My choice of wine to accompany this dish:
CALIFORNIA CLARET OR ZINFANDEL

MORGAN HILL PORK SAUSAGES

(4 servings)

Walter S. Richert, Richert & Sons, Morgan Hill

I invented this to leach out all those excessive spices used in sausage formulas. Place 1 pound link sausage in frying pan. Barely cover with California Sauterne, Chablis or other white dinner wine. Cover pan and simmer about 10 minutes. Remove cover; continue cooking over low heat until wine is evaporated and sausages are a delicate brown. Turn sausages over and lightly brown other side. Serve with hash-brown potatoes for brunch.

My choice of wine to accompany this dish:
CALIFORNIA RIESLING OR PINOT CHARDONNAY

GERMAN MEAT PIE

(8 servings)

Mrs. Justine Mirassou, Mirassou Vineyards, San Jose

This recipe has been handed down for generations in the family, to the present-day children and grandchildren. It is also a good way to cook rabbit.

        1 (6-lb.) pork shoulder roast
        2 pkgs. whole pickling spice
        2 onions, chopped
        2 cloves garlic, chopped
          Large bunch parsley
          Salt and pepper
        ¾ cup California wine vinegar
          California white dinner wine
        5 cups sifted all-purpose flour
     1¼ teaspoons baking powder
        1 teaspoon salt
        ½ cup rendered fat from meat
     1½ cups milk
        1 egg

Cut fat from roast; render fat and set aside. Cut meat in 1″ cubes. Combine pickling spice, onions, garlic, parsley, salt, pepper and wine vinegar. Pour over meat in a large glass or porcelain dish; add enough wine to cover meat. Marinate in refrigerator 3 days. Drain meat well, removing any whole spices left on meat. Sift together flour, baking powder and salt. Mix in rendered fat. Combine milk and egg; add to flour mixture. Roll out part of dough to fit a 13 x 9″ baking pan (don't roll too thin). Line pan; dough should lap well over sides. Fill with drained meat. Cover with pricked top crust, sealing with overlapping bottom crust. Bake in moderately hot oven (375°) for 1 hour, or until crust is rich brown. As the pie is quite rich, a crisp curly endive salad is all that is necessary to serve with it.

Our choice of wine to accompany this dish:
CHILLED CALIFORNIA WHITE RIESLING

SHERRY-GLAZED SPARERIBS

(4 to 6 servings)

Mrs. Bruno T. Bisceglia, Bisceglia Bros. Wine Co., Fresno

        1 side meaty spareribs
          Salt and pepper
        1 (8-oz.) can tomato sauce
        ½ cup California Sherry
        ½ cup honey
        2 tablespoons California wine vinegar
        2 tablespoons minced onion
        1 clove garlic, minced (optional)
        ¼ teaspoon Worcestershire sauce

Sprinkle spareribs with salt and pepper. Place in shallow baking pan and bake in hot oven (400°) for 40 minutes. Drain off fat. Combine remaining ingredients; pour over spareribs. Bake 1 hour longer in moderate oven (350°) or until tender. If desired, spareribs can be barbecued over low coals, brushing on the same sauce to glaze.

My choice of wine to accompany this dish:
A DRY RED CALIFORNIA DINNER WINE

LAMB STEW SANTA CLARA

(6 servings)

Mrs. H. Peter Jurgens, Almaden Vineyards, Los Gatos

        3 lbs. lean boneless lamb stew meat,
            cut in 1-inch cubes
        3 tablespoons butter or margarine
        2 level tablespoons flour
        2 cups California Mountain White, or
            Chablis or other white dinner wine
          Herb bouquet (tie together 3 or 4 sprigs
            parsley, sprig thyme and small bay leaf)
        1 large onion, sliced
        1 clove garlic, minced
          Salt and pepper

In large heavy skillet or Dutch oven, lightly brown lamb in butter. Stir in flour. Add wine and enough water to just cover meat. Add herb bouquet. Cover; simmer 1 hour, or until almost tender. Add onion, garlic, salt and pepper; continue cooking until meat is tender. Remove herb bouquet.

NOTE: *Since many stews are even better when some wine is added at the last minute, about ¼ cup of the wine called for can be saved for this purpose. The same kind of wine would also be delightful served with this succulent dish—or, perhaps, a California Rosé. Either one well chilled, of course.*

BRAISED LAMB BURGUNDY

(5 to 6 servings)

Mrs. Ferrer Filipello, California Wine Association, Lodi

        2 tablespoons bacon drippings or other fat
        2 lbs. boned lamb shoulder, cubed
        3 tablespoons flour
        1 cup California Burgundy or other
            red dinner wine
        1 cup beef stock (canned or
            bouillon-cube broth may be used)
        1 (8-oz.) can tomato sauce
          Pinch of rosemary
        ½ teaspoon salt
        ⅛ teaspoon pepper
        1 cup diced celery
        ½ cup chopped onion
        1 (4-oz.) can mushroom stems and
            pieces, drained
        2 tablespoons chopped parsley
        1 (10-oz.) pkg. frozen peas and
            carrots (optional)

Heat bacon drippings in Dutch oven or other heavy kettle; brown lamb slowly on all sides. Sprinkle flour over meat; stir well. Add ¾ cup of the wine, stock and tomato sauce; cook, stirring constantly, until mixture boils and thickens. Add rosemary, salt, pepper, celery and onion. Cover; simmer gently 1 hour, or until meat is tender, stirring occasionally. (Add a little more wine during cooking if necessary.) Shortly before serving, add mushrooms and parsley, and cooked and drained peas and carrots. At very last minute, stir in remaining ¼ cup wine.

My choice of wine to accompany this dish:
CHILLED CALIFORNIA VIN ROSÉ

MINT-STUFFED LEG OF LAMB

(6 to 8 servings)

Mrs. George Marsh, U. of Calif. Dept. of Food Technology

        1   (5 or 6-lb.) leg of lamb, boned
            Lemon juice
        ¼   teaspoon salt
            Pepper
        ⅓   cup golden or dark raisins, chopped
        1   small clove garlic, minced
        1   small onion, chopped
        ¼   cup butter or margarine
        3   tablespoons California Rosé
        3   cups soft stale bread crumbs, **or**
        1   (8-oz.) pkg. stuffing mix
        2   or 3 tablespoons chopped mint or parsley
            Pinch of dried rosemary or oregano
            Wine Lamb Baste (see below)

Rub lamb with lemon juice; sprinkle with salt and pepper. Combine other ingredients; mix well. Stuff lamb, fitting meat around mixture. Tie or hold in place with skewers. Place skewered side down in roasting pan. Roast in moderately hot oven (375°) for 2½ to 3 hours, basting often with Wine Lamb Baste.

WINE LAMB BASTE: Combine 1 cup California Rosé, ¼ cup soy sauce and ½ teaspoon **each** dried rosemary and oregano, in saucepan; simmer a few minutes before using to baste meat.

My choice of wine to accompany this dish:
CHILLED CALIFORNIA PINOT CHARDONNAY

BARBECUED LEG OF LAMB

(8 to 10 servings)

John Cadenhead, Wine Advisory Board, San Diego

        2   cups California red or white dinner wine
        2   teaspoons poultry seasoning
        2   teaspoons salt
        3   cloves garlic, peeled
        1   leg of lamb, boned and butterflied
            (spread out flat)

Combine wine, poultry seasoning, salt and garlic; pour over lamb in glass or porcelain dish. Marinate 12 to 24 hours, turning occasionally. Barbecue over charcoal, skin side up, for 30 minutes. Turn; cook 30 minutes more. Baste with remaining marinade while cooking. When done, slice across grain to serve. I prefer this with a pilaf, green salad, and strawberries in Port with brown sugar.

My choice of wine to accompany this dish:
CALIFORNIA BURGUNDY OR CLARET

NOTE: *For strawberry idea mentioned, see Dessert section.*

VINEYARD LAMB SHANKS

(4 servings)

Mrs. Fred Snyde, Woodbridge Vineyard Association, Lodi

        4   lamb shanks
        1   lemon, cut
            Salt and pepper
        1   tablespoon dry mustard
        1   medium-size onion, chopped
        1   clove garlic, chopped
        1   green pepper, chopped
        1   cup California Sauterne, Chablis
            or other white dinner wine

Rub shanks thoroughly with cut lemon; sprinkle with salt and pepper; coat with dry mustard. Put shanks in large casserole so they do not overlap. Add chopped vegetables and wine. Cover; cook in moderately slow oven (325°) for 2 hours. Turn during last hour of cooking. More wine may be added if they become dry. Serve with rice pilaf, green vegetable, tossed salad with oil and wine vinegar dressing, and lemon pie.

My choice of wine to accompany this dish:
THE SAME DRY WHITE WINE USED IN THE RECIPE

CURRIED LAMB SHANKS

(8 servings)

Mrs. E. A. Mirassou, Mirassou Vineyards, San Jose

        ½   cup cooking oil
        8   medium-size lamb shanks
        ⅓   cup flour
        1   tablespoon curry powder
        1   cup water
        1   cup California Sauterne, Chablis
            or other white dinner wine
        2   teaspoons salt
        ¼   teaspoon pepper
        ⅛   teaspoon garlic salt
        1   onion, thinly sliced

Heat oil in large, heavy skillet. Add shanks; brown well. Remove shanks from pan; blend flour and curry powder into drippings. Add water and wine. Cook, stirring constantly, until mixture is thickened and smooth. Add salt, pepper and garlic salt. Return shanks to pan; add onion slices. Cover tightly; simmer 1½ hours, or until meat is tender. Serve with rice, vegetable of the season, and green salad.

My choice of wine to accompany this dish:
A CHILLED CALIFORNIA WHITE DINNER WINE

NOTE: *California Dry Sherry flavors the lamb shanks cooked by Mrs. Herman Wente of Wente Bros., Livermore. She says Sauterne may also be used, and adds: "If dinner is delayed, add a little more wine, turn off the oven and do not worry."*

SHISH KABOB SAN JOAQUIN

(10 to 12 servings)

Zoe Vartanian, Crest View Winery, Inc., Fresno

- 1 (5 or 6-lb.) leg of lamb, boned
- 2 large onions, each cut in 6 wedges
- 6 to 8 large sprigs parsley, chopped
  Salt and pepper
- ½ cup California Burgundy or
  other dry red dinner wine
- 4 or 5 tomatoes, quartered
- 4 or 5 green peppers, cut in chunks

Trim part of fat from meat; cut meat in 2″ cubes. In large glass bowl, combine meat, onions, parsley, salt and pepper; pour over wine and mix thoroughly. Refrigerate overnight. When ready to barbecue, mix meat again; spear meat alternately with onions, tomatoes and peppers on long metal rods or small individual wooden skewers. Cook over coals to desired degree of doneness. Menu might include a rice pilaf, green beans and tossed green salad.

My choice of wine to accompany this dish:
CALIFORNIA VIN ROSÉ OR SPARKLING BURGUNDY

NOTE: *The top-quality meat, plus the marinating, makes this a melt-in-your-mouth treat. Can be cooked indoors under the oven broiler in cold weather.*

LIVER VINO BLANCO

(3 servings)

Lyman M. Cash, E. & J. Gallo Winery, Modesto

- 1 lb. beef or calf liver
  (lamb liver may also be used)
  Flour
- ¼ cup olive oil
- 1 or 2 cloves garlic
- 1 small onion, minced
  Salt and pepper
- 1 teaspoon basil, minced
- ½ cup California Sauterne, Chablis
  or other white dinner wine

Scald liver in boiling water; drain; wipe dry. Dredge with flour; brown slowly in hot oil. Remove from pan; keep warm. Split garlic in half lengthwise; place on wooden picks; brown in oil remaining in pan. Add onion; stir and cook 5 minutes. Return liver to pan; spoon over onion and garlic. Add salt, pepper and basil; pour over wine. Cover; simmer slowly ½ hour, basting every 10 minutes with pan liquid. Discard garlic before serving.

My choice of wine to accompany this dish:
CALIFORNIA CLARET, BURGUNDY OR PINOT NOIR

NOTE: *Over 200 years ago, a similar recipe for liver cooked with white wine was a favorite in England. You can't keep a good idea down! At the same winery, Mrs. Lewis Stern also makes a delicious liver-and-onion dish, but uses red wine in cooking.*

BREAST OF LAMB MENDOCINO

(4 servings)

Maynard Monaghan, Beaulieu Vineyard, Rutherford

- 3 lbs. breast of lamb, cut in
  serving-size pieces
- 1 cup California Sauterne or
  other white dinner wine
- ½ cup chili sauce
- 1 large onion, chopped
- ½ green pepper, chopped
- 1 tablespoon soy sauce
  Salt and pepper

Arrange pieces of lamb, fat side up, in single layer in shallow baking pan. Mix other ingredients; pour over lamb. Cover with pan lid or aluminum foil; let stand at room temperature 1 hour or so. Bake, covered, in moderately hot oven (375°) for 1 hour; uncover, and continue baking 1 hour more, basting often.

My choice of wine to accompany this dish:
CALIFORNIA ZINFANDEL OR GAMAY

LIVER WILLIAM

(4 servings)

Mrs. William Bonetti, Charles Krug Winery, St. Helena

This is an original recipe. It must be served immediately; better start cooking when everyone is already seated at the table.

- 1 lb. veal or calf liver
- 2 tablespoons butter or margarine
  Pinch each of rosemary and sage
  Salt
- 2 tablespoons California Dry Sherry
- 1 tablespoon California Port

Cut liver into small cubes; brown very quickly in butter. Add remaining ingredients, stirring a few minutes. Let simmer 2 or 3 minutes more; serve at once. (DO NOT OVERCOOK!) We like it with steamed rice or whipped mashed potatoes.

My choice of wine to serve with this dish:
CHILLED CALIFORNIA VIN ROSÉ

NOTE: *A different way of handling liver, and quite good.*

KIDNEY SAUTÉ

(4 to 6 servings)

Mrs. William V. La Rosa, Calif. Grape Products Corp., Delano

    12 lamb kidneys
    ¼ cup California wine vinegar
     1 medium onion, sliced
     1 cup celery, sliced
     3 tablespoons shortening
     3 tablespoons flour
     1 cup stock or water
     1 cup mushrooms, small whole or sliced
    1½ teaspoons salt
       Pepper
     1 teaspoon Worcestershire sauce
    ¼ cup California Dry Sherry

To prepare kidneys for cooking, cut each in half; remove fat and tubes from center. Cover with cold water to which ¼ cup wine vinegar has been added; soak ½ hour. Sauté onion and celery in shortening. Add kidneys; simmer 5 minutes. Stir in flour, then stock or water. When smooth, add mushrooms, salt, pepper and Worcestershire sauce. Simmer, covered, 30 minutes. Add Sherry. Serve over rice or cooked noodles. Menu might include celery, olives and carrot sticks; biscuits; crushed pineapple cole slaw; finally cookies.

My choice of wine to accompany this dish:
CALIFORNIA DRY ROSÉ OR SAUTERNE

NOTE: *Mrs. La Rosa says that veal or beef kidneys may also be prepared in this way. The larger beef kidneys should be soaked 1 hour.*

VEAL SWEETBREADS LOS GATOS

(8 servings)

Louis A. Benoist, Almaden Vineyards, Los Gatos

     2 lbs. veal sweetbreads
       Salt
    ½ lemon
    ¼ cup butter or margarine
    ¼ cup California Dry Sherry
    ½ cup beef stock (canned or
         bouillon-cube broth may be used)
     1 truffle, diced (optional)
     1 cup sliced sautéed mushrooms
    ½ cup pitted sliced green olives
       Rooster combs (optional)

Simmer sweetbreads 15 minutes in water to which salt and lemon have been added (or in Court Bouillon). Drain; plunge into ice water; clean and slice. Sauté in butter until slightly browned. Add Sherry and beef stock; reduce about ¼. Add truffle (if desired), mushrooms and olives. (Parboiled rooster combs may also be added, if you want to be very récherché.) Season to taste; serve with white rice.

My choice of wine to accompany this dish:
CALIFORNIA JOHANNISBERG RIESLING

BREADED SWEETBREADS MARSALA

(4 or 5 servings)

Mrs. Marvin B. Jones, Gibson Wine Company, Elk Grove

     2 pairs sweetbreads
     1 tablespoon vinegar or lemon juice
     1 egg, beaten
    ½ cup fine dry bread crumbs
    ½ teaspoon salt
    ⅛ teaspoon pepper
    ¼ cup melted butter or margarine
       Oil
    ½ cup California Marsala or Cream Sherry

Soak sweetbreads in cold water ½ hour, changing water twice during that time. Drain; plunge into boiling water to which vinegar or lemon juice has been added. Cook 5 minutes. Put into ice water for 10 minutes. Wipe dry, remove membranes. Cut into thick slices. Dip in beaten egg; then in bread crumbs seasoned with salt and pepper; then in melted butter. Dip again in egg; then bread crumbs. Cook to golden brown in small amount of heated oil. About 10 minutes before done, pour over wine; cover; continue cooking. A well-chilled white wine alongside brings out the delicate, delicious flavor.

My choice of wine to accompany this dish:
CALIFORNIA RIESLING OR HAUT SAUTERNE

SWEETBREADS Á LA KING

(6 to 8 servings)

Mrs. Hans Hyba, Paul Masson Vineyards, Saratoga

     2 lbs. sweetbreads
       Salt
    ⅓ cup onion rings
     1 green pepper, cut in rings
     2 tablespoons butter or margarine
     1 pimiento, cut in rings
     1 lb. fresh mushrooms, sliced
     4 teaspoons flour
    1½ cups hot milk or cream
     1 cup California Dry Sherry

Wash sweetbreads in cold water. Cover with salted water in a saucepan; bring to boiling. Reduce heat; simmer 5 minutes. Cool in broth. Meanwhile, sauté onions and green pepper in 2 teaspoons butter a few minutes; add pimiento. Remove cooled sweetbreads, reserving broth; cut in strips about 2" long and ½" thick. Add sweetbreads and mushrooms to onion mixture; stir very gently over low heat until hot (do not stir out of shape). Remove from heat. Melt remaining butter in saucepan; blend in flour. Stir in hot milk and 1 cup sweetbread broth; cook, stirring, until smooth and slightly thick. Add Sherry. Fold sauce into sweetbread mixture. Serve on toast; garnish with pieces of green pepper, mushrooms and pimiento.

NOTE: *Such a delectably rich dish deserves a kingly toast in California Champagne. If the budget interferes, serve a white dinner wine or Rosé.*

OXTAIL STEW WITH RED WINE

(6 to 8 servings)

H. Peter Jurgens, Almaden Vineyards, Los Gatos

- 3 lbs. oxtails, cut in 2" pieces
- 2 qts. water
- 1 bay leaf
- 1 large onion with 2 cloves inserted
- 4 carrots, sliced
- 4 stalks celery, sliced
- 2 sprigs parsley
- 1 tablespoon salt
- ¼ teaspoon pepper
- 6 white onions
- ¼ cup butter or margarine
- 3 level tablespoons flour
- 1 cup California Cabernet, Burgundy or other red dinner wine
- 1 teaspoon kitchen bouquet
- 2 tablespoons finely-chopped parsley

Simmer oxtails in water with bay leaf, spiced onion, carrot and celery slices, parsley, salt and pepper. Cook until tender (about 2 hours). Meanwhile, cook onions until tender; set aside. When oxtails are tender, melt butter in saucepan; stir in flour. Slowly add 2 cups of strained hot broth from oxtails and wine; stir constantly until smooth. Add kitchen bouquet. Taste; correct seasoning. Add pieces of oxtail, carrot slices and cooked onions. Simmer 10 minutes; sprinkle chopped parsley over stew before serving.

NOTE: *Utterly delicious. Liquid could be thickened slightly, if desired, or served in a bowl over French bread. Would be even more enjoyable with the same red wine served with the meal. Another who makes a good oxtail stew is Mrs. Lewis A. Stern of E. & J. Gallo Winery, Modesto, who adds this idea: "If we have company, I serve the stew from my silver chafing dish, and I heat 3 tablespoons California brandy, ignite it and pour the flaming spirits over the oxtails at the table. This bit of ceremony adds charm and delightful interest to such a dish as stew. I serve rice or mashed potatoes with this oxtail recipe, as everyone loves the gravy."*

SWEET-SOUR TONGUE

(6 servings)

Mrs. Eugene Morosoli, Wine Advisory Board, San Francisco

- ¼ cup butter or olive oil
- 1 small onion, sliced
- 1 tablespoon flour
- ¼ cup California Burgundy or other red dinner wine
- 2 tablespoons California red wine vinegar
- ½ cup sweet pickle, chopped
- ½ cup sweet pickle juice
- 1 bouillon cube dissolved in 1 cup hot water, or 1 cup broth
- 2 tablespoons catsup
- ⅛ teaspoon *each*: rosemary, thyme, sage
- 1 clove garlic, finely chopped
- 2 tablespoons chopped parsley
- 18 slices boiled beef tongue

Heat butter or oil in saucepan; sauté onion until slightly brown. Stir in flour to make a paste; add all remaining ingredients, except tongue. Simmer ½ hour, stirring occasionally. Add tongue; heat through 5 to 10 minutes.

My choice of wine to accompany this dish:
CALIFORNIA BURGUNDY OR A RED "VINO" TYPE

TONGUE NAPA VALLEY

(3 or 4 servings)

Mrs. Robert Mondavi, Charles Krug Winery, St. Helena

- 1 fresh tongue (calf or veal)
  Butter or margarine
- 1 onion, chopped
- 2 carrots, cut in small cubes
- 1 cup California Sauterne, Chablis or other white dinner wine
- 1 cup tomato sauce
  Salt and pepper
- 2 tablespoons chopped pickles or relish
- ½ teaspoon chopped oregano
- 1 tablespoon fresh chopped parsley

Cover tongue with water; bring to boiling. Reduce heat; simmer 20 minutes. Cool until easy to handle; remove skin. Brown meat in butter to which onion and carrots have been added. When brown, add wine, tomato sauce, salt and pepper. Simmer, covered, 45 minutes. Skim off excess fat. Remove tongue, keeping warm. Add chopped pickles and herbs to pan liquid. Cut tongue in thin slices, arrange on serving platter and pour sauce over all.

NOTE: *Either red or white dinner wine would be a pleasurable accompaniment — and especially a chilled Rosé.*

LAMB TONGUES BON VIN

(8 servings)

Mrs. E. A. Mirassou, Mirassou Vineyards, San Jose

This recipe has been handed down through the family for generations, through Ed's mother and grandmother.

- 12 lamb tongues
- ½ cup California wine vinegar
- 2 onions, chopped
- 6 stalks celery, chopped
- 1 clove garlic
- ¼ cup oil
- ¼ cup flour
- 2 cups beef or chicken broth
  Salt and pepper
  Chopped parsley
- ½ cup California Sauterne or other white dinner wine

Place tongues in saucepan; add wine vinegar and enough water to cover. Let stand 2 hours; bring to boiling and simmer 2 hours. Remove tongues, reserving broth. Remove skin from tongues; cut into 1" pieces. Sauté onion, celery and garlic in oil until almost soft. Add flour, blending well. Stir in broth; cook slowly until thickened, stirring constantly. Add other ingredients and pieces of tongue; heat through. Serve over rice, with fresh vegetable of the season and green salad.

My choice of wine to accompany this dish:
A CHILLED CALIFORNIA WHITE DINNER WINE

TRIPPA NOVARESE

(8 to 10 servings)

Dino Barengo, Acampo Winery, Acampo

This is a modified recipe. The original basic tripe recipe is prepared in the province of Novarra in Italy. I learned it from my father, the late Camillo Barengo, a native of this province.

    ½ cup butter or margarine
    ¼ cup olive oil
    3 large yellow onions, thinly sliced
    5 lbs. honeycomb tripe, cut in ¾ x 1½" strips
    2⅓ tablespoons salt
    2 lemons
    2 (10½-oz.) cans consommé
    1 (20-oz.) can chicken broth
    1 teaspoon pepper
    ½ teaspoon thyme
    ½ teaspoon oregano
    1 large or 2 small cloves garlic, pressed
    ¼ to ½ teaspoon cayenne pepper
    1 teaspoon monosodium glutamate
    4 bay leaves
      Dash cloves
    4 medium-size carrots, sliced ½" thick
    6 stalks celery, cut in 1" pieces
    1 small green pepper, cut in ½" squares
    1 (1-lb. 4-oz.) can solid-pack tomatoes,
      undrained and coarsely chopped
    ½ cup California Dry Sherry
    ½ cup California Sauterne or
      other white dinner wine
    2 tablespoons finely-chopped parsley
      Grated Parmesan cheese (optional)

Melt butter with olive oil in Dutch oven or large soup kettle; sauté onions until slightly browned; set aside. Cover tripe with cold water in large saucepan; add 2 tablespoons salt and juice of 1 lemon. Bring to boiling; cook 3 or 4 minutes. Drain; rinse with warm water. Drain tripe well; combine with onions, oil and butter in Dutch oven. Add consommé, chicken broth, 1 teaspoon salt, pepper, juice of other lemon and seasonings. Simmer 2½ hours. Add vegetables and wines; simmer 1 hour more. Taste and correct seasoning. Stir in parsley. Serve from soup tureen with topping of Parmesan cheese, if desired. Sour-dough Italian bread and plenty of California Burgundy are necessary complements to this dish. Menu might also include green salad with simple olive oil and wine vinegar dressing; and assorted fruits and cheeses served with California Port as a dessert.

My choice of wine to accompany this dish:
ANY CALIFORNIA DRY RED DINNER WINE

NOTE: *Two other delicious and still different tripe recipes were submitted by Mrs. William V. La Rosa of California Grape Products Corp., Delano, and Mrs. Robert Mondavi of Charles Krug Winery, St. Helena.*

TRIPE PARISIENNE

(6 to 8 servings)

Mrs. Rene Baillif, Buena Vista Vineyards, Sonoma

This old recipe originated in France in the province of Normandy, but it is served "par excellence" in Paris, where some restaurants have for many generations specialized in this dish.

    4 to 4½ lbs. honeycomb tripe,
      cut in 2" squares
    1 bottle California Sauterne or
      other white dinner wine
    1 (14-oz.) can condensed chicken broth
      Salt and pepper
    1 bay leaf
      Dash thyme
    1 onion, chopped
    3 or 4 green onions, chopped
    ½ cup chopped parsley
    1 (1-lb.) veal shank, cut in 2" cubes
    12 whole peppercorns
    3 or 4 tablespoons California brandy

Cover tripe with slightly salted water; bring to boiling; cook 30 minutes. Drain thoroughly; place in large heavy kettle. Cover with boiling water, wine and chicken broth. Season with salt and pepper. Add bay leaf, thyme, chopped onion, green onions and parsley. Bring to medium boil. Cook about ½ hour, skimming foam thoroughly. Add veal. Cover and bake in slow oven (250°) for 4 or 5 hours. Add more hot water and wine during cooking, if necessary. During last 15 minutes, add peppercorns and brandy. Carefully remove bones from veal. Serve very hot in individual oven-proof casseroles. Almost a meal in itself, it can be served with steamed potatoes and followed by green salad and cheese.

My choice of wine to accompany this dish:
CALIFORNIA GREEN HUNGARIAN OR GREY RIESLING

NOTE: *This and the Italian tripe recipe on this page could both receive the last-minute treatment indicated at the start of the Meat section: a little more wine poured in just before serving, for those who prefer a more pronounced wine flavor.*

POULTRY

Chicken, Turkey, Duck, Goose, Squab with Wine

"A hot bird and a cold bottle" sums up one of man's happiest conditions at the dining table. And as in the case of meats, the bird is juicier, tenderer than ever, when cooked as well as served with a fragrant wine from California's vineyards. Wine is indispensable for perfect poultry. You'll enjoy these time-tried recipes. (For suitable sauces and wild game bird ideas, grouped separately, see sections starting on Pages 79 and 65.)

CHICKEN ZELLERBACH

(7 or 8 servings)

J. D. Zellerbach, Hanzell Winery, Sonoma

> 2 (3-lb.) frying chickens or
> 1 (6-lb.) roasting chicken
>   Flour, seasoned with salt and pepper
> 1 cup butter or margarine
> ½ cup chopped onion
> 1 chicken bouillon cube dissolved in
>   1 cup hot water; or 1 cup chicken broth
> 1½ cups California Pinot Chardonnay
>   or other white dinner wine
> ½ cup California Marsala or Cream Sherry
> 1 teaspoon marjoram
> 1 teaspoon thyme
> ½ bay leaf
> ¼ teaspoon curry powder
> ½ teaspoon paprika

Cut chicken in serving size pieces; dredge in seasoned flour. Melt ½ cup butter in skillet; fry chicken on all sides over moderate heat until tender. Meanwhile, melt remaining ½ cup butter in saucepan; sauté onions until yellow. Add other ingredients. A few minutes before serving, add chicken to sauce; heat thoroughly. If more sauce is desired, simply add a little more wine or chicken broth.

NOTE: A rich, sound chicken of excellent flavor. Would be especially good served with chilled glasses of the same white dinner wine, or a Chablis.

QUICK FEAST FOR THE HURRIED: Pick up a barbecued chicken at the butcher's or delicatessen on your way home. Have it cut in half. In shallow baking pan, melt ¼ cup butter; add about ¼ cup California Light Muscat, Cream Sherry or Muscatel. Roll chicken halves in this mixture, then sprinkle with instant minced onion, salt and monosodium glutamate. Heat thoroughly in same pan in moderately hot oven (350 to 375°), about 20 minutes. Baste once or twice with wine-butter from pan bottom. Pour any remaining sauce over hot chicken just before serving to two hungry persons, with glasses of cold California Rhine or Rosé alongside.

ROASTED CHICKEN CALABRIAN

(8 servings)

M. J. Filice, San Martin Vineyards Co., San Martin

Delicious, exotic—one of Italy's famous, classic fryer dishes (Pollo alla Calabrese). In proper platter, has tremendous eye appeal. When garnished attractively with figs, orange slices and parsley, this dish is a composition of epicurean art.

> 2 (2½ or 3-lb.) frying chickens, quartered
>   Olive oil
> 1 teaspoon dried oregano, crumbled
> 2 teaspoons minced fresh parsley
> 2 cloves garlic, minced
>   Salt
>   Monosodium glutamate
> 1 cup California Malvasia Bianca, Light Muscat,
>   Sauterne or other white dinner wine
> 1 lemon
> 1 (1-lb. 1-oz.) can Kadota figs, drained
> 1 medium-size thin-skinned orange,
>   sliced ¼" thick
>   California Sherry

Brush chicken with oil. Sprinkle with seasonings. Place in shallow baking pan, skin side up. Bake, uncovered, in hot oven (400°) for 20 to 25 minutes, or until brown. Combine wine and juice of lemon; baste chicken often during cooking. Meanwhile, prick figs with fork; marinate figs and orange slices in Sherry. Turn chicken; brown other side 15 to 20 minutes. Taste; correct salt (should have slightly salty taste). Add figs and orange slices; continue cooking 5 to 10 minutes, or until golden. (If chicken seems dry, finish basting with Sherry marinade from fruit.) Menu may include soup, tossed green salad, spaghettini, fresh fruit, good music, and a good book or good friends in conversation.

My choice of wine to accompany this dish:
CALIFORNIA MALVASIA BIANCA
OR CHABLIS OR SAUTERNE

BAKED CHICKEN ROSÉ

(3 or 4 servings)

Mrs. Joseph S. Concannon, Jr., Concannon Vineyard, Livermore

While a dry white wine is quite appropriate in this recipe, we prefer the flavor from cooking it with a dry Rosé. With it, however, we like to serve a chilled white.

- 1 (2½ or 3-lb.) chicken, quartered or cut in large serving pieces
  Flour seasoned with salt and pepper
- 6 tablespoons butter or margarine
- 2 tablespoons flour
- ¾ cup chicken bouillon (canned or bouillon-cube broth may be used)
- ½ cup California Rosé or a white dinner wine
- ¼ cup thinly sliced green onions (including tops)
- 1 (4-oz.) can mushrooms, or ½ cup fresh mushrooms sautéed in butter
- 1 (9-oz.) pkg. frozen artichoke hearts (cooked according to pkg. directions)

Dust chicken with seasoned flour. Melt 4 tablespoons butter in shallow baking pan. Place chicken in pan, skin side down; bake, uncovered, in moderate oven (350 to 375°) 45 minutes to 1 hour, or until almost tender. Meanwhile, melt other 2 tablespoons butter in saucepan. Stir in flour. Add bouillon and wine; cook, stirring constantly, until thickened and smooth. Remove chicken from oven. Turn pieces over; sprinkle with onions, mushrooms and cooked artichokes. (Water chestnuts or thinly sliced fresh tomatoes may be substituted for artichoke hearts.) Pour over sauce. Return to oven; reduce heat to 325°; bake 25 to 30 minutes longer. We serve this usually with a rice Milanese, with chicken sauce on top, and fresh asparagus if in season.

My choice of wine to accompany this dish:
CHILLED CALIFORNIA CHABLIS OR MOSELLE

BAKED CHICKEN CALIFORNIAN

(3 or 4 servings)

Jack Pandol, Delano Growers Co-Op. Winery, Delano

- 1 (3 or 4-lb.) frying chicken, quartered or cut in large serving pieces
  Salt and pepper
- 1 onion, sliced
- 2 slices bacon, diced
- ¼ cup water
- ¼ cup California Sherry

In a shallow baking pan, place chicken pieces snugly in a single layer, skin side up. Sprinkle generously with salt, pepper; add onion and bacon. Sprinkle with water and Sherry. Cover; bake in moderate oven (350°) ½ hour. Remove cover; bake 20 to 30 minutes longer or until chicken is tender. Serve with pilaf or steamed rice, vegetable and green salad.

My choice of wine to accompany this dish:
ANY CALIFORNIA WHITE DINNER WINE

EASY ROAST CHICKEN

(8 servings)

Mrs. Herman Ehlers, East-Side Winery, Lodi

- 2 (2 or 2¼-lb.) frying chickens, quartered
- ¼ cup butter or margarine
  Salt and pepper
- 2 cups California Sauterne or other white dinner wine
- ½ cup chicken stock (canned or bouillon-cube broth may be used)
- ½ cup thinly sliced green onions
- ½ cup chopped celery
- ¼ cup finely-chopped parsley

Rub skin side of chicken with butter; sprinkle with salt and pepper. Place skin side down in shallow baking pan; bake in hot oven (425°) for 15 minutes. Combine remaining ingredients; pour over chicken. Bake 30 minutes longer, basting several times. Reduce heat to 350°, turn chicken skin side up; continue baking and basting until chicken is done and as brown as desired. Pan drippings make a good gravy.

NOTE: A most pleasing flavor, and quite simple to prepare. Serve the same wine, chilled, on the side.

CHICKEN IN THE POT

(4 servings)

Mrs. Stanford J. Wolf, Paul Masson Vineyards, Saratoga

This is even more flavorful if made the day before and reheated.

- 1 roasting chicken
- 1 lemon, cut in half
  Salt and pepper
- 2 tablespoons butter or margarine
- 2 cups chicken broth (chicken stock base broth may be used)
- 1 stalk celery
- 2 tomatoes
- 2 onions
- 2 carrots
- ¼ lb. green beans
  Small bunch parsley, chopped
- 2 cups California Sauterne or other white dinner wine

Rub chicken inside and out with cut lemon, salt and pepper. Melt butter in Dutch oven; brown chicken on all sides. Add broth; simmer 45 minutes. Meanwhile, cut vegetables in chunks. Add to chicken with wine; simmer 1 hour longer, or until chicken and vegetables are tender. Taste and correct seasoning. Preferred menu with the chicken: rice, large stuffed mushrooms, and salad of watercress and bean sprouts.

My choice of wine to accompany this dish:
CHILLED CALIFORNIA ROSÉ OR RIESLING

NOTE: Those who enjoy a particularly winey flavor can pour a little more wine into the pot immediately before serving. There are many variations on this great classic treatment for chicken (cooked in wine, with vegetables). The dish has a long history, and was a favorite of Henri IV of Navarre.

CLASSIC CHICKEN IN WINE

(4 to 6 servings)

Mrs. Frank H. Bartholomew, Buena Vista Vineyards, Sonoma

In a flower-filled garden high above the ancient old-world village of Tramin, this savory Coq au Vin was served to us in a silver bowl, on a tray garlanded with spring flowers. Cuttings from steep hillside vineyards above the town have been growing in California more than 100 years, producing one of the finest of dry white wines.

  1 (5 or 6-lb.) roasting or fricassee chicken,
    cut in large pieces
    Salt and pepper
 ¼ cup chicken fat
 ¾ cup butter or margarine
 ⅓ cup California brandy
  3 cups California Gewurz Traminer,
    Rhine or other white dinner wine
  1 cup chicken broth (canned or
    bouillon-cube broth may be used)
  1 teaspoon marjoram
12 small white onions
12 tiny new carrots
12 small new potatoes
    Chopped parsley

Wipe chicken with damp cloth; sprinkle with salt and pepper. Melt chicken fat and ¼ cup butter in large, heavy skillet or Dutch oven; brown chicken slowly on all sides (about 10 minutes). Pour over brandy; ignite. When flames die down, add wine, broth and marjoram. Cover; place in slow oven (250 to 300°) about 3 hours or until chicken is nearly tender. (Add a little more wine during cooking, if necessary.) Meanwhile, brown onions, carrots and potatoes in remaining ½ cup butter. Add to chicken; continue cooking about 30 minutes or until vegetables are tender. Sprinkle with chopped parsley. Serve with green salad and hot, crusty, sour-dough French bread.

My choice of wine to accompany this dish:
CHILLED CALIFORNIA GEWURZ TRAMINER

NOTE: *The flaming brandy treatment for chicken is also favored by Mrs. Marvin B. Jones of Gibson Wine Company, Elk Grove. Mrs. Jones' Chicken au Vin is simmered in a combination of red and white dinner wines (after first browning, then flaming). Egg yolks, cream and flour are finally added, to make a marvelous gravy. She prefers California Rosé with the dish— "a pleasing and striking accompaniment."*

STILL ANOTHER luscious brandy-and-wine treatment for chicken (unflamed) features California Dry Vermouth. Brown chicken parts in ¼ lb. butter, add salt and bare hint of chopped green onions, shallots or garlic, if desired. Pour over 1 cup Dry Vermouth and 2 or 3 tablespoons California brandy; simmer 20 minutes, covered. Result is rich and moist; good treatment also for pheasant. Leftover clear sauce can be refrigerated for later flavoring of other dishes, even vegetables.

BRANDIED FRICASSEE CHICKEN

(6 servings)

H. Peter Jurgens, Almaden Vineyards, Los Gatos

  1 (4-lb.) roasting or fricassee chicken,
    cut in serving pieces
 ¼ cup sifted flour
 ½ cup butter or margarine
  1 thin slice raw ham, diced
10 small onions, peeled
  2 tablespoons California brandy
    Herb bouquet (tie together 3 or 4 sprigs
     parsley, sprig thyme and small bay leaf)
    Salt and pepper
  1 cup mushrooms (optional)
  1 cup California Pinot Noir, Burgundy
    or other red dinner wine

Dredge chicken in flour; sauté in melted butter until nicely browned. Add ham and onions; cook until lightly browned. Pour over brandy; ignite. When flames die down, add herb bouquet, salt, pepper, mushrooms and wine. Cover tightly; simmer until chicken is very tender, about 2½ hours. Discard herb bouquet. If desired, thicken gravy with a little cornstarch mixed with cold water.

My choice of wine to accompany this dish:
CALIFORNIA PINOT NOIR

NOTE: *The brandy in cooking adds a wonderfully subtle flavor. Another using this method in a similar recipe is Mrs. Walter Staley of Western Grape Products, Kingsburg. Mrs. Staley says a package of frozen peas may be added during the last half-hour, which would add attractive color. She prefers to serve a dry white wine with her chicken, although she uses red wine in the cooking.*

SUPERB BARBECUED CHICKEN

(Any amount)

Nino Muzio, California Growers Wineries, Cutler

Remove wing tips, ends of leg bones and excess fat from chicken (quartered, halved or whole). Place chicken in wooden bowl, tub or glass container. Cover with ½ California white dinner wine and ½ California Dry Sherry (or **all** white wine or Sherry); marinate 12 hours in refrigerator. Drain off wine; dry with paper towels, brush with thin layer of olive oil, and season with salt, pepper, savory salt, onion salt and poultry seasoning. Layer chicken in bowl, with additional olive oil, salt, pepper, parsley, rosemary and a few garlic chips on each layer. Cover bowl; refrigerate 12 to 15 hours. Barbecue over medium-hot coals. When almost done, baste with a mixture of ½ soy sauce and ½ melted butter or margarine.

NOTE: *Chilled California white dinner wine or Rosé would be perfect with this—or a red dinner wine, since the chicken is highly seasoned.*

CHICKEN PARISIENNE

(4 servings)

Mrs. A. H. Burton, Roma Wine Co., Fresno

This is a good way to use leftover chicken, or stewing chicken.

  1 (10-oz.) pkg. frozen broccoli
  2 tablespoons butter, melted
  2 tablespoons flour
  1 cup milk
  ½ teaspoon salt
  ¼ cup California Sherry
  4 to 8 slices cooked chicken
     (or, turkey may be used)
  1 cup grated Cheddar cheese

Cook broccoli according to package directions. Meanwhile, in small saucepan, blend butter and flour; slowly stir in milk. Cook, stirring constantly, until mixture is smooth and thick. Add salt; stir in Sherry. Drain broccoli; place in 4 individual casseroles. Top with chicken or turkey slices. Pour over wine sauce; top with grated cheese. Broil until cheese is melted and delicately browned. With this dish we like a tossed green salad with tomatoes, rolls, and ice cream or sherbet for dessert.

My choice of wine to accompany this dish:
CHILLED CALIFORNIA GREY RIESLING

CHICKEN CACCIATORE

(4 to 6 servings)

Mrs. L. J. Berg, Mont La Salle Vineyards, Napa

  ¼ cup olive oil
  2 (3 or 4-lb.) frying chickens, cut
    in serving pieces
  2 cloves garlic, minced
  1 teaspoon salt
  ¼ teaspoon pepper
  ½ teaspoon crumbled oregano
  ½ teaspoon crumbled basil
  1 (1-lb. 4-oz.) can tomatoes
  1 (3-oz.) can mushrooms, drained
  ¼ cup California Sherry
    Parsley

Heat oil in chicken fryer or heavy skillet. Brown chicken until golden-brown. Add garlic, salt, pepper, oregano, basil, tomatoes and mushrooms. Cover; simmer about 25 minutes or until tender. Add Sherry; cook 10 minutes longer. Sprinkle with parsley.

My choice of wine to accompany this dish:
CALIFORNIA DRY SAUVIGNON BLANC
OR JOHANNISBERG RIESLING

NOTE: *Another delicious recipe with similar combination of ingredients is used by Mrs. John G. Laucci of Franzia Brothers Winery, Ripon. Her version is called CHICKEN HUNTER STYLE, and includes sage leaves and potatoes (deep-fried first, then cooked 10 minutes with chicken). Excellent Cacciatores are also made by Mrs. Frank G. Cadenasso of Cadenasso Winery, Fairfield; and Mrs. August Sebastiani of Samuele Sebastiani, Sonoma.*

CHICKEN RAPHAEL WEILL

(4 servings)

Louis A. Benoist, Almaden Vineyards, Los Gatos

This delicate chicken dish, with its melting celestial sauce, was named after the gourmet uncle of the owner of one of San Francisco's oldest department stores. It is interesting to note that a famous Paris restaurant includes this dish on its menu. Quite a feather in the culinary cap of California!

  2 (2-lb.) broiling chickens
  ½ lemon
    Salt and pepper
    Flour
  ¼ cup butter or margarine
  3 medium-size green onions, chopped
  ½ cup California Pinot Blanc, Sauterne
    or other white dinner wine
  2 tablespoons rich chicken broth
  4 egg yolks
  1 cup heavy cream
    Freshly-grated nutmeg
    Cayenne pepper
    Minced chives
    Parsley
    Chervil and tarragon (optional)
    Few drops lemon juice

Cut chickens into serving size pieces. Rub with lemon; sprinkle with salt and pepper; dust with flour. Heat butter in heavy skillet; sauté chicken until golden on all sides. Cover; simmer 10 minutes. Add onions; cook 5 minutes longer, shaking pan frequently. Pour over wine; simmer 2 minutes. Add rich chicken broth (can be made by reducing ¼ cup chicken broth by half). Cook, covered, over low heat 10 minutes or until chicken is fork-tender, shaking pan frequently (be careful not to boil). Meanwhile, beat egg yolks with heavy cream; season to taste with nutmeg, cayenne, chives, parsley and, if desired, chervil and tarragon. Just before serving, pour cream mixture over chicken in pan. Cook over very low heat, stirring or shaking pan constantly, until sauce thickens. Add a few drops lemon juice. Arrange chicken on warm platter; pour over sauce; serve at once.

My choice of wine to accompany this dish:
CALIFORNIA PINOT CHARDONNAY

LODI CHICKEN

(4 servings)

Mrs. Hubert Mettler, Guild Wine Co., Lodi

- 1 (10½-oz.) can cream of mushroom soup
- 1 cup sour cream
- 1 (4-oz.) can button or sliced mushrooms, undrained
- ½ cup California Sherry
- 1 frying chicken, quartered
- Paprika

Combine soup, sour cream, mushrooms and Sherry. Pour over chicken in baking pan. Sprinkle with paprika. Bake, covered, in a moderate oven (350°) for 1 or 1¼ hours, or until tender. Serve with baked potatoes, a hot vegetable such as peas and carrots, green tossed salad, rolls, and cookies for dessert.

My choice of wine to accompany this dish:
ANY FAVORITE CALIFORNIA WHITE DINNER WINE

NOTE: *This is an exceptionally easy recipe, providing lots of tantalizing gravy for the potatoes (or perhaps noodles or rice). Many good cooks like the combination of sour cream, mushrooms and California Sherry with baked chicken. It's an ever-pleasing blend, recommended also by Mrs. A. Jensen of Gemello Winery, Mountain View; and Mrs. Alvin Ehrhardt of United Vintners, Inc., Lodi.*

CHICKEN AND RICE CREOLE

(6 servings)

Mrs. William Perelli-Minetti, A. Perelli-Minetti & Sons, Delano

- 1 (4-lb.) fricassee chicken, cut in serving-size pieces
- ½ cup flour
- 2 teaspoons salt
- ¼ teaspoon white pepper
  Heated shortening or cooking oil
- 2 cups canned tomatoes
- ¼ cup instant minced onion
- ¼ cup dried sweet pepper flakes
- 1½ cups water
- ½ cup California Chablis or other white dinner wine
- ½ bay leaf
- 1 tablespoon dried parsley flakes
- ½ teaspoon thyme
- 1 teaspoon salt
  Hot cooked rice

Coat chicken with flour seasoned with salt and pepper. Brown in hot shortening. Add tomatoes, onion, sweet pepper, water, wine and bay leaf; cover tightly; simmer 1 hour. Add parsley, thyme and salt; simmer 15 to 20 minutes longer, or until chicken is fork-tender. Serve over hot cooked rice, with menu including green peas and tossed salad.

My choice of wine to accompany this dish:
CALIFORNIA SAUTERNE OR CHABLIS

CHICKEN ALMOND

(6 to 8 servings)

Mrs. Joseph S. Concannon, Jr., Concannon Vineyard, Livermore

I've found this to be one of the simplest chicken recipes, especially handy when supervising our three pre-school children.

- 1 (10½-oz.) can cream of mushroom soup
- 1 (10½-oz.) can cream of celery soup
- 1 cup grated Cheddar cheese
- ¾ cup California Sauvignon Blanc, Chablis or other white dinner wine
- 2 (3-lb.) frying chickens, quartered or cut in large serving pieces
- ⅓ cup sliced almonds

Combine soups, cheese and wine in large shallow baking pan. Add chicken, bone side down. Cover pan with foil; bake in moderately slow oven (325°) 2½ hours. Remove foil; add sliced almonds. Bake 30 minutes longer. The recipe sauce is good as a gravy on rice or mashed potatoes.

My choice of wine to accompany this dish:
CALIFORNIA SAUVIGNON BLANC OR WHITE RIESLING

SMOTHERED CHICKEN

(4 servings)

Mrs. Harold E. Roush, Guild Wine Co., Lodi

You can also use this same easy mushroom sauce to enhance the flavor of Swiss steak or pork chops as they bake.

- 1 (4-lb.) frying chicken, cut in serving pieces
- ¼ cup flour
  Salt
- 3 tablespoons oil
- 1 cup diced celery
- ½ cup diced onion
- 1 (10½-oz.) can cream of mushroom soup
- ¼ cup California Cream Sherry

Coat chicken with flour seasoned with salt. Heat oil in heavy skillet; brown chicken. Combine remaining ingredients; pour over chicken. Cover; bake in a moderate oven (350°) for 30 minutes. Uncover; bake 15 minutes longer. The menu with this might include baked rice (using broth from neck, wing tips, etc., for liquid); buttered green beans; crisp apple-celery-pineapple salad and toasted French rolls.

My choice of wine to accompany this dish:
CALIFORNIA WHITE DINNER WINE

CHICKEN MARSALA

(2 to 4 servings)

Harry Baccigaluppi, Calif. Grape Products Corp., Delano

4 chicken breasts
3 tablespoons flour
½ teaspoon seasoned salt
Dash of pepper
Pinch of oregano
3 tablespoons olive oil
3 tablespoons butter or margarine
½ cup California Marsala or Cream Sherry

Remove skin from chicken breasts. Dredge in flour seasoned with salt and pepper. Sprinkle oregano over breasts. Heat oil and butter in heavy skillet. Brown chicken, cavity side first. When browned on both sides, add wine. Cover and simmer about ½ hour or until tender. Serve with risotto or buttered rice.

My choice of wine to accompany this dish:
CALIFORNIA NEBBIOLO, OR ROSÉ OR CHABLIS

CHICKEN IN THE VINE

(4 to 6 servings)

J. B. Cella, II, Cella Wineries, Fresno

12 halved chicken breasts
Flour seasoned with salt and pepper
6 tablespoons butter or margarine
1 (6-oz.) can sliced mushrooms, undrained
2 tablespoons flour
½ teaspoon salt
¼ teaspoon pepper
2 tablespoons grape juice
1 cup chicken stock (canned or bouillon-cube broth may be used)
1 cup seedless grapes
Paprika
1 cup California Cream Sherry

Remove skin from chicken breasts. Dust chicken with seasoned flour. Sauté in melted butter, turning occasionally until tender and slightly browned. Place in casserole. Stir undrained mushrooms into rich brown drippings left in pan. Combine flour, salt and pepper; mix with grape juice to form smooth paste. Stir into mushrooms and drippings; add chicken stock, grapes and paprika. Simmer gently 10 minutes, stirring occasionally. Pour in wine; let sauce simmer 1 minute. Pour sauce over chicken; bake in moderate oven (350°) for 30 minutes.

My choice of wine to accompany this dish:
CALIFORNIA RIESLING OR DRY SAUTERNE

NOTE: *If a less-sweet chicken flavor is desired, California Dry or Medium Sherry can be used in the cooking instead of Cream Sherry. Either way, it's a flavorful and interesting dish.*

SAUTÉED CHICKEN IN CREAM

(6 servings)

Mrs. Klayton Nelson, U. of Calif. Dept. Viticulture & Enology

This is an excellent choice for a buffet luncheon or even a hearty dinner. Sauce is rich and good, but not complicated, and economical to prepare.

12 chicken breasts or thighs, boned
½ cup butter or margarine
12 medium-size fresh mushroom caps
3 tablespoons butter or margarine
7 tablespoons flour
2⅓ cups chicken broth (canned or bouillon-cube broth may be used)
¼ cup California Dry Sherry
1 cup light cream

Sauté chicken gently in ½ cup butter until slightly brown, turning occasionally, until almost tender. Add mushroom caps; cook, covered, until done. Meanwhile, melt 3 tablespoons butter in saucepan; stir in flour and chicken broth; cook, stirring constantly, until very thick. Remove chicken and mushrooms to warm serving dish. Add Sherry to pan in which chicken was cooked; scrape up browned bits in bottom and on sides of pan; stir in cream. Blend wine-cream sauce into thickened white sauce. Strain sauce; spoon over chicken and mushrooms. Nice with frozen peas or beans, or any other bright green vegetable, and buttery baked potatoes.

My choice of wine to accompany this dish:
ANY CALIFORNIA DRY WHITE OR DRY ROSÉ

CHICKEN JUBILEE

(6 to 8 servings)

Esther Gowans, Glen Ellen Winery & Distillery, Glen Ellen

6 to 8 chicken breasts
½ cup flour
¼ teaspoon garlic salt
½ teaspoon paprika
1½ teaspoons salt
¼ cup butter or oil
1 cup California Sauterne, Chablis or other white dinner wine
2 cups canned pitted Bing cherries
½ cup California brandy

Shake chicken breasts in bag with flour, garlic salt, paprika and salt. Sauté slowly in butter or oil to rich golden-brown. Arrange in casserole or baking pan; pour over wine. Cover; bake in moderately hot oven (375°) 20 minutes. Remove cover; add cherries. Return to oven; bake, uncovered, 15 to 20 minutes longer or until chicken is tender. Place on top of stove over very low heat. Pour over brandy; do NOT allow to boil. Set aflame; when flames die down, serve chicken with cherries and sauce. I usually serve this with buttered noodles; green peas; tossed salad with olive oil and wine vinegar dressing, and beets pickled in wine vinegar; and finally cheese cake.

My choice of wine to accompany this dish:
CHILLED CALIFORNIA RIESLING

BREASTS OF CHICKEN AU PORTO

(6 servings)

Mrs. Joseph Heitz, Heitz Wine Cellar, St. Helena

6 boned chicken breasts
4 blades tarragon
2 tablespoons butter or margarine
6 small white onions, thinly sliced
1 cup sour cream
½ cup California Port
3 tablespoons California Sherry
½ cup very rich chicken broth
(2 cups broth over high heat
reduced to ½ cup)
Salt and freshly ground pepper
Dash nutmeg

In a skillet, sauté chicken breasts lightly in butter until tender. Meanwhile, prepare sauce, as follows: Parboil tarragon in water; drain; pound to a paste with 2 tablespoons butter. Melt flavored butter; add onions; cook until delicately colored, stirring constantly. Put pan over hot water; stir in sour cream; heat 5 minutes. Stir in wines and broth; simmer 5 minutes more. Place chicken breasts in sauce, cover and simmer gently 5 to 10 minutes, or until sauce is thick. Season with salt, pepper and nutmeg.

My choice of wine to accompany this dish:
CALIFORNIA JOHANNISBERG RIESLING
OR CABERNET SAUVIGNON

NOTE: *This unusual, flavorful recipe, also known as Supremes de Volaille au Porto, is ideal for a chafing dish.*

SUPREME DEVILED CHICKEN

(4 to 6 servings)

Earle M. Cobb, California Growers Wineries, Cutler

1 (3-lb.) broiling or frying chicken,
cut in serving-size pieces
Paprika
Salt and pepper
½ cup oil or melted shortening
2 tablespoons flour
1½ teaspoons dry mustard
1 cup soup stock or chicken broth
(canned or bouillon-cube broth may be used)
2 teaspoons Worcestershire sauce
2 teaspoons catsup
½ cup California Sherry

Sprinkle chicken with paprika, salt and pepper. Brown in heated oil; remove from pan. Stir flour and mustard into fat remaining in pan. Slowly stir in stock. Cook, stirring constantly, until thick. Add remaining ingredients. Return chicken to pan. Simmer, covered, 1 hour.

NOTE: *This would be spicy enough for any type of dinner wine to accompany it — white, Rosé or red.*

GOLD RUSH CHICKEN LIVERS

(4 to 6 servings)

Mrs. Gerta Wingerd, U. of Calif. Med. Center, San Francisco

1 lb. chicken livers
½ teaspoon salt
⅛ teaspoon pepper
½ cup sifted flour
¼ cup bacon fat
½ cup California Sauterne, Riesling,
or other white dinner wine
6 slices crisply-fried bacon, crumbled
Finely-chopped fresh parsley

Dredge chicken livers in mixed salt, [...] brown lightly in hot bacon fat. Turn [...] wine; cover and steam 5 minutes, [...] Sprinkle with bacon and parsley. S[...] or noodles, with watercress or tom[...]

NOTE: *Either red or white wine would be hi[...] with this piquant dish: the same used in [...]ong [...]laret.*

[...]N LIVERS IN PORT

(2 or 3 servings)

[...]d B. Ficklin, Ficklin Vineyards, Madera

[...]icular favorite of ours for chafing dish cookery, [...]ood when done "top of the stove." We like it for a [...] evening, cooked and served before the fireplace.

2 small green onions, finely chopped
¼ cup butter or margarine
½ lb. chicken livers
¼ teaspoon fresh sage, or
⅛ teaspoon ground sage
¼ teaspoon salt
1 tablespoon lemon juice
⅓ cup California Port
⅛ teaspoon freshly ground pepper

Sauté onions in melted butter a few minutes. Add livers; sauté 3 to 5 minutes, depending on size of livers. Bruise sage; add along with salt, lemon juice, Port and pepper. Cook slowly about 8 minutes, stirring occasionally. Correct seasoning and serve it forth on toast! Menu might include a tossed green salad with oil and wine vinegar dressing; toasted French bread; and dessert of Port, apple wedges and a few walnuts.

My choice of wine to accompany this dish:
CALIFORNIA PINOT NOIR

SQUABS IN RED WINE

(2 servings)

Mrs. Joseph J. Franzia, Franzia Brothers Winery, Ripon

- 4 slices bacon, diced
- 2 (1-lb.) squabs, prepared for roasting
- 3 tablespoons flour
- 1 teaspoon salt
- ¼ teaspoon pepper
- 1 cup California Burgundy, Claret or other red dinner wine
- ½ cup chicken stock (canned or bouillon-cube broth may be used)
- 8 small white onions, peeled
- 2 carrots, peeled and sliced
- ½ bay leaf
- 2 tablespoons chopped parsley
- 2 squab livers, chopped
- ¼ lb. fresh mushrooms, sliced, or 1 cup shelled fresh peas

In heavy skillet, fry bacon until golden brown, then put in large casserole or covered roaster. Sprinkle birds with flour seasoned with salt and pepper. Brown all over in bacon drippings remaining in skillet. Add any remaining flour; blend well. Put birds in casserole. Add ½ to ¾ cup wine and all the stock to drippings in skillet. Bring to boiling; reduce heat; simmer, stirring to scrape up all browned bits in bottom and on sides of pan. Cook 5 minutes, stirring constantly. Pour over squabs. Add onions, carrots, bay leaf, parsley, livers and remaining wine. Cover; bake in moderate oven (325 to 350°) for ½ hour. Add mushrooms (or peas); cook, covered, 40 to 45 minutes longer, or until squabs are tender. If mushrooms are used, then menu might include steamed buttered rice or baked potatoes; and tossed green salad with wine vinegar and olive oil dressing.

My choice of wine to accompany this dish:
CALIFORNIA BURGUNDY OR SPARKLING BURGUNDY

QUICK ROAST TURKEY CHABLIS

Mrs. Frank G. Cadenasso, Cadenasso Winery, Fairfield

This method shortens the cooking time of your bird. After cooking many turkeys, we find this wine-and-butter treatment gives a moist white meat and a rich, really elegant gravy that needs only slight thickening with flour.

- Roasting turkey, stuffed with favorite dressing
- Oil
- Salt
- California Sauterne, Chablis or other white dinner wine
- ½ cup butter or margarine

Place turkey, oiled and salted, breast side up on rack in large roasting pan in moderately hot oven (400°); brown. Turn turkey breast side down; cover with cheesecloth dampened thoroughly with wine. Reduce heat to 300 to 325°. Melt butter; brush cheesecloth with butter and wine frequently as turkey cooks. An 18 to 20-lb. bird takes only about 3½ hours. Serve with any traditional turkey dinner menu.

My choice of wine to accompany this dish:
CHILLED CALIFORNIA RHINE WINE OR CHABLIS

STUFFED ROASTED SQUABS

(8 servings)

Mrs. Eugene P. Seghesio, Seghesio Winery, Cloverdale

My father has always raised squabs for as long as I can remember. He gives them special attention; and we, as children, helped in their care. For Sunday dinner and on many special occasions, we enjoyed squab prepared in a variety of ways by my parents, and always with wine in the recipe.

- 8 (1-lb.) squabs (cavities salted)
- Wild Rice Stuffing
- Butter
- Salt and pepper
- ½ cup California Sauterne, Chablis or other white dinner wine, or
- ⅓ cup California Dry Sherry

Stuff each squab with Wild Rice Stuffing (see below). Rub birds generously with butter or margarine; season with salt and pepper. Place in roasting pan in hot oven (400°) 10 minutes. Reduce heat to 325°; cook 50 minutes longer, basting frequently with pan juices. During last 15 minutes, pour over wine. This is one dish I especially enjoy serving to guests. The following menu would be for a **special** dinner party: Hors d'oeuvre such as Camembert cheese and crackers, and small cantaloupe wedges wrapped in prosciutto slices, with California Champagne. Then as first course, homemade antipasto (made with red wine vinegar) and California Chablis or Johannisberg Riesling. Next, tortellini with a meat sauce made with ½ cup red or white dinner wine. Then the squab with wild rice, fresh asparagus, sautéed mushrooms and mixed green salad. With this main course a California Pinot Noir. For dessert, fresh strawberries in Burgundy, flamed with brandy and spooned over coffee ice cream. Finally, coffee with California brandy.

WILD RICE STUFFING: Chop ½ medium onion, ½ clove garlic and 2 stalks celery; saute in ¼ cup butter or margarine until onion is clear. Combine with 2 cups cooked wild rice, ⅓ cup California Sauterne or other white dinner wine, salt and pepper.

NOTE: *Such an epicurean menu, for a special occasion, would certainly deserve California Champagne at the beginning. One kind of wine (such as a Burgundy) throughout the dinner would still be correct, if desired. For those on budgets, delicious brown rice stuffing might be made same way.*

BREASTS OF CORNISH GAME HEN

(6 servings)

Brother Timothy, Mont La Salle Vineyards, Napa

We served this menu several years ago to a group of visiting food editors, and it met with such enthusiasm that we serve it, with small variations, at many of our luncheons for distinguished visitors. It never fails to call forth much praise.

> 6 boned breasts of Cornish game hens
>   (chicken breasts may be used)
>   Monosodium glutamate
> ¼ cup flour
>   Salt and pepper
> ¼ cup butter or margarine
> ¼ cup finely-chopped green onions
> ½ cup California Light Muscat or
>   other light sweet white wine
> 1 cup chopped fresh mushrooms
> 2 cups chicken broth
>   (chicken stock base broth may be used)
> ¾ cup light cream
>   Chopped parsley

Sprinkle game hen breasts with monosodium glutamate; dredge in flour seasoned with salt and pepper. Sauté in melted butter until lightly browned. Add onions; cook until onions are tender but not browned. Add wine and mushrooms. Simmer gently, covered, 15 minutes. Add chicken broth; simmer 20 minutes longer, or until tender. Remove breasts to warm platter. Stir cream into pan juices; heat thoroughly. Pour sauce over breasts; sprinkle with parsley. Serve with rice pilaf; hearts of artichokes Parmesan; a simple green salad with wine dressing; hot rolls; fresh strawberries or pineapple flavored with a Light Muscat; and thin wafers.

My choice of wine to accompany this dish:
CALIFORNIA DRY SAUVIGNON BLANC
OR JOHANNISBERG RIESLING

CHESTNUT TURKEY STUFFING

(For 10 to 15-lb. turkey)

Mrs. Tulio D'Agostini, D'Agostini Winery, Plymouth

> 1 lb. large chestnuts
> ¼ cup shortening
> 1 teaspoon salt
> 1 egg, beaten
> 1 cup ground pork sausage, lightly browned
> 1 cup soft stale bread crumbs
> 1 teaspoon chopped parsley
> ½ teaspoon basil, chopped or powdered
> ½ teaspoon oregano
> 1 small onion, chopped
> ½ cup California Light Muscat or
>   other light sweet white wine

Boil chestnuts about 20 minutes; remove shells and skins. Re-boil shelled chestnuts in salted water until tender; drain and put through ricer or sieve. Combine with other ingredients; mix well. Use to stuff cavity of 10 to 15-lb. turkey.

My choice of wine to accompany this dish:
A CALIFORNIA BURGUNDY

ROAST TURKEY ROSÉ

Mrs. Joseph Roullard, Petri Wineries, Escalon

Prepare favorite stuffing using California Rosé wine as part of the liquid. Rub inside of bird with ⅛ teaspoon salt per pound. Fill neck cavity with stuffing; fasten neck skin to back with skewer. Stuff rest of bird well, but do not pack. Fasten opening with skewers, lacing if necessary. Rub entire bird with soft butter or margarine. Place on rack in large roasting pan, breast side up. Prepare basting liquid of half California Rosé and half chicken bouillon (begin with ½ cup of each, preparing more as necessary). Pour over turkey; cover with foil. Place in a moderate oven (325 to 350°). Baste several times during cooking. Remove foil last 20 minutes to brown. A 10 to 14-lb. bird requires 3½ to 4 hours. Serve with crab cocktail; mashed potatoes with giblet gravy; hot buttered rolls; peas with mushrooms; cabbage-apple-raisin salad and pumpkin pie. Makes a wonderful Thanksgiving dinner, though I serve turkey other times, too.

My choice of wine to accompany this dish:
CHILLED CALIFORNIA ROSÉ OR RIESLING

NOTE: Mrs. Alvin Ehrhardt of United Vintners, Inc., Lodi, also has a special fillip for roasting fowl: turkey, chicken, squab, pheasant, etc. Before stuffing the bird, she places California brandy in the cavity: from ¼ cup up, depending on bird size. Simply swish brandy around a little, then add stuffing and roast in usual manner. "This enhances the flavor," she says.

BARBECUED TURKEY

(10 to 15 servings)

Mrs. Don Rudolph, Cresta Blanca Wine Co., Livermore

> 1 (15-lb.) turkey
> 2 cups California Sherry
> 2 cups California Sauterne or
>   other white dinner wine
> 3 medium onions, cut in eighths
> 1 cup olive oil
> 5 cloves garlic, finely chopped
> 2 green peppers, cubed
> 1 tablespoon oregano
> 1 teaspoon poultry seasoning
>   Salt and pepper

Disjoint turkey. Combine other ingredients; pour over turkey in large glass or porcelain dish. Marinate in refrigerator 2 to 5 days, turning meat twice a day. Barbecue on a spit, basting with strained marinade. Preferred menu with this would be rice, buttered carrots, green salad and hot rolls.

My choice of wine to accompany this dish:
CALIFORNIA GREY RIESLING OR SAUTERNE

NOTE: The remaining strained marinade can also be made into a good accompanying sauce, to spoon over the rice. Thicken slightly, if desired, and heat thoroughly.

RAISIN TURKEY STUFFING

(For turkey 14 to 18 lb. size)

Harry Baccigaluppi, Calif. Grape Products Corp., Delano

½ cup chopped onion
2 cups chopped celery
1½ cups butter or margarine
  (part turkey fat may be used)
4 qts. (16 cups) bread crumbs
  (use 2 or 3-day-old bread)
2 cups seedless raisins, plumped in
  boiling water
½ cup chopped parsley
1 tablespoon salt
2 teaspoons poultry seasoning
1 cup California Burgundy or other
  red dinner wine (approximately)

Sauté onion and celery gently in melted butter, stirring occasionally, just until onion is soft. Add to crumbs. Add raisins, parsley and seasonings; mix lightly but thoroughly. Gradually add just enough wine to moisten stuffing slightly. Stuff turkey and roast in usual way, preferably covered with oiled cheesecloth, and basted with mixture of additional Burgundy with melted butter.

My choice of wine to accompany this dish:
CALIFORNIA BURGUNDY, NEBBIOLO OR PINOT NOIR

TURKEY STUFFING MUY BUENO

(For turkey about 16-lb. size)

Inez Bueno Wargo, Wine Advisory Board, San Francisco

This is a very old family recipe from Mexico, richly flavored and interestingly different.

Gizzard, heart and liver of turkey
4 cups water
1 teaspoon salt
1 clove garlic
3 tablespoons oil
½ pound ground pork
½ cup blanched almonds, halved and toasted
½ cup raisins, plumped in hot water
½ cup pitted chopped green olives
1 tablespoon chopped green pepper
1 tablespoon chopped onion
1 tablespoon chopped parsley
1 tablespoon chopped celery
¼ teaspoon oregano
½ cup tomato sauce
1 cup California Sherry
1 teaspoon California wine vinegar
  Strained broth from giblets
  Salt (additional)
¼ teaspoon black pepper
  Garlic (additional)
1 large pkg. bread cubes for stuffing

Simmer turkey gizzard, heart and liver in water seasoned with salt and garlic, until tender. Remove giblets; chop well; strain and reserve broth. Heat oil in heavy skillet; brown ground pork with giblets. Combine with other ingredients. Rub turkey cavity with mixture of salt, pepper and garlic; stuff loosely. Roast turkey in usual way, timed according to size, and basted with additional Sherry if desired.

Our choice of wine to accompany this dish:
ANY CALIFORNIA RED DINNER WINE

DUCK AU VIN

(Allow 1 lb. per person)

Mrs. Robert Mondavi, Charles Krug Winery, St. Helena

1 duck (domestic)
  Salt and pepper
2 tablespoons olive oil
1 cup orange juice
1 cup California Burgundy, Claret
  or other red dinner wine
1 tablespoon lemon juice
1 large onion, thinly sliced
1 tablespoon grated lemon or orange rind
½ teaspoon *each:* marjoram and rosemary
  Pinch of oregano
2 tablespoons orange curacao

Cut duck into serving-size pieces; season with salt and pepper. Brown in hot olive oil. Remove to a hot casserole with tight-fitting lid. In same skillet, add orange juice, wine, lemon juice, onion, rind and herbs. Bring to boiling, scraping up browned bits in bottom and on sides of pan. Pour mixture over duck; bake, covered, in a slow oven (275°) for 2½ to 3 hours, or until tender. Remove duck to heated platter. Strain and measure remaining pan juices; taste and correct seasoning. Add orange curacao and enough red wine to bring liquid to 2 cups. Thicken to desired consistency with flour stirred smooth in a little wine. Add to measured liquid; cook, stirring constantly, until thickened. Pour over duck. Serve with rice.

NOTE: *Mrs. Mondavi says domestic goose is good this way, too — also wild duck or goose. Wild rice may be used if desired. Your favorite California Burgundy or Claret would be most fitting with such a memorable dinner.*

ROAST GOOSE

(8 servings)

Charles van Kriedt, California Wineletter, San Francisco

1 (10-lb.) frozen goose
  California brandy
  Salt
2 cups small cubes or pieces white toast
1 medium onion, diced
2 stalks celery with leaves, finely cut
1 cup *each:* dried prunes & dried apricots
½ cup melted butter
  Salt, pepper, thyme and oregano
  California Sherry
2 cups California Burgundy, Claret
  or other red dinner wine
2 cups stock (canned or
  bouillon-cube broth may be used)

Thaw goose; rub with brandy and sprinkle with salt. Combine toast cubes, onion, celery, prunes, apricots, butter, salt, pepper, thyme and oregano. Moisten with Sherry. Stuff goose, reserving a little dressing for use in gravy. Prick skin all over with sharp fork to let out melting fat. Roast uncovered on rack in slow oven (300°), allowing 25 to 30 minutes per lb. Combine wine and stock; use to baste bird frequently. As fat and liquid accumulate in bottom of roasting pan, draw off with basting syringe. Place in jar and cool; skim off fat. Use liquid for gravy, combining with reserved dressing and simmering about 1 hour.

NOTE: *Such a richly-flavored masterpiece deserves a fine California Claret or Burgundy alongside.*

WILD GAME

Venison, Pheasant, Dove, Rabbit, Goose, Duck with Wine

California's beautiful wine country abounds in game, as well as grapes—so it's natural that winemaking families should be especially interested in wild game cookery of all sorts. Here, again, wine adds the touch of grace, making gamey flavors more delicate, and coarser textures more tender. That is why marinating plays a major part in many of these flavorful recipes. Add a glass or two of your favorite California wine at the table, and a game dish can become a wondrous experience.

ROAST SADDLE OF VENISON

(Allow ½ to ¾ lb. per person)

Mrs. Frank Franzia, Franzia Brothers Winery, Ripon

Our menfolks love to hunt wild game. This is one of our favorite venison dishes.

 1 saddle of venison
 1⅓ cups water
 2⅔ cups California Burgundy or
    other red dinner wine
 2 teaspoons mustard seeds
 2 bay leaves
 1 teaspoon thyme
 2 onions, sliced
 ½ teaspoon pepper
 2 cloves garlic, slivered
 1 tablespoon salt
 ½ cup sour cream
 1 cup red currant jelly
 1 tablespoon California brandy

Trim all fat off venison. Combine water, wine, mustard seeds, bay leaves, thyme, onions and pepper; pour over meat in glass or porcelain dish. Marinate in refrigerator 24 hours, turning occasionally. Insert slivers of garlic in meat; sprinkle with salt. Place in moderate oven (350°); roast, uncovered, 2 to 4 hours, depending on size, or until tender, basting often with marinade. Remove meat to warm platter. Skim off excess fat from meat drippings; stir in sour cream, jelly and brandy; cook until mixture thickens. Spoon sauce over meat or serve separately. Serve with wild rice and tossed green salad with wine vinegar in the dressing.

My choice of wine to accompany this dish:
CALIFORNIA CLARET OR ROSÉ, OR ANY
FAIRLY LIGHT, DRY RED WINE

NOTE: *Mrs. Franzia sometimes uses a simpler treatment for venison, first marinating overnight just in California Claret. Next day she removes roast to pan containing 1 cup olive oil and marinates again, turning several times throughout the day. While roasting, venison is basted with the oil and melted butter. She says venison of almost any age becomes a good roast when treated this way.*

VENISON STEAKS À LA TEDESCHI

(Any amount)

Bill Bagnani, American Industries Corp., Geyserville

 Venison steaks
 California red dinner wine
 Fine dry bread crumbs
 Olive oil

Cut steaks from hind leg of deer (thickness as desired). Pound lightly. Marinate in red dinner wine for several hours, turning occasionally. Remove steaks. Pat dry with paper towels. Coat with bread crumbs; fry in hot olive oil. Or, broil 10 minutes at 550°.

My choice of wine to accompany this dish:
CALIFORNIA DRY RED DINNER WINE

NOTE: *Mr. Bagnani says this type of wine is a "must" with venison.*

VENISON STEW KUKOLSKY

(4 servings)

Dr. Wm. V. Cruess, U. of Calif. Dept. of Food Technology

 1½ lbs. venison stew meat
 1 onion, sliced
 2 to 6 cloves garlic, as desired
 2 whole cloves
 2 whole allspice
 1 teaspoon salt
 12 dried prunes, pitted
 ½ cup California red or white
    dinner wine, or Dry Sherry

Combine all ingredients; cook slowly until prunes are well-cooked and lose shape and venison is tender, about 2 hours. Taste; add salt if needed.

NOTE: *Most venison stew-lovers would probably prefer a California red dinner wine with this richly-flavored dish. See also the tip at the bottom of Page 35, on how to enhance the wine flavor in any stew by adding extra wine at the last minute.*

SONOMA VENISON STEW

(6 servings)

Mrs. August Sebastiani, Samuele Sebastiani, Sonoma

This is my own recipe. It is also very rich and good made with beef, as a Beef Burgundy.

    1½ lbs. venison, cubed
    2   tablespoons flour
    ½   teaspoon *each*: salt, pepper, garlic salt
    ¼   cup *each*: oil and butter or margarine
    2   stalks celery, chopped
    1   onion, chopped
    2   cloves garlic, chopped
    4   sprigs parsley
    1½ cups California Burgundy, Claret
        or other red dinner wine
    ½   cup water

Coat venison in flour seasoned with salt, pepper and garlic salt. In a large heavy skillet, brown meat in oil and butter. Add celery and onion; brown well. Add garlic and parsley; brown slightly. Pour over wine and water. Simmer, covered, over low heat or in moderately slow oven (325°) for 1 to 1½ hours, or until meat is tender. This stew is delightful served over rice or noodles, and with a green salad it makes a very nourishing dinner.

My choice of wine to accompany this dish:
CALIFORNIA DRY RED OR ROSÉ

VENISON SWISS STEAK

(4 or 5 servings)

Mrs. Dorothy Winneberger, U. C. Dept. Viticulture & Enology

This is my own invention.

    2   (1½-lb.) venison steaks, cut in half
        Flour
        Butter or margarine
    1   (1⅜-oz.) pkg. dry onion soup mix
    2   teaspoons spaghetti sauce seasoning
    2   small bay leaves
        Salt and pepper
    1   cup California Burgundy, Claret
        or other red dinner wine
    1   (8-oz.) can tomato sauce

Dredge meat in flour. Melt butter in heavy skillet; brown meat over medium heat (350° in electric skillet). Add soup mix, spaghetti sauce seasoning, bay leaves, salt and pepper; pour over wine and tomato sauce. Simmer, covered, 30 to 45 minutes, or until tender. If sauce seems too thick, add a little more wine or water. Serve with buttered fluffy rice to which pine nuts have been added. With this I like a very simple green salad, possibly just lettuce, Parmesan cheese and wine vinegar and oil dressing. A wine pudding dessert might do nicely with this dinner.

My choice of wine to accompany this dish:
CALIFORNIA CHIANTI OR BURGUNDY

NOTE: This makes an exceptionally good gravy with the rice.

WILD DUCKS are sometimes marinated in red dinner wine, with a little olive oil, sliced onion, chopped parsley and seasoning added. Jack Pandol of Delano Growers Co-Op. Winery, Delano, marinates ducks 2 to 4 hours, then broils over charcoal, basting with strained marinade. He serves the same type of California red wine with the dinner.

VENISON MT. MADONNA

(4 to 6 servings)

M. J. Filice, San Martin Vineyards Co., San Martin

This recipe was developed by the early Italian settlers of the Mt. Madonna area of the Santa Cruz mountains, in Santa Clara County. Venison was then the dish for Sunday dinner. Deer, rabbit, quail and other game were very plentiful, and it was a rare Sunday when they ate "store" meat.

    2   cups California red wine vinegar
    3   cups California Sauterne or
        other white dinner wine
    2   large cloves garlic, crushed
    2   tablespoons chopped parsley
    2   cloves
    1   medium-size onion, chopped
    4   lbs. venison (rack, loin or leg)
        Salt and pepper
    3   tablespoons flour
    4   slices salt pork or bacon
    1   cup California Sherry

Combine wine vinegar and white wine in a saucepan; bring to boiling. Remove from heat; add garlic, parsley, cloves and onion; cool. Place venison in glass or porcelain dish; pour over cooled marinade. Marinate in refrigerator for 10 hours. Remove meat from marinade; dry with paper towels. Sprinkle with salt and pepper; rub with flour. Place meat in baking pan; top with slices of salt pork or bacon (and onion slices, if desired). Brown in hot oven (400°) on both sides (about 30 minutes). Add 1 cup marinade; reduce heat to 350°; roast about 1½ hours, or until tender. (Add more marinade as needed.) When tender, pour over Sherry; simmer slowly about 10 minutes. Serve hot, with a pasta dish (spaghetti, lasagna or ravioli), salad, fruit in season and ice cream.

My choice of wine to accompany this dish:
CALIFORNIA SPARKLING BURGUNDY,
RUBY CABERNET OR BURGUNDY

NOTE: Mr. Filice says that spring lamb can also benefit from this treatment. The marinating not only heightens flavor, but — in the case of tougher meat cuts — tenderizes, as well. Not all Wine Land cooks marinate a leg of venison, however. Mrs. Guy Baldwin, Jr., of Mont La Salle Vineyards, Napa, simply lards hers with salt pork and roasts it long and slowly, basting with Burgundy (which also enriches the gravy).

PHEASANT AU VIN

(4 servings)

Mrs. James Concannon, Concannon Vineyard, Livermore

    1   large pheasant, cleaned and prepared
        Flour
        Marjoram
    2   tablespoons chopped parsley
    ½   cup butter or margarine
    4   to 8 small white onions, peeled
    1   stalk celery
    ½   cup canned consommé
    ½   cup California Burgundy, Claret
        or other red dinner wine

Quarter pheasant. Flour lightly; place in oiled roasting pan. Sprinkle lightly with marjoram and parsley; dot with butter. Add onions and celery; pour over consommé and wine. Cover tightly; bake 30 minutes in hot oven (450°), basting often. Reduce heat to 325°; cook 1½ hours. Uncover last 15 minutes to brown. We enjoy this recipe with a rice pilaf and green vegetable.

My choice of wine to accompany this dish:
CALIFORNIA CABERNET SAUVIGNON

PHEASANT WITH MUSHROOMS

(6 servings)

Mrs. E. L. Barr, Sr., Western Grape Products, Kingsburg

      3 pheasants, split
  ½ cup butter or margarine
      2 cups sliced fresh mushrooms
      1 cup California Sauterne, Chablis
         or other white dinner wine
      2 tablespoons lemon juice
  ½ cup chopped green onions
      1 teaspoon salt
         Freshly ground pepper

Sauté pheasant in butter over moderate heat 10 minutes. Remove pheasant; sauté mushrooms in butter remaining in skillet for 10 minutes or until golden brown. Return pheasant to skillet. Add wine, lemon juice, green onions, salt and pepper. Cover; simmer 1 hour or until tender. Good with rice pilaf, any vegetable, green salad and toasted French bread.

My choice of wine to accompany this dish:
CALIFORNIA DRY WHITE OR RED DINNER WINE

NOTE: Two others who particularly recommend pheasant cooked with mushrooms and white dinner wine are Mrs. Stanley Strud, California Wine Association, Lodi, and Jessica McLachlin Greengard, public relations consultant on wines and food.

PHEASANT JUBILEE

(8 servings)

J. B. Cella, II, Cella Wineries, Fresno

      4 pheasants, quartered
         Flour
  ½ cup butter or margarine
      1 onion, chopped
  ½ cup seedless raisins
      1 cup chili sauce
  ½ cup water
  ½ cup brown sugar (packed)
      2 tablespoons Worcestershire sauce
  ¼ teaspoon garlic powder
      1 cup California Sherry
      1 (1-lb.) can pitted dark sweet
         cherries, drained

Dust pheasants with flour. Melt butter in heavy skillet; brown birds thoroughly. Place pheasants in a deep casserole. In same skillet, combine onion, raisins, chili sauce, water, brown sugar, Worcestershire sauce and garlic; boil briefly, scraping browned meat from bottom and sides of pan; pour over pheasants. Bake, covered, in a moderately slow oven (325°) for 1½ hours. Remove cover; add Sherry and cherries. Continue baking 20 minutes longer. To serve, transfer to a deep chafing or warming dish.

My choice of wine to accompany this dish:
CALIFORNIA DRY RED DINNER WINE—CHIANTI TYPE

WESTERN DOVE DINNER

(4 to 5 servings)

Mrs. Joseph S. Concannon, Jr., Concannon Vineyard, Livermore

    10 doves
         Flour seasoned with salt, pepper,
         paprika and basil
         Butter or margarine
      1 cup consommé
      1 cup California Burgundy, Claret
         or other red dinner wine
      1 cup sliced fresh mushrooms, or
      1 (6-oz.) can sliced mushrooms
  ½ teaspoon celery salt
  ⅛ teaspoon freshly ground pepper
  ⅔ cup orange juice, strained

Draw and clean doves, reserving livers and gizzards; wash well and drain. Split birds; dust with seasoned flour. Brown quickly in melted butter in Dutch oven or deep heavy skillet that will hold birds comfortably. Add livers and gizzards to bottom of pan. (They are delightfully delicate to the taste.) Mix consommé and wine; pour over birds. Add celery salt, and pepper. Bring to boiling; reduce heat; add mushrooms. Cover; simmer, stirring frequently, for about 35 minutes or until birds are tender (prick leg to test). When tender, pour in orange juice; cook 5 minutes longer. We usually serve our doves with just plain mashed potatoes and fresh green beans, with sometimes a simple tossed salad and a light dessert, such as chilled fruit or sherbet.

My choice of wine to accompany this dish:
CALIFORNIA CABERNET SAUVIGNON

NOTE: This same method could be used for little Cornish game hens. Still another interesting dove treatment is recommended by Mrs. John Paul, California Products Co., Fresno. Mrs. Paul rolls doves in seasoned flour, dips them in beaten egg, then browns doves in butter and simmers them in Sauterne. She prefers Sauterne as accompanying beverage.

SMOTHERED DOVES

(3 or 4 servings)

Mrs. V. Petrucci, Fresno State College Dept. Vitic. & Enology

This is an old family recipe.

      6 to 8 doves
      3 tablespoons flour
  ½ teaspoon salt
  ¼ teaspoon pepper
  ½ cup olive oil
      1 or 2 cloves garlic
      1 cup California Burgundy, Claret
         or other red dinner wine

Dust doves with flour seasoned with salt and pepper. In a heavy skillet, lightly brown doves in heated oil with garlic. When browned, remove garlic and discard. Add wine and enough water to barely cover birds. Simmer about 1½ hours, or until tender. Thicken pan juices with a little of the remaining seasoned flour. Serve with rice, zucchini steamed with butter, tossed green salad, garlic bread, and chilled grapes or other fresh fruit for dessert.

My choice of wine to accompany this dish:
CALIFORNIA DRY SEMILLON OR WHITE RIESLING

BAKED DOVE BONANZA

(12 to 15 servings)

Mrs. E. L. Barr, Sr., Western Grape Products, Kingsburg

> 30 doves
> 3 cloves garlic, very finely chopped
> Salt and pepper
> ¼ cup meat sauce
> ¼ cup Worcestershire sauce
> 2 cups California Burgundy, Claret
> or other red dinner wine
> ¼ cup oil
> 4 slices bacon, diced
> Paprika

Place birds breast side down in shallow baking pan. Combine garlic, salt, pepper, meat sauce, Worcestershire sauce, wine and oil; pour over birds. Dot with bacon; sprinkle with paprika. Bake in very hot oven (550°) for 20 minutes. Reduce heat to 350°; bake at least 10 minutes longer or until tender. (I allow about 45 minutes total cooking time.) Serve with rice pilaf, any vegetable, green salad and toasted French bread.

My choice of wine to accompany this dish:
CALIFORNIA DRY RED OR WHITE DINNER WINE

BREAST OF WILD GOOSE

(8 servings)

Mrs. John B. Ellena, Regina Grape Products Co., Etiwanda

This is a sweet-sour sauce, which is equally delicious for venison chops or steak.

> 3 average-size wild geese
> 3 eggs, beaten
> 1 cup bread crumbs
> Butter and bacon drippings
> 1 teaspoon salt
> 1 teaspoon pepper
> ¼ teaspoon paprika
> 2 bay leaves
> 3 whole cloves
> 2 cloves garlic, finely chopped
> ¼ cup California wine vinegar
> ½ cup catsup
> 2 tablespoons Worcestershire sauce
> 1 tablespoon meat sauce
> 1 teaspoon kitchen bouquet
> ½ cup California Burgundy or
> other red dinner wine
> 1 (10-oz.) glass red currant jelly

Fillet each breast; if large, cut into 3 or 4 pieces lengthwise. Use only the breasts and legs. Dip in beaten eggs, then in bread crumbs. Brown on all sides in butter and bacon drippings. Add salt, pepper, paprika, bay leaves, cloves and garlic. In mixing bowl, blend the wine vinegar, catsup, Worcestershire sauce, meat sauce and kitchen bouquet; pour over meat. Bake, covered, in moderate oven (350°) for 1 hour or until tender. The last 10 minutes, add wine and jelly. Garnish serving platter with parsley. Good with wild rice, or any favorite rice recipe.

My choice of wine to accompany this dish:
CALIFORNIA SPARKLING BURGUNDY OR
PINK CHAMPAGNE, OR BARBERA

BARBECUED RABBIT SELMA

(6 servings)

Kenneth Knapp, Selma Winery, Inc., Selma

This method can also be used to barbecue chicken.

> 1 (3-lb.) rabbit, cut in
> serving-size pieces
> California Dry Sherry, or Sauterne
> or other white dinner wine
> 1 cup chicken broth (canned or
> bouillon-cube broth may be used)
> Salt and pepper
> ½ cup butter or margarine
> 4 or 5 drops garlic juice
> ½ teaspoon oregano or rosemary

Place pieces of rabbit in deep glass or stainless steel bowl. Cover with wine; marinate overnight or at least 5 hours. Before barbecuing, prepare baste by combining other ingredients with 1 cup of wine used to marinate rabbit. Place rabbit about 8 inches above coals; cook slowly 45 minutes to 1 hour, turning and basting constantly. (Racks that allow you to turn a dozen pieces at a time work best.) When done, brown as desired by moving rabbit closer to coals. Continue basting; do not allow to become dry. Serve with pink beans, green salad and French bread.

My choice of wine to accompany this dish:
CALIFORNIA ROSÉ

NOTE: A very good method. The marinating in wine, plus slow barbecuing and constant basting, makes a juicy and tender rabbit (or chicken).

BURGUNDY BAKED RABBIT

(2 or 3 servings)

Karl L. Wente, Wente Bros., Livermore

> 1 cup California Burgundy or
> other red dinner wine
> 2 tablespoons California red wine vinegar
> ½ medium onion, sliced
> 1 bay leaf
> 1 sprig *each*: rosemary and thyme, *or*
> ½ teaspoon *each*: dried rosemary
> and thyme
> 4 peppercorns, crushed
> 1 rabbit, cut in serving-size pieces
> 2 tablespoons olive oil
> Salt

Combine wine, wine vinegar, onion, bay leaf, herbs, and peppercorns; pour over rabbit; marinate several hours. Remove rabbit; dry with paper towels. In heavy skillet, brown meat in heated olive oil. Place browned meat in a casserole. Strain marinade; pour over meat; add salt. Cook, covered, in slow oven (300°) for 1 to 1½ hours. After 40 minutes, add more wine if necessary. To complete the meal: brown rice, green beans or zucchini, a cabbage-and-grated-carrot coleslaw, and apples and cheese for dessert.

My choice of wine to accompany this dish:
THE SAME CALIFORNIA BURGUNDY

FISH

And Shellfish...with Wine

The green vineyards of California are never very far away from rivers, lakes, bays or the sea; hence the wide interest among winemakers in the ancient sport of angling. And they love to cook their catch with their own good California wines, for in this field of cookery wine is particularly helpful. The sometimes "fishy" oils or tastes are eliminated by the addition of a white dinner wine or Sherry. At the same time, bland flavors are delicately enriched. To make the dining pleasure complete: put California wine on the table, as well.

BAKED FISH CUCAMONGA

(6 servings)

Cesare Vai, Cucamonga Vineyard Company, Cucamonga

    4 lbs. whole fresh fish (sea bass, barracuda, corbina, bonita, etc.)
    Lemon juice
    Salt and pepper
    A few *each:* parsley leaves, celery leaves, onion slices
    ½ lb. fresh mushrooms, thinly sliced
    2 tablespoons *each:* butter and olive oil
    1 medium onion, minced
    2 stalks celery, minced
    1 cup California Chablis or other white dinner wine
    2 tablespoons chopped parsley

Wash, dry and split fish. Rub inside and out with lemon juice, salt and pepper. Place parsley and celery leaves and onion slices in cavity. Place a few more slices onion on bottom of oiled baking dish; cover with a few of the mushroom slices; top with fish. Bake, uncovered, in moderate oven (350°) for 15-20 minutes. Meanwhile, heat butter and oil; slowly brown minced onion and celery; add mushrooms, wine and parsley. Pour over fish; bake 30 to 45 minutes longer, basting fish frequently. Add more melted butter and wine during cooking, if necessary. Serve garnished with fresh chopped parsley and lemon wedges. Menu might include new potatoes in parsleyed butter, asparagus vinaigrette, broiled tomatoes au gratin, and a lemon-gelatin cake.

My choice of wine to accompany this dish:
CALIFORNIA DRY WHITE, PREFERABLY CHABLIS

NOTE: *This is a really simple treatment, with a fresh pleasing flavor. Mr. Vai says that dried mushrooms may be substituted for the fresh ones, if they are soaked in warm water 30 minutes before adding to the dish.*

POACHED SOLE WITH GRAPES

(6 servings)

Mrs. Kerby T. Anderson, Guild Wine Co., Lodi

    1½ lbs. fillet of sole
    1½ cups milk
    3 tablespoons butter
    4 tablespoons flour
    ½ lb. sharp Cheddar cheese, grated or cubed
    ½ teaspoon salt
    Dash *each:* pepper and paprika
    ½ cup California Sauterne or other white dinner wine
    1 cup fresh or canned seedless grapes (drained if canned)

Roll fillets; secure with wooden picks. Poach in hot milk a few minutes. Remove fish to a buttered casserole, reserving liquid. Melt butter in saucepan; mix in flour. Slowly add milk used to poach fish; cook, stirring constantly, until mixture is slightly thickened. Add cheese; stir until melted. Add salt, pepper, paprika and wine. Pour sauce over fillets; sprinkle with paprika. Bake in moderately slow oven (325°) for 25 minutes. Just before serving, pour grapes over fish. This can be served with rice pilaf or baked potatoes, green vegetable for color contrast, tossed green salad with tart herbed dressing, and pineapple sherbet for dessert.

My choice of wine to accompany this dish:
CALIFORNIA RIESLING

NOTE: *A most enjoyable variation on the classic combination of sole with grapes (Sole Veronique). Still another is recommended by Brother Gregory of Mont La Salle Vineyards, Napa. He likes the grapes browned in butter, with a California Light Muscat added, plus a touch of curry powder. This is boiled until reduced one-half (but left unthickened), then poured over cooked fish.*

ST. HELENA SOLE

(6 servings)

Mrs. Joseph Heitz, Heitz Wine Cellar, St. Helena

> 6 tablespoons butter or margarine
> 2 tablespoons flour
> 1½ cups milk, heated
> 2 fresh sole
> 2 cups California Chablis or other
>   white dinner wine
> ½ lb. fresh mushrooms
> 6 tablespoons heavy cream
>   Salt and pepper

Melt 3 tablespoons of the butter in a saucepan; stir in flour; gradually add heated milk. Cook, stirring constantly, until thickened. Remove from heat; cool, stirring occasionally to prevent a skin from forming. Meanwhile, clean and fillet fish. Place in fairly deep baking dish; cover with wine. Bake in moderate oven (350°) for 30 minutes. Wipe mushrooms with damp cloth; cut off earthy part of stems. Chop mushrooms finely. Combine with ½ of the white sauce; pour into serving dish and keep warm. Carefully remove fillets and place on top of mushroom sauce. To remaining white sauce, add the cream, remaining 3 tablespoons butter, salt and pepper. Heat, but do not boil. Pour sauce over fish.

My choice of wine to accompany this dish:
CALIFORNIA JOHANNISBERG RIESLING

SHERRY-ALMOND SOLE

(4 servings)

Mrs. Joe Cooper, Wine Advisory Board, San Francisco

> 4 large fillets of sole,
>   about ¾" thick
> 2 green onions (including part
>   of tops), chopped
> ½ cup fresh mushrooms,
>   cleaned and chopped
> ¼ teaspoon salt
>   Pinch dried rosemary
> ⅔ cup California Dry Sherry or
>   Sauterne or other white dinner wine
> ½ cup heavy cream
> 1 tablespoon butter or margarine
> ⅓ cup chopped almonds

Combine fish, onions, mushrooms, salt, rosemary and wine in small frying pan. Simmer over low heat 10 minutes. Place fillets in shallow casserole. Reduce liquid remaining in pan by half, over high heat. Lower heat; add cream and butter; bring to boiling. Pour over fish, distributing onions and mushrooms evenly. Sprinkle almonds over top. Broil under medium heat for about 10 minutes, watching carefully to avoid burning.

My choice of wine to accompany this dish:
CALIFORNIA CHABLIS OR SAUTERNE

FILLET OF SOLE MONTEREY

(4 servings)

Mrs. Stanford J. Wolf, Paul Masson Vineyards, Saratoga

The leftover sauce from this dish can be used to make a gourmet soup the following day.

> 1 medium-size onion, sliced
> 1 bunch parsley, chopped
> 1 teaspoon salt
>   Few whole white peppercorns
> 2 lbs. fillet of sole
> ¼ lb. fresh mushrooms (caps only)
> 2 tablespoons chopped shallots
>   or chopped green onions
> ¼ cup butter or margarine
> 1 cup small oysters
> 1 cup heavy cream
> ½ cup chicken broth
> ½ cup California Sauterne or other
>   white dinner wine
> 1 cup fresh cooked or
>   canned shrimp

Fill large heavy skillet ¼ with water; add onion slices, parsley, salt and peppercorns. Simmer ½ hour. Carefully place fillets in pan; simmer 10 minutes. Carefully remove fish to ovenproof dish; set aside. Peel (but don't wash) and slice mushroom caps; sauté with shallots or green onions in melted butter for 2 minutes. Add oysters; cook 1 minute longer. In top of double boiler, heat cream over hot water (do not boil). Add chicken broth and wine; heat thoroughly. Place sautéed mushrooms, onions, oysters and shrimp over and around fish. Pour over sauce. Bake in moderate oven (350°) for 20 minutes. Serve **immediately.** This is good with small new potatoes, boiled and parsley-buttered; baby carrots and buttered toasted crackers.

My choice of wine to accompany this dish:
CALIFORNIA RIESLING OR PINOT CHARDONNAY

HERBED FISH SAUTERNE

(6 servings)

S. Martinelli, S. Martinelli & Company, Watsonville

> ½ cup butter or margarine
> ½ cup California Sauterne, Chablis
>   or other white dinner wine
> ⅓ cup lemon juice
> 1 clove garlic, chopped
>   Generous pinch of rosemary
>   Chopped parsley
>   Chopped chives or green onions
> 6 servings halibut, salmon,
>   bass, trout, etc.

In a saucepan, melt butter; add wine and lemon juice; bring to boiling. Add garlic, rosemary, parsley and chives. Use to baste fish frequently while frying, baking, broiling or barbecuing. (If desired, marinate fish in the wine ½ hour; drain off; combine as above.)

My choice of wine to accompany this dish:
CALIFORNIA SAUTERNE, OR A VERY DRY SHERRY

FROZEN FISH STICKS are special when marinated 15 minutes in ½ cup California Rhine or other white dinner wine, ¼ cup California wine vinegar, ¼ cup water, plus salt. Drain fish sticks well; dip in crumbs if not already breaded. Arrange in oiled shallow baking dish; cover with mixed sour cream, mayonnaise and chopped onion. Dust with paprika; bake in hot oven (500°) for 10 minutes. Serve with lemon wedges.

SOLE WITH SHELLFISH

(10 servings)

Mrs. Frederick H. McCrea, Stony Hill Vineyard, St. Helena

This makes an ideal Saturday or Sunday luncheon in the country, especially since it can be prepared the day before (except for final heating) and refrigerated. In this case, let stand at room temperature a couple of hours before baking. If you are lucky enough to have any left over, freeze it for another day. (Seafood used can be fresh, frozen or canned.)

    4½ lbs. fillets of sole, uncooked
        Salt and pepper
    ⅔ cup butter or margarine
    5 tablespoons sifted flour
    1 cup cream or chicken broth
    ½ cup California Chablis or other
        white dinner wine
    ½ lb. small cooked shrimp
    ½ lb. cooked crabmeat
        Dash cayenne pepper
    2 tablespoons Worcestershire sauce
        Paprika

Cut fillets in 20 serving-size pieces; sprinkle with salt and pepper. In large casserole, oiled, arrange fish one piece on top of another (so that there are 10 nice double pieces for serving). Bake in moderate oven (350°) for 35 to 40 minutes. Meanwhile, melt ½ cup of the butter, browning slightly. Add flour, stirring until smooth. Drain fish liquid from casserole; add enough cream or broth to make 2½ cups liquid. Stir liquid into butter-flour mixture. Cook over low heat, stirring constantly, until thickened and smooth. Add wine, shrimp, crab, cayenne and Worcestershire sauce. Sprinkle fillets with paprika; dot with remaining butter; spoon sauce over fish. Bake, covered, in moderate oven (350°) until bubbling hot. Serve with rice or narrow noodles, a good green salad and a loaf of French bread.

My choice of wine to accompany this dish:
CALIFORNIA GEWURZ TRAMINER OR PINOT CHARDONNAY

NOTE: *There are many variations on baked sole with seafood-and-wine sauce, most of them rich and sumptuous. Mrs. Herbert Cerwin of Cerwin Vineyards, Sonoma, started making the dish in Rio de Janeiro, where fresh shellfish is plentiful. She likes lobster or mussels as well as shrimp in her sauce, with California Riesling or Traminer accompanying the dish.*

OVEN-FRIED FISH

(6 to 8 servings)

Mrs. Tulio D'Agostini, D'Agostini Winery, Plymouth

This is an original recipe. My family does not like the usual pan-fried fish, so I tried the drier way of oven-frying, and it is a favorite with family and friends. Any white wine may be used, but the Dry Muscat gives a special zest.

    2 lbs. fish fillets
    1 cup California Dry Muscat,
        Sauterne or other white dinner wine
    1 tablespoon salt
    1 cup toasted bread crumbs
    ⅓ cup oil
    1 tablespoon chopped parsley
    4 lemons, quartered

Cut fillets in serving-size pieces. Dip in wine; roll in salted bread crumbs; place on well-oiled baking sheet. Sprinkle with oil and remaining wine. Bake in a hot oven (450°) about 15 minutes, or until fish flakes easily. Serve sprinkled with parsley and garnished with lemon quarters. Good with baked cauliflower, tossed green salad, and peach compote for dessert.

My choice of wine to accompany this dish:
CALIFORNIA DRY MUSCAT OR SAUTERNE

RUSSIAN RIVER STEELHEAD

(2 servings per lb.)

Mrs. Edward Seghesio, Seghesio Winery, Cloverdale

Healdsburg, our home, is of course on the banks of the Russian River. Ed always looks forward to the steelhead run, and is often lucky. We believe the steelhead is an especially good fish, and this recipe is our favorite way of preparing it. The recipe is very flexible as to ingredients, however; I have never made it exactly the same way twice, yet it is always tasty.

    1 large baking-size steelhead (or,
        other fish, such as bass, cod,
        salmon, etc., may be used)
        Salt and pepper
    ⅓ cup olive oil
    1 onion, chopped
    ½ cup chopped parsley
    1 clove garlic, finely chopped
    ½ cup minced canned tomatoes
    ½ cup tomato sauce
    ¾ cup California Sauterne, Chablis
        or other white dinner wine

Place fish in shallow baking dish; season with salt and pepper. Cover with oil. Place in moderate oven (350°) until oil is hot. Add onion, parsley and garlic. When brown, add tomatoes, tomato sauce and wine. Continue baking about 45 minutes, or just until fish flakes easily. We like it served with baked potatoes, tossed green salad and French bread.

My choice of wine to accompany this dish:
CALIFORNIA SAUTERNE OR CHABLIS

STRIPED BASS AU VIN BLANC

(4 servings)

Mrs. James Riddell, Vie-Del Grape Products Co., Fresno

There are many ways to prepare striped bass, but I never fully appreciated the fish until I had this recipe. It was given to me by a close friend, Mrs. Joe Couly, who is an excellent cook of French descent, and an ardent admirer of California wines.

- 4 **thick slices striped bass** (about 1 to 1½ lbs.)
- 1 **teaspoon salt**
- ½ **teaspoon pepper**
- 1 **tablespoon *each*: very finely chopped parsley, celery and green onion**
- ½ **cup California Sauterne or other white dinner wine**
- ¼ **cup buttered bread crumbs**

Remove skin from bass; cut fish into 1-inch cubes. Sprinkle with salt and pepper. Place cubes in a well-buttered casserole in a single layer. Sprinkle with parsley, celery and green onion. Pour in wine (should be about ½-inch deep). Top with buttered bread crumbs. Bake, uncovered, in a moderate oven (350°) for about 20 minutes or until fish flakes easily. Serve with new potatoes and peas, and coleslaw or vegetable salad. Dessert might be a caramel custard, or plain cake with a wedge of Monterey Jack cheese.

My choice of wine to accompany this dish:
CALIFORNIA RIESLING

NOTE: *Exceptionally good eating. Any other firm-fleshed fish, such as halibut or salmon, could be prepared this way.*

BROILED FISH NORTH COAST

(4 to 6 servings)

Don Gregg, Mendocino Grape Growers, Inc., Ukiah

This is a good, easy treatment for almost any kind of fish: salmon, sea bass, trout, etc.

- 2 **lbs. fish (slices, fillets or whole small fish)** Salt and pepper
- 1 **tablespoon lemon juice**
- 1 **onion, thinly sliced**
- 2 **tablespoons butter or margarine**
- 1 **cup California Sauterne, Chablis or other white dinner wine**
- 1 **tablespoon flour**
- 3 **tablespoons California white dinner wine or water, warmed**
- 6 **stuffed olives, sliced** Few drops onion juice

Place fish slices or fillets in buttered shallow pan. (If whole fish is used, split lengthwise and place skin side down in pan.) Sprinkle with salt, pepper, and lemon juice; spread onion slices over whole surface. Dot with butter; place under broiler. When butter begins to melt, baste with wine. Broil, basting frequently, until fish flakes with a fork. Remove fish to hot platter. Thicken liquid in pan with flour mixed with warm wine or water. Add olive slices and onion juice; pour sauce over fish.

My choice of wine to accompany this dish:
A CALIFORNIA WHITE DINNER WINE

POMPANO EN PAPILLOTTE

(6 servings)

Albert E. Moulin, Jr., Wine Advisory Board, New Orleans

Fish with a rich wine sauce, cooked in a sealed parchment paper, is a very old New Orleans method. One famous restaurant here has featured pompano in this manner for generations.

- 3 **pompano or medium-size trout** Salt
- 2 **cups water**
- 2 **green onions, chopped**
- 6 **or 7 tablespoons butter or margarine**
- 2 **cups California Sauterne, Chablis or other white dinner wine**
- 1 **cup crabmeat**
- 1 **cup small or diced cooked shrimp**
- 1 **teaspoon garlic puree**
- 1½ **cups chopped red or white onions**
- 1 **bay leaf** Pinch thyme
- 2 **tablespoons flour**
- 2 **egg yolks** Parchment paper

Clean fish; cut into 6 fillets. Simmer heads and backbones in salted water to make 2 cups fish stock; set aside. Sauté green onions and fillets in 2 or 3 tablespoons butter. Add wine; cover and simmer gently 5 to 8 minutes, or until tender. Drain, saving wine stock. Meanwhile, sauté crab, shrimp and ½ teaspoon garlic in 2 tablespoons butter. Add chopped red onions and remaining ½ teaspoon garlic; cook 10 minutes. Add 1¾ cups fish stock, bay leaf and thyme; cook 10 minutes longer; remove bay leaf. In a large, heavy skillet, blend together 2 tablespoons butter, flour and remaining ¼ cup fish stock. Add crab mixture along with wine stock. Cook, stirring constantly, until thickened. Beat egg yolks with some of the hot sauce; add to skillet, mixing thoroughly. Taste; correct seasoning. Chill sauce until firm. Cut 6 parchment paper hearts (8 x 12″). Oil well. Place a tablespoon sauce on parchment, top with a fillet. Fold over; hand seal. Place on oiled baking sheet; bake in a hot oven (450°) until brown. Serve in paper hearts. (Small paper bags tied close with string may be used in place of parchment hearts.) With this dinner I'd prefer a turtle or onion soup, potatoes (soufflé or French-fried) and green salad with olive oil and wine vinegar dressing.

My choice of wine to accompany this dish:
CALIFORNIA DRY SAUTERNE

BAKED ROCK COD WITH POTATOES

(6 to 8 servings)

Mrs. Frank Franzia, Franzia Brothers Winery, Ripon

This is almost a meal in itself, and delicious. The recipe has been in our family since 1920, when a friend brought us the fish and cooked it for us. We have been using the recipe ever since, and hope you'll enjoy it, too.

        2 tablespoons olive oil
        5 potatoes
          Salt and pepper
        2 tablespoons finely chopped parsley
        2 cloves garlic, chopped
      ½ onion, chopped
        1 (4 to 5-lb.) rock cod
        1 (8-oz.) can tomato sauce
      ¾ to 1 cup California Sauterne,
          Chablis or other white dinner wine

Pour oil into baking dish (13 x 9"). Peel and slice potatoes lengthwise about ½" thick; arrange on bottom of dish; season with salt and pepper. Combine parsley, garlic and onion; sprinkle half of mixture over potatoes. Salt the cod; place over potatoes. Sprinkle with remaining half of onion mixture. Pour over tomato sauce, then pour over wine. Bake, uncovered, in moderate oven (375°) for 1½ hours, basting occasionally. Could be served with a tossed green salad made with wine vinegar, and, for dessert, baked apple in California Sauterne.

My choice of wine to accompany this dish:
CHILLED CALIFORNIA SAUTERNE, CHABLIS OR VIN ROSÉ
(My husband prefers a California Claret)

TROUT IN WINE

(Any amount)

Kenneth Knapp, Selma Winery, Inc., Selma

Place each trout (or other favorite fish) in center of large sheet of foil; cup foil up around fish. Sprinkle with salt and pepper; top with 2 tablespoons butter or margarine and 2 thin slices lemon. (Dash of dill or rosemary may be added, if desired.) Pour 2 to 4 tablespoons (depending on size of fish) California Dry Sherry or white dinner wine over **each** fish. Pull foil edges together; seal well, leaving small air space inside. Bake in moderately hot oven (400°) for 30 minutes; or, cook over coals of barbecue or campfire for 30 to 40 minutes. Serve with baked potatoes, green salad using wine vinegar, and dessert.

My choice of wine to accompany this dish:
CALIFORNIA SAUTERNE OR ROSÉ

NOTE: *A dependable and easy way of cooking trout. Mr. Knapp says he has tried many types of wine in the cooking (except red, which can discolor the white meat of the fish), always with completely different yet pleasing results in taste. It's fun to experiment.*

ANOTHER GREAT FAVORITE is fresh salmon, barbecued outdoors or grilled indoors wrapped in foil. The Marquise de Pins, of Beaulieu Vineyard, Rutherford, specifies Chablis and a bay leaf to be added to salmon cooked this way, with the butter, lemon juice, salt, freshly ground pepper and any other favorite seasoning. (For directions, follow those above for TROUT IN WINE.) She favors California Chablis as accompanying beverage with the salmon.

BAKED FISH PIMIENTO

(4 servings)

Mrs. Harold Roush, Guild Wine Co., Lodi

        1 (10½-oz.) can tomato soup
      ⅓ cup California Sauterne, Chablis
          or other white dinner wine
        1 cup shredded process
          pimiento cheese
        2 tablespoons chopped parsley
        1 small onion, minced
        4 fish steaks (salmon,
          halibut or sole)

Combine soup, wine and cheese in saucepan. Stir over low heat until cheese melts and is blended. Add parsley and onion. Arrange fish steaks in shallow baking pan; pour over sauce. Bake in moderately hot oven (375°) about 25 minutes, or until fish flakes with fork. Enjoyable with baked potatoes, tossed green salad and toasted French rolls.

My choice of wine to accompany this dish:
CALIFORNIA VIN ROSÉ

POACHED FROZEN TROUT

(2 servings)

Mrs. Herman L. Wente, Wente Bros., Livermore

        1 cup California Chablis or other
          white dinner wine
        4 frozen trout
        1 lemon
        1 tablespoon butter
          Salt and pepper

In large skillet, bring wine to boiling. Place trout in single layer in boiling wine; cover. Reduce heat; simmer gently 5 to 10 minutes. Turn fish carefully; simmer about 5 minutes longer or just until tender. Remove to hot plates. Add juice of lemon, butter, salt and pepper to liquid in pan. Pour over fish; serve at once. Sprinkle with parsley, if desired.

My choice of wine to accompany this dish:
THE SAME CALIFORNIA CHABLIS OR OTHER WHITE

NOTE: *A refreshing change from frying, and very easy.*

SALMON COURT-BOUILLON

(4 servings)

Rene Baillif, Buena Vista Vineyards, Sonoma

This is from a fisherman's long experience. If proportions and TIMING are correct, the dish will be perfect.

  1 qt. water
  1 large bottle California Sauterne or
     other white dinner wine
  1 onion
  7 or 8 sprigs parsley
     Thyme
  1 bay leaf
  1 teaspoon seasoned salt
  8 to 10 whole peppercorns
  1 (2-lb.) piece salmon
     (trout may also be used)

Combine water, wine, onion, parsley, thyme, bay leaf and seasoned salt in large saucepan or kettle. Simmer 45 minutes; add peppercorns 10 minutes before end of simmering. Cool broth completely; strain. Place piece of salmon on rack in cold prepared broth (Court-Bouillon). **Very, very slowly** bring liquid to simmering (takes about ½ hour). Simmer 25 minutes. When cooked, peel off skin. Serve hot with white sauce with capers, if desired, using part of the cooking broth as sauce liquid. Or, serve salmon cold, decorated with anchovy fillets, sliced pickles, sliced hard-cooked eggs and a green sauce (thinned mayonnaise with chopped parsley and chopped tarragon leaves added).

My choice of wine to accompany this dish:
CALIFORNIA WHITE JOHANNISBERG RIESLING

NOTE: Mrs. Jack F. M. Taylor of Mayacamas Vineyards, Napa, has a delicious addition for salmon simmered or poached in wine-flavored bouillon. She makes dumplings from prepared biscuit mix with herbs added. She removes cooked salmon from bouillon (easy when it's been cooked in cheesecloth) and keeps it warm in the oven, on a heated platter, then drops dumplings by teaspoonful into simmering bouillon. Dumplings should cook 15 minutes, covered; do not lift lid. Remove and place dumplings around fish. Sprinkle with chopped onion and chopped anchovies which have been sautéed in skillet in butter and added to a little of the bouillon.

SALMON SNACK CHABLIS

J. R. Lazarus, Wine Institute, San Francisco

Drain a can of salmon and turn the fish into a bowl. Pour on a little California Chablis, some salad oil, soy sauce and wine vinegar. Sprinkle with chopped green onion, chopped canned pimiento and seasoned salt. Chill well for several hours. Serve with sliced tomatoes, potato salad, and buttered rye or pumpernickel bread. Very refreshing on a warm day.

My choice of wine to accompany this dish:
CHILLED CALIFORNIA CHABLIS OR ROSÉ

POACHED SALMON FREMONT

(2 servings)

Richard Elwood, Llords & Elwood Wine Cellars, Fremont

  1 lb. salmon steak
     Salt
     White pepper
  4 thin slices cooked tongue
  3 tablespoons butter or margarine
  ¾ cup California Cream Sherry
  ¼ cup boiling water
  8 mushrooms, quartered

Place salmon in shallow saucepan; season with salt and pepper; cover with tongue slices. Dot with 2 tablespoons butter. Add Sherry and boiling water. Cover tightly; simmer until fish is tender. Sauté mushrooms in remaining tablespoon butter. Slide salmon onto hot platter without disturbing tongue; place mushrooms around fish.

NOTE: Very good indeed, and different from the usual poached fish. A chilled California white dinner wine or Rosé would be perfect with it, at the table. Still another interesting salmon method is used by Mrs. Karl L. Wente, Wente Bros., Livermore. She bakes her salmon in white dinner wine, then adds wine sauce including baby clams, shrimp and mushrooms.

FIESTA FISH CASSEROLES

(6 servings)

Mrs. Frank Garbini, Wente Bros., Livermore

This recipe is my own; I just kept adding as I went along.

  ½ cup butter or margarine
  ½ cup sifted all-purpose flour
  1 teaspoon salt
  ⅛ teaspoon pepper
     Dash paprika
  2 cups rich milk
  1 tablespoon soy sauce
  2 tablespoons finely chopped parsley
  ½ cup California Dry Sherry
  1½ cups grated Parmesan cheese
  1 (4-oz.) can sliced mushrooms,
     drained
  6 small slices salmon, halibut or
     striped bass, or 3 large slices halved
  ¾ lb. uncooked prawns or
     large shrimp, shelled and cleaned
  1 (10-oz.) can baby clams

Melt butter in saucepan; stir in flour, seasonings and milk. Cook, stirring constantly, until thickened and smooth. Add soy sauce, parsley, Sherry, 1 cup cheese and mushrooms. Place small slice of fish in each of 6 greased individual casseroles. Top with prawns and clams, divided equally. Cover fish with sauce; sprinkle with remaining cheese and paprika. Bake in moderate oven (350°) for ½ hour. Serve with a tossed green salad, sour French bread and dessert.

My choice of wine to accompany this dish:
CALIFORNIA GREY RIESLING

NOTE: A really elegant combination, unusually good. Sauce can also be used for pasta, substituting ¾ cup California Claret or Burgundy for the Sherry called for above.

SHRIMP NEWBURG

(4 servings)

Mrs. James L. Riddell, Vie-Del Grape Products Co., Fresno

I used this recipe several years ago on a television program. Cooked in a fancy chafing dish and served in individual colorful ramekins, the Newburg sauce makes an appetizing appearance for any shellfish (lobster or crab may also be served with it). If the cream is warmed beforehand, it speeds up the preparation of the dish.

 ¾ cup butter or margarine
 2 tablespoons flour
 3 cups cooked and shelled shrimp,
   cut into bite-size pieces
 ⅛ teaspoon nutmeg
   Dash of paprika
 ½ teaspoon salt
 ½ cup California Sherry
 3 egg yolks
 2 cups cream
   Buttered bread crumbs

Melt butter in top of chafing dish or top of double boiler over hot water. Stir in flour; add shrimp, seasonings and Sherry. Beat egg yolks slightly; add cream; mix well. Stir slowly into shrimp mixture. Cook slowly, stirring until slightly thickened. Spoon into individual ramekins or baking shells; sprinkle with buttered bread crumbs. Brown under broiler a few minutes. Serve with sliced tomatoes and lettuce salad and sour dough bread. Finish with a light dessert, such as a sherbet or sponge cake ring with fresh strawberries.

My choice of wine to accompany this dish:
CALIFORNIA JOHANNISBERG RIESLING

NOTE: *A touch of nutmeg is used in another version of this tempter, by Mrs. Alvin Ehrhardt of United Vintners, Inc., Lodi. Mrs. Ehrhardt says the nutmeg is optional, but "very rakish in flavor." She also recommends the sauce for oysters or sweetbreads.*

WINEMAKER'S SHRIMP

(4 to 6 servings)

Mrs. Harold Berg, U. C. Dept. of Viticulture & Enology

 2 lbs. raw shrimp in shells
 ½ cup tomato sauce
 1 tablespoon chopped parsley
 ¼ teaspoon oregano
   Salt
 ¼ cup butter or margarine
 2 cloves garlic, chopped
 1 (10½-oz.) can consommé
 1 cup California Dry Sherry

Boil shrimp 10 to 20 minutes, or just until tender. Shell and devein. Meanwhile, combine and simmer tomato sauce, parsley, oregano, salt, butter, garlic and soup. Just before serving, add shrimp and Sherry. Heat thoroughly. Serve with plain rice, tossed green salad and sour French bread.

My choice of wine to accompany this dish:
CALIFORNIA SAUVIGNON BLANC

SHERRIED SHRIMP

(6 servings)

Robert S. McKnight, Di Giorgio Wine Company, Di Giorgio

 1 clove garlic
 ⅓ teaspoon tarragon
 ⅓ teaspoon parsley
 ⅓ teaspoon minced shallot
 ⅓ teaspoon minced onion
 ½ cup butter or margarine
 1 cup fine dry bread crumbs
   Salt and pepper
   Dash *each:* nutmeg and thyme (optional)
 ¼ to ⅓ cup California Dry Sherry
 2 lbs. shelled cooked shrimp
   Buttered bread crumbs

Mash garlic to paste; add seasonings. Combine with butter and dry bread crumbs; mix until thoroughly blended, using electric beater or blender. Season with salt and pepper and, if desired, nutmeg and thyme. Blend in Sherry. In 6 buttered shells or individual casseroles, alternate layers of mix with layers of cooked shrimp. Top with buttered crumbs. Bake in moderately hot oven (400°) for 15 to 20 minutes.

My choice of wine to accompany this dish:
CALIFORNIA BRUT CHAMPAGNE OR ROSÉ

NOTE: *A delectable dish, similar to the famous Shrimp de Jonghe.*

RIESLING SEAFOOD SHELLS

(6 to 8 servings)

Mrs. Ze'ev Halperin, Mt. Tivy Winery, Reedley

This is an American adaptation of a dish served by a European airline. All sorts of seafoods may be added, or substituted. It may be served over rice instead of in the pastry shells.

 1 pkg. frozen puff pastry shells
 1½ to 2 cups cooked lobster meat, or
   2 (9-oz.) pkgs. frozen
   lobster tails, cooked
 ¾ lb. boiled shrimps, shelled
   and deveined
 20 canned clams
 1 cup fresh or canned mushrooms
 1 tablespoon flour
 2 tablespoons butter or margarine
 1½ cups California Riesling, Sauterne
   or other white dinner wine
 1 cup light cream
 ½ teaspoon salt
 ⅛ teaspoon pepper
 ½ teaspoon seasoned salt
 ½ cup chopped parsley

Bake puff pastry shells according to package directions; remove centers and save for topping. Break or cut seafood and mushrooms into small pieces; dust with flour; sauté lightly in butter. Add wine; simmer 10 minutes. Add cream and seasonings. Pour into pastry shells; sprinkle with parsley. Top with reserved pastry "covers." Serve with tossed green salad and hot buttered rolls. For dessert, an icebox cake, with chocolate frosting flavored with California brandy.

My choice of wine to accompany this dish:
CALIFORNIA RIESLING

SCAMPI TRECATE

(6 servings)

Mrs. Dino Barengo, Acampo Winery, Acampo

¾ cup butter or margarine
¾ cup olive oil
2 lemons
1 large clove garlic, crushed
6 green onions, minced
1 carrot, minced
3 stalks celery, minced
1 large tomato, cut in small pieces
2 lbs. large raw shrimp, unshelled
½ cup California brandy
2 cups California Dry Sauterne or
    other white dinner wine
2 tablespoons California
    red wine vinegar
½ teaspoon salt
¼ teaspoon black pepper
1 teaspoon Tabasco sauce
½ (10½-oz.) can consommé
½ cup water
3 tablespoons flour

In large, heavy saucepan, melt ½ cup of the butter; add oil, peel of 1 lemon, garlic, green onions, carrot, celery and tomato. Sauté 5 minutes. Add shrimp; cook, stirring over medium heat 10 minutes. Add brandy; flame. Remove shrimp; when cool enough to handle, shell and devein; set aside. Strain cooked vegetable mixture into saucepan. Add juice of lemons, wine, wine vinegar, salt, pepper, Tabasco sauce, consommé, water and cleaned shrimp; cook 10 minutes. Remove shrimp to serving bowl. Melt remaining ¼ cup butter in small saucepan; blend in flour. Add some of liquid in which shrimp was cooked, 2 tablespoons at a time, stirring constantly, to make a thin paste. Return to remaining shrimp-cooking liquid; boil a few minutes. Pour over shrimp. Serve with thin slices of sour dough Italian bread.

My choice of wine to accompany this dish:
WELL-CHILLED CALIFORNIA DRY WHITE DINNER WINE

NOTE: *Even to read it makes you want to start cooking—and this shrimp bowl is really much easier than it sounds.*

ABALONE LIVERMORE

(4 servings)

Mrs. Herman L. Wente, Wente Bros., Livermore

Instead of deep fat cooking for abalone try deep wine cooking. Since the sauce should be ready before cooking the abalone, make the sauce first, as follows:

2 tablespoons butter
1 tablespoon flour
½ cup California Sauterne, Chablis
    or other white dinner wine
1 tablespoon lemon juice
2 tablespoons finely chopped parsley

Melt butter in saucepan; blend in flour. Pour in wine slowly, stirring constantly. Add lemon juice and parsley. Cook, stirring, until thick and smooth. Pour over poached abalone, which you now cook as follows:

TO POACH ABALONE: In heavy pan, bring 1" of California white dinner wine to boiling. Add slices of well-pounded abalone, one at a time. Cook each slice 1 minute, keeping wine boiling.

NOTE: *The same type of California white dinner wine, well chilled, would be perfect served at the table.*

LOBSTER NEWBURG

(4 servings)

Mrs. Fred Snyde, Woodbridge Vineyard Association, Lodi

2 lobsters, cooked, cleaned
    and cut in half
⅓ cup California Dry Sherry
¼ cup butter or margarine
3 level tablespoons flour
2 cups rich milk or thin cream
1 teaspoon seasoned salt
    Dash *each*: pepper, cayenne,
    nutmeg

Remove lobster from shell, saving shells. Cut meat in bite-size pieces. Pour over Sherry; refrigerate 2 or 3 hours. Meanwhile, melt butter in saucepan; blend in flour. Gradually blend in milk; cook, stirring constantly, until thickened and smooth. Add lobster, Sherry and seasonings; heat thoroughly. Fill lobster shells with mixture; place under broiler until slightly browned. Serve with stuffed baked potatoes, fresh peas and a tomato aspic salad.

My choice of wine to accompany this dish:
CALIFORNIA WHITE DINNER WINE

NOTE: *If a thicker sauce is preferred, add a little more flour, or use heavy cream. For an excellent, easy tomato aspic, see VINTAGE ASPIC in the section on Salads.*

COQUILLE ST. JACQUES

(6 to 8 servings)

Mrs. Kerby T. Anderson, Guild Wine Co., Lodi

2 lbs. fresh scallops
2 cups California Dry Sherry
1 bay leaf
1 lb. fresh mushrooms, sliced
1 medium onion, diced
¾ cup butter or margarine
3 tablespoons flour
2 tablespoons lemon juice
1 teaspoon salt
½ teaspoon paprika
⅛ teaspoon pepper
    Dash cayenne
    Bread crumbs
    Grated Parmesan cheese

Simmer scallops 10 minutes in Sherry with bay leaf. Drain, saving broth. Sauté mushrooms and onion in butter. Add flour; stir in wine broth and lemon juice. Cook, stirring constantly, until thickened. Season with salt, pepper, paprika and cayenne. Add scallops. Place in buttered casserole or individual baking shells. Sprinkle with bread crumbs, Parmesan cheese and paprika. Bake in moderately slow oven (325°) for 25 minutes. This goes well with rice pilaf or baked potatoes, green vegetable for color contrast, tossed green salad with tart herbed dressing, rolls, and pineapple sherbet dessert.

My choice of wine to accompany this dish:
CALIFORNIA RIESLING

NOTE: *Many original or individual variations appear in the various scallop recipes favored by California winemaking families. Mrs. Stanley Strud, California Wine Association, Lodi, adds chopped green pepper and pimientos to her version, and California Chablis. Mrs. A. D. Webb, U. C. Dept. of Viticulture & Enology, has a simple method, baking scallops in a sauce including grated Swiss cheese and California Flor Sherry.*

CRAB-ARTICHOKE CASSEROLE

(6 to 8 servings)

Mrs. E. L. Ely, Jr., Italian Swiss Colony, Asti

2 (7½-oz.) cans crabmeat, drained
¼ cup butter or margarine
¼ cup flour
2 teaspoons salt
⅛ teaspoon pepper
1 teaspoon paprika
1 teaspoon instant minced onion
3¼ cups milk
1¼ cups uncooked macaroni shells
1 (9-oz.) pkg. frozen artichoke hearts, or
1 (8½-oz.) can artichoke hearts
⅓ cup California Dry Sherry
¼ cup grated sharp Cheddar cheese

Flake crabmeat, removing any cartilage; set aside. Melt butter in medium-size saucepan. Remove from heat; stir in flour, salt, pepper and paprika until smooth. Add onion. Gradually stir in milk; bring to boiling, stirring constantly. Reduce heat; simmer 5 minutes. Remove from heat; set aside. Prepare macaroni according to package directions; drain well. Cook artichoke hearts according to package directions; drain well. Combine crabmeat, Sherry, macaroni and artichoke hearts with sauce; mix well. Turn into 2 to 2½-qt. casserole. Sprinkle with grated cheese. Bake in a moderate oven (350°) about 20 minutes or until bubbly. We prefer this as the hot dish for a buffet supper, with green salad, French bread, and assorted cheeses and crackers.

My choice of wine to accompany this dish:
CALIFORNIA RIESLING OR CHABLIS

NOTE: *Mrs. Albert Cribari of Evergreen Vineyards, San Jose, serves a similar crab-artichoke casserole as a luncheon dish. Her version adds mushrooms. For a heartier meal, she suggests serving the mixture over rice.*

WINE LAND CRABMEAT

(4 servings)

Karl L. Wente, Wente Bros., Livermore

1 tablespoon grated onion
¼ cup butter or margarine
¼ cup sifted flour
1 cup milk
½ cup California Dry Semillon, Chablis or other white dinner wine
½ cup California Sherry
1 teaspoon salt
Dash Tabasco sauce
2 tablespoons thinly sliced mushrooms
1 egg yolk, beaten
2 cups cooked or canned crabmeat

Sauté onion in melted butter; blend in flour, but do not brown. Gradually blend in milk and wines, stirring constantly, until thickened. Add salt, Tabasco sauce and mushrooms. Remove from heat when bubbles appear; quickly stir in egg yolk and crabmeat. Serve over toast triangles or fluffy rice. Or, if desired, place in ramekins or baking shells, sprinkle with paprika and brown lightly in oven. Good with a green salad and fruit for dessert.

My choice of wine to accompany this dish:
CALIFORNIA SEMILLON OR PINOT BLANC

CRAB ACAPULCO

(8 servings)

Mrs. Bruno T. Bisceglia, Bisceglia Bros. Wine Co., Fresno

¼ cup butter or margarine
¼ cup sifted all-purpose flour
1⅔ cups milk
¾ teaspoon salt
1 teaspoon Worcestershire sauce
Dash cayenne pepper
2 tablespoons fresh lime or lemon juice
3 tablespoons California Sherry
⅓ cup grated sharp American cheese
2 cups cooked or canned crabmeat
4 avocados
Salt
Toasted sesame seeds or toasted coconut

Melt butter in saucepan; blend in flour. Gradually blend in milk; cook, stirring constantly, until thickened and smooth. Add salt, Worcestershire sauce, cayenne, lime juice, Sherry and cheese; mix well. Add crabmeat; cook just until heated. Cut avocados in half; remove seeds and skins. Place in shallow baking dish; sprinkle with salt and heap with crab mixture. Sprinkle with sesame seeds or coconut. Bake in a slow oven (300°) for 15 minutes only, or JUST UNTIL WARM. Serve as luncheon entrée, with hot bread or toasted muffins and whole spiced peaches.

My choice of wine to accompany this dish:
CALIFORNIA RIESLING

EASY DEVILED CRAB

(4 servings)

Mrs. August Sebastiani, Samuele Sebastiani, Sonoma

This recipe was handed down to me from my grandmother. It is a very old one, and especially delicious, either as a main course dish or as a salad.

3 tablespoons butter or margarine
2 tablespoons flour
1 cup milk, heated
1 teaspoon salt
Dash cayenne pepper
1 teaspoon Worcestershire sauce
2 egg yolks, slightly beaten
2 cups crabmeat, fresh cooked, frozen or canned
¼ teaspoon lemon juice
¼ cup California Dry Sherry
⅔ cup buttered crumbs
4 lemon slices
Paprika

Melt butter; stir in flour and heated milk. Season with salt, cayenne and Worcestershire sauce; cook, stirring constantly, until thick. Add slightly beaten egg yolks and crab; cook 3 minutes. Stir in lemon juice and Sherry. Spoon mixture into individual baking shells or ramekins; cover with buttered crumbs. Top with a lemon slice and sprinkling of paprika. Bake in a hot oven (450°) about 20-25 minutes or until brown.

My choice of wine to accompany this dish:
ANY CALIFORNIA DRY WHITE OR ROSÉ

TUNA TETRAZZINI

(6 servings)

Mrs. Edmund Accomazzo, Cucamonga Winery, Cucamonga

This recipe is supposed to have been named for the famous opera diva, Tetrazzini. I serve it often for bridge luncheons.

    ½ (8-oz.) pkg. spaghettini
    3 tablespoons bottled garlic spread
      (or less, to taste)
    ¼ cup sifted all-purpose flour
    1 cup milk
    ¼ cup California Dry Sherry
    2 (4-oz.) cans button mushrooms
    1 (8-oz.) pkg. process American cheese,
      grated
    ½ teaspoon seasoned salt
    ¼ teaspoon pepper
    2 (6½ or 7-oz.) cans chunk-style tuna,
      drained
    2 tablespoons grated Parmesan cheese

Cook spaghettini according to package directions; drain and set aside. In top of double boiler, melt garlic spread over boiling water. Stir in flour; gradually add milk. Add Sherry and ½ cup liquid drained from mushrooms. Cook, stirring constantly, until thickened. Add grated American cheese, salt and pepper; stir until cheese is melted. Stir in spaghettini, tuna and mushrooms. Pour into 1½-qt. shallow baking dish; sprinkle with Parmesan cheese. Bake in moderate oven (350°) for 20 minutes or until light golden. Serve with green salad.

My choice of wine to accompany this dish:
CALIFORNIA DRY SAUTERNE OR GRIGNOLINO ROSÉ

QUICK CLAM-CORN DINNER

(4 to 6 servings)

John Lockett, Wine Advisory Board, San Francisco

This is an easy main dish for a bachelor cook. All you need is to keep plenty of wine and canned foods on hand.

    2 (7-oz.) cans minced clams
    4 tablespoons butter or margarine
    6 tablespoons flour
    ½ cup milk
    ⅓ cup California Sauterne, Rhine
      or other white dinner wine
      Salt, garlic salt, pepper
    1 cup canned whole-kernel corn, drained
    2 tablespoons chopped parsley
      Buttered fine bread crumbs
      Paprika

Drain clams, reserving liquid. Melt butter and stir in flour; add ⅔ cup reserved clam liquid and the milk and wine. Cook, stirring constantly, until sauce boils and thickens. Season to taste with salt, garlic salt and pepper. Cool slightly. Stir in clams, corn and parsley. Spoon mixture into 4 or 6 greased baking shells or individual casseroles. Sprinkle with bread crumbs and paprika. Bake in moderately hot oven (400°) about 20 minutes, or until bubbly and browned.

My choice of wine to accompany this dish:
CALIFORNIA SAUTERNE, VERY WELL CHILLED

NOTE: *Mrs. Harold Berg, University of California Dept. of Viticulture & Enology, also has an interesting clam casserole, combining sour cream, noodles, mushrooms and white wine with the clams.*

DEVILED CLAMS MORRO BAY

(8 servings)

Marjorie Riley, Mont La Salle Vineyards, Napa

This recipe can be altered to suit the whim of the cook. It is my own version of a way of preparing clams which I first tasted near Morro Bay, where the old-time residents do a lot of clamming. A wonderful Italian woman showed me how to prepare them. Mine never tasted quite like hers, but I think that's because she sang while she cooked, and that makes a difference. Also, she put in "a little of this, a little of that, never the same," and like many truly delicious things, it was almost impossible to figure out the exact ingredients.

    2 cups finely ground fresh clams, or
    3 (7½-oz.) cans clams,
      drained and ground
    ½ cup ground onion
    ⅓ cup ground green pepper
    ⅓ cup ground celery
    1⅓ cups dry French bread crumbs,
      toasted and ground
    1 cup whipping cream
    2 eggs, beaten
    2 tablespoons butter or margarine, melted
    2 teaspoons prepared mustard
    1½ teaspoons salt
    1 teaspoon pepper
    ½ cup California Dry Semillon, Sauterne
      or other white dinner wine
      Grated Parmesan cheese
    4 slices bacon

Using a meat grinder, grind clams, onion, green pepper, celery and toasted bread crumbs. Measure and combine. Stir in cream, eggs, melted butter, mustard, salt, pepper and wine. (Mixture should be thick, rich and creamy.) Scoop mixture into large clam shells or other individual baking dishes. Bake in moderate oven (350°) for 20 minutes. Remove; sprinkle heavily with grated Parmesan cheese. Top with ½ slice bacon; return to oven until bacon is crisp and brown. We love to serve these clams with a green salad and garlic French bread.

My choice of wine to accompany this dish:
CALIFORNIA RIESLING, CHABLIS,
PINOT CHARDONNAY OR SEMILLON

TUNA CHO-CHO-SAN brings delicate Oriental flavor and color to a luncheon or supper menu. To make 6 to 8 servings: Drain and slice water chestnuts (5-oz. can). Drain liquid from 4-oz. can sliced mushrooms into measuring cup; add enough California Chablis or other white dinner wine to bring to 1 cup level. (Will take about ⅔ cup wine.) Cook ¼ cup **each** finely chopped green onions and celery in ⅓ cup butter, until crisp-tender but not brown. Blend in ⅔ cup sifted flour, 1 teaspoon **each** seasoned salt and soy sauce, and ¼ teaspoon grated lemon rind. Slowly stir in 2 cups thin cream. Cook, stirring, until mixture starts to thicken; stir in wine-mushroom liquid. Bring to boil, stirring now and then; add water chestnuts, mushrooms and chunk-style tuna (9½-oz. can). Heat slowly a few more minutes. If desired, add 2 tablespoons **each** chopped pimiento and parsley. Spoon into baked patty shells, toast cups, or serve over toast, cornbread or rice, with the same wine accompanying.

SAUCES

Including Basic Bastes and Marinades with Wine

The suave, sumptuous flavor imparted to meats, poultry, game or fish by a good sauce or baste plays a major role in our most pleasurable dinner memories. Wine is often essential to the blending of a memorable sauce, since it is, after all (in terms of kitchen use), a liquid seasoning as basic as salt, pepper and herbs. Many main dishes reach new heights in taste when merely basted with California wine alone. But for those who enjoy trying special individual approaches, here are some favorite recipes from experienced cooks. (See also the marinating ideas on Page 120.)

UNIVERSAL B.B.Q. WINE BASTE

(2⅔ cups)

N. C. Mirassou, Mirassou Vineyards, San Jose

This sauce can be used on any kind of meat, fowl or fish that is barbecued. Leftover sauce can be frozen and used at a future date. Let thaw one day before using.

    ¾ cup California red or white
        dinner wine, **or** brandy
    ½ cup California wine vinegar
    ½ cup olive oil
    1 cup finely chopped chives
    1 cup finely chopped parsley
  1½ teaspoons crushed or
        finely chopped garlic
    1 tablespoon salt
    1 tablespoon pepper
    1 tablespoon monosodium glutamate

A day ahead, combine all ingredients in a glass or ceramic dish; let stand at room temperature. Baste meat, poultry or fish on one side 1 hour before barbecuing. Place basted side down on grill; while first side cooks, brush sauce on unbasted side.

My choice of wine to accompany the meal:
CALIFORNIA RED OR WHITE DINNER WINE
(CALIFORNIA CHAMPAGNE WITH HORS D'OEUVRE)

CUCAMONGA SPAGHETTI SAUCE

(2 quarts)

Mrs. John B. Ellena, Regina Grape Products Co., Etiwanda

    4 medium-size onions, chopped
    ½ cup margarine, or
        ¼ cup oil and ¼ cup butter
    3 cloves garlic, finely chopped
    ½ cup chopped parsley
    1 cup chopped celery tops
    1 green pepper, finely chopped
    1 (4-oz.) can mushrooms, chopped
    1 teaspoon rosemary
    1 teaspoon basil
    ½ teaspoon pepper
    2 teaspoons salt
    2 lbs. ground beef
    1 (1-lb. 4-oz.) can solid-pack tomatoes
    1 (6-oz.) can tomato paste
    1 cup California Zinfandel, Burgundy
        or other red dinner wine

Sauté onions in margarine until tender and golden. Add garlic; sauté about 2 minutes. Add parsley, celery tops, green pepper, mushrooms and seasonings; sauté well, stirring often. Brown meat in Dutch oven or heavy skillet, stirring until crumbly and no redness remains. Add sautéed vegetables; mix well. Add tomatoes, tomato paste and wine, stirring until well mixed. Bring to boiling; lower heat; simmer 3 hours, then serve on spaghetti.

My choice of wine to accompany this dish:
CALIFORNIA ZINFANDEL

NOTE: A hearty, aromatic flavor-blend, perfected by the wine and the patient slow cooking. Appetizing spaghetti sauces with individuality are also made by Mrs. Frank J. Pilone of Cucamonga Vineyard Co., Cucamonga, and Mrs. Dale R. Anderson of Di Giorgio Wine Co., Di Giorgio. Mrs. Pilone includes white wine and Italian sausage (or ground pork sausage), as well as ground beef, in hers. Mrs. Anderson prefers red wine in the sauce, and diced bacon.

MY FAVORITE SPAGHETTI SAUCE

(1½ qts.)

Mrs. Albert J. Puccinelli, Puccinelli Vineyards, San Mateo

 1 lb. ground beef
 1 (1-lb. 4-oz.) can tomato puree
 3¾ cups water
 1 cup California Sherry
 ¼ teaspoon *each*: oregano,
 thyme and marjoram
 ½ cup chopped parsley
 ¼ cup instant minced onion
 1 (6-oz.) can mushrooms
 1 tablespoon salt
 ½ teaspoon pepper

Sauté ground beef, stirring until brown and crumbly. Add remaining ingredients, mixing well. Simmer, covered, over low heat 4 to 6 hours. May be used with spaghetti, noodles, tagliarini, lasagna or risotto. (If used with lasagna or risotto, layer the pasta and sauce until dish is full; cover with grated cheese; bake until cheese is melted and dish heated through.)

NOTE: A thick rich sauce, with extra flavors brought out by the long slow simmering. With any of the dishes mentioned, a California red, Rosé or "vino" type would be delightful.

EASY ALL-PURPOSE WINE SAUCE

(About ⅔ cup)

Mrs. Dale R. Anderson, Di Giorgio Wine Co., Di Giorgio

This all-around barbecue sauce and marinade was a favorite recipe of our neighbor in Kerman, Mrs. Louise Fike, who was fond of cookouts. We have enjoyed it many times. It can be used for roasts, steaks, fowl or salmon.

 ¼ cup oil
 ¼ cup California Sherry
 2 tablespoons soy sauce
 1 teaspoon Worcestershire sauce
 1 teaspoon garlic powder
 Freshly ground pepper

Combine all ingredients. Marinate roast 24 to 48 hours; steaks 4 hours; poultry or salmon 2 hours. Use remaining marinade to baste while cooking.

NOTE: A simple, always-good combination. Serve your favorite California dinner wine with the meal, according to the dish.

NO-MIX BARBECUE SAUCE

(Any amount)

J. B. Cella, II, Cella Wineries, Fresno

This sauce is the simplest one I know. It involves no mixing, but merely a trip to your store for a bottle of your favorite California Dry Vermouth. This can be used to baste all forms of fowl, steaks and hamburger. In this you have the wine flavor of the Vermouth and the herbs that are blended into the Vermouth.

NOTE: Smart cooks are discovering that both Dry and Sweet California Vermouth can do much for cooking, and deserve more experimenting. At the table, serve whichever wine you prefer with the particular finished dish.

EVEN APPLESAUCE can gain in interest from a touch of wine. Next time you slice a pound of peeled cooking apples into the pan, add a few teaspoons sugar, to taste; 1 large onion, chopped; salt and pepper; and 2 tablespoons California Cream Sherry. Cover; simmer gently (stirring now and then) until tender. Serve with any pork dish, duck or goose. A bottle of chilled California white dinner wine on the table makes the dinner unforgettable.

BASIC WINE SAUCE

(2½ cups)

Brother Timothy, Mont La Salle Vineyards, Napa

Crush 2 cloves garlic in 2 tablespoons salt. Add 1 cup California dinner wine (Chablis for fish, **or** Claret for red meats, pork or game); ¼ cup lemon juice, 1¼ cups olive oil, 1 teaspoon freshly ground black pepper and 1 teaspoon crushed or powdered herb seasoning (thyme for fish, **or** oregano for red meats, pork or game). Use as marinade and also for basting.

NOTE: As versatile as it is flavorful. With dinner, serve the same wine as used in the sauce.

GINGER-VERMOUTH MARINADE

(1⅔ cups)

Mrs. W. W. Owen, California Grape Products Corp., Delano

    1 teaspoon tarragon
    1 tablespoon ground or grated fresh ginger
    ½ cup California Dry Vermouth
    1½ cups California Sauterne, Chablis
        or other white dinner wine
    1 tablespoon lemon juice
    1 tablespoon monosodium glutamate
    1 teaspoon salt

Combine all ingredients; pour over a cut-up chicken. Marinate several hours, turning occasionally. Bake or broil as desired, basting with remaining marinade.

NOTE: *A tantalizing flavor. Either white or Rosé would be fine served with chicken marinated in this manner.*

A FLAVORSOME MEAT LOAF SAUCE is recommended by Mrs. Myron S. Nightingale of Roma Wine Co., Fresno. Mrs. Nightingale mixes California Claret or other dry red dinner wine with brown sugar, canned whole cranberry sauce and ground cloves, spreading most of this mixture over the meat loaf. A small amount is reserved and blended with cornstarch and pan drippings, to be served as sauce at the table. The same red wine or a California Rosé would be ideal as accompaniment.

BARBECUED POULTRY PLEASER

(1½ cups)

Mrs. Keith V. Nylander, Di Giorgio Wine Co., Di Giorgio

    ¼ cup oil or melted butter or
        margarine
    ¾ cup California Sauterne, Chablis
        or other white dinner wine
    1 clove garlic, finely minced
    1 large onion, grated
    1 teaspoon salt
    1 teaspoon celery salt
    ¼ teaspoon black pepper
    ¼ teaspoon dried thyme
    ⅛ teaspoon dried tarragon
    1 tablespoon chopped parsley

Mix all ingredients together thoroughly. Let stand overnight. Marinate chicken or turkey in sauce several hours before broiling or barbecuing. Baste with remaining marinade during cooking. Chilled artichokes that have been cooked in boiling water with salt, garlic, white wine vinegar and tarragon go beautifully with chicken or turkey barbecued with this sauce. The menu could also include a pilaf, tossed green salad, garlic bread, and dessert combining fresh fruit with orange sherbet and California Champagne float.

My choice of wine to accompany this dish:
CALIFORNIA WHITE DINNER WINE

NOTE: *The "float" of Champagne, as topping for the fruit-and-sherbet dessert, deserves to be poured at the table, in front of guests. It's a colorful and dramatic touch, adding flair to the dinner.*

WILD DUCK BARBECUE SAUCE

(About 3 cups)

J. W. Fleming, Lockeford Winery, Lodi

This sauce is also very good with spareribs or any other barbecued pork.

    1 cup California brandy (or, ½ cup
        brandy and ½ cup California Sherry)
    1 cup soy sauce
    1 cup honey
    1 tablespoon salt

Combine all ingredients, heating slightly to blend well. Marinate ducks in sauce for 3 or 4 hours, depending on size. Cook in Chinese oven or on motor-driven spit in barbecue with hood, for about 1½ hours or until tender (legs will move easily from body). Baste occasionally during cooking.

NOTE: *A wonderfully rich glaze and flavor. If the dish is wild duck, a California red or Rosé dinner wine might be especially enjoyable; if domestic duck or pork, Rosé or white. Another interesting wild duck marinade is made by Mrs. W. W. Owen of Calif. Grape Products Corp., Delano. She uses dry white wine and ground mace in her recipe, and prefers this type of wine served with the wild duck. (See also note at bottom of Page 66, on red wine with wild duck.)*

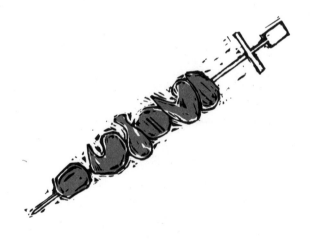

TURKEY BARBECUE SAUCE

(1½ cups)

Leonard P. LeBlanc, California Growers Wineries, Cutler

    1 cup California Sherry
    ¼ cup olive oil
    2 tablespoons butter or margarine
    1 medium onion, very finely minced
    1 clove garlic, crushed
    1½ teaspoons salt
    ¼ teaspoon paprika
    1 teaspoon fines herbs
    1 teaspoon minced parsley
        Freshly ground pepper

Combine all ingredients; simmer 15 minutes. Use to baste turkey barbecued on a spit, basting often.

NOTE: *Unusually appealing. With the turkey, serve your usual preference: California red, white or Rosé dinner wine.*

CLASSIC CUMBERLAND SAUCE

(About 1 cup)

Karl C. Krupp, Wine Advisory Board, Los Angeles

This sauce is traditional with wild or domestic duck, goose, cold turkey or chicken, or hot or cold ham.

⅓ cup red currant jelly
¼ cup California Port
¼ cup orange juice
2 tablespoons lemon juice
2 teaspoons dry mustard
1 teaspoon paprika
½ teaspoon ground ginger
1 teaspoon cornstarch
2 tablespoons grated orange rind

Stir jelly over low heat until melted. Blend remaining ingredients; add to jelly. Bring to boiling; reduce heat and simmer, stirring constantly, for 5 minutes. Let stand an hour or longer before serving, preferably with hot roast goose.

My choice of wine to accompany this dish:
CALIFORNIA CLARET OR ZINFANDEL

SHERRIED RAISIN SAUCE

(About 2 cups)

Mrs. Jake Rheingans, Sanger Winery Association, Sanger

This may be served on baked ham, corned pork or tongue.

¾ cup seedless raisins
1½ cups water
½ cup brown sugar (packed)
1½ tablespoons cornstarch
¼ teaspoon cloves
½ teaspoon salt
1 tablespoon butter or margarine
½ cup California Sherry

Rinse raisins and drain. Add raisins to water; simmer 10 minutes. Mix together brown sugar, cornstarch, cloves and salt; stir into raisins. Cook, stirring constantly, until clear and thickened. Blend in butter and Sherry; heat thoroughly.

NOTE: *A chilled California Rosé would be perfect with any of the dishes suggested with this spicy sauce.*

SPARERIBS BARBECUE SAUCE

(For 5 or 6 lbs. spareribs)

S. Martinelli, S. Martinelli & Co., Watsonville

1 cup California red or white dinner wine
¼ cup catsup
1 teaspoon brown sugar
1 teaspoon Worcestershire sauce
1 teaspoon salt
¼ teaspoon dry mustard
¼ teaspoon dry celery seed
¼ cup chopped onion
Dash pepper

Combine wine, catsup and seasonings; mix well. Baste spareribs frequently with sauce during the barbecuing.

My choice of wine to accompany this dish:
CALIFORNIA DRY RED OR WHITE DINNER WINE

NOTE: *Mrs. Jake Rheingans of Sanger Winery Assn., Sanger, barbecues spareribs with a sauce that includes molasses and California Sherry. This would be tops with any pork. Crushed pineapple and Port are among the sparerib sauce secrets of Marvin B. Jones, Gibson Wine Co., Elk Grove.*

STEAK SAUCE BORDELAISE

(4 servings)

Mrs. A. D. Webb, U. of Calif. Dept. of Viticulture & Enology

There are two schools of thought about this classic sauce in Bordeaux—one prefers garlic, while the other prefers shallots. In any case, enough is used that the flavor is unmistakable.

3 tablespoons chopped garlic or shallots
1 cup California Burgundy, Claret or other red dinner wine
½ cup pan drippings from steaks

Gently simmer garlic or shallots in wine until volume is reduced by one half. Set aside. After steaks are broiled, stir the rich brown pan drippings into sauce. Spoon warm sauce over steaks just before serving. Accompany steaks with green salad and French bread, with cheese and fresh fruit for dessert.

My choice of wine to accompany this dish:
CALIFORNIA CABERNET OR ZINFANDEL

NOTE: *For another traditional steak sauce, the Marchand de Vin or Wine Merchant sauce, see recipe for PAPER-THIN STEAKS on Page 41.*

LEMON-CHABLIS FISH SAUCE

(1¼ cups)

Mrs. Walter Richert, Richert & Sons, Morgan Hill

    2 lemons
    1 tablespoon cornstarch
    1 cup California Chablis or other
      white dinner wine
    ¼ teaspoon salt
    1½ tablespoons butter or margarine

Remove peel from 1 lemon; slice lemon very thinly. Squeeze juice from second lemon. Make a smooth paste of cornstarch, wine and salt. Melt butter in small saucepan; add paste; cook, stirring constantly, until mixture is clear and slightly thickened. Add lemon juice and slices; heat a few minutes longer. Serve over baked, broiled or poached fish.

NOTE: *Most people would like a California Rhine, Chablis or Sauterne with the fish served with the sauce.*

UNCOOKED WINE HOLLANDAISE

(About 1½ cups)

Otto E. Meyer, Paul Masson Vineyards, Saratoga

    4 egg yolks
    ½ teaspoon salt
      Dash cayenne pepper **or** Tabasco sauce
    1 cup melted butter or margarine
    ¼ cup California Riesling or other
      dry white dinner wine
    1 tablespoon lemon juice

Beat egg yolks until very thick and light yellow (takes about 8 to 10 minutes). Blend in salt and cayenne or Tabasco, beating well. Add butter, a tablespoon at a time, beating well after each addition, until 6 tablespoons have been added. Combine wine and lemon juice; beat in very slowly, alternating with remaining butter. Spoon over hot cooked asparagus or broccoli. **(Do not heat sauce, however.)** Store leftover sauce in refrigerator. It will solidify upon storing. You can use it later as is, or let it soften at room temperature to its original airy texture.

NOTE: *A vegetable with a sauce as luxurious as this would befit the most festive dinner — accompanied by California Champagne.*

QUICK ROSÉ-CHEESE SAUCE

(About 1⅓ cups)

Helen Junker, Wine Advisory Board, San Francisco

This is a fast, easy sauce to serve over a hot cooked vegetable, such as asparagus, broccoli or cauliflower.

    ½ lb. process American cheese
    ½ cup California Rosé
    3 or 4 drops Tabasco sauce

Cut cheese into chunks; place all ingredients in top of double boiler over hot (not boiling) water. Heat, stirring now and then, until blended and smooth. We enjoy this vegetable and sauce with a steak dinner.

My choice of wine to accompany this dish:
CALIFORNIA ROSÉ OR BURGUNDY

CHEESE & EGGS

Also Pastas and Rice Recipes with Wine

It has been widely noted that wine and cheese have an ancient affinity. Both typify man's quest for a more enduring and portable form for perishable foods. The transmuting of grapes into wine, and milk into cheese, were two of the brighter beacons in civilization's history. They proved to the old wandering tribes that Nature's own wonders (of wine fermentation and milk curding) could be controlled and improved upon by man. Not trivially, wine and cheese also bestowed upon the world a superlative companionship of taste: no two food products have ever done more for each other. Today's cooks still find the combination an irresistible one.

MACARONI & CHEESE WITH WINE

(About 6 servings)

Mrs. Ted Yamada, American Society of Enologists, Anaheim

- 2 cups uncooked macaroni
- 2 tablespoons soft butter or margarine
- 1½ cups cubed sharp Cheddar cheese
- ½ teaspoon salt
- ½ teaspoon dry mustard
- 2 eggs, beaten
- 1½ cups rich milk or thin cream
- ½ cup California Sauterne or other white dinner wine
- 2 or 3 tablespoons chopped canned green chiles
- ½ cup stale bread crumbs mixed with 2 tablespoons melted butter or margarine

Combine all ingredients except crumbs; mix well. Place in buttered 1½-qt. baking dish. Sprinkle with buttered crumbs. Bake, covered, in moderate oven (350°) for 40 to 50 minutes. Let stand 5 to 10 minutes before serving, to thicken liquid in casserole.

NOTE: *Quickly made, and especially pleasing with a well-chilled California Rosé served on the side. Another easy idea for macaroni is offered by Mrs. Clifton Chappell of Thomas Vineyards, Cucamonga. She suggests substituting California Sauterne for all or part of the milk in your favorite recipe for macaroni and cheese—a "delightful variation for a standard recipe."*

EGGS ARE LUSCIOUS when poached or fried very gently in California Sherry. Sprinkle with Parmesan cheese and serve on hot buttered melba toast. A glass of chilled Chablis is ideal on the side.

BAKED SPAGHETTI UKIAH

(6 servings)

Mrs. John Parducci, Parducci Wine Cellars, Inc., Ukiah

This dish may be made the day before and refrigerated. It is also excellent for freezing. If frozen, allow 6 hours in refrigerator for thawing before baking.

- 1½ lbs. ground beef
- 1 medium-size onion, minced
- 1 clove garlic, mashed or finely chopped
- ¼ cup oil
- 3 (8-oz.) cans tomato sauce
- 1 cup California Burgundy, Claret or other red dinner wine
- 1 teaspoon dried Italian or mixed herbs
- ½ teaspoon dried parsley (optional)
- 1 tablespoon sugar
- ½ teaspoon salt
- ¼ teaspoon pepper
- ½ lb. spaghetti, broken in 2" lengths
- 1½ cups grated American cheese

Sauté meat, onion and garlic in heated oil. Add tomato sauce, wine, herbs, parsley, sugar, salt and pepper. Simmer, covered, 1 hour, stirring occasionally. Cook spaghetti according to package directions; drain. Add spaghetti and ½ cup cheese to sauce. Turn into 3-qt. casserole; sprinkle with remaining 1 cup cheese. (If made ahead, do not sprinkle cheese on top until ready to bake.) Cover; bake in a moderately slow oven (325°) for 45 minutes. Uncover; bake 30 minutes longer.

NOTE: *A meaty, full-flavored dish, that would be at its best with California Burgundy or Claret on the table.*

LIVERMORE SPAGHETTI

(6 servings)

Mrs. Don Rudolph, Cresta Blanca Wine Co., Livermore

- ½ lb. ground pork
- ½ lb. ground lamb
- 1 lb. ground beef
- 5 medium onions, finely chopped
- 4 cloves garlic, finely chopped
- 1 cup grated Parmesan cheese
- 1 cup California Burgundy or other red dinner wine
- 1 cup fine dry bread crumbs
- ½ teaspoon Tabasco sauce
- 1 tablespoon Worcestershire sauce
- 2 eggs, beaten
- 2 tablespoons chili powder
- 1 (1-lb. 4-oz.) can tomatoes
- 1 (10½-oz.) can tomato soup
- 2 (8-oz.) cans tomato sauce
- 2 (4-oz.) cans mushrooms
- 2 tablespoons sugar
- 1 teaspoon garlic powder
- 1 tablespoon oregano
- Salt and pepper
- ¼ cup California Sherry

Combine pork, lamb, beef, 2 onions (chopped), garlic, cheese, wine, bread crumbs, Tabasco sauce, Worcestershire sauce, eggs and 1 tablespoon chili powder; mix well. Form into balls; arrange in baking pan. Bake in a moderate oven (350°) until brown, turning once or twice. Meanwhile, combine other ingredients and remaining 3 onions (chopped) and 1 tablespoon chili powder, in large saucepan. Cook 1½ hours, or until thick. Enrich sauce with drippings from meat balls, if desired. Combine meat balls with sauce; serve with spaghetti. Also on menu: green peas, tossed green salad and French bread browned with garlic and butter.

My choice of wine to accompany this dish:
CALIFORNIA BURGUNDY OR CLARET

SAVORY BARBECUE RICE

(5 or 6 servings)

Marjorie Lumm, Wine Institute, San Francisco

- ⅓ cup finely-chopped green pepper
- ½ cup sliced green onion
- ¾ cup regular rice, uncooked
- 3 tablespoons butter or margarine
- 1½ teaspoons salt
- 1 (1-lb.) can tomatoes
- ½ cup California Sauterne or other white dinner wine
- 1 cup cubed Cheddar cheese

Sauté green pepper, onions and rice in butter over moderate heat until rice is slightly browned and vegetables soft. Add salt, tomatoes and wine. Cook, covered, over low heat until rice is tender and liquid absorbed (about 25 minutes). Stir in cubed cheese; remove from heat and let stand, covered, a few minutes until cheese softens and melts slightly.

NOTE: *This dish could help enliven any barbecue menu, with a favorite red, white or Rosé dinner wine poured for guests.*

RISOTTO ALLA CUCAMONGA

(4 to 6 servings)

Mrs. John B. Ellena, Regina Grape Products Co., Etiwanda

- 1 medium-size onion, finely chopped
- ½ cup butter or margarine
- 1 cup regular rice, uncooked
- 1 (10½-oz.) can beef consommé
- ¾ cup water
- ¼ cup California Sherry
- 1 cup grated Parmesan cheese

Sauté onion in ¼ cup butter until tender and golden. Add rice; sauté until yellow. Stir in consommé, water and Sherry. Bring to boiling; lower heat; simmer, covered, 25 minutes or until all liquid is absorbed. Add remaining ¼ cup butter and cheese; mix gently but well. This is delicious with broiled or fried chicken. Or, it can be served as a meat substitute, with green vegetable and crisp green salad.

My choice of wine to accompany this dish:
CALIFORNIA WHITE WINE, CHILLED

NOTE: *The Sherry makes this different from the traditional risottos cooked with dinner wines. A most appealing flavor.*

NEXT TIME you make a pilaf or other rice dish, try adding a few raisins (first steamed over hot water, or soaked in a little wine, to soften) shortly before serving. It adds exotic flavor and a new color accent.

RISOTTO MILANESE

(6 servings)

Mrs. Eugene Morosoli, Wine Advisory Board, San Francisco

- ½ cup butter or margarine
- 1 large onion, chopped
- 1½ cups long-grain rice, uncooked
- ⅓ cup California Chablis or other white dinner wine
- 4¼ cups boiling hot chicken broth (canned or bouillon-cube broth may be used)
- ¼ teaspoon powdered saffron
- Salt and pepper
- ¼ cup chopped dried or button mushrooms
- 1 cup grated Parmesan or Swiss cheese

Melt butter in heavy skillet; sauté onion until soft. Add rice, stirring constantly, until rice begins to brown. Add wine and 2 cups of the boiling chicken broth; bring to rapid boiling. Stir in saffron, salt, pepper and mushrooms. Keep mixture boiling, stirring frequently; add remaining hot chicken broth as needed until all used up (takes about 25 minutes). When all the liquid is absorbed and rice is tender, stir in cheese.

My choice of wine to accompany this dish:
A VERY COLD CALIFORNIA WHITE DINNER WINE

WINE CHEESE FONDUE

(4 servings)

Mrs. Walter S. Richert, Richert & Sons, Morgan Hill

This recipe is of authentic Swiss origin. I have all of the ingredients ready ahead of time. After an evening of cards, a chafing dish is placed on the table and the fondue is cooked before all eyes. Each person is provided with a plate, fork, napkin and WINE glass. The same WINE used in cooking is served. This recipe is also useful for wine tasting parties, omitting the garlic and nutmeg.

    1 clove garlic
    2 cups California Riesling, Chablis
      or other white dinner wine
    1 lb. Swiss cheese, shredded
    3 tablespoons flour
    ½ teaspoon salt
    ⅛ teaspoon pepper
      Dash nutmeg
    3 tablespoons California brandy
      (optional)
    1 loaf French bread, cut in bite-size
      pieces with crust

Rub cooking utensil with garlic or force garlic through press. Pour in wine. Place over very low heat until air bubbles rise to surface. **(DO NOT BOIL!)** Coat cheese with flour. Stir wine, adding cheese by handfuls; completely melt each handful before adding the next. Keep stirring until mixture starts bubbling lightly. Add salt, pepper and nutmeg. Stir in brandy; place on table heating element. Guests should spear a piece of bread with a fork, dunk in fondue with a stirring motion, and eat heartily.

My choice of wine to accompany this dish:
CALIFORNIA RIESLING OR CHABLIS

NOTE: The flavor of the grape comes through most agreeably in this fondue. Mrs. Richert's omission of garlic and nutmeg when serving it at a wine tasting party stems from a customary practice at this very specialized type of gathering. The practice is to avoid any highly seasoned food accompaniments. Where many wines are to be tasted, with their subtle flavor distinctions studied minutely, it is best to serve only the blandest of cheese complements. This saves the taste buds for the business at hand: the appreciation of good wines.

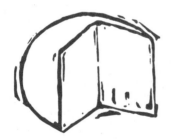

ANOTHER SWISS FONDUE VERSION (called American style), for a dinner or late supper dish, is used by Mrs. Rose Marie Pangborn, of the U. C. Dept. of Food Science and Technology, Davis. Mrs. Pangborn adds a little sharp Cheddar cheese to the Swiss cheese which dominates the recipe, plus extra nutmeg. She too prefers California Riesling (Johannisberg or Grey) served with hers.

CALIFORNIA RAREBIT

(4 or 5 servings)

Doris Paulsen, Wine Institute, San Francisco

For brunch, lunch, supper or snack, this is hard to beat.

    1 (10½-oz.) can cream of celery
      soup, undiluted
    ¼ cup California Sauterne or other
      white dinner wine
    ½ teaspoon mustard
    ½ teaspoon Worcestershire sauce
    1½ cups grated sharp Cheddar cheese
    1 egg, lightly beaten

In a saucepan, blend together soup, wine, mustard and Worcestershire sauce; heat thoroughly. Add cheese, stirring over low heat until melted. Slowly stir in lightly beaten egg; cook 2 or 3 minutes longer, stirring constantly, over very low heat until thickened. Serve at once over crisp toast or crackers.

My choice of wine to accompany this dish:
CALIFORNIA SAUTERNE OR ROSÉ

BAKED EGGS IN SPINACH NESTS gather compliments at Sunday suppers. To serve 6 generously: First make a cheese sauce. (Melt 3 tablespoons butter, stir in same amount flour, add 1 cup milk; cook, stirring constantly, until mixture boils and thickens. Stir in 1 cup shredded process Cheddar cheese, stirring until melted. Now add ¼ cup California Sherry to sauce, plus ½ teaspoon Worcestershire sauce, ¼ teaspoon prepared mustard, salt and pepper to taste.) Place 2 cups cooked or canned spinach (well-drained and chopped) in 6 oiled individual casseroles; depress each center to form a nest. Break an egg into each. Spoon some of cheese sauce over each egg; dust with paprika. Bake in moderately hot oven (375°) about 15 minutes, or until eggs are set. Serve with chilled California Rosé.

STUFFED EGGS GOURMET are an easy and different touch for a luncheon. To serve 6, cut 6 hard-cooked eggs lengthwise in halves; remove yolks. To yolks add 1 cup cottage cheese with chives; 3 tablespoons California Sherry; 2 tablespoons mayonnaise; and ¼ teaspoon **each** Worcestershire sauce and prepared mustard. Add salt and pepper to taste and blend well. Heap mixture high in whites; sprinkle with paprika. Chill well before serving, with sliced cold meats or cheeses, sliced tomatoes (marinated in California wine vinegar and oil), hot buttered rolls and glasses of chilled California Rosé.

HOPPIN' JOHN

(4 servings)

Mrs. J. C. Russell, Almaden Vineyards, Los Gatos

This is a meal in itself, an old South Carolina dish.

        1 cup long-grain rice, uncooked
        2 teaspoons bacon fat
        2 onions
        1 cup broth (bouillon cube
            may be used)
        ½ teaspoon savory or fines herbs
        6 red pepper pods (optional)
        1 tablespoon butter
            Salt
        3 tablespoons California Burgundy or
            other red dinner wine
        2 (1-lb.) cans black-eyed peas

Cook rice according to package directions until tender and liquid is absorbed; stir in bacon fat. Simmer onions in broth until liquid evaporates. Combine rice with onions and remaining ingredients; heat through.

My choice of wine to accompany this dish:
A CALIFORNIA RED DINNER WINE

ADD SHOWMANSHIP to a weekend brunch party with a Wine Country Parmesan Omelet. (This makes about 5 servings.) Beat 6 egg whites with 1 teaspoon salt, until stiff. Beat 6 yolks separately until thick, then beat in ⅓ cup California Rhine or other white dinner wine. Now fold yolk mixture into whites and pour into hot oiled skillet. Cook over low heat about 8 to 10 minutes, or until omelet is puffy and golden on underside. Transfer to moderately slow oven (325°); bake until surface is dry and center springs back when pressed (about 10 to 15 minutes). Sprinkle with ½ cup shredded Parmesan cheese. Run spatula around inside skillet edge to loosen omelet. Fold over to enclose cheese, or cut into pie-shaped wedges. A great show-off dish, with currant jelly or a mushroom sauce, and chilled glasses of the same wine.

CHEESE SOUFFLÉ CHABLIS

(4 or 5 servings)

Kenneth E. Vogt, Wine Advisory Board, Milwaukee

Cheese and wine traditionally go together. This recipe adds showmanship when you have dinner guests.

        3 tablespoons butter or margarine
        3 tablespoons flour
        1 teaspoon salt
        ¼ teaspoon dry mustard
        ½ cup milk
        ½ cup California Chablis or other
            white dinner wine
            Dash Tabasco sauce
        1 cup grated sharp Cheddar cheese
        4 eggs, separated

Melt butter; blend in flour, salt and mustard. Stir in milk and wine (mixture may curdle a little but will smooth out on cooking). Cook and stir until mixture boils and thickens. Add Tabasco sauce and cheese; stir over low heat until cheese melts. Remove from heat. Beat egg yolks lightly; stir into cooked mixture. Beat whites until stiff; fold into mixture. Turn into 2-qt. baking dish. Set in pan of hot water. Bake in slow oven (300°) for 1 hour. Serve at once from same baking dish.

My choice of wine to accompany this dish:
ANY CHILLED CALIFORNIA WHITE DINNER WINE

SHERRIED SHRIMP RAREBIT

(6 to 8 servings)

Ralph H. Winters, Wine Advisory Board, New York City

This is a simple recipe that I worked up myself to use on television appearances. It is easy to remember and, best of all, very tasty.

        1 lb. aged Cheddar cheese,
            grated or diced
        1 (10-oz.) can frozen cream of
            shrimp soup, thawed
        ¼ cup California Cream Sherry

Combine cheese and soup in top of double boiler; heat over hot water, stirring, until cheese melts and is blended. Just before serving, stir in Sherry. Serve over toast points as a main course, or, in a chafing dish as a hot dip for potato chips.

NOTE: As a supper dish, this might be accompanied by a chilled California Rosé. As a cocktail hour dip, it would be perfect with Sherry or Dry Vermouth on-the-rocks.

SCRAMBLED EGGS SAUTERNE

(About 4 servings)

Mrs. Myron Nightingale, Roma Wine Company, Fresno

        6 eggs
        ½ teaspoon salt
        2 tablespoons cream
        ¼ cup California Sauterne, Chablis
            or other white dinner wine
        ⅛ teaspoon dried dill, rosemary
            or basil
        2 tablespoons butter or margarine
        ¼ cup coarsely crumbled blue cheese
        1 tablespoon chopped chives,
            parsley or pimiento

Beat eggs slightly. Stir in salt, cream, wine and seasoning. Melt butter in medium-size skillet; coat bottom and sides of pan. When hot enough to make drop of water sizzle, pour in egg mixture; reduce heat. Cook slowly, gently lifting eggs from bottom and sides with a spoon as mixture sets, so liquid can flow to bottom. (Do not overstir.) Add cheese and chives while eggs are still creamy. Cook to desired moistness. Serve at once, for a late breakfast or luncheon.

My choice of wine to accompany this dish:
THE SAME CALIFORNIA SAUTERNE

SHERRIED EGGS

(2 to 4 servings)

Sylvia Elwood Preiss, Llords & Elwood Wine Cellars, Fremont

        3 egg yolks
        1 cup cream
            Salt and pepper
        4 hard-cooked eggs, quartered
        ½ cup California Dry Sherry

Beat yolks in cream; season with salt and pepper. Cook over hot water in top of double boiler until thick. Add quartered eggs. When ready to serve, stir in Dry Sherry. Serve in hot ramekins.

NOTE: *This would be good for a Sunday brunch or late supper. A chilled white dinner wine or Rosé would be particularly pleasant as beverage.*

VEGETABLES

New and Refreshing Treatments with Wine

Far too often, alas, the great taste potential of vegetables has been overlooked. Dull, waterlogged and soggy, or overcooked—these sad traits have exiled many an innocent vegetable dish from the family table, denounced as "rabbit food" or worse. But crisp-tender green vegetables or creamy-rich root vegetables, buttery and hot, and sauced or seasoned with California wine, are another matter. Wine cookery here is notably rewarding because of the welcome variations it brings. Vegetables take on a new distinction, a brightness of flavor. They become, at last, fully as enjoyable as the main dish itself—in perfect harmony with the good dinner wine on the table.

MODESTO POTATOES

(4 servings)

Lyman M. Cash, E. & J. Gallo Winery, Modesto

> 3 tablespoons butter or olive oil
> 1 tablespoon flour
> 4 medium-size potatoes, peeled and sliced
> 1 medium-size onion, sliced
> 1 clove garlic, minced
> Salt and pepper
> ⅓ cup California Sauterne or other white dinner wine
> ⅓ cup chicken or beef broth (canned or bouillon-cube broth may be used)
> ½ teaspoon minced thyme or marjoram
> 1 tablespoon minced parsley

Melt butter or heat oil in heavy skillet; mix in flour; brown quickly. Add potatoes, onion, garlic, salt and pepper. Fry, turning often, until slightly brown. Add wine, broth and thyme; cover tightly. Simmer until potatoes are tender and liquid is absorbed. Add parsley; mix well. Serve with a baked fish dinner (fillet of rock cod, fillet of sole, bass or salmon).

My choice of wine to accompany this dish:
CALIFORNIA SAUTERNE

NOTE: Exceptionally good with any menu calling for potatoes. Shows what wine can do to make vegetables more interesting.

SHERRIED CORN LUCULLUS

(6 to 8 servings)

Mrs. Edmund A. Rossi, Jr., Italian Swiss Colony, Asti

> 2 (10-oz.) pkgs. frozen whole-kernel corn
> ¼ cup butter, melted
> ¼ cup water
> Salt
> Pepper
> ¼ cup cream
> ¼ cup California Sherry

Cook corn in melted butter and water about 4 minutes, stirring constantly. Add seasonings; stir in cream and Sherry. Heat thoroughly, stirring, and serve at once. Particularly good with a steak dinner.

NOTE: With a hearty California Claret or Burgundy on the table!

WINE-GLAZED CARROTS

(About 4 servings)

Brother Gregory, Mont La Salle Vineyards, Napa

Peel enough carrots for about 4 servings, and slice lengthwise, very thin. Parboil in salted water until just tender, still a little crisp. Drain and saute in 1 tablespoon butter until lightly browned. Add 2 tablespoons California Light Muscat and simmer until wine has evaporated.

NOTE: A delightful new flavor; would win compliments from guests. Try serving this dish with roast chicken or barbecued duck, and a chilled California Rhine or Sauterne.

CARROTS IN SHERRY

(6 to 8 servings)

Mrs. Lewis A. Stern, E. & J. Gallo Winery, Modesto

    2 lbs. carrots, scraped and quartered
    ¼ cup butter or margarine
    1 teaspoon salt
    ⅛ teaspoon pepper
    ¼ teaspoon sugar
    ½ cup California Sherry
    Minced parsley

Sauté carrots in melted butter, turning until well coated. Sprinkle with salt, pepper and sugar. Add Sherry; simmer gently about 5 minutes. Add water just to cover; simmer, covered, 15 to 25 minutes or until tender. (Small young carrots take only about 15 minutes.) Remove cover; cook over medium heat until most of liquid has evaporated. Sprinkle with parsley. These go well with baked ham with pineapple; boiled potatoes with parsley-butter sauce; coleslaw; and chilled fruits with cookies for dessert.

My choice of wine to accompany this menu:
CALIFORNIA ROSÉ, CHABLIS OR SAUTERNE

CARROTS ALSO take to California Sauterne. Add 4 cups shredded carrots and 1 chopped onion to 2 tablespoons butter that you have melted in saucepan. Salt and pepper to taste, then add ½ cup Sauterne. Cover; cook 10 minutes, or just until tender. Or, can be baked in casserole in moderate oven (350°) about 25 minutes. Makes 4 servings. A nice change with a roast beef or leg of lamb, and California Rosé as beverage.

CALIFORNIA FRIED TOMATOES

(6 servings)

E. L. (Ted) Barr, Western Grape Products, Kingsburg

    6 medium-size firm tomatoes
    ¼ cup sifted flour
    1 teaspoon garlic salt
    ½ teaspoon rosemary or thyme
    ¼ cup butter or margarine
    2 teaspoons brown sugar
    ⅔ cup California Burgundy or
      other red dinner wine

Core tomatoes; remove skin if desired. Cut each tomato in half. Combine flour, salt and rosemary (or thyme). Dredge tomatoes in seasoned flour. Sauté on both sides over moderate heat in melted butter. Add sugar and wine; continue cooking until tomatoes are tender, about 5 minutes. Serve with any remaining liquid. Fine with wild game or steaks or any hearty dinner.

NOTE: The same Burgundy or other red dinner wine would be enjoyable with such a menu.

BROILED SHERRIED TOMATOES

(1 or 2 halves per serving)

Robert D. Rossi, Jr., United Vintners, Inc., San Francisco

    Medium large firm tomatoes
    California Sherry
    Salt
    Pepper
    Dried dill
    Mayonnaise
    Grated American cheese

Cut tomatoes in halves, crosswise. Pierce with fork and sprinkle with Sherry. Season with salt, pepper and dill. Broil 5 to 7 minutes or until heated through. Combine equal amounts of mayonnaise and cheese; put a spoonful on each tomato half. Return to broiler and brown lightly. Excellent with barbecued meats or chicken.

NOTE: Try a chilled California Rosé with the menu: a sure pleaser.

CAULIFLOWER SANTA ROSA

(5 or 6 servings)

Elmo Martini, Martini & Prati Wines, Inc., Santa Rosa

- 1 large head cauliflower
- ¼ cup butter or margarine
- ¼ cup flour
- 1 cup rich milk
- ½ cup California Rhine, Sauterne or other white dinner wine
- ½ cup water
- ½ cup shredded, blanched almonds
  Salt and pepper
- ¼ cup grated Cheddar cheese

Trim and wash cauliflower; separate into flowerets. Drop into boiling, salted water; cook 10 to 15 minutes, or just until tender when pierced with a fork. Meanwhile, prepare sauce. Melt butter and stir in flour. Add milk, wine and water; cook, stirring constantly, until mixture is thickened and smooth. Add almonds, salt and pepper. Drain cauliflower carefully; place in greased baking dish. Pour over sauce and sprinkle with grated cheese. Bake in moderately hot oven (375°) for 20 minutes.

NOTE: *Deserves a good steak or roast beef, with California Claret or Rosé served with the dinner.*

GLAZED CELERY SAN JOAQUIN

(4 to 6 servings)

Lawrence Quaccia, Guild Wine Co., Lodi

- 4 cups 1" pieces of celery
- ½ cup chicken broth
- 2 teaspoons cornstarch
- ¼ cup California Sauterne or other white dinner wine
  Salt
  Slivered toasted almonds (optional)

Combine celery and chicken broth in saucepan; cook, covered, about 15 minutes, or until tender but still crisp. Stir cornstarch into wine; add to celery. Cook over low heat until mixture boils and thickens. Add salt. Serve hot. May be sprinkled with toasted slivered almonds, if desired.

NOTE: *This is an elegant treatment, suited to the most festive dinner menu, and served with any California dinner wine or Champagne.*

RED CABBAGE ETIWANDA

(6 to 10 servings)

Mrs. John B. Ellena, Regina Grape Products Co., Etiwanda

- 1 medium head red cabbage
- 5 cooking apples
- 2 tablespoons sugar
- 3 tablespoons California red wine vinegar
- 1 tablespoon butter
- 1¼ teaspoons salt
- ¼ teaspoon pepper
- ¼ cup California Burgundy, Claret or other red dinner wine

Shred cabbage finely; core and cut apples in small pieces. Combine with sugar, vinegar, butter, salt and pepper in saucepan. Cook slowly, covered, 45 minutes to 1 hour or until soft, stirring occasionally. Add wine last 10 minutes of cooking. This is delicious with roast pork.

My choice of wine to accompany this menu:
WELL-CHILLED CALIFORNIA WHITE DINNER WINE
SUCH AS FRENCH COLOMBARD OR RIESLING

NOTE: *Cabbage cooked with wine is also a favorite of Mrs. Don McColly, Wine Institute, San Francisco; Mrs. H. L. Archinal of Mt. Tivy Winery, Reedley; and Mrs. L. J. Berg of Mont La Salle Vineyards, Napa.*

BACCHANALIAN BRUSSELS SPROUTS

(3 or 4 servings)

Jessica McLachlin Greengard, Public Relations, Wines & Food

- 1 lb. fresh or 1 (10-oz.) pkg. frozen Brussels sprouts
  California Chablis or other white dinner wine
- ¾ cup white seedless grapes
  Butter
  Salt and pepper

Cook Brussels sprouts, using wine for all or part of cooking liquid. Drain; add grapes. Season with butter, salt and pepper. Heat through. This vegetable is especially good with wild duck, venison or turkey.

NOTE: *Really delicious, a magic touch for sprouts. A velvety California Burgundy would be just right with the types of menus indicated.*

SHERRIED WINTER SQUASH (acorn squash) with pineapple is delightful. Cut squash into small squares and cook until tender in salted water. Drain; remove rind. Place squash in shallow baking dish and top with drained crushed pineapple and brown sugar. Drizzle with California Sherry and dot with butter. Bake in moderate oven (350°) about a half hour. Good with baked ham, served with chilled California Rosé.

GLORIFIED ZUCCHINI

(6 to 8 servings)

Mrs. Leo Demostene, Soda Rock Winery, Healdsburg

This same mixture may also be stirred into French-cut green beans, baked the same way.

- 4 or 5 medium zucchini, sliced 1" thick
  Salt
- 1 large onion, chopped
- 2 tablespoons butter or margarine
- 2 tablespoons flour
- ½ cup California Sauterne, Chablis or other white dinner wine
- 1 (10½-oz.) can cream of mushroom soup
  Grated cheese

Parboil zucchini slices in boiling salted water. Drain; place in single layer in buttered (9 x 11") baking dish. In saucepan, brown onion in butter; stir in flour. Add wine and soup; mix well. Pour over zucchini; sprinkle with grated cheese. Bake in moderate oven (350°) for 30 to 40 minutes. This is very good with any menu.

NOTE: And your favorite California dinner wine (red, white or Rosé) accompanying.

SPRING SQUASH IN WINE

(8 to 10 servings)

Mrs. Ernest A. Wente, Wente Bros., Livermore

- 2 tablespoons butter
- 2 tablespoons olive oil
- 1 medium onion, minced
- 2 large stalks celery, thinly sliced
- 1 lb. yellow crookneck squash, diced in ½" cubes
- 1 lb. scalloped or summer squash, thinly sliced
- 1 lb. zucchini, thinly sliced
- ½ cup California Sauterne, Chablis or other white dinner wine
- ¼ teaspoon basil, crumbled
- ½ teaspoon salt
- ⅛ teaspoon pepper
  Nutmeg

Heat butter and oil in large saucepan. Sauté onion, celery and squashes until onion is clear. Add wine and seasonings; cover; simmer about 20 minutes or until tender. Season with additional butter before serving, if desired.

NOTE: Cheerful in color, with a fresh cheerful flavor. Would combine well with spring lamb chops or leg of lamb, served with California Rosé.

CREAMED SHERRY SPINACH

(6 servings)

Joseph J. Franzia, Franzia Brothers Winery, Ripon

- 1 (12-oz.) pkg. frozen chopped spinach
- ¼ cup butter or margarine
- ¼ cup flour
- ¾ cup canned condensed cream of mushroom soup
- ¼ cup California Sherry
- ½ cup grated process Cheddar cheese
- ½ cup (firmly packed) soft bread crumbs
- 3 eggs, slightly beaten
- 1 teaspoon grated onion
- ¼ teaspoon nutmeg
  Salt
  Pepper

Cook spinach according to package directions; drain well. Melt butter, stir in flour, add soup and wine. Cook, stirring, until mixture boils and thickens. Add cheese; stir over low heat until melted. Remove from heat. Add spinach and other ingredients. Turn into 6 well-greased custard cups. Set in shallow pan of hot water. Bake in moderate oven (350°) about 45 minutes, or until firm. Remove from oven; let stand 5 minutes or so before unmolding, to unmold easily.

NOTE: Even spinach-haters enjoy this recipe. Attractive and good for any kind of dinner menu, with California red or white dinner wine alongside.

GARBANZOS IN WHITE WINE

(8 servings)

Frank I. Pirrone, F. Pirrone & Sons, Inc., Salida

- 2 (1-lb.) cans garbanzos
- ½ cup California Sauterne or other white dinner wine
- ¼ cup oil
- ¼ cup California wine vinegar
- ¼ cup catsup
- ¼ cup finely chopped green onion
- 2 tablespoons finely chopped fresh parsley
- 1 tablespoon finely chopped pimiento
- 1 teaspoon salt

Drain garbanzos; combine with all other ingredients. Mix lightly; cover and refrigerate several hours or overnight. Serve garbanzos with some of the marinade. An easy way to serve a vegetable, cold, with a barbecue or buffet dinner.

NOTE: Would be especially appealing with any red meat dinner, with a California Claret or Zinfandel accompanying.

VINTNER'S BEANS

(10 to 12 servings)

Mrs. David Ficklin, Ficklin Vineyards, Madera

We use this dish traditionally for summertime outdoor suppers. It can be baked ahead and reheated easily. Excellent for pot-luck or buffet suppers as well as barbecues.

    1 lb. navy beans
    ½ lb. salt pork, thinly sliced
    1 medium-size onion, chopped
    ½ teaspoon dry mustard
    1 tablespoon salt
    ½ cup brown sugar (packed)
    1½ cups California Port
    1 cup strong hot coffee

Soak beans in cold water overnight. Place salt pork, onion and drained beans into bean pot or heavy casserole. Add mustard, salt, sugar, 1 cup Port and enough water to barely cover. Bake in slow oven (275°) for about 4 hours; add a little more water during last half hour, if necessary. Add remaining ½ cup Port and cup of strong hot coffee. Continue baking 1½ to 2 hours longer.

My choice of wine to accompany this dish:
CALIFORNIA CLARET

GREEN PEAS GOURMET

(5 or 6 servings)

Robert D. Rossi, Jr., United Vintners, Inc., San Francisco

    2 cups shelled fresh peas
      (about 2 lbs.)
    1 cup thinly sliced celery
    1 teaspoon seasoned salt
    1 cup chicken broth
    ¼ cup California Sauterne
      or other white dinner wine
    3 tablespoons butter or margarine
      Pepper
    2 or 3 teaspoons cornstarch (optional)

Combine peas, celery, salt and broth in saucepan. Cover and cook gently until peas are tender. Stir in wine, butter, pepper and additional salt to taste. Thicken liquid with cornstarch mixed with a little water, if desired. Serve in sauce dishes with the richly flavored sauce.

NOTE: An epicurean treatment. Choose the dinner wine according to the main dish on the menu — usually red wine for red meats, white wine for white meats. Rosé or Champagne with anything.

DON'S FAVORITE BEANS

(3 or 4 servings)

Mrs. Don W. McColly, Wine Institute, San Francisco

These are easy and very good. Green beans are a favorite in our household, because both Don and I grew up on farms and enjoyed them fresh from the field. These days, we still like the old-fashioned bacon and onion flavors in the frozen wine-cooked beans.

    1 (9-oz.) pkg. frozen French-cut
      green beans
    1 teaspoon instant minced onion
    ½ teaspoon seasoned salt
      Dash or two seasoned pepper
    1 strip crisp cooked bacon
    ¼ cup California Riesling, Chablis
      or other white dinner wine
    3 tablespoons butter or margarine

Place frozen beans in saucepan. Sprinkle on onion, salt and pepper; crumble on bacon. Pour wine over all; cover closely. Cook over moderately high heat 6 to 10 minutes or just until beans are crisp-tender. Add butter, stir to blend and serve at once. (For those who like more liquid, another tablespoon or two of wine may be stirred in along with the butter.) We prefer these with leg of lamb, salad of butter lettuce and mandarin oranges, and a frozen lemon dessert with brownies.

Our choice of wine to accompany this menu:
CALIFORNIA RED, WHITE OR ROSÉ DINNER WINE

BEETS BURGUNDIAN

(6 to 8 servings)

Mrs. J. H. M. Elwood, Llords & Elwood Wine Cellars, Fremont

      Freshly cooked beets
    2 tablespoons butter or margarine
    1 tablespoon flour
    ½ to 1 cup California Burgundy
      or other red dinner wine
    1 teaspoon sugar
      Grating of nutmeg
      Pinch cloves
      Salt and pepper

Peel beets; grate enough to make 3 cups. Melt butter in saucepan; stir in flour. Stir in ½ cup wine. Add beets, sugar and seasonings. Simmer over low heat until tender. Add more wine during cooking, if needed.

NOTE: Serve them with a steak, buttery baked potatoes, hearts of lettuce with oil and wine vinegar dressing, and the same California red wine for a dinner-winner. The classic dish, Harvard Beets Burgundy, is similar in flavor but includes wine vinegar in the preparation.

LEEKS COUNTRY STYLE

(6 servings)

Mrs. A. D. Webb, U. of Calif. Dept. of Viticulture & Enology

This recipe was collected during a visit to Bordeaux. It's especially good with lunches including cold meat cuts, French bread and the more flavorful white wines. However, the dish is flavorful enough to be accompanied by either red or white wine.

    2 bunches leeks
    ¼ cup butter or margarine
    3 tablespoons flour
    ½ cup California Chardonnay, Chablis
      or other white dinner wine
    ¾ teaspoon salt
    ⅛ teaspoon pepper
    4 egg yolks, lightly beaten
    ½ cup grated Swiss cheese
      Bread crumbs

Cut leeks in ¾" lengths, including part of green tops. Cook until tender in about 1¼ cups water; drain, saving cooking water. Melt butter in small saucepan; stir in flour. Add wine and 1 cup of the cooking liquid; cook, stirring constantly, until thickened. Season with salt and pepper. Add beaten egg yolks very gradually, stirring constantly. Add cheese, stirring until melted. Place leeks in casserole; cover with cheese sauce; dust lightly with bread crumbs. Bake in a moderate oven (350°) for 15 minutes. Serve as vegetable with entrée.

JERUSALEM ARTICHOKES

(4 servings)

Mrs. Herbert Cerwin, Cerwin Vineyards, Sonoma

As Jerusalem artichokes are a root vegetable, belonging to the sunflower family, they usually take the place of potatoes. They are highly regarded by many trying to diet, as they are not starchy.

    1 small onion, chopped
    2 tablespoons oil
    1 pound Jerusalem artichokes,
      pared and sliced
    2 cups California Riesling or
      other white dinner wine
      Garlic salt
      Pepper
      Salt
      Nutmeg
    2 tablespoons finely-chopped
      parsley
      Parmesan cheese (optional)

Sauté onion in oil until clear. Add sliced artichokes and wine. Cover and simmer just until tender, about 25 to 30 minutes. Season to taste with garlic salt, pepper, salt and a dash of nutmeg. Just before serving, sprinkle with chopped parsley. You may like to add a sprinkling of Parmesan cheese. A garnish of a few sprigs of watercress, mint or tarragon is nice. This dish seems to go best with beef and a mixed green salad.

My choice of wine to accompany this menu:
CALIFORNIA CLARET, CABERNET OR ZINFANDEL
(OR RIESLING IF A WHITE IS PREFERRED)

COMPANY ONIONS

(About 4 servings)

Mrs. Stanley Strud, California Wine Association, Lodi

    1 (1-lb.) can small whole onions, drained
    ⅔ cup light cream
    2 teaspoons cornstarch
    2 tablespoons butter or margarine
      Dash of mace or nutmeg
    ¼ cup California Sherry
    ¼ cup fine dry bread crumbs

Place drained onions in shallow baking dish. Combine cream and cornstarch; cook and stir until thickened. Add 1 tablespoon butter, mace and Sherry; pour over onions. Melt remaining butter; blend with crumbs. Sprinkle over onions. Bake in moderate oven (350°) about 20 minutes, until well-heated and lightly browned. Serve with steak, roast or chops, with any favorite California dinner wine—red, white or Rosé.

LEEKS ARE ALWAYS a refreshing change as a vegetable dish. Another cooking method, extremely simple, is to poach them in California Sauterne (or other white) and melted butter. First slit the leeks in half, lengthwise, keeping part of the green tops. Wash carefully, so that the halves hold their shape. Lay them in loaf pan, barely covering with wine and butter. Cover tightly with foil; simmer until tender. Dust with paprika and serve hot with any meat dish and your favorite California dinner wine. (The leftover cooked leeks may be refrigerated, to enrich a salad the next day.)

MUSHROOMS NEWBURG

(6 servings)

Mrs. Emil M. Mrak, University of California, Davis

This makes a good Friday lunch dish on toast.

    1 lb. fresh mushrooms
    ¼ cup melted butter or margarine
    ½ cup California Dry Sherry
    3 cups Cream Sauce (see below)
    ½ cup blanched almonds, slivered

Wash mushrooms; drain. Simmer 10 minutes in small amount of salted water; drain. Slice; toss with melted butter. Stir Sherry into Cream Sauce. Pour layer of sauce in a 1½-qt. casserole; add layer of mushrooms; top with almonds. Repeat layers, ending with a layer of white sauce and sprinkling of almonds. Bake in moderate oven (350°) for 20 minutes.

CREAM SAUCE: Melt 6 tablespoons butter or margarine in saucepan; stir in 6 tablespoons flour. (DO NOT LET BROWN.) Add 1½ cups chicken broth, 1 cup light cream and ½ cup California Chablis or other white dinner wine; cook, stirring constantly, until thickened. Season with 1 teaspoon salt, ½ teaspoon monosodium glutamate and dash of pepper.

NOTE: Mrs. Mrak makes her own chicken broth, adding sliced onion and various herbs to the simmering chicken bones. However, canned chicken broth or bouillon-cube broth may be used instead, in making the rich Cream Sauce. The same California white dinner wine would be a delightful accompaniment. The dish would be equally good for a Sunday night supper.

BAKED MUSHROOMS CONTRA COSTA

(6 servings)

Judy Hibel, Wine Advisory Board, San Francisco

These are delicious and not at all difficult. They may accompany a very special chicken dinner, with chilled California Chablis on the table. Or, they're equally good as a hot appetizer, served at cocktail time with Dry Sherry.

    12 large mushrooms
       Lemon juice
    2 tablespoons butter
    2 tablespoons Swiss cheese, grated
    ¼ cup bread crumbs
    2 tablespoons minced parsley
    ½ clove garlic, minced
    1 tablespoon minced onion
       Salt and pepper
    2 to 4 tablespoons California Sherry

Wash mushrooms; remove stems, leaving caps intact. Sprinkle few drops lemon juice on each cap; set aside. Prepare stuffing as follows: Mince stems very fine; sauté in butter. Meanwhile, combine cheese, bread crumbs, parsley, garlic, onion, salt and pepper in a bowl. Add sautéed mushroom stems; mix thoroughly. Add enough Sherry to moisten mixture. Pile stuffing into mushroom caps; sprinkle with additional bread crumbs and dot with butter. Bake in moderate oven (350°) for 15 minutes. Serve piping hot!

MUSHROOMS BOURGUIGNON

(4 to 6 servings)

Mrs. Ernest C. Haas, East-Side Winery, Lodi

    ⅓ cup butter or margarine
    2 small green onions, chopped
    1 clove garlic, crushed
    1 lb. fresh mushrooms, sliced
    1 cup California Burgundy or other
       red dinner wine
       Freshly ground black pepper
    ½ teaspoon salt
    2 tablespoons chopped fresh parsley

Melt butter in saucepan; add chopped onion, garlic and mushrooms. Saute until tender, then add other ingredients. Simmer until wine is reduced by half. (Mushrooms will be quite dark.) Serve as accompaniment to broiled steak.

NOTE: With a California Claret or Burgundy on the table, this would make dreamy dining.

A 200-YEAR-OLD English recipe for a "fricassee of mushrooms" calls for 1 cup of Champagne or white wine, ½ cup or less of beef broth, butter mixed with flour, onions, herbs and mace. Simmer fresh mushrooms in this for 15 minutes. Just before serving, add mixed egg yolks and cream, and heat briefly. Squeeze some orange or lemon juice over the top and serve. We don't know the type of beverage wine preferred by the creator of this delectable dish, but a California white dinner wine would have been perfect with it. And not too far-fetched, either —the first wine grapes were planted in California in 1769.

AN EXOTIC CHINESE EFFECT can be given canned sauerkraut, using California wine. Cook the kraut only 3 or 4 minutes, covered; drain. Pour a little medium Sauterne over, and add small fillets of fresh white-meat fish on top of kraut. Sprinkle with dill and caraway seed. Cover tightly and simmer, to steam fish until done (5 to 15 minutes, depending on thickness of fillets). Just before serving, mix **very** lightly; fish should not take on sauerkraut flavor. This unusual and subtle recipe is from a wine industry supplier noted for his cooking.

SPRING ASPARAGUS ROSÉ

(About 2¼ cups sauce)

Alice Nelson, Wine Institute, San Francisco

This is an easy main dish for a luncheon or light supper.

 1 lb. process American cheese
 ¾ cup California Rosé
 ½ teaspoon mustard
 1 tablespoon instant minced onion
  Hot cooked asparagus
  Toast or toasted hamburger buns

Cut cheese into medium-size pieces. Place in top of double boiler; add wine, mustard and onion. Cook over hot water, stirring frequently, until cheese melts and mixture is smooth. Arrange hot buttered asparagus stalks on lightly buttered toast or buns. Spoon cheese sauce over each serving. Good accompanied by sliced tomatoes marinated in oil and wine vinegar, and any favorite dessert.

My choice of wine to accompany this dish:
THE SAME CALIFORNIA ROSÉ, CHILLED

FESTIVAL SWEET POTATOES

(6 servings)

Roy Petersen, Foote, Cone & Belding, San Francisco

 3 large sweet potatoes or yams
 6 slices canned pineapple
 4 tablespoons butter or margarine
 ½ cup brown sugar
 ½ cup California Sherry

Boil sweet potatoes in their skins 20 to 30 minutes, or until tender. Peel; cut lengthwise in halves. Arrange pineapple in single layer in shallow baking dish. Top each pineapple slice with a potato half, cut side down. Heat butter or margarine, sugar and Sherry together until sugar is dissolved; pour over potatoes and pineapple. Bake in moderately hot oven (375°) 30 minutes, basting often with syrup in pan. Serve with the festive holiday turkey or a baked ham dinner anytime.

My choice of wine to accompany this menu:
CALIFORNIA RED, WHITE OR ROSÉ DINNER WINE

BROCCOLI IN SHERRY-ALMOND SAUCE is an interesting new treatment. Cook broccoli in usual manner until tender. Meanwhile, make your own white sauce, or use canned type if you prefer. Heat, stirring. Blend California Sherry to desired consistency into thickened white sauce, and cook only a minute longer. Pour sauce over hot drained broccoli and sprinkle with chopped or slivered almonds.

SALADS

And Salad Dressings...with Wine

A crisp, zestful salad can be made doubly enjoyable by an artfully seasoned dressing. The greatest chefs and best home cooks know this calls for *wine* vinegar— aristocrat of vinegars, the oldest known to man. Wine vinegar adds the desirable lively tang without the harshness. Its smooth mild character and beguiling bouquet make all the difference in the fresh taste of any salad. When your recipe also includes a touch of wine, as well as fine California wine vinegar, you explore a whole new world of varied flavors.

BEAN SALAD ESCALON

(10 to 12 servings)

Mrs. Joseph Roullard, Petri Wineries, Escalon

This recipe has been used on a number of occasions at the winery, and is very popular.

    1 (1-lb.) can cut green beans
    1 (1-lb.) can red kidney beans
    1 (1-lb.) can garbanzo beans
    1 (8-oz.) can pitted ripe olives
        (optional)
    1 red onion, thinly sliced
    ½ cup minced green pepper
    ½ cup oil
    ⅓ cup California red wine vinegar
    ¼ cup California Burgundy, Claret
        or other red dinner wine
    ½ cup granulated sugar
    ¼ teaspoon basil, or
        ¼ teaspoon mixed salad herbs
    ¼ teaspoon garlic powder

Drain beans and olives; combine with onion and green pepper. Combine remaining ingredients; pour over bean mixture. Cover; refrigerate several hours or overnight. Good with menu including prime rib roast with horseradish sauce, rice pilaf, platter of fresh raw vegetables (carrots, green onions, tomatoes, etc.), garlic bread and an apple pie dessert.

My choice of wine to accompany this dish:
CALIFORNIA SPARKLING BURGUNDY OR
BURGUNDY OR PINOT NOIR

POTATO SALAD SAUTERNE adds the touch of elegance to a picnic—with no muss or fuss. Simply marinate the boiled potatoes in California Sauterne while they are still hot, then follow up with your usual potato salad recipe. Pack a thermos jug of chilled Sauterne or Rosé along with the salad, cold cuts and French bread, and you'll picnic with a flair.

PACIFIC CRAB SALAD

(6 to 8 servings)

Al Pirrone, F. Pirrone & Sons, Inc., Salida

This is a meal in itself, good on a warm day.

    1 cup chili sauce
    1 tablespoon prepared horseradish
    1 to 2 tablespoons fresh lemon juice
    ⅛ teaspoon garlic powder, or 1 small
        clove garlic, crushed
    1½ teaspoons instant minced onion, or
        2 tablespoons chopped green onion
    ⅛ teaspoon dried dill
    ½ cup California Sauterne or Rosé
    1 lb. fresh crabmeat
        Crisp romaine lettuce or other greens
        Hard-cooked egg slices
        Ripe olives

Combine chili sauce, horseradish, lemon juice, garlic, onion, dill and wine; refrigerate several hours. Add half of crab to sauce. Arrange crisp lettuce on serving plates; top with remaining crabmeat. Spoon on crab cocktail sauce (or serve in individual lemon cups). Garnish with egg slices and olives; serve very cold.

My choice of wine to accompany this dish:
CHILLED CALIFORNIA GREY RIESLING

NOTE: *For a creamy or Louis-type dressing, add ½ cup mayonnaise or sour cream.*

ANOTHER LUSCIOUS LOUIS dressing uses California Sherry, with commendable results. (It keeps well in the refrigerator, too.) To make about 1½ cups: Combine 1 cup mayonnaise, ½ cup chili sauce, 3 tablespoons medium Sherry, ½ teaspoon Worcestershire sauce, salt and pepper. Chill well, and enjoy on any seafood or lettuce salad.

OLD-FASHIONED HOT POTATO SALAD

(4 servings)

Jim Morse, Beringer Bros., Inc., St. Helena

This is a delicious old-time salad, and an easy way to serve potatoes when you're serving a cold meat plate or frankfurters. It's especially good for buffet meals (if kept hot) or barbecues.

        4 medium-size potatoes
        4 slices bacon
      ¼ cup chopped onion
        1 teaspoon salt
            Pepper
        3 tablespons California wine vinegar
        2 tablespoons California Chablis
            or other white dinner wine
        2 teaspoons sugar
        2 hard-cooked eggs, chopped

Boil potatoes in skins until tender; peel and dice, keeping hot. Fry bacon until crisp; drain and crumble. Measure ¼ cup bacon fat and return to skillet. Sauté onions lightly in measured fat. Add salt, pepper, vinegar, wine and sugar. Heat; pour over hot potatoes. Add chopped eggs; mix lightly to blend the dressing through salad. Serve immediately, while hot.

NOTE: This would make almost any meat or poultry menu a distinguished one — served with any favorite dinner wine, red, white or Rosé.

SPINACH SALAD & DRESSING

(8 servings)

Phil Hiaring, Wine Institute, San Francisco

      ⅔ cup salad oil
      ¼ cup California wine vinegar
        2 tablespoons California Chablis or
            other white dinner wine
        2 teaspoons soy sauce
        1 teaspoon sugar
        1 teaspoon dry mustard
      ¼ to 1 teaspoon curry powder
      ½ teaspoon salt
      ½ teaspoon garlic salt
        1 teaspoon freshly ground pepper
        2 bunches (about 4 qts.) young spinach
        1 pound bacon
        2 hard-cooked eggs, coarsely grated

Combine oil, wine vinegar, wine, soy sauce, sugar and seasonings in a covered jar. Shake well; chill; Meanwhile, thoroughly wash the spinach; tear into pieces, removing stems. Dice bacon; fry until crisp. Mix the bacon and eggs with spinach. Shake dressing again; pour over spinach.

NOTE: This would be good with many types of meat or poultry menus. Choose the accompanying wine according to the main dish served. Most people usually like a red dinner wine with red meats, white with white meats; Rosé with anything.

RANCHER'S TURKEY SALAD

(4 servings)

Mrs. H. T. Woodworth, Allied Grape Growers, Lodi

For a luncheon or Sunday night supper, this could serve as the main course, with hot rolls and dessert. It's an excellent way to use leftover turkey or chicken.

      1½ cups diced cooked turkey or chicken
      1½ teaspoons instant minced onion, **or**
            2 tablespoons finely chopped raw onion
        ¼ cup California Sauterne or other
            white dinner wine
        1 tablespoon fresh lemon juice
        ½ teaspon salt
        1 cup sliced celery
        2 hard-cooked eggs, diced
        3 tablespoons salad oil
        2 tablespoons drained sweet pickle relish
        1 tablespoon mayonnaise
            Salt
            Shredded lettuce

Combine turkey, onion, wine, lemon juice and salt; let stand 1 hour or longer. Drain, saving marinade. Add celery and eggs to turkey. Combine marinade with oil, relish and mayonnaise; blend well. Pour over turkey mixture; mix lightly. Salt to taste. Serve over crisp shredded lettuce.

My choice of wine to accompany this dish:
CALIFORNIA DEMI-SEC CHAMPAGNE

PORT-CHERRY SALAD MOLDS

(6 to 8 servings)

Mrs. E. Jeff Barnette, Martini & Prati Wines, Inc., Santa Rosa

I live at Blossom Hill Ranch, a half mile from the winery. We grow three kinds of cherries and we always have many kinds of wine on hand. I try to use our ranch produce, and in this recipe I am combining it with good California wine. This salad is perfect with so many kinds of food that I always use the accompanying meat as guide to the type of wine to be served.

        1 cup cherry juice, **or** cherry juice
            and water to make 1 cup
        1 (3-oz.) pkg. cherry or
            orange-flavored gelatin
        1 cup California Port
        2 cups cooked pitted black cherries,
            drained, **or** 1 (1-lb.) can
            pitted black cherries, drained
        1 cup chopped nuts

Heat cherry juice to boiling. Add gelatin; stir until dissolved; cool. Add Port; chill until slightly thickened. Fold in cherries and nuts. Turn into individual molds or 1 large mold. Chill until firm. This is good with almost any menu. I sometimes make the salad in an open ring mold and fill the center with chicken salad. This with a hot bread makes a delicious lunch.

NOTE: With such a luncheon, a chilled California Sauterne or Rosé would be delightful. (Mrs. Barnette also says of this recipe that Muscatel may be substituted for Port, if Royal Anne cherries are preferred in making salad.)

SPRING SALAD BUFFET MOLDS

(6 servings)

Mrs. Stanley Strud, California Wine Association, Lodi

- 1 (3-oz.) pkg. lemon-flavored gelatin
- 1 cup hot water
- ¾ cup California Sauterne or other white dinner wine
- 3 tablespoons California wine vinegar
- 2 tablespoons sugar
- Salt
- 1 (10-oz.) pkg. frozen mixed vegetables, cooked and drained
- ½ cup finely diced celery
- 2 tablespoons grated onion
- 2 tablespoons chopped parsley

Dissolve gelatin in hot water; add wine, wine vinegar, sugar and salt. Stir well; chill. When mixture begins to thicken, stir in other ingredients. Spoon into 6 individual molds that have been rinsed in cold water or lightly oiled. Chill until firm. Unmold on crisp salad greens; serve with mayonnaise flavored with prepared horseradish. Tomato or pickled beet slices make a nice garnish. This goes well with almost any type of meat or poultry; is attractive for buffet service, with favorite California dinner wine accompanying.

VINTAGE ASPIC

(5 or 6 servings)

Marjorie Lumm, Wine Institute, San Francisco

The most endearing feature of this salad is the fact that it improves with age. It's an excellent tomato aspic to serve as soon as it has set; but refrigerate it for one or two days (carefully covered, of course) and the flavor becomes spectacular.

- 1¼ cups tomato juice
- ⅛ teaspoon crushed basil
- ¼ teaspoon salt
- 1 (3-oz.) package lemon-flavored gelatin
- ¾ cup California Sauterne or other white dinner wine
- 3 tablespoons California wine vinegar
- ⅓ cup crumbled blue cheese

Heat the tomato juice, basil and salt to boiling; add gelatin and stir until dissolved. Remove from heat; blend in wine and wine vinegar. Chill until mixture begins to thicken; stir in crumbled cheese. Turn into individual oiled molds or small ring mold; chill until firm. Serve on crisp salad greens, with topping of sour cream sharpened with a little grated horseradish. I like this with beef or veal sauté, wheat pilaf, buttered peas, and for dessert fresh strawberries in Champagne.

My choice of wine to accompany this menu:
A CALIFORNIA CLARET WITH BEEF, OR
DRY SAUTERNE WITH VEAL

CRANBERRY-PORT SALAD

(10 to 12 servings)

Mrs. Myron S. Nightingale, Roma Wine Company, Fresno

- 1 medium-size whole orange, coarsely ground
- ¾ cup California Port
- 1 (3-oz.) pkg. raspberry-flavored gelatin
- 1 (1-lb.) can whole cranberry sauce
- 1 cup coarsely chopped walnuts
- 1 cup sour cream

Combine ground whole orange (including peel and juice) with Port in small saucepan. Boil 1 minute. Remove from heat; add gelatin, stirring until dissolved. Add cranberry sauce and nuts. Pour into mold; chill until firm. Unmold; serve with sour cream for dressing.

NOTE: *An ideal salad to go with cold sliced turkey, for a buffet supper or luncheon, with California Rosé as beverage. Another delicious molded cranberry salad is made by Mrs. Joseph S. Concannon, Jr., of Concannon Vineyard, Livermore. She uses Claret in hers, with lemon gelatin, chopped celery and crushed pineapple.*

SALMON SAUTERNE MOLD delights the eye and appetite. Soften 1 envelope unflavored gelatin in ¼ cup cold water; dissolve in 1 cup hot chicken stock or broth. Add ½ cup California Sauterne or other white dinner wine, 2 tablespoons lemon juice, and grated onion, salt and pepper to taste. Chill until mixture starts to thicken, then fold in 1 (1-lb.) can salmon, drained and flaked. Pour into oiled 1-quart mold, fish-shaped if available. Unmold on crisp lettuce and serve with mayonnaise. Excellent for luncheon main dish.

MOLDED FRUIT MEDLEY

(10 to 12 servings)

Janet Laird, Wine Institute, San Francisco

- 1 (3-oz.) pkg. lime-flavored gelatin
- 1 cup hot water
- ½ cup California Sauterne, Chablis or other white dinner wine
- ¼ cup sugar
- 1 teaspoon lemon juice
- ¼ cup orange juice
- 1 tablespoon grated orange rind
- 1 cup whipping cream, whipped
- 2 medium-size avocados, diced
- 1 (1-lb.) can grapefruit sections, drained
- 1 (1-lb.) can Royal Anne cherries, drained
- 1 (8½-oz.) can crushed pineapple, drained
- ¼ cup sliced almonds (optional)

Dissolve gelatin in hot water. Stir in the wine, sugar, lemon juice, orange juice and rind. Fold in whipped cream. Fold in the remaining ingredients. Pour into individual molds or a 2-quart mold. Chill until firm. Unmold on crisp salad greens.

NOTE: *This would be an attractive main-dish salad for a luncheon, with hot buttered rolls and chilled California Sauterne or Rosé accompanying.*

TANGY BLUE CHEESE DRESSING

(5 cups)

Mrs. Frank Lico, San Martin Vineyards Company, San Martin

- ⅓ cup chopped green onions, including tops
- 2 cups mayonnaise
- 1 cup sour cream
- ⅓ cup California wine vinegar
- 2 tablespoons California Sauterne or other white dinner wine
- 2 tablespoons lemon juice
- ½ lb. blue cheese, crumbled
- 1 or 2 cloves garlic, mashed or crushed
- ½ cup chopped parsley
- ½ teaspoon salt
- ¼ teaspoon pepper

Combine all the ingredients; mix with electric beater. Good with barbecued steak, baked potato, green beans and apple pie for dessert.

My choice of wine to accompany this menu:
CALIFORNIA BURGUNDY OR CLARET

NOTE: Flavorsome and easy. If stronger vinegar flavor is desired, just increase wine vinegar and slightly decrease amount of wine.

DE LUXE PARMESAN DRESSING

(About 2 cups)

Jim Morse, Beringer Bros., Inc., St. Helena

- 1 cup salad oil
- ¼ cup California Rhine or other white dinner wine
- ½ cup California wine vinegar
- ½ cup grated Parmesan cheese
- 2 raw eggs
- 1 teaspoon salt
- ½ teaspoon *each*: onion salt, garlic salt, paprika and coarsely ground black pepper
- ¼ teaspoon Worcestershire sauce

Combine all in mixing bowl. Beat with rotary beater until well blended, or whirl in electric blender. If you do not plan to use the dressing immediately, store in covered jar in refrigerator, and beat well just before serving. Good on tossed green or mixed vegetable salad, with a hearty beef dinner.

NOTE: And glasses of California Claret, Burgundy or Zinfandel.

TUSH DRESSING

(About 1½ cups)

Mario Lanza, Wooden Valley Winery, Suisun

- ½ cup catsup
- ⅓ cup salad oil
- ¼ cup California wine vinegar
- ⅓ cup California Sauterne or other white dinner wine
- 2 tablespoons granulated sugar
- ½ teaspoon salt
- ½ teaspoon paprika
- 1½ teaspoons grated onion
- 1½ teaspoons pressed or grated garlic, or 1 whole clove garlic

Combine all ingredients. Mix well.

NOTE: What Mr. Lanza really said was "Shake the devil out of it — now eat it." And that's easy to do; it's delicious, as well as simple to make. Good on mixed cold vegetables or lettuce, with lamb chops, Claret.

POOR MAN'S SALAD DRESSING

(4 servings)

Bill Bagnani, American Industries Corp., Geyserville

- ½ cup California red wine vinegar
- ½ cup mayonnaise
- ½ cup catsup
- 2 tablespoons prepared mustard
- 2 to 4 tablespoons California Dry Sherry
  Salt and pepper
- 1 head lettuce

Let not the little woman throw out dregs of empty mayonnaise, catsup and mustard jars. Store in rear of refrigerator. Disregard the precise measurements above. When sufficient jars are available, rinse each jar with a little wine vinegar. Pour the rinsings into the mayonnaise jar with Sherry, salt and pepper. Shake real well till dressing is smooth, light pink in color and delightful to taste. Quarter lettuce head, pour over dressing and serve.

NOTE: Mr. Bagnani's directions, above, are as lucid and flavorful as the California wine and wine vinegar used in recipe. A good, practical idea.

RIESLING SALAD DRESSING

(1½ cups)

Brother Timothy, Mont La Salle Vineyards, Napa

This is an original recipe.

- ½ cup California Riesling, Rhine or other white dinner wine
- ¼ cup lemon juice
- ¾ cup salad oil
- 1 teaspoon salt
- ½ teaspoon freshly ground pepper
  Dash garlic salt

Combine all ingredients; mix well.

NOTE: A simple, satisfying blend on crisp greens. Perfect with game hen menu suggested on Page 63 — with the same wine accompanying.

AVOCADO DRESSING LIVERMORE

(1¾ cups)

Mrs. Charles Rezendes, Cresta Blanca Wine Co., Livermore

- 1 ripe medium-size avocado
- ¼ cup sour cream
- ½ teaspoon onion salt
- ¼ teaspoon Worcestershire sauce
  Dash Tabasco sauce
- 1 teaspoon lemon juice
- ½ cup blue cheese
- ¾ cup oil
- ¼ cup California white wine vinegar
- ¼ cup California Sauterne, Rhine or other white dinner wine

Remove seed and peel avocado; mash until smooth. Blend in sour cream, onion salt, Worcestershire sauce, Tabasco sauce and lemon juice. Mash cheese until fairly smooth; blend in oil, wine vinegar and wine. Combine with avocado mixture; chill. Serve over crisp lettuce wedges or toss with salad greens.

NOTE: Smooth and creamy, pleasantly different. Particularly good with barbecued chicken and the same white wine, or a Rosé.

SANDWICHES

Also Toast, Waffles and Bread with Wine

Throughout the occidental world, bread and wine are the age-old symbol of hospitality. A jug of wine, a loaf of bread, have summed up in poetry the essentials of man's daily diet. But wine is also used effectively in *concocting* many bread dishes, for a savory new flavor. For snack-time, lunch or brunch or supper, a wine-sauced sandwich can become a robustly satisfying meal. With a glass of California wine accompanying, all of the good old classic elements are present, and the joy of the diner is great indeed.

TURKEY SANDWICHES DAVIS

(4 servings)

Mrs. George Marsh, U. C. Dept. Food Science & Technology

Thin slices cooked turkey
Thin slices American cheese
8 slices buttered bread
3 eggs, slightly beaten
1½ cups milk
½ cup California sherry
Salt, celery salt and pepper

Prepare 4 turkey-cheese sandwiches; arrange in greased shallow baking pan. Combine remaining ingredients; pour over sandwiches and let stand for about 1 hour. Bake in moderately slow oven (325°) for 1 hour. To serve, separate sandwiches with a sharp knife and lift onto plates with a broad spatula. Good for lunch or a Sunday night supper.

My choice of wine to accompany this dish:
CALIFORNIA SAUVIGNON BLANC

NOTE: A convenient recipe to remember, during the holidays especially, when most people have the leftover turkey problem.

BUON GUSTO SANDWICHES

(4 or 5 servings)

Ernest C. Haas, East-Side Winery, Lodi

Mix 2 slightly beaten eggs, ⅓ cup milk, ⅓ cup California Sherry, ¼ teaspoon Worcestershire sauce and salt. Prepare 4 or 5 cheese sandwiches, using white bread and thin slices of processed American or Cheddar cheese. Dip sandwiches in egg mixture, then sauté slowly in small amount of bacon drippings, butter or margarine. Brown sandwiches nicely on one side; turn with a spatula. Cover skillet and continue cooking until browned on other side. Serve at once with crisp bacon garnish. This makes a hearty and satisfying lunch.

NOTE: Especially when glasses of chilled California Rosé or white dinner wine (such as Sauterne, Chablis or Rhine) are on the table.

PARMESAN WINE BREAD

(6 to 8 servings)

Paul Huber, E. & J. Gallo Winery, Fresno

- 2 cups biscuit mix
- 1 tablespoon sugar
- 1 teaspoon instant minced onion **or**
  1 tablespoon finely chopped mild onion
- ½ teaspoon crushed oregano **or**
  ¼ teaspoon powdered oregano
- ¼ cup melted butter or margarine
- ¼ cup California Sauterne, Chablis or other white dinner wine
- 1 egg, beaten
- ½ cup milk
- ¼ cup shredded Parmesan cheese

Combine biscuit mix, sugar, onion and oregano. Add melted butter, Sauterne, beaten egg and milk. Beat until blended. Turn into a well-greased 8″ round cake pan. Sprinkle Parmesan cheese over top. Bake in hot oven (400°) for 20 to 25 minutes. Serve warm, in pie-shaped wedges.

NOTE: Simple, yet different, with a show-stealing airy texture and tantalizing aroma. Could be served at either a dinner (with red, white or Rosé dinner wine, according to the menu)—or at a luncheon, with a main-dish type of salad, or creamed crab or chicken. In this case, a chilled California white dinner wine or Rosé would probably be preferred.

ZESTY FRENCH BREAD

(1 loaf)

Edward R. Oberlander, Woodbridge Vineyard Assn., Lodi

- 1 (5-oz.) jar American or Cheddar cheese spread
- ¼ cup California Sherry
- 2 tablespoons mayonnaise
- ½ teaspoon prepared mustard
- ½ teaspoon Worcestershire sauce
- 1 long loaf French bread

Combine cheese spread and Sherry in bowl; blend thoroughly. Add mayonnaise, mustard and Worcestershire sauce; mix well. Cut bread in half, lengthwise; slice crosswise, not quite all the way through. Spread cheese mixture over cut surfaces of bread; broil slowly until delicate brown. Serve hot. Good with barbecued chicken or any hearty indoor meal, as a change from the usual garlic bread. (Halves of French rolls or hamburger buns may also be used with the same spread.)

My choice of wine to accompany the menu:
CALIFORNIA GREY RIESLING

SANDWICH SURPRISE

(5 or 6 servings)

Mrs. Dan C. Turrentine, Wine Advisory Board, San Francisco

These are really quite easy, with lots of appetite-appeal for a luncheon, Sunday night supper, or any meatless dinner.

- ¼ cup butter or margarine
- ¼ cup flour
- 1 cup milk
- ½ cup chicken stock (canned or bouillon-cube broth may be used)
- 1 teaspoon grated onion
- ½ teaspoon Worcestershire sauce
  Salt and pepper
- 1 (6½-oz.) can chunk-style tuna
- 1 (4½-oz.) can chopped ripe olives
- 10 to 12 slices white bread
- 2 eggs mixed with ½ cup milk
  Butter, margarine or other fat
- ⅓ cup California Sauterne or other white dinner wine
- ½ cup grated Cheddar cheese
- 2 tablespoons chopped parsley

In a saucepan, melt ¼ cup butter; stir in flour; add milk and chicken stock. Cook, stirring constantly, until mixture boils and thickens. Add onion, Worcestershire sauce, salt and pepper. Mix ½ cup of sauce with tuna and olives. Use tuna mixture and bread to make 5 or 6 sandwiches. Dip sandwiches quickly on both sides in egg-milk mixture; sauté them slowly in heavy skillet, in small amount of butter, until nicely browned on both sides. Add wine, cheese and parsley to remaining thickened sauce; stir over low heat until cheese melts and sauce is piping hot. Cut sandwiches in half diagonally; place on individual plates. Pour sauce over sandwiches and serve at once, garnished with watercress or tomato slices that have been marinated in oil and wine vinegar.

My choice of wine to accompany this dish:
CHILLED CALIFORNIA SAUTERNE

FOR AFTERNOON or evening refreshment time, make tiny open-faced sandwiches. Blend cream cheese with California Sherry, chopped mint and chopped fresh dates. Spread on nut bread or thin slices of whole wheat bread. Serve with chilled Sherry or other dessert wine.

VALLEY FIG WAFFLES

(6 to 8 servings)

Mrs. Charles M. Crawford, E. & J. Gallo Winery, Modesto

    ¾ cup dried figs
    Batter for 6 to 8 waffles
    (use favorite recipe or mix)
    Sherry Sauce (see below)

Cover figs with boiling water; let stand 10 minutes. Drain thoroughly. Clip off stems with scissors; cut figs fairly fine. Add figs to waffle batter. Bake in hot waffle iron as usual. Serve with Sherry Sauce. Delicious with ham or bacon for a brunch or supper.

SHERRY SAUCE: Mix 1 tablespoon cornstarch with 1½ cups brown sugar (firmly packed) and dash of salt, in saucepan. Gradually add ½ cup **each** California Sherry and water, stirring until smooth. Cook and stir over medium heat until mixture boils, thickens and becomes clear. Add 1 tablespoon lemon juice, 1 teaspoon grated lemon rind and ¼ cup butter or margarine. Serve piping hot over hot Fig Waffles.

NOTE: *As a brunch or supper feature, the waffles could be accompanied by a chilled California Sauterne or other white dinner wine.*

SHERRY SNACK TOAST

(4 to 6 servings)

Secondo P. Meda, Wine Broker, San Francisco

This toast is my own creation, and can be served for lunch or as an afternoon snack or evening party refreshment. It is also good as a dessert after dinner.

    4 egg yolks
    3 tablespoons powdered sugar
    ¾ cup California Cream Sherry,
       Marsala or other dessert wine
    ¼ cup butter or margarine, melted
    ¼ cup California brandy or rum
    4 to 6 slices cornbread or white bread,
       cut in 5 x 3 x ½" slices
    1 teaspoon grated lemon peel
    1 teaspoon cinnamon

Cream together eggs, sugar and wine. Add melted butter and 2 tablespoons brandy or rum. Dip both sides of bread slices in mixture. Combine lemon peel and cinnamon with remaining brandy or rum; spread on top of dipped bread. Place in warm buttered skillet. Bake in very slow oven (200°) until golden brown on both sides. (Pure maple syrup could be poured over at serving time, for those who like more sweetness in the dish.)

My choice of wine to accompany this dish:
CALIFORNIA CREAM SHERRY OR MARSALA

NOTE: *Unusual and flavorful — like a gourmet French toast.*

JELLIES & JAM

Also Fruit Conserves and Nuts with Wine

As garnish for meat and poultry, wine jellies or condiment fruits add a subtle complementary flavor that can hardly be topped. They are colorful, too, and make thoughtful gifts for gastronomy-minded friends. One of the many charms of wine jelly is its vast range of flavor and color. Simply follow the basic recipe below, and you can come up with some highly original delicacies.

BASIC WINE JELLY

(About 5 glasses, 6-oz. size)

Mario Lanza, Wooden Valley Winery, Suisun

    2 cups California Burgundy or other
       red dinner wine
    3 cups sugar
    ½ bottle liquid fruit pectin

Combine wine and sugar in top of double boiler. Place over rapidly boiling water; heat about 3 minutes, or until sugar is completely dissolved, stirring constantly. Remove from heat; stir in pectin. Quickly pour into glasses; paraffin immediately. For a change of color and flavor, a white dinner wine (such as Sauterne) or Vin Rosé may be used in place of Burgundy.

NOTE: And dessert or appetizer wines, such as Port or Sherry, are also delicious used in the basic recipe. This jelly makes a delightful and attractive gift, especially when poured into inexpensive wine glasses. Adds piquant flavor when served with wild game, meats or poultry (and your favorite California dinner wine).

EASY PORTED FRUITS

(1 quart)

Mrs. E. F. Handel, East-Side Winery, Lodi

Fill a quart jar with pitted dates, prunes, golden figs and dried apricots. Half fill jar with California White Port. Cover; shake. Refrigerate several days, shaking jar now and then to distribute liquid. A delicious treat to accompany rich meats and poultry.

NOTE: Would be a glamorous touch for the festive holiday dinner, with California Champagne or a beautiful Rosé accompanying.

PORT-HERB JELLY

(About 5 glasses, 6-oz. size)

Elmo Martini, Martini & Prati Wines, Inc., Santa Rosa

Follow recipe for Basic Wine Jelly, using California Port as the wine. Add 1 or 2 tablespoons of dried marjoram to wine and sugar before heating. Strain jelly through a fine sieve into glasses to remove herb. (Or, if a more pronounced herb flavor is preferred, pour jelly without straining.) Good to accompany meats, or on toast as a snack anytime.

NOTE: Still another pleasing variation on the Basic Wine Jelly recipe is recommended by Mrs. Richard D. Dettman of Mont La Salle Vineyards, Napa. Mrs. Dettman uses a California Light Muscat as the wine, which provides a particularly delicate and different flavor. Any of these jellies, when served with meats, would harmonize beautifully with the red, white or Rosé dinner wine chosen to accompany the menu.

GRAPE GARNISH for meat or poultry platter is a delight to see as well as eat. Cut tiny clusters of fresh seedless grapes, dip in egg whites (beaten slightly until fluffy), then dredge in granulated sugar. Sugar will stick, adding frost or "bloom."

MINTED WINE JELLY

(About 5 glasses, 6-oz. size)

E. L. (Ted) Barr, Western Grape Products, Kingsburg

    2 cups California Muscatel
      Green food coloring
    3 cups sugar
    ½ bottle liquid fruit pectin
    12 drops mint or spearmint extract

Place wine in top of double boiler; tint slightly with green coloring. Stir in sugar. Place over rapidly boiling water. Heat 2 minutes, or until sugar is thoroughly dissolved, stirring constantly. Remove from water and at once stir in pectin. Add mint extract. Pour quickly into glasses and paraffin immediately.

NOTE: *Would be perfect with roast lamb or lamb chops, and any California dinner wine preferred with this particular meat — Rosé, white or red.*

HARVEST PEAR JAM

(Makes 1 pint)

Ernest C. Haas, East-Side Winery, Lodi

    1 cup sugar
    ¼ cup California Sherry
    1 teaspoon *each* grated orange and
      lemon peel
    ¼ cup orange juice
    1 tablespoon lemon juice
    2 cups coarsely ground pears (firm - ripe)

Combine all ingredients except pears. Simmer 5 minutes. Add pears, and simmer 15 minutes, stirring occasionally. Pour immediately into hot sterilized jars and seal.

NOTE: *This would make a good evening TV snack, on toast or a hot buttered muffin, with a glass of Sherry on the side.*

VINEYARD APPLE BUTTER

(About 1½ quarts)

Frank I. Pirrone, F. Pirrone & Sons, Inc., Salida

    1 large bottle California Port
    1 quart water
    2 quarts sliced, peeled apples
    1½ cups sugar
    ¼ teaspoon salt
    ½ teaspoon cinnamon
    ¼ teaspoon cloves
    ¼ teaspoon allspice

Heat wine and water to boiling in large kettle; add apples and cook slowly, stirring often, for 1½ to 2 hours, or until mixture starts to thicken. Add sugar, salt and spices; cook rapidly, stirring constantly, until thick enough to spread. Pour quickly into hot sterilized jars and seal with paraffin.

NOTE: *An ideal spread for toast, while watching the late TV show, with a glass of Port accompanying. Good also to serve at brunch parties, as a change from the usual jellies or jams.*

FESTIVE FRUIT GARNISH

(12 to 16 servings)

Mrs. Rose Marie Pangborn, UC Dept. Food Science & Technology

    1 cup honey
    ¾ cup California wine vinegar
    10 whole cloves
    3 inches stick cinnamon
    ¾ cup California Port or Muscatel
    1½ qts. fresh or drained canned fruits

Simmer honey, vinegar and spices together 5 minutes. Add wine and fruits; simmer 15 minutes, or until fruits (if fresh) are tender. Cool; store in refrigerator. Good fruits to use are apple quarters; peach, pear or apricot halves; or a mixture of fruits. A wonderful relish or garnish for roasts or chops or turkey.

NOTE: *With California red, white or Rosé wine as beverage!*

WINE LAND PRUNES

(1 quart)

A. A. Vetriolo, Wine Advisory Board, San Francisco

Soak prunes for 24 hours in California Port or flavored wine. Pour all into quart jar and store in refrigerator, using as needed. Prunes will absorb some of wine; keep them covered by adding more wine from time to time. Delicious served with meats, or as a salad or dessert, or on top of cereal for a late brunch.

SHERRY SPICED NUTS

(About 1 pint)

Mrs. Jake Rheingans, Sanger Winery Association, Sanger

    1 cup granulated sugar
    ¼ cup California Cream Sherry
      Pinch cream of tartar
    1 teaspoon cinnamon
    1 teaspoon vanilla
    2 cups nutmeats (walnuts or pecans)

Combine sugar, Sherry and cream of tartar in a small saucepan; boil until syrup threads; remove from heat. Add cinnamon and vanilla; mix well. Add nuts; stir until cold. Turn out onto buttered platter. Separate with a fork.

NOTE: *Wonderful anytime as a refreshment — afternoon or evening, when serving Sherry or other California dessert or appetizer wines.*

DESSERTS

Simple or Spectacular...with Wine

Never underestimate the most basic of all final menu courses: a glass of dessert wine by itself. A California Port, Muscatel or Cream Sherry, rich with only the natural grape-sweetness, crowns any dinner and needs no bolstering by prepared desserts. (Many prefer a bit of cheese as complement, an unsurpassed combination.) If family tradition calls for a special dessert, it can still be as simple and easy to serve as wine-topped fruit or ice cream or pudding. But for more festive occasions, wine of course adds immeasurably to the making of elaborate pies or cakes or flaming desserts. The extra preparation here is often part of the fun. Whatever your pattern, the helpful thing is to have wine on hand—then you're ready for anything.
These recipes suggest the many variations in desserts cooked and served with wine.

DELANO PEACH DELIGHT

(4 servings)

Harry Baccigaluppi, Calif. Grape Products Corp., Delano

This dessert caps any meal. Italian macaroons or amaretti served with the following will add a final touch of elegance.

     4 nectar peach or Elberta peach halves
       Vanilla ice cream
    ½ cup California Muscatel, Port
       or Sherry
     4 maraschino cherries

Place a peach half in bottom of each of 4 sherbet glasses. Cover with ice cream. Pour 2 tablespoons wine over each serving; top with a cherry.

NOTE: *Simple, but so good; another proof of the great ease of adding wine to make food even better. Any favorite dessert wine would be suitable accompanying, or to end the dinner.*

CHAMPAGNE DESSERTS need not be extravagant. Buy small bottles, to pour over drained fruits at the table. Or, pour the Champagne on the fruits from a large bottle, then serve the rest as beverage. If served promptly, the Champagne bubbles are retained in any uncooked dessert. Even in a cooked dessert dish, Champagne flavor remains.

SARATOGA FRUIT CUP

(6 to 8 servings)

Mrs. Otto E. Meyer, Paul Masson Vineyards, Saratoga

     4 cups fresh fruit in season (apples,
       oranges, grapes, cherries, melon,
       etc.— peeled, pitted and sliced)
    ¼ cup California brandy
     1 cup California Riesling, Chablis or
       other white dinner wine
     2 tablespoons orange flower water
    ¼ cup sugar

Combine equal parts of several kinds of fruit in a glass or ceramic bowl. Sprinkle with liquids and sugar. Cover; refrigerate at least 4 hours.

NOTE: *Equally refreshing and eye-appealing: a glass of California Champagne or a Rosé as accompaniment.*

CANNED FRUITS become something special when wine is added. Try a little California Sherry over canned kadota figs.

FRESH SEEDLESS GRAPES are a charming addition to fruit compotes or other fruit desserts, in summer. In winter, remember that you can buy grapes in small buffet-size cans.

BAKED PEARS SAN GABRIEL

(6 servings)

Domenic E. Viotti, Jr., Viotti Winery, San Gabriel

This is a family dessert recipe, taught to me by my mother, Mrs. Virginia Viotti.

    6   brown baking pears
    18 whole cloves
    2   cups California Port
    1½ cups sugar
    3   cinnamon sticks

Wash pears, leaving in stem. Insert 3 cloves in lower half of each pear. Place pears in shallow baking dish. Pour over wine; sprinkle over sugar. Break cinnamon sticks into wine. Bake, uncovered, in slow oven (300°) about 2 hours, or until pears are very tender. Baste frequently. Remove cloves just before serving. Serve hot or cold, spooning wine sauce over pears.

NOTE: *Sour cream or vanilla ice cream would be good with the pears, and a glass of California Port. (In making the recipe, Burgundy may be substituted for Port. In this case, increase the sugar to 2 cups.)*

STRAWBERRIES AMERICO

(Any amount)

Joseph Ghianda, Ghianda's Winery, Oroville

Americo Ghianda, the founder of our winery, grew both Zinfandel grapes and navel oranges, and he concocted this simple dessert as he was very proud of his fruit. This dish is good following a rich dinner, or to start a meal.

Wash and hull the best strawberries you can buy; sprinkle with powdered or granulated sugar. Pile into sherbet glasses and pour about ¼ cup fresh orange juice over each glass of berries. Fill the rest of the glass with California Zinfandel or other red dinner wine. (If a sweeter wine is preferred, use Port.)

NOTE: *Really good, with either the dry or sweet wine. Another who likes a California Burgundy to marinate sugared berries is Mrs. Joe Cooper of Wine Advisory Board, San Francisco. The same wine used on the berries would be fine for beverage accompaniment.*

SERVE WHOLE STRAWBERRIES with stems on, with a bowl of brown sugar on the side, and glasses of California Port. Using stems as handles, guests dip strawberries into Port, then in brown sugar. This dessert is a favorite of John Cadenhead, Wine Advisory Board, San Diego.

SHERRIED ORANGES

(Any amount)

Mrs. Louis P. Martini, Louis M. Martini Winery, St. Helena

This is an easy light dessert after a rich meal. The dish is especially good with plain pound cake.

Place drained, canned mandarin orange sections in individual serving dishes. Pour a little California Cream Sherry over each serving. (If the Cream Sherry is quite heavy, use 1 part Dry Sherry to 2 parts Cream Sherry.) Let stand in refrigerator 2 to 3 hours before serving. If desired, top with whipped cream.

My choice of wine to accompany this dish:
CALIFORNIA CREAM SHERRY

NOTE: *Delectable. Sour cream could also be used. Another nice combination is diced oranges with grapes, in California Light Muscat, as recommended by Brother Gregory of Mont La Salle Vineyards, Napa.*

STRAWBERRIES IN CHAMPAGNE

(4 to 6 servings)

Louis A. Benoist, Almaden Vineyards, Los Gatos

Stem a quart of large strawberries. (Do not wash; rinse with California white dinner wine.) Sprinkle with California brandy; chill. Before serving, sprinkle with sugar. At the table, pour California Brut Champagne over the berries; serve at once.

My choice of wine to accompany this dish:
THE SAME CALIFORNIA BRUT CHAMPAGNE

NOTE: *An excellent treatment. And rinsing the berries in white wine is a good idea; water often makes them watery in flavor. (Many cooks avoid washing fresh mushrooms in water, for the same reason.) This is a popular dessert among California winemaking families, with variations. Mrs. Stanley Strud of California Wine Association, Lodi, marinates her strawberries in Champagne for 1 or 2 hours. Mrs. Alvin Ehrhardt of United Vintners, Inc., Lodi, uses frozen strawberries and adds frozen pineapple chunks. She removes fruit still frosted from packages, pours Champagne over fruit in serving bowl, stirs gently until frost is thawed, then serves immediately while the Champagne is still bubbling. An easy, refreshing dessert after a festive dinner.*

PORT VOLCANO

(1 serving)

Dick Davis, Wine Advisory Board, San Francisco

This is good any time, any place—a simple answer to anyone who fears wine cookery is involved or time-consuming. In a wine glass (any wine glass), make a mountain of vanilla ice cream. Spoon out a crater in the ice cream mountain. Into the crater pour deep red California Port. The striking color of the Port overflowing onto the white ice cream makes a beautiful dish. Quick and delicious.

My choice of wine to accompany this dish:
CALIFORNIA RUBY PORT

WINE TASTER'S BANANAS

(4 servings)

W. W. Owen, California Grape Products Corp., Delano

> 4 bananas
> 2 tablespoons melted butter
> 1/3 cup California Muscatel
> 2 tablespoons brown sugar
> 1/8 teaspoon ground cloves
> Pinch of salt
> 4 tablespoons lemon juice

Arrange 4 peeled bananas in shallow pan. Combine all other ingredients and pour over bananas. Bake under broiler, basting frequently, until fruit is delicate brown.

NOTE: *A new twist on an old favorite. The same dessert wine served on the side would be a flavorful dinner finale.*

LISA FRUIT CUP

(6 servings)

Mrs. William Bonetti, Charles Krug Winery, St. Helena

This is an original recipe.

> 1 apple
> 1 pear
> 1 orange
> 1 banana
> 1/2 cup fresh strawberries
> 1 (buffet-size) can apricots, drained
> 1/4 cup orange juice
> 1 tablespoon lemon juice
> 1/4 cup sugar
> 1/4 cup California Port

Grate apple and pear; dice remaining fruit. Combine in large bowl. Sprinkle with orange and lemon juice. Add sugar and Port; toss lightly. Keep at room temperature 2 hours, then chill.

NOTE: *Mrs. Bonetti says that some fruits could be substituted for the above, but that the apple and orange should never be omitted. This would be particularly appealing with a glass of California Port.*

HOT DESSERTS are especially welcome in cold weather. And they can be fast. Turn a can of peaches with half the syrup into a skillet or saucepan. Add a nip of California Port or Sherry and heat until piping hot. Great with cookies.

GRAPEFRUIT ALASKA

(3 servings)

Kenneth B. Fry, Calif. State Fair & Exposition, Sacramento

This is a good dessert to serve after a rather heavy dinner, as it is not actually what you would call a "rich" dessert. The tartness of the grapefruit serves to give it the lightness one seeks after a heavy meal.

> 3 large grapefruit
> 6 tablespoons California White Port
>   or other dessert wine
> 3 small scoops vanilla ice cream
> 2 egg whites
> 1 teaspoon sugar
>   Dash salt

Cut grapefruit across 1/3 from stem end. With a sharp knife, loosen each segment from membrane. Cut membrane loose from bottom of fruit; remove. In each cavity formed, place a scoop of ice cream; pour over 2 tablespoons wine. Beat egg whites until stiff but not dry; add salt and sugar. Top each fruit with 1/3 of the meringue. (Be sure edges are sealed with meringue, and top is well covered.) Bake in moderately hot oven (400°) for 3 to 4 minutes or until meringue is nicely browned. Serve immediately.

My choice of wine to accompany this dish:

CALIFORNIA DEMI-SEC OR SWEET CHAMPAGNE,
OR A SWEET ROSÉ

NOTE: *This is not only delicious, but spectacular — a dessert to delight your guests. It's quite easy to make. Grapefruit may be prepared in advance, with the wine added, then stored in refrigerator, covered. When ready to add ice cream and meringue, first stir the grapefruit segments gently, to blend the wine flavor throughout.*

SAUTERNE FRUIT COMPOTE

(6 servings)

Mrs. Herman L. Wente, Wente Bros., Livermore

This is a good dessert after a hearty meat course.

> 3 ripe peaches
> 6 apricots
> 1 cantaloupe
> 1/4 cup orange juice
> 2 cups California Sweet Semillon,
>   Haut Sauterne or other
>   light sweet wine
>   Maraschino cherries

Peel peaches; cut into thick slices. Cut apricots in half, removing pits. Trim rind from melon, remove seeds and cut meat into chunks or balls. Place fruits in shallow dish; pour over orange juice and wine. Marinate for at least 1 hour. (Keep it cool, but do not refrigerate.) Garnish with cherries at serving time. Accompany with very plain cake slices, cookies or lady fingers.

My choice of wine to accompany this dish:

CALIFORNIA SWEET SEMILLON OR SAUTERNE

EPICUREAN BAKED APPLES

(6 servings)

Mrs. Edmund A. Rossi, Jr., Italian Swiss Colony, Asti

```
  6  baking apples
     Spices
     Butter
 ¾   cup California Muscatel
     or Port
     Sour cream (optional)
```

Bake apples in usual way, adding spices and/or butter as desired. Just before removing from oven, pour 2 tablespoons wine over each apple. Serve hot or cold. A spoonful of sour cream is wonderful on each apple, added at the very last.

NOTE: *The same dessert wine would be good accompanying.*

HONEYED GREEN GRAPES

(4 servings)

Mrs. Robert Weaver, U. of Calif. Dept. Viticulture & Enology

This is good after any heavy dinner requiring a light, refreshing dessert.

```
  1  lb. Thompson seedless grapes (about 2½ cups)
     OR 2 buffet-size cans seedless grapes
  1  teaspoon lemon juice
 ¼   cup honey
  2  tablespoons California Sherry or brandy
 ½   cup sour cream
```

Wash grapes; remove stems. Mix lemon juice, honey and Sherry or brandy; pour over grapes. Refrigerate overnight and serve in tall crystal sherbet glasses. Just before serving, top with sour cream.

NOTE: *Ideal after-dinner drink to follow this would be a Cream Sherry.*

FRUTTA AMABILE

(4 to 6 servings)

Mrs. Louis P. Martini, Louis M. Martini Winery, St. Helena

```
  1  fresh ripe pineapple
     Sugar
     California Light Sparkling Muscat
     or Champagne
     Maraschino cherries
```

Split pineapple in half, lengthwise through fruit and green top. With a grapefruit knife, remove core; cut pineapple in chunks. (Save shells for serving.) Place pineapple chunks in glass bowl; add sugar to taste. Pour over wine; marinate for 2 to 3 hours. To serve, return fruit to shells, add a little more wine and garnish with cherries.

My choice of wine to accompany this dish:
CALIFORNIA LIGHT SPARKLING MUSCAT

STUFFED PEACHES PIEMONTESE

(6 servings)

Mrs. Cesare Vai, Cucamonga Vineyard Co., Cucamonga

This is a wonderful dessert for barbecued suppers.

```
  7  fresh peaches
  2  egg yolks, beaten
  2  teaspoons ground cocoa
  6  to 8 macaroons or amaretti, dried and crumbled
  3  or 4 ground peach nuts (from inside peach seed)
  1  tablespoon melted butter
  2  tablespoons California brandy or Sherry
 ½   cup California Sauterne, Chablis or
     other white dinner wine (optional)
```

Cut 6 of the peaches in half; remove pit; do not peel. Arrange face up in buttered shallow baking pan. Mash pulp of remaining peach; add egg yolks, cocoa, macaroon crumbs, ground peach nuts, melted butter and brandy or Sherry. Fill peach halves with mixture. Bake in moderately slow oven (325°) for 1 hour. Increase heat to 400° last 10 minutes to brown. Pour white dinner wine over peaches while baking if more sauce is desired. Serve hot or cold.

My choice of wine to accompany this dish:
A CHILLED CALIFORNIA SPARKLING MUSCAT
OR MOSCATO SPUMANTE

NOTE: *Mrs. Frank J. Pilone of the same winery makes another version of the same dessert, from an old family recipe that includes almond extract and vanilla instead of peach nuts. She prefers a sweet Champagne as accompaniment. Still another version, much simpler, is favored by Mrs. J. B. Cella, II, Cella Wineries, Fresno. Mrs. Cella fills canned peach halves with crushed macaroons mixed with brandy and peach syrup.*

WINE-SPICED PRUNES

(8 to 10 servings)

Myrtle F. Cuneo, Regina Grape Products Co., Etiwanda

These prunes make a good dessert served with cheese and crackers—but may also be served for breakfast, or as a salad, with cottage cheese.

```
 1½  cups prunes
  2  cups water
  1  (3-inch) stick cinnamon
 ½   teaspoon allspice
 ¼   cup brown sugar
 ½   cup California Port
```

Combine prunes, water, cinnamon and allspice in saucepan; cook until tender, about 25 to 30 minutes. Stir in brown sugar and Port. Cover tightly and let stand until cold.

NOTE: *The prunes become even more plump and flavorful if they stand overnight before using. Would be especially good with a glass of the same Port alongside.*

PUDDING-IN-A-HURRY

(6 servings)

Mrs. Fred Perelli-Minetti, A. Perelli-Minetti & Sons, Delano

    1 (3¼-oz.) pkg. vanilla pudding mix
 1½ cups milk
    1 teaspoon shredded orange rind
  ¼ teaspoon salt
  ¼ cup California Sherry
  ½ cup whipping cream
    1 box fresh strawberries or
       2 large bananas

Make pudding mix as directed on package, but using only 1½ cups milk. Add salt, orange rind. Remove from heat; stir in Sherry; cool. Beat cream until stiff; fold into cooled pudding. Wash and hull berries (or peel and slice bananas). Divide fruit in 6 dessert dishes; top each serving with pudding. Garnish with extra whipped cream and fruit, if desired.

NOTE: *This is a light, fresh dessert to which the wine contributes a very subtle richness. A glass of California Cream Sherry on the side would be highly suitable.*

PEACHES IN WINE

(Any amount)

Mrs. Herman Ehlers, East-Side Winery, Lodi

Slice as many fresh or frozen peaches as desired into a deep glass bowl, alternating layer of peaches and layer of sugar. When desired amount is ready, pour over California Haut Sauterne or other light sweet wine, until almost covered. Cover tightly; chill 3 hours or longer. (Wine keeps peaches from turning brown.) Serve as dessert or pre-dinner fruit cocktail, adding whatever fruit is in season — strawberries and bits of pineapple are very good.

NOTE: *If you freeze your own peach slices, Mrs. Ehlers suggests that you do not add the wine in advance, before freezing. Pour it over fruit later, while thawing. This is an exceptionally good dessert, and would be pleasant indeed with the same wine served on the side.*

SHERRIED GRAPEFRUIT

(2 servings)

Otto Gramlow, Beaulieu Vineyard, Rutherford

Cut grapefruit in half and section. Pour in just enough California Sherry to be level with tops of sections. Sugar to taste and serve chilled. Or, cover each Sherried grapefruit half with 2 tablespoons brown sugar and dot with ½ teaspoon butter. Place under broiler until lightly browned; serve hot. Hot or cold, Sherried Grapefruit is fine for first or final course at luncheon or dinner.

NOTE: *If served at the end of a meal, accompany the grapefruit with a glass of California Cream Sherry or other dessert wine.*

RHINE FARM LEMON CREAM

(8 to 10 servings)

Mrs. Otto Dresel, Rhine Farm Vineyards, Sonoma

(This recipe was contributed with Mrs. Dresel's permission by Mrs. Frank H. Bartholomew of Buena Vista Vineyards, Sonoma, who writes:)

This pudding is light as air—perfect climax to a heavy dinner. The Dresel Champagne family of Germany planted the great Rhine Farm Vineyards in Sonoma, which were ended by Prohibition. But laws could not abolish good living among the vineyards of Sonoma. Of enduring fame are the Dresel recipes, of which this is one. (Before 1890, leaf gelatin was used, if available; or you boiled meat bones and skimmed off the gelatin. Then came Mr. Knox.) Garnish this with a lemon leaf and blossom, if a lemon tree grows in your garden.

    5 eggs, separated
    1 cup plus 2 tablespoons granulated sugar
       Juice and grated peel of 1 lemon
    1 envelope plain gelatin
  ¼ cup cold water
  ¾ cup California White Riesling (Johannisberger)
       or other white dinner wine, heated

Combine egg yolks, sugar, lemon juice and grated peel; beat 10 minutes. Soften gelatin in cold water; dissolve in hot wine. Add slowly to egg mixture. Beat egg whites until stiff; fold into gelatin mixture. Chill; serve mounded high in parfait or sherbet glasses.

My choice of wine to accompany this dish:
CALIFORNIA WHITE RIESLING (JOHANNISBERGER)

PLUM FLUFF

(6 servings)

Mrs. Edmund Accomazzo, Cucamonga Winery, Cucamonga

This recipe is Polish in origin, but has been used in our family for years. It is satisfying but not filling — delicious after a heavy meal.

    1 cup California Burgundy, Claret
       or other red dinner wine
 1¼ cups sugar
    2 lbs. fresh plums
    4 egg whites
  ½ teaspoon vanilla

Combine wine and 1 cup sugar in a saucepan; bring to boil, stirring until sugar is dissolved. Add plums; cover and simmer 20 to 25 minutes, or until plums are soft. Beat whites until they form soft peaks; gradually beat in remaining ¼ cup sugar and vanilla until stiff and glossy. Pour hot plums and juice into baking dish or 6 individual casseroles. Spread meringue over fruit. Bake in moderately hot oven (375°) about 12 minutes. Serve hot.

NOTE: *A fruity-flavored Port could follow this, for after-dinner sipping.*

PORT OF NAPA GELATIN

(8 servings)

Brother Timothy, Mont La Salle Vineyards, Napa

- 2 envelopes unflavored gelatin
- 1¼ cups water
- ¼ cup lemon juice
- 1 cup sugar
- 1 cup orange juice
- 1 cup California Port
- Red food coloring (optional)
- Whipped or sour cream
- Seedless grapes

Soften gelatin in ½ cup cold water; add ¾ cup boiling water; stir until gelatin dissolves. Add lemon juice, sugar, orange juice and Port. If desired, add a few drops of red food coloring to intensify the color. Pour gelatin into large wine glasses (or other serving dishes); chill until firm. Served topped with whipped cream and a seedless grape.

NOTE: *A glass of Port or a Light Muscat would be pleasurable accompanying this dessert.*

SHERRIED CARAMEL CUSTARD

(6 servings)

Paul Huber, E. & J. Gallo Winery, Fresno

- 3 eggs
- ⅓ cup sugar
- ¼ teaspoon salt
- 1⅓ cups evaporated milk
- 1 cup water
- 6 tablespoons California Sherry
- Caramel Sauce (see below)

Beat eggs lightly; stir in sugar, salt, milk and water, stirring until sugar is dissolved. Blend in Sherry. Pour into custard cups; set in pan of hot water. Bake in moderate oven (350°) about 1 hour, or until barely set. Cool. Turn out in dessert dishes and top with Caramel Sauce.

CARAMEL SAUCE: In saucepan, mix 1 tablespoon cornstarch, ⅓ cup brown sugar and dash of salt. Gradually add ⅔ cup California Sherry and ⅓ cup cold water, stirring until mixture is smooth. Stir over low heat until sauce boils and thickens; continue cooking another minute or two until it is clear. Remove from heat and add 2 tablespoons butter or margarine. Cool. Pour over custards and top with ½ cup toasted coconut. (This makes about 1 cup of sauce.)

NOTE: *Would be perfection followed by a glass of California Cream Sherry as after-dinner drink.*

ROSÉ STRAWBERRY CREAM

(6 servings)

Viola Moehrle, Wine Advisory Board, San Francisco

- 1 (8½-oz.) can crushed pineapple
- California Rosé wine
- 1 (3-oz.) package strawberry gelatin
- Few grains of salt
- 1 pint vanilla ice cream

Drain pineapple thoroughly. Add wine to pineapple juice to make 1 cup liquid; heat to boiling. Combine liquid with gelatin and salt, stirring until dissolved. Blend in ice cream. Chill until slightly thickened; fold in pineapple. Spoon into individual serving dishes; chill until firm. Serve topped with whipped cream.

My choice of wine to accompany this dish:
A SEMI-SWEET CALIFORNIA ROSÉ

PEACHES sprinkled with California Muscatel and chopped almonds are a great flavor-team.

CHAMPAGNE JELLY

(8 servings)

Kenneth B. Fry, Calif. State Fair & Exposition, Sacramento

- 2 envelopes plain gelatin
- ½ cup California strawberry wine
- ½ cup granulated sugar
- Dash salt
- 2 cups hot water
- 1½ cups California Champagne, chilled
- Whipped cream
- Maraschino cherries or strawberries

Soften gelatin in strawberry wine. Add sugar, salt and hot water; stir until gelatin and sugar dissolves. Chill until mixture begins to thicken. Whip Champagne quickly into slightly thickened gelatin; pour into parfait glasses. Chill until firm. Top with whipped cream and a maraschino cherry or fresh strawberry before serving.

NOTE: *Some of the Champagne bubbles are retained in this airy dessert, if Champagne is whipped into thickening gelatin as directed. An attractive climax to a festive dinner, with Haut Sauterne or Champagne accompanying.*

BRANDY PUDDING SELMA

(12 servings)

Mrs. Walter Staley, Western Grape Products, Kingsburg

We enjoy this for Christmas or other holiday meals. Top of pudding can be decorated with candied fruit, if desired.

- 1½ cups chopped pitted dates
- 1 teaspoon soda
- ⅓ cup California Sherry
- ⅔ cup boiling water
- ¼ cup butter or margarine
- 1 cup sugar,
- 1 egg, beaten
- 1¼ cups sifted all-purpose flour
- ¼ teaspoon baking powder
- Dash of salt
- 1 cup chopped nuts
- Brandy Sauce (see below)

Combine dates and soda; pour over Sherry and boiling water; let stand. Meanwhile, cream butter and sugar; beat in egg. Sift together flour, baking powder and salt; add to creamed mixture. Add date mixture and nuts. Pour into a buttered 8 x 12" pan; bake in slow oven (300°) for 1 hour. Pour Brandy Sauce over hot pudding. Serve with whipped cream.

BRANDY SAUCE: Combine 2 cups sugar, 1 cup water and dash of salt in a saucepan; bring to boil; cook 5 minutes. Add 1 teaspoon butter or margarine, 1 teaspoon vanilla and ¼ cup California brandy.

NOTE: *A glass of California Muscatel, Port or Cream Sherry would be appropriate with this festive, rich-looking dessert.*

FOOD FOR THE GODS

(6 to 8 servings)

Mrs. Kurt G. Opper, Paul Masson Vineyards, Saratoga

- 2 cups California Riesling, Chablis or other white dinner wine
- ¾ cup sugar
- 1 teaspoon vanilla
- 6 eggs, separated
- 2 tablespoons cornstarch
- ¼ teaspoon salt
- 24 macaroons or vanilla wafers
- 2 tablespoons powdered sugar

Combine wine, sugar, vanilla, egg yolks, cornstarch and salt in a saucepan; bring to boiling, stirring constantly; remove from heat. Cover bottom and sides of a 8½" square casserole with macaroons or vanilla wafers. Beat egg whites until stiff; fold half into cooked mixture; pour over cookies. Sweeten other half of egg whites with powdered sugar; spread evenly over mixture in casserole. Bake in moderate oven (350°) about 15 minutes, or until meringue is lightly browned. Remove from oven; cool.

NOTE: *Rich, yet exquisitely light and fluffy. A glass of Haut Sauterne or Champagne would be a fitting accompaniment.*

ZABAGLIONE CLASSIC

(4 servings)

Mrs. August Sebastiani, Samuele Sebastiani, Sonoma

This is a very old Italian dessert, good after a heavy dinner or any lunch. It is especially nice because it can be made on the spur of the moment.

- 3 egg yolks
- ½ cup sugar
- ¼ cup California Sherry
- Grated rind and juice of 1 lemon

Measure ingredients into top of double boiler; place over boiling water. Beat constantly with a rotary beater until mixture thickens and mounds like whipped cream. Remove from heat. Serve hot or chilled in tall parfait glasses by itself, or as a topping for sponge cake or canned fruit.

My choice of wine to accompany this dish:

CALIFORNIA CHAMPAGNE

NOTE: *Mrs. Bruno T. Bisceglia of Bisceglia Bros. Wine Co., Fresno, recommends spooning Zabaglione as a sauce over Sherry-soaked sponge cake, or similar plain cake. This is one of the most popular desserts among California winemaking families.*

EASY ZABAGLIONE

(8 servings)

Mrs. Albert J. Puccinelli, Puccinelli Vineyards, San Mateo

- 3½ cups cold milk
- 2 (4 ½-oz.) pkgs. instant vanilla pudding mix
- ½ cup cold California Sherry

Measure milk into a bowl; add pudding mix. Beat slowly with rotary beater 1 minute. Add Sherry; beat ½ minute longer. Pour into serving dishes. Top with whipped cream, as a pudding dessert.

NOTE: *This version of Zabaglione could also be used as a cake sauce. Sherry or Champagne would be a welcome flavor-mate.*

APPLE CHARLOTTE FLAMBÉ

(10 to 12 servings)

Dr. J. F. Guymon, U. of Calif. Dept. of Viticulture & Enology

This is especially recommended for a Thanksgiving dinner dessert—or for any fall or wintertime party when good apples are available. It is very easy to flame, and is as tasty as it is spectacular.

            3 lbs. apples
            2 cups granulated sugar
            2 tablespoons California Sherry
          ¼ cup butter or margarine
          ⅓ cup California brandy
         1½ to 2 cups fine dry bread crumbs

Pare apples, halve and seed; slice thinly. Place slices in a bowl; add about ⅓ cup sugar and Sherry. Cover; let stand 2 to 3 hours, turning occasionally with a large spoon. In buttered shallow baking dish, place layer of apples; sprinkle with part of the bread crumbs and remaining sugar; dot with butter. Repeat layers until dish is filled (should be closely packed). Place dish in shallow pan of hot water; bake in moderate oven (350°) for 1½ hours. Remove and place dish on tray or platter. Pour over brandy which has been sweetened and warmed. Set aflame and serve. Top servings with sweetened whipped cream flavored with vanilla and brandy.

My choice of wine to accompany this dish:
A FRUITY-FLAVORED CALIFORNIA MUSCATEL
OR HAUT (SWEET) SAUTERNE

WARM THE BRANDY very slightly in a double boiler before you ignite it, when you want to serve a flaming dessert. To keep the flame burning longer, set a lump of sugar on top of the dessert, and pour the warmed brandy over all. Touch your match to the sugar.

OTHER TRICKS with California brandy are numerous. Make a layer cake with your favorite packaged mix. Sprinkle first layer with brandy, then cover with whipped cream. Repeat with second layer, then serve at once. Or, marinate pitted prunes in brandy for 1 week. Or, blanch glacéed cherries for 1 or 2 seconds to remove the glacé; drain well, cool, and cover with brandy to serve.

ROYAL WINE TORTE

(10 to 12 servings)

Mrs. Edmund Accomazzo, Cucamonga Winery, Cucamonga

This dessert is of Hungarian origin. It may also be made with a red dinner wine, such as Burgundy.

          ¾ cup California Rhine, Chablis
            or other white dinner wine
          ¾ cup sugar
            1 teaspoon fine dry bread crumbs
         1½ cups very finely chopped walnuts
            1 (6-oz.) pkg. semi-sweet
            chocolate pieces
            6 eggs, separated

Combine wine, sugar, crumbs, nuts and chocolate pieces in a saucepan. Cook over low heat, stirring constantly, until chocolate is melted and mixture thickens, about 15 minutes. Cool to lukewarm. Beat egg whites until stiff, but not dry. With same beater, beat yolks until light. Stir yolks into cooled chocolate mixture; fold in whites. Spread this batter in a well-buttered, lightly floured 9 x 12" loaf pan. Bake in moderately slow oven (325°) for 50 to 60 minutes. Cool in pan; serve cut in squares. Top with whipped cream or vanilla ice cream, and sprinkle with chopped nuts, if desired.

My choice of wine to accompany this dish:
CALIFORNIA CHAMPAGNE OR CHABLIS

THIRSTY TORTE

(8 servings)

Mrs. Herman Ehlers, East-Side Winery, Lodi

            4 eggs, separated
          ¾ cup sugar
            1 cup sifted all-purpose flour
            1 teaspoon baking powder
          ½ teaspoon salt
          ⅓ cup melted butter
            1 teaspoon vanilla
              Wine Sauce (see below)

Beat egg whites to soft peaks; gradually add ¼ cup sugar, beating until stiff. Beat yolks with remaining ½ cup sugar until thick and lemon colored; fold into meringue. Sift dry ingredients together; fold into eggs. Gently fold in melted butter and vanilla. Pour into 2-qt. casserole. Bake in moderately hot oven (375°) for 30 minutes or until done. When done, poke holes all over cake with a fork or a skewer; spoon over Wine Sauce. Sprinkle with coconut or chopped nuts. Top with whipped cream or ice cream.

WINE SAUCE: Combine 2 cups sugar and 2 cups water in a saucepan; bring to boil; cook until soft ball forms in cold water. Add ½ cup California Sherry.

NOTE: *Tantalizing with a glass of Cream Sherry, as dessert or mid-afternoon refreshment.*

PORT-PINEAPPLE FRUIT CAKE

(2 loaves or 1 large tube pan)

Mrs. E. Sonnikson, Sonoma County Co-Op Winery, Windsor

Make this cake before Thanksgiving, and it will be nicely mellowed by Christmas.

> 2 cups (1 pkg., 16-oz. size) mixed candied fruits
> 2 cups seedless raisins
> 1 cup chopped dates
> 1 cup chopped walnuts
> 1 (No. 2) can crushed pineapple, drained
> 1 cup California Port
> ¾ cup shortening
> 1 cup brown sugar, firmly packed
> ¼ teaspoon cinnamon
> ¼ teaspoon nutmeg
> ¼ teaspoon cloves
> 4 eggs, well beaten
> 2½ cups sifted all-purpose flour
> 1 teaspoon baking powder
> 1½ teaspoons baking soda
> 1 teaspoon salt

In large bowl, mix together candied fruits, raisins, dates, nuts and pineapple. Pour Port over fruits; set aside, stirring occasionally. Meanwhile, cream shortening, brown sugar and spices until light and fluffy; blend in beaten eggs. Sift dry ingredients together; add to creamed mixture. Stir in fruit and wine mixture, mixing well. Grease and flour 2 (9x5x3") loaf pans or 1 large tube pan. If 2 pans are used, divide batter equally or pour into large pan. Bake in slow oven (300°) for 2 hours or until wooden cocktail pick inserted in center comes out clean. Remove from pans; cool thoroughly. Wrap in cloth moistened with brandy, then in heavy waxed paper or foil. Store in covered container or in cool place for at least 1 week before cutting.

My choice of wine to accompany this dish:
CALIFORNIA SHERRY

THIN some raspberry, strawberry, boysenberry or cranberry jelly or jam with California Port. Heat and serve over pound or angel food cake. It's terrific, and so easy.

———

QUICK CAKE DESSERT: Sprinkle slices of leftover sponge or pound cake with Port, Muscatel or Cream Sherry. Or, pile pieces of angel food cake in sherbet glasses; moisten with any of these wines and top with whipped or ice cream.

CREAMY REFRIGERATOR CAKE

(12 servings)

Mrs. Charles M. Crawford, E. & J. Gallo Winery, Modesto

This is a good dessert for company dinners, as it is made the day before and easy to serve, although very elegant. Since it is rather rich, we prefer to serve it after a fairly plain meal, such as roast beef or lamb, with rice or potatoes and tossed green salad.

> 24 macaroons
> ½ cup sugar
> 1 tablespoon plain gelatin
> ¼ teaspoon salt
> ¼ teaspoon nutmeg
> 1 cup milk
> 3 eggs, separated
> ½ cup California Dry Sherry
> 1 cup whipping cream

Butter an 8" or 9" cakepan; line with macaroons. Crumble remaining macaroons and make bottom crust (filling in any holes). Save some crumbled macaroons for top. Mix together sugar, gelatin, salt and nutmeg in top of double boiler; add milk and slightly beaten egg yolks; cook until thickened, stirring constantly. Cool slightly; stir in Sherry. Chill. Beat egg whites until stiff. Whip cream and fold it and egg whites into gelatin mixture. Decorate top with remaining macaroon crumbs. This cake is better after standing overnight in the refrigerator.

My choice of wine to accompany this menu:
CALIFORNIA ROSÉ OR BURGUNDY

NOTE: *A luscious cake, that could also shine as a mid-afternoon or late-evening refreshment, with glasses of Cream Sherry.*

QUICK EASY WINE CAKE

(16 to 20 servings)

Mrs. W. H. Lubsen, Wine Advisory Board, Washington, D.C.

The flavor here can be varied in successive bakings, by using Dry, Medium or Cream Sherry. The cake has a light, spongy, pound-cake texture.

> 1 (1-lb. 3-oz.) pkg. yellow cake mix
> 1 (3¾-oz.) pkg. vanilla instant pudding mix
> 4 eggs
> ¾ cup oil
> ¾ cup California Sherry
> 1 teaspoon nutmeg

Combine all ingredients. Mix with electric beater about 5 minutes at medium speed. Pour batter into greased angel food cake pan. Bake in moderate oven (350°) about 50 minutes or until done. Cool in pan about 5 minutes before turning out on rack. Sprinkle with powdered sugar.

My choice of wine to accompany this dish:
A CALIFORNIA SHERRY

ALMOND SHERRY COOKIES

(About 3 doz.)

Joseph Ghianda, Ghianda's Winery, Oroville

- ½ cup butter or margarine
- ⅓ cup granulated sugar
- 2 egg yolks, unbeaten
- 1 cup almonds, coarsely ground
- ½ teaspoon grated lemon rind
- ¼ teaspoon vanilla
- ¼ cup California Sherry
- 1 cup sifted all-purpose flour
- ⅛ teaspoon salt

Cream butter; add sugar gradually. Add egg yolks; beat until light and fluffy. Add ½ cup almonds, lemon rind and vanilla. Stir in Sherry alternately with flour and salt, sifted together. Drop by tablespoon onto remaining almonds sprinkled on waxed paper. Toss dough until coated with nuts. Quickly shape into balls, about 1" in diameter. Place on lightly greased baking sheet. Place on upper rack of moderate hot oven (400°); bake 12 to 15 minutes, or until delicately browned.

My choice of wine to accompany this dish:
CALIFORNIA SHERRY

NOTE: *These are not sweet cookies, and could be served with any wine at any time, as a refreshment. A similar cookie is made by Mrs. Leo Demostene of Soda Rock Winery, Healdsburg, who uses anise extract instead of the vanilla.*

APRICOT-WINE COOKIES

(About 9 dozen)

Mrs. Laura M. Quaschnick, Bear Creek Vineyard Assn., Lodi

- 1 cup butter or margarine
- 1 cup sugar
- 1 cup brown sugar
- 2 eggs
- 2 teaspoons vanilla
- 3½ cups sifted cake flour
- 2 teaspoons baking powder
- ½ teaspoon salt
- Apricot-Wine Filling (see below)

Cream butter and sugars. Beat eggs with vanilla until light. Sift dry ingredients; add to creamed mixture alternately with eggs. Chill dough. Divide dough in half; roll out each half on lightly floured board to oblong shape (14 x 10 x ¼"). Spread each half with Apricot-Wine Filling; roll like a jelly roll. Wrap in waxed paper; chill several hours or freeze. Slice about ¼" thick with thin-bladed sharp knife. Place on greased baking sheet; bake in hot oven (400°) for about 8 minutes.

APRICOT-WINE FILLING: Combine 1 (7-oz.) pkg. dried apricots, chopped, ¾ cup sugar, juice of 1 lemon and ¾ cup California Muscatel in a saucepan. Let stand 1 hour to soften. Bring to boiling; cook, stirring constantly, until mixture thickens. Cool. Add 1 cup chopped walnuts and, if necessary, a little additional Muscatel to bring to spreading consistency.

NOTE: *A very good cookie; would be worth freezing a batch, to have on hand. California Muscatel would be the ideal beverage.*

MENDOCINO NUT DROPS

(About 4 doz.)

Mrs. John Parducci, Parducci Wine Cellars, Inc., Ukiah

This is our favorite cookie.

- 1½ cups butter or margarine
- 1¾ cups sifted powdered sugar
- ¼ teaspoon salt
- 3⅓ cups sifted flour
- ½ cup California Dry Sherry
- 1 cup finely chopped walnuts

Cream butter thoroughly. Gradually add sugar, beating until well blended. Mix in salt. Add flour alternately with Sherry, mixing well. Stir in nuts. Drop by small teaspoonfuls on greased baking sheet. Bake in moderate oven (350°) for 20 to 25 minutes.

NOTE: *Delicious with any light sweet wine or dessert wine, for dessert or an afternoon refreshment.*

SHERRY BALLS

(About 60 balls, 1" size)

Mrs. Albert J. Puccinelli, Puccinelli Vineyards, San Mateo

- 2 (7¼-oz.) pkgs. vanilla wafers, finely crushed
- ½ cup honey
- ¾ cup California Sherry
- 4 cups finely ground walnuts
- Granulated sugar

Combine wafer crumbs, honey, Sherry and walnuts; mix well. Shape into round balls (about 1" in diameter); roll in sugar. Store in metal can or cookie jar. Flavor improves with age.

NOTE: *With these on hand, unexpected guests would be no problem. A good mid-afternoon or evening refreshment with glasses of California Cream Sherry or other dessert wine. Raymond H. Mettler of Bear Creek Vineyard Association, Lodi, makes a similar delicacy, Brandy Balls, mixing 2½ cups vanilla cookie crumbs, 1 cup sifted powdered sugar, 2 tablespoons cocoa, ¼ cup California brandy, 1 cup walnut meats (chopped fine) and 3 tablespoons corn syrup. He recommends similar procedure and storing.*

PORT-DATE PINWHEELS

(3 to 5 doz.)

Mrs. Laura M. Quaschnick, Bear Creek Vineyard Assn., Lodi

Actually any basic ice box cookie recipe will do here for the cookies themselves. Using the Port-Date filling is my own experiment.

> ½ cup butter or margarine
> ½ cup granulated sugar
> ½ cup brown sugar (packed)
> 1 egg, beaten
> ½ teaspoon vanilla
> 2 cups sifted all-purpose flour
> ½ teaspoon soda
> 1 teaspoon salt
> Port-Date Filling (see below)

Cream butter and sugars thoroughly. Add egg and vanilla; mix well. Sift dry ingredients together; add to creamed mixture; mix well. Chill dough. Divide dough in half; roll out one half into rectangle ¼" thick. Spread with ½ chilled Port-Date Filling; roll up like a jelly roll. Repeat with remaining half of dough. Wrap rolls in waxed paper; chill several hours. Slice ¼" thick; place on greased cookie sheet. Bake in moderately hot oven (400°) for 8 minutes.

PORT-DATE FILLING. Combine 1 lb. chopped pitted dates, ½ cup sugar and ½ cup California Port in saucepan. Bring to boiling; cook, stirring constantly, until mixture thickens slightly. Cool. Add ½ cup chopped walnuts just before ready to spread on dough. If mixture seems too thick to spread easily, thin with little additional Port.

NOTE: *A delightful cookie, served either with ice cream, as a dessert, or with glasses of California Port as an anytime refreshment.*

DESSERT WINE DUMPLINGS

(10 to 12 servings)

Mrs. Kurt G. Opper, Paul Masson Vineyards, Saratoga

> 3 eggs, separated
> 3 tablespoons cornstarch, or flour or fine dry bread crumbs
> 3 tablespoons sugar
> Shortening
> 3 cups California Haut Sauterne or other light sweet wine

Beat egg yolks until thick and lemon colored; add cornstarch, flour or crumbs and sugar. Beat whites until stiff; fold into yolk mixture. Heat kettle of shortening to just below boiling. Drop egg mixture a teaspoonful at a time into hot shortening; cook 1 or 2 minutes. Remove dumplings to a bowl. Sweeten wine to taste, if desired; heat and pour over dumplings. Serve hot.

NOTE: *Light and delicate. An unusual dessert that would harmonize beautifully with a glass of Haut Sauterne, Sweet Semillon or Champagne.*

BABS' BABA

(10 servings)

Mrs. D. C. Turrentine, Wine Advisory Board, San Francisco

> 1 (1-lb. 1-oz.) pkg. pound cake mix
> ⅓ cup California Sherry
> ⅓ cup orange juice
> ½ cup sugar
> ½ teaspoon grated orange rind

Following package directions, bake pound cake. While baking, combine other ingredients in small saucepan. Bring to boil, lower heat and simmer about 10 minutes; cool. Cool baked cake in pan until lukewarm; gently poke holes all over top surface, inserting fork tines as far as possible. Carefully spoon orange syrup over cake top. Slice; serve warm or cold, plain or topped with whipped cream.

NOTE: *Delicious, interesting and quick. A glass of California Cream Sherry would be good either on the side or following the dinner.*

DAVIS DATE BARS

(About 16 bars)

Mrs. Klayton Nelson, U. of Cal. Dept. Viticulture & Enology

> 1 cup dates, finely cut
> 1 cup granulated sugar
> ½ cup California Sherry
> ¼ cup water
> 1 tablespoon lemon juice
> 1 teaspoon lemon rind
> 1 cup chopped nuts
> 1 cup brown sugar
> ¼ teaspoon salt
> 1 teaspoon baking soda
> 1¾ cup uncooked quick-cooking rolled oats
> 1½ cups flour
> ½ cup butter or margarine

Combine dates, sugar, Sherry and water in saucepan. Bring to boil; reduce heat and simmer, stirring frequently, until mixture is quite thick. Remove from heat; add lemon juice, rind and nuts. Cool. Meanwhile, mix dry ingredients. Work in butter to make a crumbly mixture. Spread half or crumbs in greased 8" pan; pat down firmly. Spread cooled date mixture evenly over crumbs; top with remaining crumb mixture, patting down firmly. Bake in moderate oven (350°) for 30 minutes. Cool in pan; cut into small squares.

My choice of wine to accompany this dish:
CALIFORNIA MUSCATEL OR PORT

SHERRY CREAM PIE

(8 servings)

Mrs. Lewis A. Stern, E. & J. Gallo Winery, Modesto

This is really a company dessert, and gets lots of oh's-and-ah's from guests who love good eating.

        1½ cups fine graham cracker or
              zwieback crumbs
        1¼ cups sugar
         ½ cup butter or margarine, melted
          6 egg yolks
         ½ teaspoon salt
          1 envelope unflavored gelatin
         ½ cup cold water
          2 cups whipping cream
         ½ cup California Sherry
              Finely sliced almonds

Combine crumbs, ¼ cup of sugar and melted butter. Press into a buttered 9" pie plate; chill 20 minutes. Meanwhile, beat egg yolks until light; stir in remaining cup of sugar and salt. Soften gelatin in cold water; dissolve over boiling water in top of double boiler. Pour gelatin over egg mixture, stirring constantly. Whip cream until stiff; fold into egg mixture. Stir in Sherry. Cool mixture until it begins to thicken; pour into pie shell. Chill until firm. Sprinkle with almonds.

NOTE: *Rich, high and handsome. Mrs. John Parducci of Parducci Wine Cellars, Inc., Ukiah, makes a similar Sherry Cream Pie, using chocolate cookie crumbs in the crust. She recommends the dish as a bridge dessert. A Cream Sherry would be good sipping after such a pie.*

SHERRIED FRESH PEACH PIE

(1 pie, 9" size)

Sandra Hancock, Wine Institute, San Francisco

        4½ cups sliced fresh peaches
         ¾ cup sugar
         ¼ teaspoon salt
          3 tablespoons flour
         ¼ cup California Sherry
          2 tablespoons butter or margarine
              Pastry for double 9" pie crust

Thoroughly wash and slice fresh peaches. Combine sugar, salt and flour; sprinkle over peaches in saucepan. Add Sherry and butter and heat just to boiling. Turn into pastry-lined pie pan. Cover with top pastry, sealing edges together well. Cut a few slits in the top. Bake in hot oven (400°) 35 to 40 minutes, until pastry is golden.

My choice of wine to accompany this dish:
CALIFORNIA CREAM SHERRY

FROZEN BRANDY PIE

(1 pie, 9" size)

Mrs. J. F. Guymon, U. of Calif. Dept. Viticulture & Enology

Guests always comment on the flavor surprise here, since this Bisquit Tortoni dessert looks like cheesecake.

        20 graham cracker squares, finely crushed
         3 tablespoons brown sugar
         ⅓ cup soft butter or margarine
         1 cup whipping cream
         ½ cup sifted powdered sugar
         2 tablespoons *each* California Sherry
              and brandy; *or,* ¼ cup brandy
         4 egg yolks

Combine graham cracker crumbs, brown sugar and soft butter; mix thoroughly. Press firmly into 9" pie pan, reserving about 2 tablespoons crumbs for topping. Chill. Meanwhile, whip cream until stiff; blend in powdered sugar, Sherry and/or brandy (at low speed, if mixer is used). Beat egg yolks until light-colored and thick; fold into cream mixture. Pour filling into chilled crust; top with reserved crumbs. Freeze. Serve frozen.

My choice of wine to accompany this dish:
CALIFORNIA CREAM SHERRY

VINEYARD HOLIDAY PIE

(6 servings)

Mrs. James Concannon, Concannon Vineyards, Livermore

         2 cups canned pumpkin
         1 (15-oz.) can (1⅓ cups)
              sweetened condensed milk
         1 egg
         ½ teaspoon salt
         ½ teaspoon cinnamon
         ¼ teaspoon ginger
         ¼ teaspoon nutmeg
         ½ cup California Sherry
         ½ cup hot water
         1 (9") unbaked pastry shell

Combine pumpkin, condensed milk, egg, salt, spices, Sherry and water in a large bowl. Beat or stir vigorously until well blended. Pour into unbaked pastry shell. Bake in moderately hot oven (375°) for 50 to 55 minutes. Cool. Serve topped with sweetened whipped cream.

NOTE: *It is important to use the sweetened condensed milk in this recipe, NOT evaporated milk. The pie is delicious for any festive occasion. Follow it with a glass of Cream Sherry as after-dinner beverage.*

SOFTEN Cheddar cheese spread with California Sherry, to top apple pie. (Or use some Sherry in the apple filling.) Serve with Cream Sherry on the side: a perfect dessert.

VALLEY MINCE PIE

(Any amount)

Evins Naman, Wine Institute, Fresno

This idea couldn't be any simpler, but it makes all the difference in that festive holiday pie. Follow the pie directions given on the mincemeat package, adding 1 or 2 tablespoons of California Muscatel or Sherry for each cup of mincemeat used. I guarantee your guests will enjoy it.

My choice of wine to accompany this dish:
CALIFORNIA MUSCATEL OR CREAM SHERRY

RAISINS added to desserts are easily softened or "plumped" first, by soaking for a couple of hours in a little Port or Muscatel or other dessert wine. This also adds to the flavor.

TANGY LEMON-RAISIN PIE

(6 servings)

Mrs. James E. Roberts, Bakersfield

1½ cups sugar
¼ cup flour
1 egg
⅛ teaspoon salt
3 tablespoons lemon juice
1½ teaspoons grated lemon peel
1 cup water
1 cup California Sherry
1 cup raisins
1 (9") unbaked pie crust

Mix sugar, flour and egg. Add all other filling ingredients and cook over hot water in top of double boiler for 15 minutes, stirring constantly. Cool. Pour into unbaked pie crust. Bake in hot oven (450°) for 10 minutes. Reduce heat to moderate (350°); bake 20 minutes longer.

NOTE: Wonderfully rich; would be good with sour cream topping. Port, Cream Sherry or any other dessert wine could follow for after-dinner enjoyment.

SEAFOAM PUDDING SAUCE

(2 cups)

Mrs. Fred Snyde, Woodbridge Vineyard Association, Lodi

½ cup soft butter or margarine
1 cup brown sugar (firmly packed)
1 egg, well beaten
Few grains salt
¼ to ½ cup California Sherry

Cream butter and sugar thoroughly until fluffy. Add egg and salt; beat well. Just before serving, gradually beat in Sherry. Place over hot water in top of double boiler; heat, beating constantly, until soft but not syrupy (about 1 minute or so).

NOTE: A light, thin, foamy sauce, different and most enjoyable. Serve a glass of California Cream Sherry as the after-dinner drink.

ANOTHER TOPPING is suggested by Brother Gregory of Mont La Salle Vineyards, Napa, who likes a Light Muscat poured over vanilla ice cream. And Kenneth Knapp of Selma Winery, Selma, recommends adding 2 tablespoons California Sherry or Muscatel per pint to your favorite recipe for homemade vanilla ice cream, or the prepared mix.

PORT WINE SUNDAE SAUCE

(4 or 5 servings)

Dan C. Turrentine, Wine Advisory Board, San Francisco

A panel of 48 wine men tried this sauce on vanilla ice cream. It was rated excellent by 34, good by 11, and fair by 3.

¼ cup sugar
1 tablespoon cornstarch
1 cup California Port
1 teaspoon lemon juice
2 teaspoons grated orange rind

Mix sugar, cornstarch. Add to Port in saucepan and cook, stirring frequently, until thickened and clear, 5 to 10 minutes. Add lemon juice and orange rind. Chill. Pour over vanilla ice cream or pineapple sherbet. More or less sugar may be used, according to taste. For an especially fruity, delightfully different flavor, use Muscatel in sauce instead of Port.

My choice of wine to follow this dish, with demitasse:
THE SAME WINE TYPE USED IN THE SAUCE

NOTE: See also PORT VOLCANO recipe, on Page 107, for an even easier topping: Port alone. Muscatel is good the same way, simply poured over ice cream by itself. Another who prefers a cooked Port sauce similar to the above is Mrs. Myron Nightingale of Roma Wine Company, Fresno. Her recipe includes butter and nutmeg instead of the lemon juice and grated orange rind; she recommends her sauce especially for puddings or custards.

NECTAR FOR FRUITS

(1½ cups)

Myrtle F. Cuneo, Regina Grape Products Co., Etiwanda

This syrup for fruits makes a very light and refreshing dessert.

- ¾ cup honey
- 1 tablespoon grated lemon peel
- 2 tablespoons lemon juice
- 2 tablespoons orange juice
- ⅓ to ½ cup California Sherry

Combine all ingredients in small saucepan. Cook, stirring constantly, over low heat for 5 minutes. Remove from heat; cool slightly; pour over fruit. (Any variety of fresh fruit, cut in serving or bite-size pieces, may be used. If grapes are used, cut in half to absorb syrup.) Allow fruit to marinate in syrup several hours before serving. Garnish with fresh mint leaves for color and flavor, if desired.

NOTE: *A sip of Sherry or any other favorite dessert wine would be a pleasing accompaniment.*

GALA DESSERT TOPPING

(About 1½ cups)

Mrs. Leonard Maullin, Paul Masson Vineyards, Saratoga

This topping will keep several days, refrigerated and covered. It is delicious on fresh or canned fruits or cake slices, and unique on chocolate or coffee ice cream.

- 8 to 10 coconut macaroons (dry type)
- 1 tablespoon brown sugar
- ½ cup California Cream Sherry
- 1 cup sour cream
- 3 tablespoons chopped roasted almonds

Crumble dry macaroons into very small pieces; add sugar and Sherry. Let stand 30 minutes. Add sour cream and nuts; blend thoroughly. Chill at least 2 hours before serving as a topping for one of the desserts indicated.

NOTE: *Choose the accompanying wine according to the dessert. If the topping is served on fruit or plain cake, a sweet dessert wine would please guests.*

IT'S EASY TO COOK WITH WINE

QUICK TIPS FOR BEGINNING COOKS

If you keep wine on hand just for cooking, remember that once the bottle is opened, some wines have a storage time limit, just as milk does. For storage tips, see Page 124.

Even the busiest cook can turn out a delicious dinner in no time and with little effort. Stir up a package of instant vanilla pudding using ¼ cup California Sherry for part of the liquid. Add a pinch of salt and a bit of grated lemon or orange rind.

Whether you're frying meat or fish, a little California white dinner wine (such as Sauterne or Chablis) stirred into the pan drippings makes a quick, easy sauce. The rest of the bottle of wine does double duty **with** dinner.

For best-ever spaghetti, cook your favorite kind as you like it, soft or firm. Heat canned spaghetti sauce with a bit of California Claret and a pinch of rosemary or oregano. Combine sauce and spaghetti with plenty of Cheddar or Parmesan cheese—and serve with glasses of the same red dinner wine.

Easiest way to enhance grilled poultry, lamb or fish is with a simple wine-butter baste. Combine equal parts butter and California Rosé, or a white dinner wine such as Sauterne or Rhine. Add squeeze of lime and pinch of your favorite herb. Heat in small pan, and brush often over meat while cooking.

Beef stew tastes extra good zipped up with California Claret, a bouillon cube or two, and a pinch of curry or herbs to your liking. Use your favorite canned stew as base; add about ½ cup red dinner wine. If gravy is a trifle thin, stir in a little cornstarch mixed with water. A tablespoon of butter or bacon drippings does wonders for the flavor.

Every wine type known can be—and is—used for cooking. Wines labeled as "cooking wines" are wines with a little salt added. If you are using one of these, you may want to reduce the amount of salt called for in the recipe.

Almost any fresh fruit or melon will be delicious as a salad or appetizer if it is molded in gelatin flavored with white dinner wine. Substitute ½ cup of California Chablis or Sauterne for ½ cup of the water. To make the jellied base as refreshing as the fruits themselves, allow a few sprigs of fresh mint to simmer in the hot water used to dissolve the gelatin. Lemon juice will add piquancy, too.

Improvise with canned soups for a hearty chowder. Start with creamed soup such as mushroom, chicken, shrimp or celery. Add canned mushrooms, shrimp or other seafoods. Then flavor with California Sherry, 1 to 2 tablespoons per cup of chowder.

To give added flavor and texture to less expensive cuts of meat (pot roasts, stews, etc.), before cooking marinate them overnight in California dinner wine (either red or white) to cover. Turn meat occasionally. Add seasonings as desired: salt, whole peppercorns or ground pepper, onion and garlic, bay leaves and other herbs, cloves and other spices, etc. When you're ready to cook the meat, strain this marinade, if necessary, and use some of it as all or part of the liquid in cooking the meat. You'll be well rewarded with extra flavor and a new tenderness in the finished dish.

Chicken that is to be broiled or barbecued is especially good if marinated in white dinner wine for several hours before cooking.

Smoked Sausages, browned quickly, then poached in California Sauterne, are delicious fare any meal of the day. Thicken the rich pan liquid slightly with a little cornstarch in water, and spoon over sausages and eggs.

When you want to try California wine in your own recipes, this quick-reference chart will serve as a "safe" general guide to the wine type and amount to be added. However, there are no hard-and-fast rules. Don't be afraid to experiment. It's easy, rewarding and fun — and can make you famous with your friends!

WINE COOKERY CHART

	FOODS	AMOUNT	WINES
SOUPS	Cream Soups	1 T. per cup	Sauterne or Sherry
	Meat and Vegetable Soups	1 T. per cup	Burgundy or Sherry
SAUCES	Cream Sauce	1 T. per cup	Sherry or Sauterne
	Brown Sauce	1 T. per cup	Sherry or Burgundy
	Tomato Sauce	1 T. per cup	Sherry or Burgundy
	Cheese Sauce	1 T. per cup	Sherry or Sauterne
	Dessert Sauce	1 T. per cup	Port or Muscatel
MEATS	Pot Roast	¼ cup per lb.	Burgundy
	Gravy for Roasts	2 T. per cup	Burgundy, Sauterne or Sherry
	Stew—Beef	¼ cup per lb.	Burgundy
	Stew—Lamb or Veal	¼ cup per lb.	Sauterne
	Ham, Baked	2 cups (for basting)	Port or Muscatel
	Liver, Braised	¼ cup per lb.	Burgundy or Sauterne
	Tongue, Boiled	½ cup per lb.	Burgundy
FISH	Broiled, Baked or Poached	½ cup per lb.	Sauterne
POULTRY AND GAME	Chicken	¼ cup per lb.	Sauterne or Burgundy
	Gravy for Roast or Fried Chicken, Turkey	2 T. per cup	Sauterne, Burgundy or Sherry
	Duck, Roasted	¼ cup per lb.	Burgundy
	Venison	¼ cup per lb.	Burgundy
	Pheasant	¼ cup per lb.	Sauterne, Burgundy or Sherry
FRUIT Fresh, Canned or Frozen	In syrup or juice (Fruit cups, compotes, etc.)	2 T. per cup *over fruit or in syrup or juice*	Port, Muscatel, Sherry, Rosé, Sauterne or Burgundy
	(or) Drained	*At the table, pour over fruits without dilution*	Champagne or other Sparkling Wines

NOTE: Where Sauterne is suggested above, any California white dinner wine, such as Rhine or Chablis, may be substituted. Where Burgundy is suggested, any red dinner wine may be used instead, such as California Claret or Zinfandel.

(T = TABLESPOON)

Wine is one of the easiest things to serve at a dinner—far less complicated than carving a roast, for example. Simply set your wine glasses to the right of the water glasses, as shown below. Put the bottle on the table, or near at hand, so guests may be invited to help themselves. In this case, the wine is usually passed as soon as the first course is begun.

First step in opening a bottle is to **cut** the foil or cellulose band just below the bottle lip, using a small sharp knife. This keeps the bottle neat-looking. Wipe the bottle mouth before inserting corkscrew, and again after cork is pulled.

A good corkscrew **is** important, and can make wine serving really simple. In shopping for a corkscrew, look for one with rounded worm-edges, as shown below. (A sharp-edged worm tends to tear or break the cork.) A good corkscrew will also have its point in line with the worm-spirals, and an **open** space down the center of the worm. (Several newer-type cork-pullers are now on the market which eject corks instantly by means of a harmless gas. These are fast, efficient, and spark conversation.)

Champagne service is a little different, of course—requiring no cork-puller but you. Untwist, loosen and remove the wire hood; the foil comes off with it. Hold your thumb on the cork meanwhile, so it won't pop out. Slant the bottle, pointed away from guests. Twist the cork gently, or work it from side to side if needed; hold onto it as it leaves the bottle. (It will still pop!) Have a glass handy to catch the first foam.

If you like to be a bit ceremonious, pour a little wine into your own glass first, as host or hostess. This old traditional custom allows the host to taste first, to assure that the wine is sound. It also gives him, not his guests, any cork bits in the bottle.

Another, more important custom is never to fill a dinner wine glass more than half or two-thirds full. Air space above the wine gathers aroma and bouquet, necessary to full enjoyment of the wine. It also lessens chance of spilling. This is why a **large** wine glass is preferable. (See opposite page.)

Give the bottle a slight twist before raising it from the glass. This catches drops on bottle-lip, avoiding drip. Or, use one of the dripless metal wine pourers; or, one of the foam-lined flower-wreaths around the bottle neck, to catch stray drops.

When do you need a wine cradle, or serving basket, as shown below? Hardly ever, unless you like wine accessories. A cradle merely helps you to handle a **very old, red wine** gently, to avoid stirring up any sediment in the bottom of the bottle. Another method is to decant or pour off an old red wine into another bottle or decanter, slowly, without shaking sediment.

When do you need an ice bucket? Again, hardly ever, unless you simply like the looks of one. A bucket **will** chill faster; but most people prefer the refrigerator. If you use a bucket, keep it handy to the dinner table, and wipe bottle with napkin before pouring. Never wrap napkin clear around bottle, hiding label. (For temperature tips, see Page 124.)

A large bottle of **dinner wine or Champagne** ("fifth" size—see Page 8) will pour 6 servings, averaging 4 ounces or more. A gallon jug will give 32 servings this size. The sweeter **dessert and appetizer wines** are usually poured in smaller, 2½- to 4-ounce servings. In this case, a large bottle will provide as many as 10 servings, and a gallon jug as many as 50.

WINE GLASSWARE

Wine may be served in any glass, even a tumbler — but somehow it seems to taste much better in a stemmed glass. This is more than the beauty of the stemmed glass on your table; it's also because a stem keeps your hand from warming the wine.

In searching for wine glasses, first of all look for a **large** size — so that the glass may be poured only about half-full. A slight tulip shape, with the top of the glass a little narrower than the widest part of the bowl, helps to hold the wine's aroma and bouquet in the empty space above the wine.

The next thing to look for is absolute clarity — no colored glass, and preferably no etched pattern. This is to let you enjoy the clarity and color of the wine itself, another part of its full enjoyment.

Traditional glass shapes are shown below, but few people indulge themselves in all these types today. Experts agree that a single type of **all-purpose** wine glass makes more sense. The glass shown actual size at the right is just such a glass. It's **large,** with 9-ounce capacity, allowing the desirable amount of "fill" indicated. It's **shaped right,** to catch and hold the wine's bouquet. It's **plain** sparkling crystal — perfect setting to show off a jewel-colored wine, and harmonious with any other crystal, china or silverware.

This is the all-purpose glass selected and recommended by California's wine-growers for use with **any** wine type: for entertaining, or daily mealtime pleasure. For information on where to find such wine glasses, write Wine Advisory Board, San Francisco 3.

Fill to here for Dinner Wine or Sparkling Wine

Fill to here for Appetizer or Dessert Wine

ALL-PURPOSE GLASS
(Shown here actual size)

Traditional Glasses

(On-the-Rocks)

APPETIZER WINES

Red   Rhine   Other White

DINNER WINES

DESSERT WINES

Saucer   Tulip

SPARKLING WINES

YOUR WINE DESERVES CARE

WINE is a living thing, and as such is subject to change. (For example, wine is the only beverage that can continue to improve after bottling.) After the bottle is opened, a few simple precautions will help to protect the wine's flavor, color, aroma and bouquet, so that it will give maximum pleasure.

DINNER WINES (such as Burgundy, Sauterne or Rosé), because of their low alcohol content, averaging about 12%, are perishable once they are exposed to air, as is milk. Once opened, such wines should be used within a few days, even though the bottle is recorked or recapped and stored in the refrigerator. Gallon dinner wines may be decanted, or transferred after opening to sterilized smaller bottles, if they are not to be used within a few days. (Fill to ¾" or 1" from the top, to allow for expansion, then recork or use a screw-cap bottle.) In many families, dinner wine left over from meals or entertaining is used later in the kitchen, for cooking.

AN OLD TRICK that helps keep dinner wines longer, if intended for cooking use, is to float a thin film of cooking oil on the wine's surface—just enough to seal off the wine from the air in the top of the bottle. (Or, pour wine for cooking into smaller bottles and cork tightly.)

SPARKLING Wines should of course be used immediately after opening, before their sparkle is lost. If you do have leftover Champagne, however, the same rules apply as above; it will still be good for a few days, even without the bubbles. If recorked and returned to a refrigerator within a few minutes after opening and serving a portion, the remainder of the bottle will probably have a fair amount of bubbles the next day.

DESSERT or Appetizer Wines (such as Port or Sherry), because of their higher alcoholic content, averaging about 20%, will keep up to several months opened, in partly-filled bottles. Store them in the refrigerator in very hot weather.

IF NATURAL sediment should appear in wine as a result of aging (more likely in a red dinner wine than in other types), stand the bottle upright for 1 or 2 hours before serving. Avoid shaking the bottle. This harmless sediment will then settle to the bottom, and the clear wine may be poured gently. Such wine may be decanted, or transferred from the original bottle to another clean bottle, if desired.

RED Dinner Wine is at its best an hour or so **after** opening the bottle. The flavor really comes up if the wine is opened this far in advance of dinner, to allow the wine to "breathe."

IT'S ALWAYS wise to store wines in a cool, relatively dry place, where temperature is fairly even, with no sudden changes or extremes. **Ideal** storage temperature is between 50° and 60°—with 70° considered the highest safe temperature for long-term storage. (If your

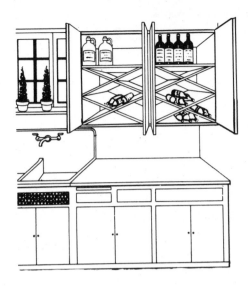

Any cupboard or closet can be converted easily to wine storage. For free booklet of do-it-yourself diagrams, "Little Wine Cellar All Your Own," write Wine Appreciation Guild, 1377 Ninth Ave., San Francisco, Calif. 94122

Or, you may be able to find ready-made wine racks, of metal or wood, at a reasonable price in local stores. Most of these will fit inside a cupboard or closet.

cellar, closet or wine cupboard gets warmer than 70°, line it with insulating material such as wallboard. The important thing is to avoid extreme changes.)

THIS MEANS wine should not be stored near furnaces, hot water heaters, steam pipes or radiators. It should be kept out of sunlight. Since wall temperatures tend to change sharply, do not store wine right up against an outside wall.

CORKED wines should rest on their sides, if stored long, so that corks will stay moist and air-tight. If you leave corked bottles in their case, turn the case on its side. Screw-cap bottles may stand upright.

IF YOU have a wine cellar or closet, store Sparkling and White Dinner Wines in the lowest racks or bins, because it is cooler there; and Red Dinner Wines in the next section up. Dessert and Appetizer Wines may be stored on top, because they are the least affected by higher temperatures.

WHITE and Rosé Dinner Wines are generally chilled in the refrigerator 1 to 3 hours before serving, and Sparkling Wines 4 to 6 hours. Red Dinner Wines are best at **cool** room temperature. (Not above 70°—in very hot weather, you may want to put a Burgundy into the **refrigerator** for a while.) There is no rule for Dessert or Appetizer Wines, but the same general customs are preferred by most people: the whiter types like Sherry or Muscatel chilled, **the** red like Port at cool room temperature. Many persons prefer **all** wines chilled. Your own personal taste is the best guide.

WINE may be stored in the refrigerator, but some authorities feel it is best to use it within 1 or 2 weeks, to avoid slight impairment of flavor. Once it is chilled, however, do not store it again at room temperature. Never chill wine below 35°.

WINE IN THE DIET

W ine (like vanilla) loses its alcoholic content in cooking; thus the entire family can enjoy many delicious wine-flavored dishes. For example, when wine is added to a sauce or soup to be cooked over direct heat, the alcohol passes off in the form of vapor at the low simmering stage (172.4°). This is well before the boiling point (212°) is reached. If wine is added to a casserole dish, or used as a baste for roasting meat, the heat of the oven will have the same effect. (Even in a low 300° oven, a cup of wine in a shallow pan will lose all its alcohol in 10 minutes.) Only the subtle wine flavor is left, to enhance and blend with the other food flavors.

W ith the alcohol, most of the calories disappear, too. A dry dinner wine such as Burgundy or Sauterne will lose 85 percent of its original calories when subjected to enough heat to lose all the alcohol. The remaining 15 percent of the calories are from non-alcohol substances in the wine, such as the natural grape sugar.

S ince dessert or appetizer wines such as Port or Sherry contain more alcohol and natural grape sugar than do the dinner wines, they are higher in caloric value. But used in cooking, they also will lose both alcohol and calories. If they are cooked for a longer period, more than an hour in a 300° oven (as in the case of a ham, roast or casserole), most of their sugars are caramelized. If the caramelization is sufficient, the material will not be oxidized by the body. (Only in California, incidentally, does the law require that the sweetness of these appetizer and dessert wines be provided by natural grape sugar alone. No cane or beet sugar may be added to California wines.)

R esearch programs under recognized authorities have established much factual information pertaining to the properties of wines (such as the B-vitamins and iron) and to the therapeutic use of wines in specific fields (such as in low-salt or slimming diets).

C aloric values shown below for various California wine classes are based on averages, and apply to wines served as **beverages,** uncooked.

WINE CLASS	ALCOHOL CONTENT BY VOLUME (%) (average)	CALORIES PER OUNCE
Red Dinner Wines	12%	24 to 25
White Dinner Wines	12%	22 to 26
Champagnes & Other Sparkling Wines	12%	24 to 25
Sherries	20%	38
Dessert Wines	20%	44 to 48

INDEX TO RECIPES

First printing Sept., 1963
Second printing Nov., 1963
Third printing April, 1964
Fourth printing August, 1964
Fifth printing Oct., 1964
Sixth printing May, 1965
Seventh printing June, 1966
Eighth printing June, 1967
Ninth printing Sept., 1967
Tenth printing April, 1969
Eleventh printing Jan., 1971
Twelfth printing Feb., 1973
Fourteenth printing Sept. 1981